STRANGER FICTIONS

STRANGER FICTIONS

A HISTORY OF THE NOVEL IN ARABIC TRANSLATION

Rebecca C. Johnson

CORNELL UNIVERSITY PRESS
Ithaca and London

Publication of this book was made possible, in part, by a grant from the Alice Kaplan Institute for the Humanities, Northwestern University.

First published 2020 by Cornell University Press

Library of Congress Cataloging-in-Publication Data

Names: Johnson, Rebecca C. (Rebecca Carol), author.
Title: Stranger fictions : a history of the novel in Arabic translation / Rebecca C. Johnson.
Description: Ithaca [New York] : Cornell University Press, 2020. | Includes bibliographical references and index.
Identifiers: LCCN 2020013041 (print) | LCCN 2020013042 (ebook) | ISBN 9781501753060 (hardcover) | ISBN 9781501753077 (ebook) | ISBN 9781501753305 (pdf)
Subjects: LCSH: Arabic fiction—European influences. | Arabic fiction—1801—History and criticism. | Translating and interpreting.
Classification: LCC PJ7577 .J64 2020 (print) | LCC PJ7577 (ebook) | DDC 892.7/35094—dc23
LC record available at https://lccn.loc.gov/2020013041
LC ebook record available at https://lccn.loc.gov/2020013042

For Nadim

Contents

Figures

Acknowledgments

What I have learned from writing this book is this: one cannot write without translating. One carries others'—and mostly strangers'—ideas across languages, times, and spaces, to bring them into one's own work. And if we are lucky, some of those strangers become mentors and friends.

I have been so lucky, above all in finding advisors and mentors to shepherd this project. At New York University, where these inchoate questions were first formed, Philip Kennedy's support, incisiveness, and precision set an impossible standard for my scholarship as for my mentorship. And Elias Khoury's ability to simultaneously provoke and encourage was beyond compare. At Yale University, it was Katie Trumpener who saw value in the work and encouraged the most expansive of thinking. It would not be an exaggeration to say that she taught me to read. She, and Richard Maxwell, set a standard for generosity of mind and spirit, and I am indebted to them and to Richard's memory.

Several grants have made the research and writing of this book possible. Research in Egypt, the United Kingdom, and Lebanon were funded by the Social Science Research Council, the Council on Library and Information Resources, and the Fulbright Foundation. Research in the United States was funded by a Beinecke Rare Book and Manuscript Library Summer Fellowship, and a year of my research writing was funded by the American Council of Learned Societies. Equally important was a Faculty Fellowship from Northwestern University's Alice Kaplan Institute for the Humanities. I would like to thank the staffs of the Egyptian National Library, the American University in Cairo Library, the Jafet Library at the American University of Beirut, the British Library, the School of Oriental and African Studies Library, the Bibliothèque nationale de France, the Cadbury Research Library at the University of Birmingham, UK, the Archives of the Church Mission Society, the Beinecke Rare Book and Manuscript Library, Yale University Library, and Princeton University Library. At Cornell University Press, I would like to thank all who helped bring this book to press, but above all Mahinder Kingra.

I have been most fortunate to have rich conversations with too many brilliant teachers and colleagues to enumerate. Sinan Antoon, Shareah Taleghani, Sherene Seikaly, Hanan Kholoussy, Jeffrey Sacks, Liat Kozma, and Hussein Fancy made New York the most exciting place in the U.S. for Middle East Studies. At Yale, I need to thank Annette Damayanti Lienau, Bilal Orfali, Beatrice Gruendler, Christopher Miller, Jill Campbell, and Wai Chee Dimock. And I am indebted to the interlocutors and friends who have shaped my ideas at conferences, research sites, and by correspondence over the years: Shaden Tageldin, Tarek El-Ariss, Samah Selim, Elliott Colla, Marina Warner, Humphrey Davies, Robyn Creswell, Kamran Rastegar, Margaret Litvin, Elizabeth Holt, Heather Badamo, On Barak, Julie Kleinman, David Faris, Stefanie Boyle, and Yannick Dupraz.

As I turned the dissertation into a book, my colleagues at Northwestern University buoyed me and threw me the occasional lifesaver. I owe an unpayable debt to Brian Edwards and his boundless energy and unflagging encouragement. And I am grateful to the English Department as a whole for its ability to not only welcome a comparativist foundling such as myself but nurture her. I especially thank Katy Breen, John Alba Cutler, Kasey Evans, Jim Hodge, Jules Law, Andrew Leong, Susan Manning, Juan Martinez, Emily Rohrbach, Laurie Shannon, Julie Stern, Helen Thompson, Wendy Wall, Kelly Wisecup, and Tristram Wolff. In the Program for Middle East and North African Studies, I have found unwavering interdisciplinary support in Katherine Hoffman, Henri Lauzière, Wendy Pearlman, Carl Petry, and Emrah Yildiz.

There were times when I did not think that this book would be a book; in those times it was Nick Davis and Susie Phillips that carried me back to myself and to the work. Jessica Winegar's insights sharpened my focus and my resolve. Hannah Feldman read every page, and I can only hope that her brilliance and elegance is somehow refracted in them. Harris Feinsod, comrade-in-arms and source of seemingly endless insights, enlightening critiques, and reality-checks, improved *Stranger Fictions* beyond measure.

I carried more than ideas while writing this book. I carried Lina, Maïa, and Salim, who by the time of printing will be able to recognize a few words from among the many on its pages. Here are the most important ones: je vous aime. Ce livre est dédié à Nadim, avec qui j'ai commencé cette vie traduite, et parfois mal traduite. À mon grand bonheur.

Note on Translation and Transliteration

Translations in what follows are my own, with the caveat being that no translation work is possible entirely alone. Much of translation relies on previous translator's work, and this book is no exception. If an English-language translation exists, therefore, I have attempted to engage with it, and if I depart from its translator's decisions I have indicated as much. In transliteration, the text follows in general the standards of the *International Journal of Middle East Studies* (*IJMES*), except that I have not elided prepositions or conjunctions that are followed by the definite article (I use *Al-Sāq ʿalā al-sāq* rather than *Al-Sāq ʿalā ʾl-sāq*). Place and personal names with accepted English spellings are rendered in English, but are otherwise transliterated as usual. In quotations I have retained other author's transliterations even when they depart from this system.

STRANGER FICTIONS

Introduction

A History of the Novel in Mistranslation

This is a book about a largely forgotten corpus of literature, Arabic translations of French and English novels that in some cases have themselves been forgotten and the traces of which I have pieced together from multiple libraries in Europe and the Middle East. And so it seems fitting to open the book with a pair of ephemeral emblems from those archives. First is a handwritten inscription that sweeps diagonally across the first page of a partial 1882 Arabic translation of Victor Hugo's *Les Misérables*. Addressed to the book's translator, Nagīb Gharghūr, it reads, "C'est très mal Monsieur Gargur, . . . traduit très très mal" (It is very bad, Mr. Gargur, . . . translated very, very poorly).[1] The second is a never-reprinted essay appearing as the preface to an 1886 translation of Abbé Prevost's *Manon Lescault*, entitled *Al-Janūn fī ḥubb Mānūn* (The madness of loving Manon), "On the Truth of the Development of the Art of Novel-Writing." Its author, the translator Mīkhā'īl 'Awrā, writes of *The Thousand and One Nights*, "The Europeans translated it and count it among the greatest works written by the Arabs—for, in their opinion, all of the East as well as its customs and morals are contained within its pages. . . . They consider the Arabs to be the finest narrators and novel-writers, and so followed their example."[2] Together, these two quotations attest that the process of translation can be understood as central to the genre of the novel. It can also be understood as precarious: translation is how works of European literature like *Les Misérables* circulated in Arabic to influence the development of the Arabic novel and how works of Arabic literature circulated to influence the development of the European novel before that. Yet even as translation acts as the very channel of literary circulation, it is also the tripwire on which it most easily founders. Important works are imperfectly transmitted: *Les Misérables* appears as a "badly translated" attempt, and *The Thousand and One Nights*—as 'Awrā argues—circulated as a text misunderstood by its European transmitters as an ethnographic document. Translation, and perhaps even more importantly *mistranslation* (the *mal traduit*), is foundational to the development of the Arabic novel. What is more, 'Arwā notes, it is foundational to the history of the genre as a whole.

These quotations come from works that have until now appeared as curious footnotes to the history of the Arabic novel. What scholars have long identified as the first Arabic novel, Muḥammad Ḥusayn Haykal's novel of rural Egyptian life *Zaynab*, first appeared in 1913, yet hundreds of works calling themselves novels and translated from English and French were published in the eight previous decades and have been ignored either because they represent foreign—rather than Arab—places, people, or customs or because they were "bad translations" produced by unskilled hacks. And yet they are cited as the most important influences on celebrated authors: Naguib Mahfouz recollects devouring British detective fiction in his youth; Jurjī Zaydān cites Walter Scott as an important influence; Sonallah Ibrahim describes himself as infatuated with *Arsène Lupin*.[3] As the Moroccan philosopher Abdelfattah Kilito has mused, the "derivative" translations of Muṣṭafā Luṭfī al-Manfalūṭī inspired most Arab authors in their youth, even if they later "turn against him," ashamed by their former bad taste.[4] What would our account of modern Arabic literature look like if we incorporated these works as part of the history, rather than the shameful prehistory, of the Arabic novel? Accounting for the wide range of translation practices—including "bad translation," mistranslation, and pseudotranslation—that make up this corpus might indeed change our account not only of the Arabic novel but of how aesthetic form circulates to form transnational canons.

These Arab translators, who themselves produced the earliest novels to appear in Arabic, offer such an alternative account, and *Stranger Fictions* follows their own theorizations of the global literary sphere and their place within it. 'Awrā's essay, in fact, forms one of the very first Arabic theses on the history of the novel, describing the transnational proliferations of the form and highlighting the role of translators at every juncture. He traces it from Greek and Roman novels—which incorporated Phoenician geographical information and Ancient Egyptian mythology—to medieval European narrative. Among those, he identifies Boccaccio's *Decameron* as foundational but as a text that had already inherited structures from nested Arabic animal fables like *Kalīla wa Dimna*. These he traces to the modern novelists Honoré de Balzac and Georges Sand writing in French and their contemporary Aḥmad Fāris al-Shidyāq writing in Arabic, all of whom he points to as examples of a global trend of affixing moral and social import to literary work. In his account, the novel is a constantly circulating form, developing from translations of translations and the incorporation of foreign tradition. Readers looking for the location of the form's "origins" will instead find a history of infinite regress: Balzac wrote in the wake of the popularity of *The Thousand and One Nights*, but ʿAwrā points out that the *Nights* was already "not original to the Arabic language" but partially derived from translated Persian sources. As for the Arabic text that he argues informed the *Decameron*, *Kalīla wa Dimna*, ʿAwrā notes that it too was translated first from Persian and then from Sanskrit.[5] All were derived, at least in part, from the fictions of strangers.

This sketch may surprise readers acquainted with a history of the novel as it has been recounted in the Anglo-American academy. In ʿAwrā's account, the genre does not follow the itinerary familiar to most scholars today, in which the novel rises in eighteenth-century England and then travels belatedly from this center to the world's peripheries via routes of empire, colonization, and government-mandated modernization. Instead, ʿAwrā describes the novel as polygenetic, transhistorical, and itinerant. He understands the novel as always *in translation*. Yet, though his essay may seem singular from our contemporary perspective, it was by no means unusual in its own time. By 1886, when ʿAwrā published this elaborated argument, the preface explaining the history and purpose of what we understand as the novel to its Arabophone audience had itself become somewhat of a genre. As one early translator of French into Arabic explains in 1858, "the art known as *rūmāntīk*" [novelistic] is the name given to *qiṣaṣ shaʿriyya* [poetic stories]" that have social import; another in 1866 traces the novel to "the beginning of human composition," which was then "transferred from one generation to another until today"; and, in 1884, a translator elaborates yet further on the novel's transhistorical and translinguistic history, warning against defining the genre too narrowly, lest "we simplify those aspects . . . that both the East and the West brought to it."[6] Even Khalīl Muṭrān, whose accessibly erudite translations of the early twentieth century deliberately turned away from the popularizing translations of the preceding decades, did not simply choose fidelity over infidelity: he claimed that the name Othello was itself a mistranscription of the Arabic ʿUṭayl, a diminutive of ʿAṭīl, hypothesizing that Shakespeare's version must have derived from an original Arabic source or at least from "an Arab spirit."[7] He claimed to be translating it "as if returning it to its origin" in the Maghrib; he would restore the "Bedouin aspects" of Shakespeare's soul.[8] Instead of a literary transfer from West to East, Muṭrān imagines his translation as merely the latest in a long-standing and bidirectional history of literary contact.[9]

Like ʿAwrā, many nineteenth-century translators offered their own labors as the latest entries in the form's transnational development—entries that they characterized as potentially erring and unworthy: "I ask those readers of discernment to let the curtain fall on those contradictions and imperfections that might be found in the translation or Arabization," one translator pleads; "I urge the reader to turn a blind eye to my mistakes," writes another.[10] Error, each reminds us, is inherent in this process, and "infallibility belongs to God alone."[11] They emphasize that translation is only possible through great labor and that it is always incomplete, provisional, or incorrect: "Every language has its own qualities that the other cannot match, except with some kind of damage done to it."[12] Over and again, in prefaces to translations, imaginative depictions of translation, and periodical articles on translation, Arabic translators of the nineteenth century highlighted discrepancies between languages as differences that are impossible to resolve even while they undertake the laborious task of resolving them.

Aḥmad Fāris al-Shidyāq, one of the nineteenth century's best-known Arab writers and least-known translators, defines the problem in a poem:

> He who has missed out on translation knows not what travail is:
> None but the warrior is scorched by the fire of war!
> I find a thousand notions for which there is none akin
> Among us, and a thousand with none appropriate;
> And a thousand terms with no equivalent.
> I find disjunction for junction, though junction is needed.[13]

The tropes of disjunction and junction highlighted by al-Shidyāq loomed over much of the period that writers in the nineteenth and early twentieth centuries called "the New Age" (*al-ʿaṣr al-jadīd*) of literary modernity and that later came to be known as the *nahḍa* (often translated as "revival"). As scholars have repeatedly noted, the nineteenth and early twentieth centuries saw an increase in communications and transportation between parts of the world that were before thought to be distant from each other. "The Age of Steam and Print" brought distant peoples together in "reading publics" that forged disperse regions and diasporic communities into an integrated temporality.[14] Steamships integrated markets and transported travelers, workers, and tourists far from home, while the telegraph transported information between cooperating governments and new agencies on a scale not seen before, creating a global information network.[15] Yet, as detailed analyses of these technologies have proven and my own research has borne out, they were rife with interruptions and failures: telegraph wires fell prey to tides, sea creatures, and faulty installation practices; steamships and steam engines regularly fell behind schedule; and newspapers printed discrepant accounts of events, used discrepant calendars, and suffered frequent print and delivery interruptions.[16] Each, as this book argues, relies on translation to bring (often tenuous) "junction" where there was disjunction. Translation, I argue, was yet another underlying technology understood to bridge communication problems as well as cultural and linguistic difference, even when such junctures were impossible. The nineteenth century—which elsewhere has been theorized as the advent of modern globalization—not only centered on translation but made translation necessary as a means to bridge these gaps and mediate between peoples and locations that are imperfectly connected. To quote an important essay of Jacques Derrida's, translation in these instances is always "necessary and impossible"—necessary to bridge gaps of linguistic and cultural difference but also impossible because, in his account, languages are fundamentally and a priori alien to each other.[17] The very strangeness of one language to another makes translation not only necessary and impossible but necessary *because* it is impossible.

My use of these virtually unknown Arab translators of sometimes-forgotten European works to paraphrase Derrida's "law of translation"—or, rather, my use of Derrida's writing to explicate the complex ideas of these translators—demonstrates the methodology that drives the argument of this book. *Stranger Fictions* reads these translators as de facto translation theorists and informed commentators on literary history. Through their prefaces, their journalistic writing, and their translation choices and techniques, they organized a transnational canon for an Arab readership, and they reinterpreted and recontextualized European originals within a longer arc of exchange in regions that were largely underemphasized in European accounts. They give readers a new account of the movement of novels in global literary space and describe an alternative history of European literature that bypasses accepted ideas about the division of subgenres and periods; they make European literary history strange. This book follows their theorization of the novel in translation as they compose literary history between languages, classifications of forms, and systems of literary value and as they insert their own labors—sometimes tentatively—as part of this long and ongoing history. More than just interpreters, these translators were also *producers* of novels, working decades before scholars have understood the genre as having arrived. Their literary productions, I argue, are theorizations and ones that are relevant to more than just the history of literature in Arabic. Taking into their scope European literature and even "the world," they have implications for discussions about world literature, the transnational novel, and the field of translation studies. Far from understanding the works of these translators as literary curiosities or footnotes to a "pre-history" of the novel, I write with them and follow them as theoreticians of the very modernity that they produced.

(Arabic) Translation in the World

Every several years, scholars of comparative literature encounter a call for an increased attention to translation in their critical methodology.[18] Rather than a derivative product unworthy of attention (at worst) or a literary curiosity (at best), they are periodically told, they should treat translations as complex literary objects. The "State of the Discipline" reports commissioned by the American Comparative Literature Association (ACLA) offer an excellent window on this phenomenon: while in the 1965 "Levin Report" and the 1975 "Greene Report" translations are treated as paraliterary objects that offer a disgraceful shortcut to students who cannot read in more than one or two languages, the 1993 "Bernheimer Report" argues that "the old hostilities toward translation should be mitigated" in order to broaden the field of inquiry in graduate programs.[19] Indeed, the mid-1990s might be seen as a watershed moment for the field, as landmark interventions posited the work of translation as a form of interpretation itself. Gayatri Spivak called translation "the most intimate act of reading." Lawrence Venuti argued that translation was a "double writing" that "rewrit[es] the foreign text according to values in the receiving culture," requiring a "double reading" in turn.[20] Indeed, in Susan Bassnett's 1993 survey of the field, she argued that literary scholars should "look upon translation studies as the principal discipline from now on, with comparative literature as a valued but subsidiary subject area."[21]

Subsequent ACLA reports reflect a growing consensus about this translational turn: the 2004 report includes an entire essay arguing for "recasting the work of translation . . . as rereading and rewriting engaged with the production of meaning."[22] The most recent report (2017) includes both an essay calling for "understanding, appreciating, and valuing translations . . . as their own elucidations, representations, and performances of texts" and an entire section of responses ("Languages, Vernaculars, Translations") that emphasizes translation's importance to the field.[23] Such scholars have hailed Translation Studies as comparative literature's methodological and political lifeline, a force for renewal for fields in crisis. As Spivak and Emily Apter have both argued in their articulations of a "new comparative literature," translation's attention to what Venuti calls "the ethics of location," or the way that language itself is culturally and politically produced, can point the way out of (the old) comparative literature's entrenched Eurocentrism by highlighting the "import of the translator's choice" as it exists in fields of discursive and material power, or the multilinguistic practice of "minor" and "marginalized" literary producers who engage the canon from below or afar.[24]

At the same time, the destigmatization of studying works in translation has helped pave the way for the emergence of the field of World Literature. Whether one thinks of that field as being constituted by "world" objects ("literary works that circulate beyond their culture of origin," as David Damrosch writes) or by a methodology ("distant reading" or collaborative scholarship that does not restrict its primary sources to those read in their original language, as Franco Moretti has posed), translation has proved to be one of its underacknowledged operating concepts. Or, as Apter has argued, world literature has relied on "a translatability assumption": the tendency to exclude translation problems and instead hew toward "reflexive endorsement of cultural equivalence and substitutability, or toward the celebration of nationally and ethnically branded 'differences' that have been niche-marketed as commercialized 'identities.'"[25] The translator, as Venuti has repeatedly emphasized, is once again rendered invisible—even while providing the methodological underpinnings to these studies of the circulation of forms.

A second argumentative principle, likewise unacknowledged, often shadows the interventions just named. Many rely on examples from Arabic language or literature. Venuti's "Call to Action" that ends *The Translator's Invisibility* includes a recuperative reading of Sir Francis Burton's translation of *The Thousand and One Nights*, which he poses as an example of double writing capable of "changing reading patterns, winning acceptance for the literature of a stigmatized foreign culture while casting English cultural history in a different light."[26] Apter's "A New Comparative Literature," the manifesto that concludes *The Translation Zone*, ends with a meditation on Edward Said's "Living in Arabic," in which she uses the Arabophone's diglossia (as he or she navigates the split between Arabic's written and spoken forms) as an example of the way that monolingualism belies structures of translation; rather than a powerful, quasi-religious law by which languages are tied to people or nations (what she calls "linguistic monotheism"), "living in Arabic" shows how a single language translates itself, "thereby regrounding the prospects for a new comparative literature in the problem of translation."[27] And Steven Ungar's essay in the 2004 ACLA report grounds its call for integrating translation into literary studies in a reading of the incommensurability of Arabic and French in Francophone Arab texts. The challenges that this literature presents to the traditional dichotomy between the original and its translation, he concludes, results in "a translation pedagogy attuned to difference [that] can contribute to recasting the model and practices of a new comparative literature in line with the realities of globalization in its multiple expressions."[28] Arabic acts as a limit case for the expanding boundary of Comparative Literature, a challenge to traditional disciplinary formations and understandings of translation.[29] It is even part of the basis for Apter's understanding of the "politics of untranslatability" itself, as she cites Edward Said's observations in *Humanism and Democratic Criticism* on the singularity of the Qur'anic Arabic and Moroccan philosopher Abdelfattah Kilito's wry readings of various Arab authors' suspicion of translation or refusal to translate or be translated, in *Lan tatakalama lughatī* (Thou shalt not speak my language). Both linguistic inviolability and refusal on political or cultural grounds mark Arabic as the extreme limit of translatability.[30]

Stranger Fictions joins this unfinished work of merging translation studies and literary scholarship from the perspective of Arabic literature. Yet unlike previous efforts, it moves Arabic to the center of translation studies, rather than placing it at a distant limit. Its six chapters take the reader chronologically through nearly a century of translations published in Beirut, Cairo, Malta, Paris, London, and New York. The book begins with the first translations performed by Lebanese and Egyptian translators under the auspices of British missionary societies in Malta in the 1830s and ends in the first decade of the twentieth century with the translations of British and French sentimental and crime novels published in Cairo. Each connects the purportedly marginal enterprise of translating foreign fiction, performed by well-known and forgotten translators, to the concerns of canonical *nahḍa* thinkers and the literary and cultural debates in which they participated. Collectively, I argue, these authors developed translation techniques and writing styles that cultivated a new mode of reading that I call *reading in translation*, which required the reader to move comparatively within and among languages and with the awareness of the diverging interpretive frameworks that animated the investments of multiple audiences. Far from being mere bad translators, these authors appear as translation theorists and informed commentators on literary history. Presenting their own work as occurring within an ongoing history of translation rather than deviating from it, these translators contend—as do I—that the Arabic novel takes translation and cultural transfer as its foundation, *as does the European novel*. The novel did not "rise" in one context and "travel" fully formed to another; it emerged in and through a dynamic process of translation. In this sense, the Arabic case is not only central: it is paradigmatic.

Bad Translation; Errant Circulations

This book takes the implications of these translators' claims seriously, counterpoising them to standard accounts of the novel's supposed travels in translation. In these accounts—which emerge from within World Literature paradigms—the novel is embedded in and an exemplar of a world literary system that is "one, and unequal."[31] Influenced in equal measure by Immanuel Wallerstein's World Systems Theory and Itamar Even-Zohar's Polysystems Theory in translation studies, scholars take "the point of view of totality" with respect to the system and analyze its parts as mutually interlinked functions (rather than as distinct units that can be compared).[32] As such, these influential models attempt large-scale, relational analyses of a single system divided into cores and peripheries, using market-based metaphors to do so.[33] Translation thus appears central, a force guiding non-European authors on a circumscribed path to the novel in its paradigmatic form: "translation-waves" radiate from the center of novelistic production in western European capitals or remedy "literary impoverishment" in the periphery by gathering "literary resources" and putting them to work.[34] Building on Even-Zohar's axiom that "there is no symmetry in literary interference," translation from "stronger" literatures to "weak" ones appears as a transparent process oriented toward adequation or, at best, as variations on a standard determined by the core.[35]

These economic metaphors certainly have their place in our accounts of world literature; after all, print capitalism is a form of capitalism. As I show in chapter 3, it was inextricably tied to translators' theories of global circulation. And, as Elizabeth Holt has argued, commodity production and related investments informed the rise of the reading public in this region.[36] However, I would like to complicate the roles of producers and consumers in this model. Economies are structures of production and consumption, yet the world literary system takes a dim view of the agency of the consumer-translator as well as the consumer-reader. As Moretti conceives it in his "Conjectures on World Literature" essay, in the spread of novels from the core to the periphery, the destiny of the receiving culture is intersected and altered by the original, with little reciprocal effect.[37] The novel, once produced, travels unmolested along a current of hegemonic diffusion where the single and unequal literary economy ensures the "planetary reproduction of a couple of national literatures." The result is, at best, a "compromise" between hegemonic foreign form and local materials ("characters" and "narrative voice"); at worst, this movement ensures the "terrible solidity of successful forms."[38] The consumer receives or rearranges those reproductions, the "successful form" untouched by its travels.

As I will show throughout this book, Arabophone literary consumers were indeed interested in foreign imports, but their interests exceeded that of picking and choosing which objects were to be consumed. More important was how they were consumed and what transformations could or should occur in their consumption. "I have changed what I did not find in agreement with the taste of our age," writes one translator. "We aimed in our 'arabization' to make this work Arab and not foreignized [*mutafarnaj*]."[39] To borrow a term from Michel de Certeau's *The Practice of Everyday Life*, they recognized the use to which objects are put as a form of production, a *poiēsis*. Indeed, as Khalīl Zayniyya writes of translating a ten-page French story into a novel-length "romantic literary novel," "I have so diverged from the author in its telling . . . that I do not know whether to call it a translation or a[n original] composition."[40] Consumers, as de Certeau writes, should be understood as "unrecognized producers, poets of their own affairs."[41] It should not be surprising, then, that many *nahḍa* thinkers put the consumer at the center of their cultural analysis and often figured the consumer as a translator. Adopting foreign customs, more than one author remarks, should be regarded as a form of *iqtibās*, or adaptation (literally, "quotation").

As Zayniyya knew and de Certeau theorized, consumption as *poiēsis* is only recognized, only made visible, when the translation "diverges" from its source, having been produced by "users who are not [an object's] makers."[42] Only then, de Certeau argues, "can we gauge the difference or similarity between the production of the image and the secondary production hidden in the process of its utilization."[43] That is: consumption's production of meaning is made visible in circulation understood as translation (or secondary production), in the movement of the object outside its context of (primary) production and into contexts where use can transform it. Bill Brown refines this kind of secondary production or translation to consider the category of "misuse." It is in an object's misuse rather than in its use that its materiality and meaning "become manifest as though for the first time . . . not because of [an object's] familiar designated function but during a re-creation that renders it other than what it was."[44] As one early translator, Salīm dī Nawfal, writes, quoting Voltaire, "every translation, in respect to the original, is like the back of a cloth is to its face."[45] Such translators ambivalently seized on the realization that there can be no equivalence in translation, turning it into an opportunity. Their texts' dissimilarities from their sources not only are routine but are also the expected results of translation.

Just as it is not use but "misuse" that most often makes the agency of the consumer visible, so too with "mistranslation": it is in a text's difference from its source that translators become visible as what Brown describes as "representatives of radical difference, able as they are to reappropriate a technology produced a world away" from its origin.[46] Translations that do not conform to the norms and values of their literary source culture or their new contexts are often dismissed as "bad translations," but those are precisely the texts that concern us here. It is in the mistranslated or "*mal traduit*" (as our critic who panned Gharghūr's translation of *Les Misérables* puts it) where the fact that a work is translated becomes visible (it "smacks of translation," as Antoine Berman writes); it is where new norms and values and even forms are mediated.[47] As Lital Levy shows in her groundbreaking work in Hebrew-Arabic interlingual interactions, translation reimagines and re-creates canons, histories, and language itself.[48] It is for this reason that I prefer, in this book, to use "translation" in all of its variants rather than to follow Apter in her concern for the "untranslatable." Translation—via translation theory—has long grappled with the untranslatable and the *mal traduit* as the (often temporary) response to its inherent impossibility.[49] Rather than focusing on the difficulties if not even the impossibilities of translatability, *Stranger Fictions* excavates the vast range of responses that translators presented in the nineteenth century—including fidelity. It refuses to reify a division of labor between theorists and practitioners in this case and sees the practice of translation as itself presenting theoretical propositions.

In histories of the Arabic novel, whether written in English or in Arabic, these translators are characterized most often as uncritical hacks, and the differences between their translations and the original are negatively described. For Matti Moosa, they are "poor" and "irresponsible" translations; for ʿAbd al-Muḥsin Ṭaha Badr, in his classic *Taṭawwur al-riwāya al-ʿarabiyya fī Miṣr* (Development of the Arabic novel in Egypt), they were "stolen, but mostly disfigured [*mushawwaha*]" goods; and for Anwar al-Jundī, the entire period of literary production of the nineteenth century was a "defective [*hajīn*, literally "half-bred"] age that produced a disabled [*muʿawwaq*] offspring."[50] Badr, for example, relates a story about the prolific translator Ṭāniyūs ʿAbduh, who would read the original, "gathering with his eyes all the eloquence that the original author had offered, and not long afterward he would close the book and turn toward his translation, writing page after page without casting a glance at the lines that his right hand was tracing."[51] Muḥammad Ḥāfiẓ Ibrāhīm, whose verse translation of *Les Misérables* appeared in 1903, reportedly had such a poor command of the French language that it took him fifteen days to translate one page.[52] And perhaps the best-known translator of French literature, Muṣṭafā Luṭfī al-Manfālūṭī, is widely known to have spoken no foreign languages at all. His translations were all Arabic renderings of novels whose plots were related to him orally or rewritings of literal translations made for him by friends. As Samah Selim, whose work excavating this corpus in Egypt is indispensable, has put it, the popular fiction of the *nahḍa* often "cared nothing for origins and genealogies."[53] Translation as mistranslation, of often unattributed originals, formed the mode of unregulated circulation that created the beginning of the Arabic novel.[54]

These are the best-known examples of translators, but they by no means represent the entirety of this corpus, which is vast. Scholars number the translations of novels published before the twentieth century from several hundred to over one thousand.[55] Many translators were masters of European languages; they paid scrupulous attention to their sources and yet still stand distinct from their source texts. Al-Shidyāq, for example, who was probably responsible for a version of *Robinson Crusoe* that would be unrecognizable to most scholars of English literature (see chapter 1), was a linguistic savant who wrote English grammars for Arabic students, lived in England and France, and was employed by a missionary society to translate the New Testament. Nakhla Ṣāliḥ and Yūsuf Aṣṣāf (see chapter 6) were both trained and employed as high-ranking professional translators, Ṣāliḥ for the Egyptian railway director and Aṣṣāf for the Egyptian postmaster.[56] Others lived extensively in Europe: Salīm Bustrus, whose serialized translations appeared in *Ḥadīqat al-akhbār* (see chapter 4) and *Al-Ahrām*, opened a trading house in Liverpool, and Luwīs Ṣābūnjī, who collaborated on one of the several translations of *The Count of Monte Cristo* (see chapter 5), founded and edited a bilingual journal in London, *Al-Naḥla / The Bee* (1877–1880).[57]

Authors of original novels, too, were often also translators and produced translations of novels, incorporated translated texts into their original works, and produced translations that they passed off as original novels. Many authors freely acknowledged these blurred lines between original work and translation. As Khalīl Zayniyya explains in his preface to *Nājiyya: Riwāya Gharāmiyya Adabiyya* (Najiyya: A romantic literary novel; Beirut 1884), a work that is listed in Ḥamdī Sakkūt's bibliography as an original text, he expanded it from a ten-page French story: "I simplified it the best I could and added to its pleasures and also changed what I did not find in agreement with the taste of our age. I have diverged from the author in its telling . . . and therefore do not know if I should call it a translation or an original work, though I think that the name 'composition' is more suitable for it than 'translation,' for he who looks through the original after reading it will see that there are clear differences and a great distance between them."[58] Other authors saw their original works as resembling translations and fulfilling similar cultural functions. Yūsuf al-Shalfūn explained to his readers that he included the novel *Ḥifẓ al-widād* (The preservation of affections, 1866) in his serial *Al-Shirāka al-shahriyya fī Bayrūt*

(The monthly share in Beirut) because the translation of *The Count of Monte Cristo* before it had proved that "there is a large audience for novels" and especially those about affection.[59] Conversely, Iskandar Tuwaynī explains that he undertook his translation, *Yamīn al-armala* (The widow's oath, 1861), after being inspired by an original novel.[60]

Translation so fundamentally structured *nahḍa* literary production that even the author of the earliest extant original novel, Khalīl al-Khūrī, did not consider the publication of *Wayy, idhan lastu bi-ifranjī* (Alas, I am not a foreigner, 1858) to be something radically new, appearing as it did alongside translated novels and even substituting for them in his newspaper's fiction section. "If we are to embark upon this art [of novel-writing]," he writes, "it is not appropriate for us to stray from the path of [other] eminent authors."[61] Indeed, al-Khūrī frames modernity itself as a translation project. His novel focuses on an Aleppo merchant, Mikhālī, as he attempts unsuccessfully to marry his daughter to a mysterious European visitor and thereby become a foreigner himself. Mikhālī's attempt at what he calls "progress" via acculturation fails, as his daughter—after spurning her Arab suitor—is rejected by the Frenchman. Mikhālī's efforts at being translated into French culture do not result in his becoming a foreigner (*ifranjī*) but a *mutafarnij* (pseudoforeigner), a species—as al-Khūrī describes it—that wears foreign clothes awkwardly and speaks enough of a foreign language to have forgotten how to pronounce Arabic. If Mikhālī is a translation of a European original, he is a bad one.

Far from denying the flood of material things and immaterial ideas being imported from Europe, al-Khūrī takes these things as objects of interrogation, and he focuses on their translation and consumption—or their translation as a form of consumption—as the problematic locus of modernity. As he explains, mocking the way Mikhālī wears his *rīdinkūt* (riding coat), "the European tailor's shop isn't a school for civilization."[62] Yet cultural isolation is no path to progress either. Instead, he advocates the adaptation (*iqtibās*, another synonym used for "translation" in this period) of foreign knowledge and arts.[63] Al-Khūrī admonishes the denizens of the new age of the *nahḍa* not to be passive receivers of Western culture. Even as *Wayy* focuses on Western imports, it understands their reception as complexly tied up with questions of agency, subjectivity, and modernity.

Al-Khūrī's novel and its translated contemporaries lead us to take seriously the idea of "importing" and to understand the novel in Arabic as engaging what al-Khūrī calls "literary and material progress": a textual object in international circulation.[64] If translation cannot be understood solely as an agent of diffusion, then what models for that circulation might we be able to sketch? Understanding the novel as developing in "mobile vectors of cultural and social imaginaries," as Dilip Parameshwar Gaonkar and Elizabeth Povinelli have described cultures of circulation, we can see it as social form in motion or as an example of "things that are neither fully denizen nor citizen of their locales"—much like the figure of the pseudoforeigner.[65] Translation, as "the (im)possibility of meaningful commensuration," as they remind us, "has long been circulation's double, its enabling twin."[66] Things cannot circulate without translation, but neither perhaps can they be translated without circulating—without an attention to the "transfigurations they demand on the palpability, intelligibility, and recognizability of texts, events, and practices."[67] Focusing on the conditions under which texts move, we can answer questions about how mobility engenders transformations in form rather than enabling its terrible solidity.

Neither importation nor translation can be reduced to Westernization. Al-Khūrī and his contemporaries ask time and again what it means to buy and use Western products—be they foreign words, musical instruments, or clothing—and they mark exchange as a process that puts local and foreign scales of value on trial. In engaging what Gayatri Spivak calls the "textuality of value," translation becomes visible as a trope of *nahḍa* discourse that poses issues of progress and modernity as cultural and material exchange, where they circulate in multiple systems of valuation at once and where that exchange does not presuppose adequation or fungibility but poses their possibility and impossibility at once.[68] Understanding these circulations requires understanding postcolonial translation not simply as a site of resistance but also one of collaboration that has material and nonmaterial benefits and where—as Shaden Tageldin writes—"subjects of empire so avidly abet their cultural colonization" for their own economic, political, or ontological gain.[69]

Like other *nahḍa* thinkers, al-Khūrī meditates on what it means to be both a producer *and* a receiver in the transnational circulation of ideas, technologies, and forms. He cultivates a mode of reading in translation (and even includes extensive sections in translation in the novel) that required the reader to move comparatively within and among languages and with the awareness of the diverging interpretive frameworks that animated the investments of multiple audiences

Stranger Fictions therefore situates novel writing within the broader history of *nahḍa* thought, showing the shared foundation of translation within both. Like al-Khūrī, who was not only a journalist and printer but also a pioneering publisher of serialized translations, it recasts well-known *nahḍa* figures as participants in the purportedly marginal practice of translation. Aḥmad Fāris al-Shidyāq is known as a journalist, author, and lexicographer, but I uncover his work as a translator for the Church Missionary Society and its press, which produced an 1835 translation of *Robinson Crusoe*. Well-known thinkers like Nasīf al-Yāzijī and Saʿīd al-Shartūnī, who were conservative voices in the great debates about linguistic modernity, at times situated their arguments within the broader framework of the translation (*naql*) of Arabic into a modern language. Founders of the print public sphere like Buṭrus and Salīm al-Bustānī, I show, thought of their journals as performing the work of literal and cultural translation: the institutions of the printing press, linguistic modernization, the print public sphere, and even anticolonial nationalism—those marquee projects of the *nahḍa*—were all founded on translation's new modes of reading. Their "bad translations" cannot be dismissed as a result of their poor grasp of foreign languages or as a symptom of their incomplete modernization but should be seen as a sign of modernity itself.

This book tracks the choices, errors, and innovations in their translations as essential elements in the development of the Arabic novel, performed by translator-critics who themselves saw translation underwriting the genre of the novel as a whole. They are not alone in this assessment. Though the theory of the novel has, over the years, become dominated by paradigms related to nation-building (as William Warner writes, it has become the theory of the "English rise of the English novel"), this was by no means always the case.[70] Eighteenth-century critics like James Beattie (1783) and Clara Reeve (1785) saw the novel's origins in French romance or in the "fabulous narrative" of the East,[71] Georg Lukács (1914–1915) understood it as the genre of "transcendental homelessness,"[72] and Mikhail Bakhtin identified its distinguishing feature as its "heteroglossia," defining the novel as "an artistically organized system for bringing different languages in contact with one another."[73] For these theorists of the novel, as for the nineteenth-century Arabic translators under study here, the novel is not a purely English or French form that then gets translated elsewhere. It is a genre that is always already in translation.

A Transnational (and Translational) *Nahḍa*

If these translations are so rich, so prevalent, and so plentiful in the nineteenth century, then why have they gone unstudied for so long? Part of the answer lies in the history of the field of Middle Eastern Studies, which has folded the history of the Arabic novel into one of its main scholarly preoccupations, the history of the nation-state. Most often modeled on the Egyptian case—where the "progression" from the production of translations to adaptations to original compositions tracks Egypt's transition from Ottoman imperial province to British protectorate to independent nation—the novel is seen as one of the primary vehicles for developing national sentiment and distributing nationalist thought in the transition to modernity, during the period of the *nahḍa*.[74] Indeed, when intellectuals writing in Egypt consolidated the term *nahḍa* itself in the first two decades of the twentieth century, they fueled this appearance of symmetry between novel and nation. According to now-canonical figures like Jurjī Zaydān, Qāsim Amīn, and Rashīd Riḍā, the key to creating a modern literary culture, family structure, or paradigm of Islamic thought was through the "revival" (*nahḍa*) of Golden Age Arab culture channeled into a modern, national mold.[75] In these and later, Syrian, Palestinian Arab, and Iraqi nationalist cases, the *nahḍa*, or "awakening," as it is usually translated, was deployed as a call to develop national consciousness, what Sherene Seikaly calls, with appropriate irony, "that heterogeneous movement wherein the nation was to rise up, discard corrupt and outdated traditions, and realize the triumphant arrival of the modern."[76]

The ideologies of the later, twentieth-century part of this story, which historians have so expertly excavated, all fall under what is now often referred to as "the second *nahḍa*," a term that encompasses a period of national debate about issues such as Arab nationalism, socialism, and Marxism, and are often traced back to these foundational Egyptian intellectuals.[77] In the course of demonstrating continuity between the second *nahḍa* and the first, scholars have tended to highlight national concerns, such that the *nahḍa* comes to be understood as coextensive with these Egyptian intellectuals, and Arab modernity itself with their efforts to create national culture and literary forms. As Samah Selim argues, this has meant—in the Egyptian case—that critics of the Arab novel define the form as one that must properly construct "the basic elements of narrative fiction—time, place, character, plot—in a way that 'mirrors' the particular social, cultural and political reality [*wāqiʿ*] of the national collectivity."[78] It is therefore no coincidence that the "first Arabic novel" was long considered to be *Zaynab*, a romanticized depiction of Egyptian rural life written by an anticolonialist nationalist thinker (Muḥammad Ḥusayn Haykal).[79] Published in 1913 under the pen name "A Man of the Egyptian Soil" (*miṣrī fallāḥ*), it has been described as the first "authentically" or "purely" Arab novel and praised for its portrayal of "national reality"—unlike those "unrealistic" and even "perverse" foreign-style fantasies that the previous century had produced. Translational novels depicting foreign places and characters, which dominated the period before *and beyond* 1913, have been treated as both prenational and prenovelistic. The history of the Arab novel, then, has yoked a process of canonization to one of nationalization. Studies of *nahḍa* literary production highlight the latter half of the "first *nahḍa*" and the budding nationalist concerns of a few authors, whose ideas are often retrospectively and uniformly projected onto the authors who preceded them.[80] All *nahḍa* thought can therefore contain "the Arab nation that is always yet to come."[81] Literary modernity, according to this logic, is always already national.

Part of this is attributable to the centrality of Egypt in the field of Middle East Studies in general and in Arabic literature in particular. Napoleon, one is often reminded, brought a printing press with him on his 1798 expedition to Egypt, producing the first Arabic printed material in Egypt in the form of official proclamations of rule in classical Arabic style. Translation, as Shaden Tageldin so eloquently argues, was fundamental to the seductions of imperial rule.[82] So too was it fundamental to Egypt's state-building: Egypt's viceroy, Mehmet Ali (Muḥammad ʿAlī), soon afterward reversed Napoleon's itinerary and dispatched scientific missions to Europe to be trained in printing, languages, and scientific and military arts.[83] The Bulāq Press, run by these delegates, issued bulletins in Arabic and Turkish and focused its monolingual Arabic publications on the translations from scientific and technical European texts that the delegates were required to produce upon their return.[84] Translation was instrumental to Mehmet Ali's vision of cultural and technical revival, and in 1837 he institutionalized it in his School of Languages (Madrasat al-alsun) in Cairo, appointing as its head Rifāʿa Rāfiʿ al-Ṭahṭāwī, an Azhar-trained scholar who accompanied the first Mission égyptienne to Paris in 1824 as a religious guide. While the school neglected literature in order to focus on scholarly and scientific books that would advance the state of Egyptian learning, al-Ṭahṭāwī nonetheless played a key role in initiating the Translation Movement with his 1867 translation of François Fénelon's *Aventures de Télémaque*, *Mawāqiʿ al-aflāk fī waqāʾiʿ Tilīmāk* (The position of the spheres as they relate to what befell Telemachus). A Golden Age of translation, often called the Translation Movement and centered in Egypt under the patronage of Mehmet Ali's grandson Ismāʿīl and his successor Tawfīq, flowered in the 1870s and 1880s, serving as an offshoot of and analogue for a national modernization project, undertaken in imitation of European institutions.[85] Napoleon's torch had been passed on.

Except, of course, literary translation was already under way outside Egypt by the time of *Tilīmāk*'s publication. Commercial presses in Beirut like Khalīl al-Khūrī's al-Maṭbaʿa al-Sūriyya (Syrian Press) or Yūsuf al-Shalfūn's al-Maṭbaʿa al-ʿamūmiyya (Public Press) had printed commercially successful translations in serialized and single-volume form in 1858 and 1865, respectively. Religious presses had also begun to print religious texts and imaginative moral literature in translation (as chapter 1 explores). As early as 1826, missionary organizations (notably the Church Missionary Society, American Board of Commissioners for Foreign Missions, and a number of Catholic orders) had begun to establish presses in Malta, Beirut, Jerusalem, and Mosul. By midcentury, individual entrepreneurs had begun to open presses in Beirut, making it the center of commercial, independent, and semi-independent publishing. As Ami Ayalon details, more than a dozen such presses operated in the Levant alone, some helmed by the most recognizable names in nineteenth-century letters: Buṭrus al-Bustānī (1819–1883) founded Maṭbaʿat al-maʿārif; Khalīl Sarkīs (1842–1915) ran al-Maṭbaʿa al-adabiyya; and Khalīl al-Khūrī (1836–1907) headed al-Maṭbaʿa al-Sūriyya. In Istanbul, al-Shidyāq himself published what Ayalon calls "one of the most influential Arabic newspapers of its time," *Al-Jawāʾib*, and established a press by the same name that operated from 1871 until his death in 1887.[86] By 1900, at least twenty-two presses produced the fifty-five newspapers and journals in Beirut and Mount Lebanon, while in Egypt (which after the 1870s became the epicenter of production) at least 105 print shops produced 394 periodicals between 1850 and 1900, many of which maintained a critical and even oppositional stance vis-à-vis the Khedival, and later colonial, state.[87]

Publications from these presses situated their own reception in the context of what may be called a sort of translation-mania: in the preface to *Riwāyat ḥifẓ al-widād* (The preservation of affection, 1866), Al-Shalfūn writes that after he saw the "larger part of the young and intelligent audience of our country desiring to read *rūmān* or literary stories, especially of the French variety," he decided to present this "new Arabic novel [*riwāya*]" of his.[88] And al-Khūrī presents his *Wayy . . . idhan lastu bi-ifranjī* (Alas, I am not a foreigner, 1859) as an alternative to the translated novels he usually publishes, "in case the reader has grown bored" with them.[89] That al-Ṭahṭāwī himself elected to publish his translation of Fénelon first in al-Khūrī's Beirut-based periodical, *Ḥadīqat al-akhbār* (The garden of news, 1861–1867), and then at al-Maṭbaʿa al-Sūriyya (Syrian Press, 1867) might point as much to the robust market for translations already in existence in the Levant as to al-Ṭahṭāwī's fear of government reprisal in Egypt for its implicit critiques of the Khedive.[90] Al-Ṭahṭāwī and his Egyptian school did not initiate a literary translation movement in prose; he *joined* one that was already in progress.

Moreover, he joined a print sphere that was not exclusively nation-bound. Even within Egypt, as Michael Allan has showed us, the institutions of literary modernity and even "literature" (*adab*) developed in "the shadow of world literature," inside the normative force of transnational definitions and valuations of the literary.[91] Yet Egyptocentrism only partly accounts for the sidelining of translations in Arabic literary studies. Equally influential have been theories of print culture, which have also tended to think in national, monocultural, and monolingual modes. In the thirty years since Benedict Anderson posited the novel, along with the newspaper, as the form that created and sustained "the kind of imagined community that is the nation," the link between the novel and the nation-state has been overly emphasized, to the exclusion of other kinds of communities.[92] In the years that followed Anderson's *Imagined Communities*, a veritable "nation and narration" industry developed in the American academy, one that reinforced a tautology: the novel "rises" because of the enabling structure of the nation, while the nation rises through the collective imaginings enabled by the novel.[93] In this way, even shifting the focus to previously marginalized literatures and novelists can serve to reinforce the paradigm. Critics can argue for the reevaluation of neglected sources on the basis of their relevance to the national imaginary: early novels could be argued to constitute nationalism, but differently.

However, the record of *nahḍa* print culture everywhere challenges these models. Ayalon's extensive research into *nahḍa* publishing institutions has revealed a rich network of production beyond Egypt, one that linked local and transnational audiences.[94] Flourishing at a time of great technological and physical interconnection, Arabic printing expanded globally: westward via diasporic Arabophone communities to Europe and the Americas; and eastward via religious and scholarly reading communities to Iran and South Asia.[95] These included long-running periodicals like *Mir'āt al-aḥwāl* (1855–1877) in London, *Al-Hudā'* (1898–1971) in Philadelphia and New York, and an efflorescence of short-lived journals in Paris in the early 1880s, in São Paulo and Rio di Janeiro in the late 1890s, as well as the appearance of several Judeo-Arabic journals in Calcutta between 1873 and 1889.[96] Several periodicals were themselves transnational, including Luwīs Ṣābūnjī's *Al-Naḥla* and Ya'qūb Ṣannū''s overtly nationalist *Abū Naḍḍāra al-zarqā'*, appearing and reappearing in multiple international locations (and in the case of *Abū Naḍḍāra*, an Egyptian colloquial weekly, smuggled to its primary audience in Egypt)—a necessity created by their founders' oppositional stance to political and religious authorities.[97]

As the following chapters will demonstrate in detail, not only was Arabic print produced on at least five continents in the nineteenth century, but it was also produced by individuals who themselves traversed boundaries and engendered transnational reading publics. As Ayalon writes, "the sounds from Beirut, Cairo, and Alexandria reached other Arab provinces, and educated groups in the towns of Syria, Palestine, Iraq, and even the Hijaz became involved in the new exchange in print across provincial boundaries."[98] Chapters 3 and 4, which explore Beirut periodicals of the 1850s through 1870s, demarcate several layers of transnational print networks. First, journals frequently indicate their international agents in cities inside and outside Arabic-speaking regions (with several listing over twenty locations), showing the wide transnational circulation of Arabic print. Second, Arabic journals incorporated excerpts from foreign newspapers that had circulated to Beirut.[99] A few of these periodicals even framed their central mission around the Arabic circulation of these foreign news items: Khalīl al-Khūrī explained in the introductory essay to his periodical, *Ḥadīqat al-akhbār*, that he has "included pages of news in different languages in order to be a lantern of improvement." Journals frequently combined original journalistic writing with articles translated from foreign newspapers and serialized both original and translated novels interchangeably, sometimes side by side.[100] In fact, Arabic journalism relied so heavily on foreign periodicals that any delay in their arrival would be cause for an urgent announcement.[101]

Even from these limited examples, we might see the way the Arabic print public sphere—from its very inception—was composed of intellectual alliances across borders.[102] Readers of these journals could not help but imagine themselves as part of a transnational print network, as they read news items explicitly marked as having been translated from the European press, read reviews of new periodicals published in other Middle Eastern cities, or read articles about the news-consumption habits of readers in countries near and far.[103] Rather than entering a narrowly defined sphere of regional or protonational print influence, they joined a transnational public sphere that was *itself* composed of translation. To acknowledge the foreign texts and foreign fellow readers that circulate through *nahḍa* periodicals is to see global circulation as a fundamental condition of not just the new Arabic reading public but the print public sphere *at large*.

Therefore, this book treats the novel much like other intellectual, commercial, and technological projects of the period, which Middle East historians have increasingly identified as having been developed in larger networks of communication. Ilham Khuri-Makdisi, for example, has tracked the rise of radical leftist ideas in Beirut, Cairo, and Alexandria as part of a larger international circulation of ideas and awareness of world events, while Julia Clancy-Smith has traced "how the Muslim Mediterranean became modern" to the transnational population movements of the nineteenth century.[104] While both Khuri-Makdisi and Clancy-Smith reanimate the category of the Mediterranean (or "the central Mediterranean corridor") as the primary unit of interaction, others identify even wider ones. For Valeska Huber, the (often forced) movement of peoples, goods, and information that were channeled to construct the Suez Canal in 1869 was an example of nineteenth-century globalization; for Hala Auji, *nahḍa* printing practices were examples of the nexus of "industrialized global modernization practices and the perseverance of local customary modes of visual production."[105] James Gelvin and Nile Green bring together modern Sufi practices, networks of Islamic reform, pilgrimage travel, weapons commerce, and Iranian music under the heading "global Muslims in the age of steam and print."[106] Even evolutionary discourse—for Marwa Elshakry—afforded *nahḍa* actors an opportunity to participate in the allegedly universal "world order of knowledge."[107] For Tarek El-Ariss, the itinerant literary and actual travels of *nahḍa* authors formed the "trials" by which modernity itself was debated and transformed.[108]

This book regards the novel as a part of material culture (print technology) that circulates within and across national and imperial borders. And while it takes much of its impetus from both "global history" models and "world literature" ones, it does not formulate its analysis exclusively at the scale of the globe. Instead, it seeks to investigate modern Arabic literature as it circulates—in and as translation—at several scales at once, some smaller and some larger than the nation. These circulations—both among localities and across empires and oceans—do not negate the usefulness of the nation as an organizing category. Instead, they complicate it, transforming the nation from an a priori category or inevitable outcome of literary history into a historical and ideological problem. As Laura Briggs, Gladys McCormick, and J. T. Way have argued in their essay "The Transnational: A Category of Analysis," "the nation itself has to be a question—not untrue and therefore trivial, but an ideology that changes over time."[109] Transnationalism, as the authors argue, is not a model of international interaction but a "conceptual acid" that "denaturalizes" national, international, and global frames, "compelling us to acknowledge that the nation . . . is a thing contested, interrupted, and always shot through with contradiction."[110] Translation, similarly, provides the conceptual acid in the isomorphism between the theory of the novel and the ideology of the nation-state. The Arabic novel, for its first decades, circulated primarily in translation, in a new, partially foreign Arabic that depicted primarily foreign peoples and locations. As this book ultimately argues in its conclusion, that foreign element—what Jean-Jacques Lecercle calls translation's "remainder"—is never disciplined out of the genre.[111] Indeed, we might see the canonization of the novel in Arabic in the twentieth century as a history of a nationalization that was and always will be incomplete.

Toward a New Transnational History of the Novel

This corpus of translated novels, this book argues, is foundational to the original novel and its modern literary institutions, coeval with them, and constitutive of them. Divided into two parts, the book traces the importance of translation chronologically from the earliest extant translated novel published in 1835 to the melodramatic translations that accompanied the rise of the nationalist novel in the first two decades of twentieth century. Part 1, "Reading in Translation," looks at translations performed in the first half of the nineteenth century in the context of three central endeavors in literary and cultural modernization: the early development of print, the scholarly effort to modernize the Arabic language, and the reformist project of creating a modern reading public in Arabic. This section posits that what scholars had previously called the "Translation Movement" comprised more than a group of texts that happened to be translated from European languages in Egypt. Rather, it cultivated a new mode of reading that required the reader to move comparatively within and among languages and with the awareness of the diverging interpretive frameworks that animated the investments of multiple audiences, and this mode of reading structured literary institutions such as print culture, the public sphere, and Modern Arabic. Part 2, "The Transnational Imagination," then takes up translations of the latter half of the century, when production of such texts peaked, and reads them in the context of their transnational production and circulation while also noting how they participated in the debates framed in part 1 about Arabic literature's entrance into global and comparative literary fields. Circulating not only between Europe and the Middle East but also among multiple and overlapping Arabic reading publics, these novels demonstrate how reading in translation rereads canons and institutions of the novel *at large* as formed across linguistic and geographic borders.

The work of these translators, literary historians, and novelists constitutes a new transnational history of the novel with translation at its center and that charts new routes through familiar sources. Their work makes literary histories and subgeneric categories unrecognizable to domestic canons; they are made strange. The Arabic *Crusoe* rewrites the novel's "rise" and recasts it as yet another leg in the novel's circulation; al-Shidyāq reconfigures generic transmission and transnational literary history as the transmission of errors; translators of Verne and Dumas recast their global fictions as fragmented and circumscribed ones; and popular translators regenerate sentimental and criminal melodramas as critical discourse on national issues.

Reading in translation is more than a historical critical practice. It is also what this book asks its reader to do: to read between texts, to identify their disjunctions and their common ground. To do so often means focusing on the details of discrepancies and congruities: the register of dialogues, the small differences in geographic descriptions, the addition of one-word parenthetical definitions. Translation, it is often pointed out, requires a meditation on difference. Yet as *nahḍa* translators insist, it is not simply the difference between languages or societies that one must contemplate. In the New Age especially, there are also differences within a single language, literature, and reading public that are not containable in discrete, homogeneous unities but that proliferate within their heterogeneous and partially strange assemblages. This, they argue, is the practice of modernity: *iqtibās*, to select, quote, from foreign and domestic sources. To read in translation is to provisionally reassemble the diverse elements that constitute the text and read among them. It is to work at the impossible task of "assembling and expressing what is to be conveyed" fragment by fragment, to borrow Benjamin's image of language as a broken vessel.[112] To do so, to construct meaning by assembling the fragments, does not, he insists, require likeness.

Neither does the novel, that broken totality according to Georg Lukács, require like fragments: it carries "the fragmentary nature of the world's structure into the world of forms."[113] It is a heterogeneous assemblage itself. To read the history of the novel in translation, from the perspective of its translators, is to read along the history of assembly, fragmentation, and reassembly that theorists of the novel have long seen as its linguistic and theoretical basis. What circulates to the Middle East and elsewhere in the novel's believed-to-be-belated literary peripheries, they argue, was already in circulation. It is not therefore "the English novel" or "the French novel" that travels but the novel in translation, in assembled and reassembled fragments. Understanding the novel as these translators did, as a form that always requires comparative analysis and "reading in translation," helps to acknowledge translation and mistranslation as central not only to the novel in Arabic but to the history of the novel itself as a transnational form.

و٩ انفس . وفلورنس ١٦٧ الفًا و٩٦ نفسًا . وجن
١٢٠ الفًا و٩٧٦ نفسًا وفنيس ١٢٨ الفًا و٩٠١ .
وبولون ١١٥ الفًا و٩٥٧ . ومسين ١١١ الفًا و٨٥٤

المفاوضة المبهمة

(من قلم خليل افندي غانم ترجمان ولاية سورية الجليلة)

Bon jour بونجور خواجا كيف حالك جهفه
يان Je vais bien كثر خيرك اي موسيو فوتر بير
et M. votre père كيف حالة مبسوط ديو مرسي
Dieu mercie اي ماما Ma mère اعتراها مرض
ال كاردله لي Elle garde le lit من اكم يوم وكال
مالادي quelle maladie مرض كراف تره كراف
Grave très-grave من طبيبكم نه مي بارله بادي
مدسين Ne me parlez pas de medecin
استدعينا جميع الاطباء كي سي تروف ان فيل
Qui se trouvent en Ville كاسك فوزافه دي
نوف Qu'est-ce que vous avez de neuf
لا يوجد شي دي بيان ساليان De bien saillant
اخبرتنا النوفل تلغرافيك Les nouvelles teleg-
raphiques عن انسوكسه unsiccès الكونت دي
شامبور كونه متمسك بيرنسيبو Daus ses principes
اسك اون تروف Est-ce qui on trouve
خمرة جيدة في البلد وي Oui عند الخواجا حنا اليان
والفرموث الذي يباع دان سون ماغازين
Dans son magasin كالك شوز دوكسكي
C'est quelque chose d'exquis ما هو
فالسيفية falsifié وناهيك عن بعض كلام يستعمل
في الحديث مثل عملنا لفو بليمان Complimants
واعطيناه رانده فو Rendez vous وتكبنا اصلها
بالفرنساوية Nous sommes quittes الى غير

ذلك من الكلمات الكثيرة المستعملة بين التجار
وقصارى الامر اننا نرى المتفرنجين من اهل
بلادنا يتكلمون لغة مبهمة لا يدركها من كان جاهلا
للغة الفرنساوية فلو تكلم البنون بحضور ابائهم (الذين
يسمونهم الرجال القدم) بلغة غريبة عن لغتهم فربما
كان ذلك يسر الاباء اذ يخيل لهم بان المحروسين
اتقنوا اللغات الاوربية ولكن عندما يسمعونهم
يخلطون اللغتين كأنه لا فرق بينهما او كأنه من الواجب
ان المخاطب يعرف اللغة الفرنساوية الا يحق لهم بان
يتعجبوا ويتكدروا اما لغتنا العربية فهي لغة غنية
غير مفتقرة الى تعريب الكلام كاللغات التي يشتق
اكثرها من اللاتينية واليونانية اشتقاقا مانوسا عند
اهلها وكاللغة التركية فان ثلثيها من العربية والفارسية
وغيرها ومع ذلك هي لغة لطيفة كعروس بديعة
ذات جمال وبهاء تتيه دلالا في رياض العرب
والفرس وتقطف منها ما يحلو لها من الازهار . فان
العربية هي خير اللغات وكم من الناس ومن اعيان
الفضل اجهدوا انفسهم في سبيل خدمتها واجالوا
افكارهم بنظم قلايدها فمن اللازم ان نتعصب للعربية
نحن بنيها وان نغار عليها لنصونها من الايادي
الغريبة واذا قصرت يدنا عن تبيين جمالها واعادة
رونقها فلا نزدري بها ونجعلها اضحوكة بجعلها كالثوب
البالي والاعتناء بها من واجباتنا وكذلك ان نصرف
همنا في سبيل تعلمها وان نحافظ عليها اكثر من محافظتنا
على اللغات الاجنبية . فان لها عند الامة العربية ارفع
درجة فانها لغة الكتاب ولغة النبي صلعم وبها اتخذوا
الرشد سبيلا الى الله سبحانه وتعالى ومن المعلوم ان
اكثر القوم يسعون الى اكتساب اللغات الافرنجية في
هذا العصر غير انهم لا يتقنون لغتهم الاصلية حتى ان
بعضهم افسدوا لغة عامتهم وحولوها الى لغة مبهمة
تحاكي لسان اهالي جزيرة مالطة غيرانتا الا نخشى

FIGURE 0.1. "Confusing Chaos," article appearing in Salīm al-Bustānī's *Al-Jinān*, December 1873. (Yale University Library)

Part One

Reading in Translation

Reading in Mistranslation

To read in translation is the condition of modernity. Abdelfattah Kilito, the Moroccan literary theorist, comes to this conclusion after giving a lecture about the *maqāmāt* of Badīʿ al-Zamān al-Hamadhānī to a French audience. Anticipating how he will explain the narrative genre to a foreign audience, he decides to introduce it as having originated in the tenth century of the Christian calendar rather than the fourth century of the *hijrī* one: "I would connect Badīʿ al-Zamān al-Hamadhānī to a period known to the audience and *link* him to his contemporary European writers," he decides. But that did not quite work as he had hoped; he could only find one such author, Roswitha of Germany, with whom he doubted any would be familiar. And so he did as many scholars had done before him: he compared the *maqāmāt* to the Spanish picaresque novel of the sixteenth century.[1] "So when speaking about Abū Fatḥ al-Askandarī, I referred to *Lazarillo de Tormes*, a work of anonymous authorship, to Quevedo's *The Swindler*, and others. In other words, I translated the *Maqamāt*. . . . [I] presented them as though they were picaresque novels, I transferred them to a different genre, a different literature."[2] He had realized, like many Arabs since the middle of the nineteenth century, as he explains, that "Arabic literature is untranslatable, and that on the whole it matters only to Arabs."[3] Reading a literature that is untranslatable and therefore in need of translation, he argues, has required a special way of reading that "takes translation into account, that is, translation as comparison." Reading in translation is the "fundamental change for us in the modern age."[4]

A century and a half earlier, during the middle of the nineteenth century, in fact, others had come to similar conclusions. Buṭrus al-Bustānī, a foundational *nahḍa* thinker, literary reformer, and translator for the American mission in Beirut (as well as a principal subject of chapter 2), addressed his own "Lecture on the Culture of the Arabs" ("Khuṭba fī ādāb al-ʿarab") to a "well-attended assembly of Westerners and Arab sons of Beirut on the fifteenth of February, 1859," at which he compared Charles the V to the Caliph al-Ma'mūn.[5] An often-cited text that circulated in pamphlet form after the lecture's delivery at the Syrian Society of Arts and Sciences (1847–1852), the "Khuṭba" inaugurated a discourse of Arabic literary modernity as a future state in which literary culture will be lifted out of its current "stagnancy" through translation and comparison.[6] As he argued, just as the Golden Age of classical Arabic literature was cultivated through al-Ma'mūn's patronage of translation from Roman, Byzantine, and Persian sources, and Europe's Dark Ages were enlightened through King Alfonso X and Charles V's patronage of translations from Arabic and Latin (which oftentimes had Arabic sources), the current revival—the *nahḍa*—was already emerging in translation projects sponsored by Mehmet Ali and Sultan Abdel-Majid I, as well as in those carried out by foreign-based Orientalist presses and missionary presses in the region. Modernity, al-Bustānī argued, required reading literary history in translation and uncovering the history of translation that was contained within Arabic literary history. As al-Bustānī reminds his readers in 1860, they "are not alone in this world" but are the "middle link" "in a great global chain [that] connects and separates the Eastern and Western worlds."[7]

As with Kilito, however, al-Bustānī indicates that this history of translation was not always straightforward: inserting the *maqāma* into a comparative literary history of the picaresque required a temporal leap of six centuries and a transformation of the genre. And comparing European translators and editors of classical Arabic texts to Arab translators of Greek classical works—both of whom "preserved the middle link in the chain of knowledge which ties ancient to modern knowledge"—revealed the frequent inadequacy of that transfer:[8] "It is obvious that the Arabic presses in Europe and America are more numerous than in this country. If not for the labor of these presses, no trace of Arabic literary works would have survived. And so we see many of our Arabic books returning to us, after a long exile, printed in beautiful letters. If only we were able to say with complete accuracy and perfect soundness."[9] The knowledge that these literary links were often weak caused al-Bustānī and others to cast a suspicious eye on what Stephen Sheehi has called the "syntagm of reform," or the linguistic and logical chain that sees "the criteria of 'progress,' 'civilization,' and modernity [as] based on European predominance and mastery" and in which stagnation is overcome through knowledge imported from the West.[10] Instead of wholesale adoption, al-Bustānī argues, transmission should be carefully surveilled by intermediaries who would keep a "sharp eye" on the translation process, catching and correcting linguistic errors.[11] Translators transformed texts rather than reproduced them. And so al-Bustānī narrates the history of Arabic letters itself as a history of translation as transformation: knowledge that had circulated "from West to East coming from the direction of the North, was returning *with numerous profits* from East to the West from the direction of the South."[12] Knowledge never merely travels for *nahḍa* thinkers; it is made to travel by multiple mediators and is transformed, either in improvement or degradation (in the case of Orientalist translators), in the process.

Understanding the "New Age" (*al-ʿaṣr al-jadīd*), what many writers of the period called the *nahḍa*, required not only reading in translation but also theorizing it. As Aḥmad Fāris al-Shidyāq writes, in what has become an emblematic literary text of the period, *Al-Sāq ʿalā al-sāq fī mā huwa al-Fāryāq* (*Leg over Leg Concerning That Which Is al-Fāryāq*, 1855), the New Age is distinguished by new modes of transmission: "I tell you that the world in your late grandfather's and father's day was not what it is now. In their day, there were no steamboats or railway *tracks* to bring close far-off *tracts*, to connect the *disconnected*. . . . Then, one didn't have to learn many languages. It could be said of anyone who know a few words of Turkish—Welcome, my lord! How nice to see you, my lord!—that he'd make a fine interpreter at the Imperial court."[13] A central and polarizing figure of the *nahḍa*, al-Shidyāq was a belle-lettrist, poet, travel writer, translator, lexicographer, grammarian, literary historian, essayist, publisher, and newspaper editor; he is known as a pioneer of modern Arabic literature, a reviver of classical forms, the father of Arabic journalism, and no less than a modernizer of Arabic literature and the Arabic language itself. In this book (chapter 1), he appears most prominently as a translator, and indeed we might see translation as the central conceptual category in his writing at large. Instead of fathers and grandfathers, al-Shidyāq claims to write a modern literature of steamboats and railways: the New Age draws literary connections that emphasize horizontal over vertical connections and that require translation as well as a keen eye of a reader-in-translation.

Nahḍa authors cast the writing and reading of modern Arabic literature, literary publics (as in chapter 3) and even modern Arabic language itself, as a question of transmission in the age of new connectivity. Early presses printed numerous editions of premodern dictionaries and lexicographical studies, which in turn became the bases for new dictionaries and linguistic studies that updated or revised their predecessors. Saʿīd al-Shartūnī (1849–1912) lists among his reasons for writing his dictionary, *Aqrab al-mawārid fī al-fuṣuḥ al-ʿarabiyya wa al-shawārid* (The closest sources to the pure Arabic language and its anomalies, 1889–1893), the importance of "setting right the mistakes in printing and copying" that occur in previously published lexicons, including *Tāj al-ʿarūs* and *Lisān al-ʿarab*.[14] He catalogues many of these in his introduction, listing them by edition.[15] Al-Bustānī describes his dictionary, *Muḥīṭ al-muḥīṭ* (The ocean of oceans, 1866), as an expansion of al-Fīrūzābādī's *Qāmūs al-muḥīṭ* in which he included "the speech of recent authors and terms from the masses [*al-ʿāmma*] that have been proclaimed to be outside the foundations of the language."[16] And al-Shidyāq offered his lexicographical study, *Al-Jāsūs ʿala al-Qāmūs* (Spying on the *Al-Qāmūs*, 1882), as an extended critique of al-Fīrūzābādī, which he argues is difficult to navigate and oftentimes confusing in its explanations (they are concise, as al-Shidyāq argues, "to the point of riddling").[17] The vigorous and often vicious discussion around the *modern* usage of the Arabic language launched a series of public philosophical debates in periodical pages, critical editions, and printed pamphlets. Those on the liberal side of the debate (al-Shidyāq, Yūsuf al-Asīr, Ibrāhīm al-Aḥdab, and later Jurjī Zaydān and Yaʿqūb Ṣarrūf) advocated for reforming Arabic and making it "suitable for the tasks of this age," while conservative scholars (chief among them Ibrāhīm al-Yāzijī) believed that the deficiencies of modern language lay "not with the Arabic language but with its people" and sought to return Arabic to its purest roots in medieval grammars.[18]

This meant that scholars not only transmitted knowledge that would lead to "progress" and theorized the language in which it would conveyed but identified and corrected the mistakes in its media of delivery. To do so, they employed a mode of criticism referred to as *takhṭiʾa*, "fault-finding," derived from *khaṭaʾ*, or "error." Much in the spirit of medieval *laḥn* literature in which authors refuted unorthodox or incorrect linguistic usage with word-by-word critiques, they brought detailed charges of error in each other's grammatical explanations and linguistic usages. Saʿīd al-Shartūnī, for example, in a work that labeled itself a *takhṭiʾa*, *Al-Sahm al-ṣāʾib fī takhṭiʾat ghunyat al-ṭālib* (The accurate arrow aimed at the errors of *Ghunyat al-ṭālib*, 1874), brought seventy-six charges of error in his *takhṭiʾa* against al-Shidyāq's *Ghunyat al-ṭālib*, which supporters of al-Shidyāq—Yūsuf al-Asīr and Ibrāhīm al-Aḥdab—answered point for point using medieval counterexamples[19] A widening circle of enmities and alliances was drawn around these linguistic opinions, drawing in some of the most prominent *nahḍa* intellectuals and placing this debate in some of the most widely circulated journals.[20] Tracking transmission meant keeping a keen eye out for places where the chain broke down.

Yet despite these scholars' biting differences, what they all agreed on was that a main cause in the crisis in modern usage was foreign language itself. Many lamented the rising position of foreign-language learning and reading among educated Arabic speakers and the consequent deemphasis of Arabic proficiency, worried about eroding effects of foreign colloquialisms in everyday Arabic speech, and debated the means by which Arabic might accommodate and name the introduction of new, foreign concepts and objects while retaining its integrity. Al-Shidyāq's grammatical simplifications were geared toward this competition with European languages, which he thought were attractive because they were easier to learn.[21] He advocated for flexibility with regard to the incorporation of foreign concepts into Arabic, making an argument for the wide use of *ishtiqāq*, or derivation from existing Arabic roots, to form new terminology.[22] Conservative scholars, who also lamented the rise of European languages, meanwhile rejected the use of foreign expressions, or *taʿrīb* (Arabization and, in other contexts, "translation"), and sought to limit the use of *ishtiqāq* to only minor deployments. Both *taʿrīb* and *al-ishtiqāq al-akbar* ("major" or liberal derivations that allow the order of root consonants to be changed), he lamented, had become all too common in an age when foreign clothes, furniture, and household devices had become permanent fixtures in Arab homes, and new discoveries tested the limits of Arabic vocabularies.[23] As Salīm al-Bustānī complains, the use of foreign words like "*al-kūmsīyūn* [commission], *al-sīkūrata* [security], and *sikūzmī afandam* [excuse me, sirs]" are "opiates" that sedate Arabic speakers and prevent them from serious scholarship in Arabic philology.[24] His magazine, *Al-Jinān*, published several articles warning the greater public against the infiltration of foreign language, arguing that it creates a generation of people who can speak neither their own language nor a foreign one (figure 0.1). In the New Age, translation was an unsettling condition of linguistic modernity.

These debates cannot be simply described as occurring between modernists open to foreign influences and revivalists looking to purify Arabic of them. Al-Shidyāq presented his reforms within the frame of competition with an encroaching Europe, and even conservative scholars adopted principles from European lexicography: al-Bustānī and al-Shartūnī modeled the organization of their lexicons after those produced by European Orientalists, arranging the entries alphabetically according to the first root letter rather than the last, or rhyme, letter. Al-Shartūnī makes this connection explicit in his *Aqrab al-mawārid fī al-fuṣuḥ al-ʿarabiyya wa al-shawārid*: "As for [the book's] sequence . . . the citation of terms [appears] according to the beginning of its root, which is the same method used by translators of Arabic into Latin and other languages, like [Jacobus] Golius and [Georg Wilhelm Friedrich] Freytag. The learned late Buṭrus al-Bustānī, the model of seriousness and scholarly boldness [*al-iqdām*], followed them in his *Muḥīṭ al-muḥīṭ* and *Quṭr al-muḥīṭ*."[25] Al-Shartūnī's conservative, revivalist project of writing a dictionary that would gather only the "most trusted sources" to preserve the "purity" of the Arabic language, then, was modeled on European scholarly works that themselves translated Arabic into Western languages. The "revival" of Arabic language and literature occurred not against translation but through it. Reviving Arabic in the modern age, even for conservative scholars like al-Shartūnī and al-Yāzijī, meant reading in translation, reading translations, and uncovering a history of the translation of foreign terms into Arabic (as al-Yāzijī does in his "Al-Lugha wa al-ʿaṣr" when he roots out the ʿAbbasid precedents for Arabizing foreign terms).[26]

Whether it was with the goal of transmitting classical Arabic literary traditions to a modern audience or introducing them to new, foreign ones, translation was a dominant mode of modernity even for conservative scholars—so much so, in fact, that the word most commonly used for both transmission and translation was the same: *naql*.[27] Also meaning "transportation," *naql* relied on the mobility of texts and language across time as well as space and the ability of authors, transmitters, and translators to "seek out knowledge wherever it was found," as al-Bustānī writes, and adapt it to Arab modernity.[28] Bedouin knowledge of the past, he argues, must be transmitted (*naql*) to a modern audience, much in the way that foreign sciences were translated from Greece in the Middle Ages.[29] Yet neither was a naïve process; movement generated wandering that was productive and potentially dangerous. While the transmission (*naql*) of Arabic works via European presses and editors was an unreliable process that often introduced problems of "grammatical correctness and proper soundness," it could also produce progress.[30] As al-Bustānī writes, medieval Arab translators cannot be considered "imitators . . . as some suggest" because these translators "innovated on and added to" the foreign knowledge.[31]

In both cases, transmission and translation were understood as forms of critical reading that invited and even required more critical reading in a potentially never-ending chain of verification and error detection. As al-Shidyāq explains in *Ghunyat al-ṭālib*, his radical simplification of Arabic grammar is a "*naql*" that abridges medieval grammatical works that were themselves commentaries on earlier linguistic treatises. He cites al-Ashmūnī's commentary on Ibn Mālik's *Al-Alfīyya*, for example, which is itself modeled on Abū Zakariyā' Yaḥyā ibn Muʿṭī's *Al-Durra al-alfīyya*, as well as al-Astarābādhī's commentary on Ibn al-Ḥājib's *Al-Kāfiya fī al-naḥw*, an abridgement of al-Zamakhsharī's *Kitāb al-faṣṣal fī al-naḥw*.[32] And when he describes the translations of European Orientalists, as he does at length in both his fictional and nonfictional travelogues, *Al-Sāq* and *Kashf al-mukhabbā' ʿan funūn urūbā*, he meticulously (and often mockingly) details their inaccuracies and misunderstandings. As he describes them, the scholars at Cambridge and Oxford who acted as the transmitters of the Arabic literary tradition—storing, teaching, editing, and translating the manuscripts that could no longer be found in Ottoman libraries—often had difficulty deciphering the texts in their stewardship. Their interpretations were full of "*laḥn wa zaḥāf*," errors and miscalculations, as they misread manuscripts and mistranslated idioms (with one English scholar translating the common curse *yuḥraq dīnuhu*, or "damn him," literally as "his religion became radiant with fire," which he erroneously explained to mean "from the heat of his faith").[33] *Al-Sāq* delivers on its promise to detail the "errors of Arabic speakers both Arab and foreign" by appending a list of the "errors of the great and noble professors of the Arabic language in the schools of Paris" that include those found in "the translation [*naql*] of Persian letters by Alexandre Chodzko" (these were the translation exercises appended to his *Grammaire persane*) and in the correction of a correction: Joseph Toussaint Reinaud and Hartwig Derenbourg's 1847 revised edition of Silvestre de Sacy's translation of the *Maqāmāt* of al-Ḥarīrī.[34] Transmission and translation, for many *nahḍa* writers, were often indistinguishable forms of the critical reading required to produce modern Arabic, modern literature, and progress more generally. All necessitated an engagement with errors.

Lexicography and literary history, two central categories of New Age literary production, exhibited a more general *nahḍa*-era concern with mediation and its sometimes-faulty nodes of contact, commenting on the complex translational dynamics of Arabic literary modernity. Errors erupt in textual transmission and produce errancy: wandering. "Being wrong," as Seth Lerer points out, "is about being displaced, about wandering, dissenting, emigrating, and alienating."[35] Error, he notes, derives from the Latin word *errare*, or "to wander," and in this it shares an affinity with the Arabic *khaṭa'* (error), a word originally derived—according to Muḥammad Murtaḍā al-Zabīdī's *Tāj al-'arūs*—from *khaṭiya*, a verb used when God makes a rain star pass over a piece of land without watering it.[36] Words deriving from it also mean "to miss a mark or go astray," but since God is the verb's original subject, the act could be either a mistake or an "intentional fault" (as in *khaṭṭaya al-sahm*, "he made the arrow miss the mark").[37] Erring could be accidental or intentional, deliberate deviation from a path. While the detection of errors also took a central role, differentiating the mere misunderstanding from the productive deviation was not often possible, and modes of comparison more complex. What is clear, and what these first chapters seek to account for, is how deviations, mistranscriptions, and easily detectible errors in translation could form the foundation of entire readings, arguments, and structures of thought. They were all understood to be as unavoidable as they were productive.

Reading in translation entailed reading in and for mistranslation. Accounting for errors was for *nahḍa* authors an "infinitely laborious task," as Zachary

Sng argues in his own history of error in European literature, and one that required both genealogical work—tracing errors back to their source—and an acknowledgment of the incoherent, nonsystemic "alternative movement" that error charts in its production of new knowledge and revision of the old.[38] Errorology, one of the *nahḍa*'s primary linguistic occupations, made use of a multivalent comparative methodology that simultaneously opened onto the past and the future, entailing "multiple and repeated attempts at distinction that fail[ed] to foreclose entirely the possibility of new uncertainties and errors."[39] *Nahḍa* lexical studies that revised and preserved premodern linguistic usage did so in translation, or in conversation and contestation with European linguists and translators and with the understanding that they were not the last word on the subject. Al-Shidyāq's appendix to *Al-Sāq ʿalā al-sāq* listing the translation errors of French Orientalists, we might note, was followed by a second appendix listing the errors in his own work. It was the "middle link" on a chain of transmission constructed partially from error.

The distinction between the understandings of modernity that distinguished the two poles of the *nahḍa*—the modernizers' and translators' advocacy of epistemological rupture on the one hand and the revivalists' and neoclassicists' insistence on preservation on the other—is a false one. Both were forms of critical reception that simultaneously engaged the premodern intellectual heritage and the European comparative context. *Nahḍa* writers' focus on error in the transmission of language and texts raises debates about the origins of Arabic literary modernity (was it a European import, foreign to the Arabic literary tradition, or was it the outgrowth of a national literary past?) and reframes them as a debate about modernity's transmission—how it was gathered and translated and how it was transformed in the process. Understanding how the novel arose amid the vigorous debate about linguistic modernization as well as the scrupulous accounting of errors (*takhṭi'a*) that attended it, we might see how translation transmits the novel as part of a larger self-critical process of modernity at large, including the foundational production of "missionary translation" (chapter 1), Arabic print capitalism (chapter 2), and the *nahḍa* reading public (chapter 3). It is what Timothy Reiss describes as "a process of embedded exchange, interweaving cultural experiences and ways of seeing."[40] This mode of comparative reading as "global dialectics" posits what Buṭrus al-Bustānī called a "wide field" of literature and Salīm al-Bustānī called the "single plane" of scientific and cultural effort as one in which universal standards and generic conventions are called into question.[41] Instead, as this section shows, through translation and its errors, readers were asked to consider difference as constituting the single modern literary field, as well as the terms on which they might enter it.

Chapter 1

Crusoe's Babel, Missionaries' Mistakes

Translated Origins of the Arabic Novel

It is a partially familiar scene: partway through the earliest extant novel to be printed in Arabic, an 1835 translation of *Robinson Crusoe, Qiṣṣat Rūbinṣun Kurūzī* (The story of Robinson Crusoe), we find Robinson Crusoe, or rather Rūbinṣun Kurūzī, sitting down to eat. It is early in his island adventure, after he—like Daniel Defoe's Crusoe—has salvaged what he could from the wrecked ship, built a shelter, and discovered a small herd of goats. The two Crusoes' stay on the island, not surprisingly for a translation, is similar in many respects. But Kurūzī's culinary triumphs far outnumber those of Defoe's original protagonist: here he sits down to eat several skewers of kebab, and later he will prepare *maḥshī* (vegetables stuffed with rice and spiced ground meat) and *mulukhiyya* (a stew of meat broth and mallow), serving all with bread made "by cooking the dough over some embers in a hole . . . like the Arabs do."[1] Rūbinsun Kurūzī, it is clear, ate better than Robinson Crusoe, whose early meals consisted of dried corn, raisins, and a tortoise that gives him convulsions so violent as to cause him, for the first time since his shipwreck, to pray to God for deliverance.

Crusoe could have benefited from the kind of "Arab wisdom" that Kurūzī makes use of in feeding himself. Instead, Crusoe's meal making is the result of a time-consuming process of trial, observation, and error. Consider, for example, his project of making bread from cornmeal, which, described over several pages, requires him "to employ all [his] Study and Hours of Working to accomplish"—in mixing his dough, devising a kiln, firing clay baking dishes, and determining the correct temperature for the fire.[2] Eventually, he too learns to bake his dough over embers as Kurūzī did, but not by reproducing the techniques of Arab or even English bakers. Instead of remembering how to bake bread "as the Arabs do," Crusoe "found ways" to succeed in all of the steps of his process through observation and reason, spending the better part of a year in "Experiment" and with "no Notion of Kiln" to produce even the clay pot in which he cooks his food (*RC*, 59, 88).

The observations that emerge from setting these two versions of Crusoe's eating habits side by side might amount to a minor point but for the fact that observing Crusoe's autonomous actions on the island have played an important role in theorizing what have been called the formal and cultural institutions of the novel: individual subjectivity, formal realism, colonial accumulation, the labor theory of value, national identity, to name a few. This is why, for many decades, scholars have labeled *Robinson Crusoe* (1719) the first English novel or even the first novel, regardless of its national origin.[3] Crusoe's fantasies of autonomy have been argued to underwrite his possessive claim to the island, his assertion of mastery, his stability of self, and his "colonial alibi" as he reestablishes national and religious identity on the island by insulating himself from contamination from without.[4] As Virginia Woolf imagined him, he is as solid and solitary as the earthenware pot that he makes and that orders the world around him: "By believing fixedly in the solidity of the pot and its earthiness," she writes, "he has subdued every other element to his design; he has roped the whole universe into harmony."[5]

Autonomy might have been important to the producers of this translation, too. Published by the Anglican-founded Church Missionary Society (CMS) in Malta, it was intended as a tool for conversion, guiding what the CMS saw as the superstitious and corrupted Eastern Christians to the right path of Protestantism by emulating Crusoe's direct and individual spiritual awakening. CMS missionaries to the Levant took active steps to discourage cultural or doctrinal hybridity, even monitoring the translators and "native teachers" in their employ for signs of the Catholic influence. As a printer for the Malta Press explained, "many things may creep in unawares."[6] The fantasy of purity and process of purification were part of the foundation of the missionary movement, making Crusoe's own myth of individualism and fantasy of autonomy its perfect ideological surrogate. Just as readers followed Crusoe as he learned to make his clay pot through direct observation and reasoned inference, the CMS hoped they would find similar inspiration in his spiritual trials and error, as he moves from rebellion to punishment, repentance, and eventually religious conversion.

But what of Kurūzī, standing not alone but next to recalled Arabs and using their knowledge to survive on the island? By relying on foreign knowledge rather than Kurūzī's own autonomous powers of observation and reason, did the translator miss the point of this new genre's epistemological and cultural potential? Or should it be read as an example of "creative translation" that sought its independence from the original or even "cared nothing for origins and genealogies"?[7] Many translators of this period, as we will see in the following chapters, adapted or changed the source material. Yet regardless of the sometimes-radical changes, most—like this one—still claimed to be producing translations rather than original works (and even passed off original works *as* translations). They praised the beauty or importance or pleasure of the original version and often lamented their inability to do justice to it: they maintained and even cultivated a relationship to the text's origins in ways that are more complex than choosing between fidelity and infidelity to it. There is no autonomy for Kurūzī or *Kurūzī*, not for the character, who relies on interlocutors past and present for survival, or for its producer, who works between languages and literary conventions and indeed between techniques and ideologies of translation.

As the earliest surviving translation of a novel into Arabic that also happened to take as its source material a work often cited as the first novel to be produced in English, *Qiṣṣat Rūbinṣun Kurūzī* stands as an ideal starting point from which to understand the origins of the Arabic novel as they emerge from translation. Produced at a multilingual press at the geographical crossroads of the western and eastern Mediterranean and by a multifaith group of Arabic- and English-speaking translators, *Kurūzī* inaugurates a century of novelistic translation as neither a response to colonial expansion (or cultural imperialism) nor an expression of the consolidation of national identity. It was the product of the increased European and American missionary presence in the Middle East, whose societies operated presses, founded periodicals, opened schools, and employed some of the most influential writers of the *nahḍa* as translators, teachers, and authors. Yet these translations cannot be understood solely from the perspective of the missionary societies and their goals; the histories of their work with the missionaries and the literary texts it produced exemplify the complex and frequently problematic intellectual encounters—what one missionary translator described as "rubbing and being rubbed"—that characterized the period and produced the Arabic novel in the crucible of modernity's trials.[8] An origin that is also a copy, and a copy that works as if to transform the original, *Kurūzī* and the translation techniques it employs help begin a reconsideration of the origins of the Translation Movement.

Translation in the Missionary Age

While Napoleon's press, which later became the Bulāq Press, might have been the first in Egypt to print in Arabic, Arabic presses had been in operation in other provinces of the Ottoman Empire—notably Syria and Lebanon—from the seventeenth century onward, with imperial (Ottoman) presses only following suit after the success of the commercial and religious ones was proven.[9] Set up by congregation leaders of the major Christian churches, Maronite, Orthodox, and Greek Catholic, these early presses printed a limited number of Latin-Arabic and translated Arabic gospels, psalters, and religious tracts for their respective religious communities. In the nineteenth century, though, the role of religious presses greatly expanded. These small presses were joined in the 1820s and '30s by ones set up by two Protestant missionary groups, the American Board of Commissioners for Foreign Missions (ABCFM) and the Church Missionary Society in Beirut and Malta, and later by two Catholic presses, Maṭba'at al-abā' al-Yasū'iyīn (The press of the Jesuit fathers, founded 1847 in Beirut) and al-Maṭba'a al-Kathulikiyya (The Catholic press, founded in 1848). These presses' distribution goals far exceeded those of their forebears: publishing not only liturgical materials but also religious and linguistic primers, literary works, spelling books, translated sermons, and simplified Bible extracts, they aimed to reach, and even cultivate through literacy promotion, a wider and multidenominational Christian audience, grooming them as potential converts.[10]

Especially for Protestant missionaries, who were for many years banned from direct proselytizing both in Beirut and in Malta, the press became their instrument of speech "instead of tongues" and one that required them to speak in translation.[11] Almost none of the early American or English missionaries had learned to read or speak Arabic prior to their arrival and so relied on bilingual local residents who could translate for them, give them language lessons, and help supervise the editorial functions of the press.[12] Soon after the arrival of the American missionaries of the ABCFM in Beirut, they established schools to supply that need: their main object was to prepare young people to act as native teachers and clergy as well as to instruct them in the English language.[13] And later, they would found or help to found scholarly institutions like the Syrian Protestant College (established 1866; it would become the American University of Beirut) and the Syrian Society of Arts and Sciences (1847), an intellectual society and reading room with its own published circular.[14] The scale of impact of the missionary educational movement in general and missionary translation in particular on the literary production of the Levant can perhaps not be overstated. Many of the most recognizable and prolific

Arab scholars and authors of the *nahḍa* worked at one time as translators for one of the missionary projects. Buṭrus al-Bustānī, who besides being the director of one of the more successful presses, the editor of three prominent periodicals (*Al-Jinān*, *Al-Janna*, and *Al-Junayna*), and the author of both a multivolume Arabic dictionary and six volumes of an encyclopedia, translated *A Pilgrim's Progress* (*Ṣiyāḥa masīḥī*, 1870) and another version of *Robinson Crusoe* (*Kitāb al-tuḥfa al-Bustāniyyah fī al-asfār al-Kurūziyya aw Riḥlat Rūbinṣun Kurūzī*, 1861). Aḥmad Fāris al-Shidyāq, who vies with al-Bustānī for the title of the "Father of the Arab Enlightenment" for his wide-ranging and era-defining scholarly and lexicographical work, was the head of the translation department of the CMS Press in Malta. Ya'qūb Ṣarrūf (1852–1927), who edited the long-standing periodical *Al-Muqtaṭaf* and wrote three successful novels, translated Samuel Smiles's *Self-Help* (*Sirr al-najāḥ*, Syrian Protestant College Press, 1880).[15] The prolific translator of French fiction and literary critic As'ad Dāghir (1860–1935) translated Protestant sermons from English, including Charles Spurgeon's *All of Grace*, Thain Davidson's *Talks with Young Men*, and devotional commentaries like Frances Ridley Havergal's *Kept for the Master's Use*. Nāṣif al-Yāzijī, the poet and philologist, worked as a "corrector" at the Beirut press and, along with Khalīl al-Yāzijī, the playwright and poet; Ibrāhīm Sarkīs, the poet and historian; and the Muslim scholar Yūsuf al-Asīr, produced Arabic versified versions—and some original ones (as in the case of Nāsīf al-Yāzijī)—of psalms and hymns for the American mission.[16] The web of the *nahḍa*'s intellectual affiliations is composed in large part by the connections of missionary education and translation.

Just as Arabic translation derived in large part from the missionary movement, the modern missionary project itself relied on translation. The Church Missionary Society, which published *Kurūzī*, made foreign-language acquisition and the translation of scripture early priorities. The Mediterranean Mission in Malta, begun in 1815, was in fact established by a what the society official history calls a "Literary Representative," William Jowett, whose express purpose was "to suggest methods for translating and circulating the Scriptures, and other ways of influencing the Oriental Churches."[17] To facilitate this program, Jowett began to advocate for expanding the translation activities of the society and for establishing a printing press on the island and in this way to ensure the transmission of sound religious principles to a native population in need of guidance.[18] The CMS leadership approved Jowett's plan, and the materials for a multiscript press were sent to Malta in 1822. With the aim of reaching potential converts in five Mediterranean languages (and especially, as Jowett stressed, in Arabic), the Malta Press formed what the CMS saw as the central actor in its project to bring all of humanity under a "common faith" and a "common salvation." "The field," as the *Church Missionary Atlas* explains, "is the world": the CMS was involved in a global project of conversion that relied on translation.[19]

CMS publications and internal documents make this goal clear and figure Christian unity in linguistic terms. The *Atlas* imagined a future in which the whole world joins in "the same song" but in "a multitude . . . of tongues."[20] Elsewhere, CMS publications and documents describe translating and preaching the Bible and other religious works in each native language as working toward reversing "the curse of Babel." The future was one of absolute fungibility guaranteed by the transcendental signifier. As one CMS missionary explains, "the imagery of the Bible is nearly all taken from nature, the work of God, and thus intelligible to all, and can consequently be translated into all human languages."[21] The belief in transcendental meaning, existing prior to human articulation and derived from "the divine commerce between Father and Son," ensures the translatability of all language.[22]

Yet while CMS missionaries staunchly denied the very existence of untranslatability between languages, they did not advocate for an eradication of cultural or linguistic particularities. These societies consciously worked to prevent Westernization, instituting policies to prevent their congregation from imitating Frankish culture. The ABCFM, for example, vigilantly policed the sites of contact for signs of assimilation, "securing the pupils from adopting Frank[ish] manners and customs" and discontinuing the (popular) classes in foreign languages in order to do so.[23] As the representatives of the Abeih station in Lebanon reported, "We are still of the opinion that the plan of giving all instruction in the Arabic language . . . is the best one. . . . In thus training up our pupils in their own tongue, we preserve in a higher degree their nationality of feeling and, we hope, encourage, rather than check, their sympathies with their people, and so fit them for more efficient and useful action among them."[24] At great pains to produce not a hybrid but a "native Protestant Church" that was properly Arab, all instruction and preaching—whether performed by English, American, or "native clergy"—was to be performed in Arabic. The missionary project in the Levant, far from having an objective of Westernization, sought to ensure "nationality of feeling."

Translation was then meticulously policed for signs of Frankishness and carried out only by the missionaries to prevent unwanted cultural influence. Only a select few Arabic speakers were permitted to continue foreign-language training and translation, which they did under the direct supervision of the missionaries themselves. This resulted in complicated translation procedures. When the ABCFM retranslated the Bible beginning in 1848, for example, Arab translators' tasks were circumscribed in a four-part process: an Arab translator would first present drafts to a missionary to "check and revise," at which point the missionary would go to a monolingual Arabophone scholar who would then "eliminate words or idioms inadmissible by classical [Arabic] standards" as well as formulations that would conjure unwelcome associations with Islam, before being submitted to a council of bilingual missionaries for ultimate approval.[25] It is by policing the external boundaries and ensuring internal consistency of Arabic that the missionaries attempted to Christianize without Westernizing.

Christianizing without Westernizing poses an interesting paradox. While missionary translation in many ways seems to domesticate the foreign text, purifying its final product of any traces of the foreignness that point to its having originated in another language, that domestication was not in the service of "assimilat[ing] foreign literary texts . . . to dominant values at home" in the target language, as domestication is usually defined.[26] Though—like other domesticating translations—the translation departments of missionary presses aimed to erase the translation process itself in order to pass as a native text, they produced domesticating Arabic translations that were not "grounded in domestic [Arab] ideologies and institutions" but instead sought to reform and even replace them.[27]

That the questions that this translation process forces us to ask (What, in this case, is the domestic? Where is home?) are ones that missionary societies wanted above all to suppress might explain their seemingly paradoxical impulses. In order to preserve "the nationality of feeling" in the service of eradicating religious difference, CMS missionaries promoted an ideology of absolute translatability among what they imagined to be discrete, homogeneous, and homolingual communities that exist prior to translation itself. It was translation to reverse Babel, to bring about a unified community in Christ. As Jacques Derrida has argued, the story of Babel figures not merely the linguistic diversity or the threat of incommunicability but also the impossibility of internal stability. The tower of Babel figures an "internal limit" to "transparent and adequate inter-expression" and therefore exhibits "an incompletion, the impossibility of finishing, of totalizing, saturating, of completing something on the order of edification."[28] To reverse Babel, as the Church Missionary Society attempted, would therefore have to make invisible that internal multiplicity. It would have to ensure discrete, stable, linguistic, and religious communities that were homogeneous and without "internal limits." And it would have to erase the traces of interlingual penetration that make visible the "incompletion" of language. That is, it would have to make invisible the complex interactions between languages, religions, and societies that produce translations, as well as the inequivalence and untranslatability that they inevitably risk. They would have to perform translation purified of the very problem of translation, an antitranslation that brings about a future in which translation is no longer necessary.

This goal, of course, was challenged by practical exigencies. Despite the missionaries' desire to eradicate the problem of translation, it surrounded them. The vision of global Christian unity and uniformity they held was but one worldview in circulation in the nineteenth-century Mediterranean. That vision, articulated in terms of "enemies" and "rivals" of the missions to be "overthrown" by the righteous—be they competing denominations of missionaries or native churches[29]—competed with Ottoman political norms that regarded the mutual recognition of different religious communities as fundamental to social order in an unequal multireligious Islamic society.[30] As a CMS representative to the Levant wrote to the leadership council, the region required the urgent attention of the missionary society because "the multitudes of Christians of different denominations . . . [were] living mingled in confusion with the Turkish inhabitants."[31] The Mediterranean, as the *Missionary Register* enthused, was an "amphitheatre of nations!"[32] Facing this vast and "incalculably important" shore, Malta was seen as the ideal "watch-tower" from which to bring all of humanity into "a common faith, and a common salvation."[33]

This "mingled" but essential amphitheater required equally intricate linguistic negotiations, as multiple written, oral, liturgical, and commercial languages circulated among the religious and ethnic communities of the Ottoman Empire, as well as among its trade diasporas. Many educated Ottoman subjects, in fact, simultaneously inhabited several of these communities, reading in one of the six written languages, composing correspondence in another, and speaking yet a third language or dialect at home.[34] An Ottoman Turkish poet could speak Albanian as a mother tongue but compose part of his work in Persian, just as a Jewish poet might compose in Turkish and Hebrew but speak Greek or Judaeo-Spanish in conversation. And these languages themselves intermingled, their vocabularies rich with multilingual loan words and multiple orthographies.[35] As William Goodell's journal makes clear, missionaries in the Syrian provinces were required to have a familiarity with several of these languages not only to carry out their religious duties but to have quotidian interactions as well.[36]

Missionary field reports were therefore punctuated by urgent calls for language learning, especially Arabic: "TO SPEAK, READ, AND UNDERSTAND ARABIC FLUENTLY AND WELL—IS ESSENTIAL TO THE PROPER CONDUCT OF A MISSION IN SYRIA AND PALESTINE," Jowett emphasized in 1822.[37] Both the CMS and ABCFM missionaries began to devote much of their time to learning languages (and little else about their host cultures), but still very few became able to speak Arabic eloquently or read it with great fluency. This was particularly devastating for the workings of the press, which Jowett hoped would occupy a large share of the society's attention. In letters to the CMS secretariat, Jowett regularly lamented his lack of Arabic assistance, which greatly impeded the efforts of the Malta station as a whole. Himself unable to compose in Arabic, he managed to produce publications only by garnering the services of missionaries who passed through Malta, even those who had only begun language study months earlier.[38] The results were short primers and sermons composed in simple sentences and often set using incomplete fonts, a problem resolved only with the addition of "native readers" to "assist."

Yet this solution produced its own a range of dangers, as missionaries often worked with the very "mingled" Christians they came to save.[39] Indeed, as Hala Auji has put it, without the contributions of Arabic-speaking Syrian employees, it is "unlikely that the [ABCFM] press could have produced any Arabic books in its first three decades."[40] Jowett and his colleagues attended to first principles as best they could and attempted to fill posts at the press with those who were not only "well acquainted with Arabic, and the other Eastern languages" but more importantly "of sound Doctrine."[41] The vast majority of the Arabic-speaking tutors and translators employed by the CMS in Malta remained unconverted members of their original congregations—a fact attributable not to any ecumenicalism on the part of the missionaries but to necessity: there were simply no Protestant converts whom the societies could employ. At the time of the CMS Press's opening in 1825, there was only one Levantine convert to evangelical Christianity, Asʿad al-Shidyāq (the native tutor to Isaac Bird, an American seminarian who arrived in Malta in 1823), and he was at the time a prisoner of the Maronite Patriarchate. (He died as "the first Protestant Martyr of Lebanon" in 1830.) Five years later, the pool was not much larger; in 1830, the entire "Protestant community" of the Ottoman Empire reportedly numbered five persons.[42]

This meant that the Arabic-speaking translators of the CMS Press were as religiously and linguistically diverse as the population of the area at large, personifying the internal multiplicity of the Ottoman cultural sphere. Apart from Isa Rassām, a Chaldean Assyrian from Mosul who converted to Protestantism in Cairo and who wanted "only enough [compensation] to live," they were largely men whose primary concern seemed to be securing a salary rather than spiritual fulfillment.[43] Dr. Cleardo Naudi, a Maltese professor of chemistry and "devout Roman Catholic," was responsible for the press's earliest output, translations of religious tracts in Italian and Maltese, but left its service in "great pecuniary distress."[44] The translator who completed the bulk of the CMS Press's early Arabic publications, Ysa Petrus, was a Greek Orthodox priest native to Palestine; he sent his translations from Jerusalem and then Damietta but refused to fill the need for a resident translator in Malta after contract negotiations broke down.[45] And Fāris al-Shidyāq, the press's longest-standing translator and a Maronite skeptic who later converted to Islam (and adopted the name Aḥmad), was in frequent disputes with the society over his compensation. (When he left Malta for a final time in 1844, he composed a censorious poem accusing the society of exploitation, a document that is sadly missing from the CMS Archives.) The society's policy of securing the piety of its native readers by giving "impulse" but not material "support," as Jowett writes, was clearly at odds how those readers understood their own role in the society.[46] Missionaries complained of the "viciousness" of their workers and the "Arabic love of money," while translators demanded remuneration equal to that which they would receive in comparable secular employ.[47]

In letters and journals, missionaries interpreted for each other the signs of proper and improper religious feeling among their translators. Whether they were seen as "living in the true spirit of Christianity" was determined by observing their behavior: observers noted their love or indifference to money, their eating and drinking habits, their observation of the Sabbath, and even—in the case of a young Coptic boy being recommended as a translator-in-training—their personal hygiene habits (it was observed that his brother did not wash his face).[48] And yet, even if translators' allegiances were suspect, the missionaries could not do without them: though al-Shidyāq was the subject of voluminous consternated correspondences that detailed his illiberal spending habits (he visited a local tavern because he could not stand the austerity of the missionary diet), his want of religious "uprightness," his seeming "unbelief," and his sexual habits (he contracted a sexually transmitted disease and was subsequently turned out of one of the missionaries' homes), he was still the longest-employed member of the translation department and its most skilled philologist. He "probes things to the very bottom" when translating, as his cotranslator Schlienz writes, a thing that "one cannot do otherwise."[49]

While missionary texts were produced in order to combat the "mingled confusion" in which Levantine Christians lived, that is, presses nonetheless relied on that mingling for their very production. Al-Shidyāq's translations were enriched by the Muslim scholarly circles he joined in Cairo and the Jewish scholars he consulted on biblical vocabulary, just as it was the (doctrinally suspect) polylingual, multiethnic, and interreligious circumstances of Ysa Petros's biography that, according to Jowett, made him such a skilled translator and learned scholar.[50] The perilous religious proximity that defined the Levant in the Ottoman period was what gave these translators the knowledge needed to do the missionaries' work. These men, instead of being translated into a missionary worldview, were ambivalent agents of translation, showing that even in the context of expansionist evangelicalism, "pure transmission" might have been impossible to achieve.[51]

The missionaries, for their part, worried about the reliability of translations performed by men of ambivalent religious feeling, whose translations, "though . . . generally correct," as the head of publications in Malta, Samuel Gobat, reported, "want that decided turn of impression in Christian doctrines, command and experiences, and in general that salt, which makes impression upon, and penetrates the heart of the reader." While he could be reasonably sure that such a reader would "translate passages strictly opposed to his individual opinion as faithfully as he possibly can," there was still potential for erroneous remainders to "creep in" or zeal to be left out.[52] Rather than transmitting the certainty of conviction, the lack of missionary spirit on the part of the translators could prevent the transmission of faith. The mission, as many members of both the CMS and the ABCFM repeatedly and increasingly admitted, was failing; the project of transmission as self-replication was not being received by its Arab transmittees. Or worse, the products they were receiving—though they *seemed* to be free of errors—were rife with mistakes that were not detectable by the (missionary) reviser.

For Gobat, these translation issues had grave consequences. Word choice was not just a matter of producing correct versions of evangelical views on sacred works but ensuring hermeneutical stability and revealing the universalism of the message of Christ. In his autobiography, he voices incredulity at CMS translators who were "puzzled continuously, not knowing how to render the imagery in which the meaning was clothed in the English original," when the work of God is "intelligible to all."[53] Writing to the lay secretary about an Arabic translation of Genesis, he describes his ambiguous translation techniques as no less than a danger to the evangelical mission itself:

> The chief defect (some may call it an advantage), according to my humble view, arises from the desire of the translators to avoid frequent repetitions of the same word, so that sometimes within a few verses there are four or five so called synonyms to render one and the same word, having the same meaning in the Original; the consequence will be, that, though the meaning of a sentence be correct, the biblical student cannot rely upon the decided meaning of the individual expressions, and will be tempted to seek for a difference of meaning in the different synonymous words; for, in fact, in Arabic as well as in other languages synonymous words generally carry with them some sense peculiar to

themselves, so that here the nicety of the language will become a temptation against the clear and simple understanding of God's word.[54]

Rather than a single "decided meaning," Arabic synonyms—a standard feature of high Arabic prose—offer multiple options among which readers must deliberate on their own; in this translation, biblical interpretation becomes an open-ended and ongoing process that *un*decides decided meaning among a plurality of possibilities. And it does so through linguistic difference, or the "niceties" of other languages that carry their own "peculiar" sense into the text: it is translation itself that risks instability. These synonyms form what Venuti, after Jean-Jacques Lecercle, has called the "remainder": effects that work only in the domestic language and literature and that can call up unpredictable and often uncontainable associations and connotations. Heterogeneous and variable, these synonyms "call attention to the translation as a translation."[55] They compose what Paul Ricoeur has called the "half-silent connotations" that compose translation and that "alter the best-defined denotations of the original vocabulary, and . . . drift, as it were, between the signs, the sentences, the sequences."[56] It is not a wonder that Gobat was disturbed by this translation practice; unmoored and variable, meaning could potentially drift away from evangelical understandings. What is more, it could reveal the possibility that there is no "clear and simple understanding of God's word" that stands prior to or apart from readerly interpretation or that is "intelligible to all, and can consequently be translated into all languages."[57] Rather than being assimilated to an ideology in which all is translatable because no translation is necessary, the translation practices of the Arab translators required readers to read *in translation*, a potentially interminable process in which linguistic difference is located not between discrete, homogeneous languages but *within* them.

Fāris al-Shidyāq, Translator

That it was Fāris al-Shidyāq whose translations provoked these responses is not surprising. As Christopher Schlienz writes of working with al-Shidyāq, "Nearly in every thing I translate with him or teach him he proves a touchstone to me and though whilst rubbing and being rubbed the labour gets a little unpleasant yet when the trial is over it commonly receives sanction and encouragement."[58] In al-Shidyāq's view, he was the only skilled translator in an organization of hacks. As he explained in a letter preserved in the CMS Archives,

Malta 24 March 1844

My dear sir

I take the liberty of sending to you and to Dr. Mill an Arabic Poem expressing the ungenerous behaviours of the Society for Promotion of Christian Knowledge in not having remunerated me for ten . . . years of faithful service to them and to the Missionary Society, and in having employed in my steade an ignorant person not withstanding. I have addressed them in tow [*sic*] letters respecting the numerous grammatical mistakes he has committed, and to which I have not yet received an answer.

I remain

Sir

Your obd. Servant

Fares Shidiak[59]

Al-Shidyāq was their longest-running translator, joining the press in 1826 after his brother Asʿad had been imprisoned for his Protestant sympathies and the ABCFM Beirut mission suspended. Except for a period from 1828 to 1835, when al-Shidyāq left for Cairo to work for a mission school and briefly for a government newspaper (and continued, as records show, to work on translations), he was, as Jurjī Zaydān reports, "responsible, as the author, translator, or editor, for every single Arabic book printed at the Malta press" until it closed in 1842.[60] Afterward, he continued to work as a translator, moving to England to finish the Arabic Bible for the Society for Promoting Christian Knowledge and staying until 1857, when he left for Tunis and then Istanbul.

In addition to being the most prolific translator working for the missionaries, al-Shidyāq was also the most ambivalent about the missionary project, frequently expressing, as Daniel Temple of the ABCFM warned Jowett, "a wish to be free, and *loudly*," both intellectually and contractually.[61] While the 1827 volume of the *Missionary Herald* published by the ABCFM records "Phares, brother of Asad" among its list of persons "such as are in a state of mind more or less promising, of whom some will probably be received ere long into the church," it is not clear that he ever did formally convert.[62] He was, as an annual report describes him, a man of "strong and wayward passions."[63] It is reported in CMS correspondence in 1832 that al-Shidyāq "delivered . . . his confession of belief," but three years later, he is described as "not yet converted" and in 1840 as "sunk very deep in unbelief."[64] These letters describe him as voluble, poetical—"sputter[ing] out in divers colours like soap-bubbles"—brilliant, and learned: fitting adjectives given that he would later become one of the most prolific and celebrated thinkers of his time.[65]

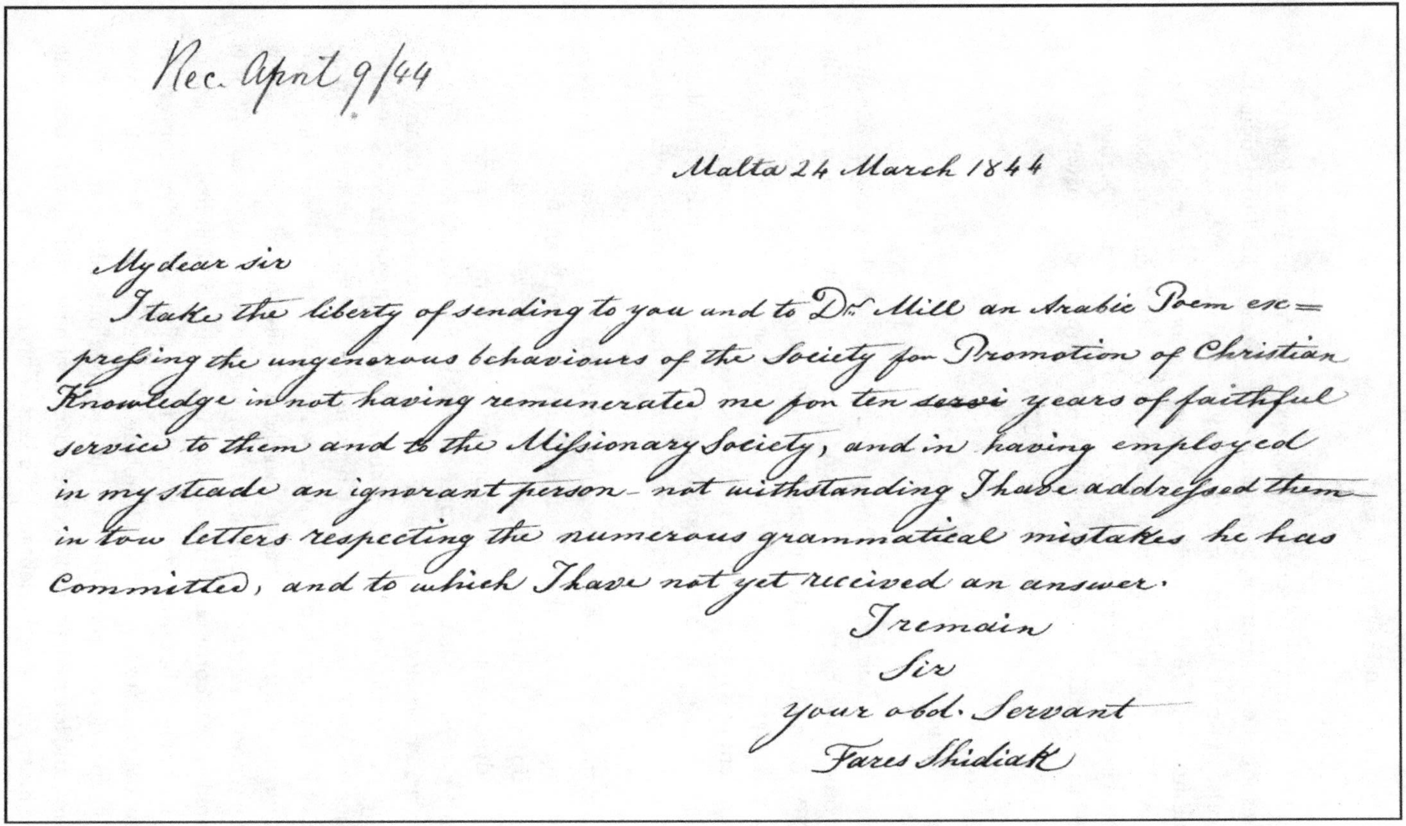
Rec. April 9/44

Malta 24 March 1844

My dear sir
I take the liberty of sending to you and to Dr. Mill an Arabic Poem ex=
pressing the ungenerous behaviours of the Society for Promotion of Christian
Knowledge in not having remunerated me for ten ~~sessi~~ years of faithful
service to them and to the Missionary Society, and in having employed
in my steade an ignorant person- not withstanding I have addressed them
in tow letters respecting the numerous grammatical mistakes he has
Committed, and to which I have not yet received an answer.

I remain
Sir
your obd. Servant
Fares Shidiak

FIGURE 1.1. Letter from Fāris al-Shidyāq to the Church Missionary Society, March 24, 1844. (Church Missionary Society Archives, Cadbury Research Library, University of Birmingham, UK)

That al-Shidyāq would produce works that recognize and even emphasize the heterogeneous effects of translation, then, is yet another manifestation of the profound skepticism that worried his CMS and Society for Promoting Christian Knowledge superiors. His "waywardness" in matters of Christian belief is well documented: *Leg over Leg* contained biting criticisms of the missionaries, whom he called "bag-men" and likened to itinerant merchants hawking their wares in the spiritual marketplace, and later (probably during his stay in Tunis in 1857–1859), he would convert to Islam and take the name Aḥmad. And a list of his unpublished and lost works contains no fewer than six treatises in refutation of either the Old or New Testament. Far from promoting the single, clear truth of God's word as it appears in the unerring Bible and interpretable in a literalistic hermeneutic, al-Shidyāq's scholarship focuses on what he called the "contradictions" of scripture that are revealed through a *comparative* analysis of texts. In *The Altercations of Interpretation in the Contradictions of the Gospel*, an unpublished treatise he composed while working with the Reverend Samuel Lee to translate the Bible, he employs this methodology, setting the Gospels side by side to reveal the "divergence and multiplicity in the narrative" of the life of Jesus.[66] The contradictions of source criticism here open up the interpretive opportunities that Gobat preferred he close in his translation of the Bible: they show that the narratives of the Gospels are not singular and "divinely inspired" (*min waḥī allah*) but are "different narratives about Jesus that had flown around in the country, and which each one transmitted [*naqalahā*] according to what he heard from the mouths of their narrators."[67]

The implications of understanding the Gospels not as *waḥī* (inspiration) but as *naql* (transmission or even translation) are profound. The four Evangelists—and by extension the evangelical preachers and missionaries—become not "witnesses" but transmitters who do not reproduce truth but produce contradicting claims, or "altercations of interpretation." Transmission itself is redefined in the process—no longer a unidirectional and hierarchical movement in which readers are figured as children, it is now figured as *ta'wīl* (interpretation or hermeneutics) to be performed by the missionaries, the translators, and the receivers of the text, whom al-Shidyāq refers to as *al-labīb*: the discerning reader.[68] Like the Arabic reader of Genesis who must discern meaning among synonyms, the reader of *Altercations* is asked to read comparatively among divergences and multiplicities.

Fostering a mode of comparative reading with and within Arabic would arguably become al-Shidyāq's central project and the explicit content of his masterwork, *Leg over Leg Concerning That Which Is al-Fāryāq* (*Al-Sāq 'alā al-Sāq fī mā huwa al-Fāryāq*, 1855). Though unacknowledged as such, it is a work that thinks in and through translation and that was in fact composed while al-Shidyāq was still working with Rev. Lee on his Arabic Bible project. *Leg over Leg* fictionalizes his travels to Malta, Egypt, and England as an exercise in cultural comparison: its semiautobiographical protagonist, al-Fāryāq, is both a condensation of his name, *Fā*ris al-Shid*yāq*, and also a verbal noun whose meaning is "he who distinguishes." While its miscellaneous style has made its generic classification an open debate among scholars, al-Shidyāq himself described it as a linguistic treatise. He wrote it, as he explains in its preface, in order to "give prominence to the oddities of the language, including its rare words," many of which he enumerates in long lexical lists interspersed throughout the text.[69] Far from digressions, al-Shidyāq saw these lists as integral features of his prose; "the enumeration of many synonymous and lexically associated words in a style clear and *admirable*, presented in a manner both fascinating and *delectable*," was part of his intent.[70]

Leg over Leg thus revels in the very literary techniques that the missionaries found so distressing. As al-Shidyāq writes, he seeks "to uncover the hidden meanings conveyed through jokes and the other excellent features . . . taking into consideration every aspect of any similar words" by juxtaposing similar words.[71] Instead of fixing meaning, he ensures that readers "seek for a difference of meaning in the different synonymous words," as Gobat feared, by in fact insisting on the differences between the synonyms he uses. This is the text's operative hermeneutic mode: it is by the juxtaposition of events, characters, and even adjectives that the plot, as nonlinear as it is, moves (and often laterally rather than forward), just as lists of synonyms act not as repetitions but nodes of association with which the reader must engage in order to construct meaning. Al-Shidyāq even goes so far as to explicitly reject the very notion of synonymity in its opening pages. He writes,

> In addition, I have imposed on the reader the condition that he not skip any of the "synonymous" words in this book of mine, many though they be (for it may happen that, on a single road, a herd of fifty words, all with the same meaning, or with two meanings that are close, may pass him by). If he cannot commit to this, I cannot permit him to peruse it and will not offer him my congratulations if he does so. I have to admit that I cannot support the idea that all "synonyms" have the same meaning, or they would have called them "equi-nyms."[72]

As al-Shidyāq points out here, the Arabic root for "synonyms," *r-d-f*, does not necessarily connote equivalence. It can mean to pile up in layers, to become stratified, to flock, to throng, to form a single line, or to follow one after another. And the adverbial phrase *sāqan ʿalā al-sāq* can mean to put one foot after another or to follow leg upon leg.[73] It is through an accumulation of linguistic nonequivalence that meaning emerges: what al-Shidyāq demands from his readers is that they read comparatively and in translation, even within the Arabic language. As his narrator tells us, "Observe, then, how people differ with regard to a single word and a single meaning!"[74] "Altercations of interpretation" abound in everyday language and not just in the holy texts. The linguistic indeterminacy ("divergence and multiplicity" in *Altercations of Interpretation*) that reigns in *Al-Sāq*—with simple definitions of words seeming to collapse under the weight of his lists of subtly differentiated synonyms—is a trial of modernity that makes visible the constitutive role of translation in all linguistic encounters.

Al-Shidyāq's experience as a translator with the CMS forms not only the epistemological foundation of the text but also its explicit content. He lampoons the missionaries and especially their weak attempts at language learning. He enumerates their translation errors, satirizes them for their hypocritical lack of scholarly goals (when staying at a monastery and in need of a dictionary to compose poetry, he inquires after a copy of *Al-Qāmūs*, only to be given answers about *jamūs* and *kabūs*, or buffaloes and nightmares), and ridicules them for their inability to communicate with their congregation in Arabic. Al-Shidyāq consistently stages encounters between Arabic speakers and non-Arabic speakers in ways that not only highlight the extent to which they rely on translation but also emphasize the productive role of nonequivalence and translation errors. As al-Shidyāq later writes,

> He who has missed out on translation knows not what travail is:
> None but the warrior is scorched by the fire of war!
> I find a thousand notions for which there is none akin
> Amongst us, and a thousand with none appropriate;
> And a thousand terms with no equivalent.
> I find disjunction for junction, though junction is needed.[75]

For al-Shidyāq, to translate is to find nonequivalence and disjunction in language; errors are therefore not an *aberration* of translation but its very foundation. *Leg over Leg* is, in this sense, a work of translation theory: al-Shidyāq presents a theory of translation to counter the CMS missionary translation practices, highlighting linguistic nonequivalence as a way of inscribing the "internal limit" within the domestic field. Translation, that is, must happen within Arabic, too. Not even synonymy can be taken for granted when all language has the potential to be "a symbol of the noncommunicable," as Benjamin writes, where all language is eternally in translation. Instead of junctions, al-Shidyāq finds only disjunctions or "divergences and multiplicity," as translation passes through the pile or flock of language's *mutarādifāt*. It passes through difference, "through continua of transformation, not abstract areas of identity and similarity" as Benjamin writes, or as al-Shidyāq figures it, it passes through (by juxtaposition) a continuum of disjointed linguistic junctures and nonequivalent synonyms.[76]

Transmission and translation, rather than tools suited only for conversion, conquest, and diffusion, become in al-Shidyāq's and other translators' hands a mode of critical reading that ensures *im*pure transmission. As I have tried to show, the press records show the extent to which the translation work of people like al-Shidyāq cannot be subsumed under the rubric of "missionary translation" or be seen as evidence of the Western origins of print culture or print modernity. As products of the religious mingling of the Ottoman Empire that these missionaries could not, try as they might, mitigate or eradicate, and as scholars in their own right who maintained an ambivalent relationship with the evangelicalism of the CMS, their translations are not reducible to the agenda of the society or to the CMS's goal of reversing the tower of Babel and eradicating the threat of singular "peculiarity." The stakes of this, of course, were high: as Derrida reminds us, the multiplicity of Babel also figures "an incompletion, the impossibility of finishing. . . . What the multiplicity of idioms actually limits is not only a 'true' translation, a transparent and adequate inter-expression, it is also a structural order, a coherence of construct": all things that the CMS Press actively sought to discourage. While Derrida laments that one of the limits of theories of translation is that they cannot account for multiplicity (and "all too often treat the passing from one language to another and do not sufficiently consider the possibility for languages to be implicated *more than two* in a text"), this was not true of the multiple and divergent method of translation used by these translators.[77] Working in tension—by "rubbing and being rubbed"—with CMS goals and the original text, these translators included the divergent and the multiple as constitutive elements of products that required their readers to read comparatively and in translation. It is with this heterogeneous and variable mode of translation that *Kurūzī* was produced, both within and in tension with missionary goals. The Translation Movement, as it arose in the missionary age, did not write back to the original or to the West but wrote with and next to it: competing with it, collaborating with it, and correcting its "ignorance" and "mistakes."

Arabic *Crusoe*

From the Church Missionary Society's perspective, *Robinson Crusoe* was a fitting early project for its Malta press. Intended as a vehicle for the dissemination of sound doctrine and the education of Christian sympathy, multiple copies of *Kurūzī* were dispatched to established missionary stations as well as sent on expeditions: Joseph Wolff packed three dozen copies for distribution in Central Asia and reported that "Robinson Crusoe's adventures and wisdom were read by Muhammedans in the market-places of Sanaa, Hodeyda, and Loheya, and admired and believed!"[78] Missionaries might have seen in *Crusoe* a parable of their own projects: the story of a "rebellious young *exempla*" finding the moral path and, as Crusoe puts it, becoming "an Instrument under Providence to save . . . the Soul of a poor Savage, and bring him to the true Knowledge of Religion, and of the Christian Doctrine."[79] Missionary biographies and accounts made regular reference to *Crusoe*. Referring to themselves as "a kind of missionary Crusoe, the monarch of all [they] surveyed" or describing themselves as feeling "as Crusoe did on observing the footsteps of a man in the sand,"[80] missionaries in diverse contexts interpolated *Crusoe* into their projects as the providential version of the colonial "alibi": presenting colonial desires as benevolent and even natural while domesticating foreign spaces and native labor into images of English domesticity and piety.[81]

Crusoe's Arabic version was no exception. The CMS Press chose for its source text an abridged edition that, like many of the nineteenth-century versions of *Crusoe*, was designed for the education of a young audience. First published 1819 and going through at least five editions by the time of *Kurūzī*'s publication, the likely source version was an anonymous abridgement published in Dublin and New York that condensed the island episode to 174 pages of relatively simple prose. Yet it was probably chosen not for its brevity or faithfulness to the original plot (it follows the plot of *Crusoe* and reproduces most of its dialogue verbatim) but for its harmony with the CMS's own pedagogical aims. Emphasizing the pleasures of domestic life, for example, or Crusoe's education of Friday over his exploration of the island and the pair's attempts to leave it, this version (like most other abridged versions) instills in its young readers the importance of home and family even while adventuring abroad.[82] "Making the away more like home" could have even proposed a solution to the problems of "going native" or permitting hybrid forms of worship (this version omits the scene in which Friday attempts to equate God with his own deity, the Benamuckee).

The source text's emphasis on the unproblematic reproduction of religious principles in foreign souls might have made it seem a perfect illustration of the CMS's iterative ideology, did we not already understand the uneasy relationship between Arabic translation and the missionaries under which it was performed. Many things may creep in unawares. Indeed, this is evident from the title page itself, which appears with an added poetic epigraph that sets up the protagonist as an allegoric figure for the unconverted reader. It features an engraving of Crusoe clinging to a rock in the stormy sea, and its second-person address offers advice that links the reader's situation with that of Crusoe:

> If you intend to rise on high
> then climb the staircase of virtues for they are the footholds.
> And if you intend to ascend without them
> then by God you will not ascend.
> And if you aim for right conduct without a guide
> then you will no doubt call out, to the West then East. (*QRK*, title page; see figure 1.2)

More than being a missionary text, this epigraph implies that *Qiṣṣat Rūbinṣun Kurūzī* is an object that missionizes: it teaches the Arabic reader the benefit of right conduct that emerges from a "guide." Yet, if the language of a "guide" to right conduct implies the importance of doctrinal fidelity, the history of the epigraph's transmission complicates a straight line of influence from the Protestant *Crusoe* to the Arabophone converts. For these verses are not a translation of an evangelical tract or an original composition by a member of the CMS staff. Instead, this three-line poem was originally written in Arabic and derived from an Eastern Catholic source: it is one of the poems of Nīqūlā Al-Ṣā'igh (1692–1756), superior general of the Basilian order at the Greek Catholic monastery of al-Shuwayr, Lebanon. Al-Sā'igh, along with others Catholic members of the learned society to which he belonged, was involved in the translation, adaptation, and printing (al-Shuwayr was one of the early sites of printing and translation in the region) of Syriac and Latin texts into Arabic, as well as intralingual translations.[83] By adding entries related to Christianity to Arabic lexicons largely designed to facilitate explication of the Qur'an, simplifying classics of Islamic philosophy, or incorporating Islamic references in their literary writings, these men created a "significant inter-religious cultural space" in their work and in the *nahḍa* at large.[84]

Yet even this transmission was not direct but a divergence. Al-Ṣā'igh's poems were known by many people (or at least those who had had some seminary education) and in circulation orally and in manuscript form.[85] The vast majority of the translators of the Malta Press had had some religious education and would have probably been exposed to *Dīwān al-khūrī* (The priest's poetry) and even memorized parts of it in school. Yet the text as it appears on

Robinson Kruse.

قصة روبنصن كروزي

اذا رمت الصعود الي علا * فشب درج الفضايل فهي مرقي
وان رمت الرقا بلا مراق * وايم الله انك لست ترقي
وان شيت الرشاد بغير هاد * لا شك تهت غربا ثم شرقا

طبع في مالطة سنة ١٨٣٥

FIGURE 1.2. Title page, *Qiṣṣat Rūbinṣun Kurūzī* (The story of Robinson Crusoe) (Malta: Church Missionary Society Press, 1835). (Beinecke Rare Book and Manuscript Library, Yale University)

Kurūzī's frontispiece is not exactly as it appeared in al-Ṣā'igh's *Dīwān* but has been amended in order to aid in clarity or correct the meter. Substituting *shubb* for *thib* ("climb"; marked not with a *shaddah* but a *sukūn*) in the first line, for example, does not change the meaning but adds a doubled consonant to make the line conform to the *wāfir* meter (the meanings of *shabba* and *wathaba* are very similar, and both mean to "leap" or to "rise"). And the final line, which reads, "And if you aim for right conduct without a trustworthy / guide then you will lose the way, West and East," in al-Ṣā'igh, is changed to clarify the adverbial case endings of "West" and "East." Like the nineteenth-century reception of premodern classics that included "updated" and "amended" versions (such as al-Bustānī's expansion of Firūzābādī's *Qāmūs al-muḥīṭ, muḥīṭ al-muḥīt*), this is not simply a quotation of al-Ṣā'igh but a correction.[86]

Beginning the translation with this epigraph, the translator signals the complex modes of mediation that brought *Robinson Crusoe* to its Arab readers. The epigraph places *Kurūzī* in a longer history of translation and printing that predated this European presence by a century and in so doing shows transmission to be a long and multilayered process that works through intermediary influences, interests, texts, and even languages. Not only was its transmission partially enacted by situating the text in a Catholic literary context, but that context was itself complexly interreligious. Not only the product of an Eastern Christian church—the church that *Kurūzī* was published in order to combat—the "foothold" on the ladder to salvation that the text offers is also produced in this interreligious space. It is the product of the "mingled confusion" in which Levantine Christians lived, traded references, and produced literary works. In this sense, we might see the divergences of this translation from Defoe's text not as an index of the resistance to or recuperation of power from the missionary societies and the imperialism for which their work served as an alibi but as continuing the longer history of the text's mediation (which began almost immediately after its publication in England) as a version of a version.

The translation of *Crusoe* that follows continues to emphasize the sedimentation of translation, correction, and adaptation that constitutes the text. This is apparent from its first lines: instead of beginning in the first person with Crusoe's account of his life and shipwreck, *Kurūzī* begins with a third-person preamble introducing the protagonist and his family history before turning to the first person with the formula *qāla sāḥib al-qiṣṣa* (and so said the narrator). Recalling the chain of transmission (*isnād*) that begins most premodern narratives and that traces the oral or written history of a particular work, this switch in narrative voice removes the narrative from the "true history" mode of narration in which an eyewitness narrates his or her account directly to the audience, and places it within an explicitly mediated narrative mode.[87] Not merely a citation of authorities, the *isnād* serves to "anchor the text to the actual instance of enunciation" that can be evaluated; the *isnād* contextualizes a work and gives a history of its transmission and its transmitters.[88] With the inclusion of this formula, the preamble to the story emphasizes the fact that the text arrives to the reader at the second degree, having been transmitted through an unknown third-person redactor who serves as an editor and interlocutor, explaining terms to the audience and giving context: "There was once a man from the land of the English called Rūbinṣun Kurūzī," the novel begins, "and he was born in the Christian year 1632 in a city called York in one of the provinces of Britain" (*QRK*, 3). This is a significant but necessary reformulation from Defoe's version ("I was born in the Year 1632, in the City of York," or "I was born in at York in the year 1632," as it appears in the abridgement). Not only is the reader marked as reading from outside England, where York must be geographically situated, but the site of mediation itself is no longer England but somewhere outside it. It is a displacement—as scholars of the non-Western reception of European literature frequently point out—that marks the difference between an original (and often implied) readership and its new one and that can demonstrate the extent to which translations were displacements themselves, not "simply products of colonialism or informers of the imperial will" but also "objects of cultural consumption."[89]

This translation, moreover, was—to paraphrase al-Shidyāq—a divergence from the original text and *a multiplication* of it. Like the synonyms that proliferated, to the missionaries' dismay, in the CMS translation of Genesis, parenthetical definitions and alternative translations make inter- and intralingual translation visible throughout. In the shipwreck, for example, Kurūzī finds "*damnajānāt (ayy qurābāt)*" (jars), "*parkalīn (ayy bīkārīn)*" (compasses) and "*darābīn (ayy naẓārāt)*" (spyglasses), and he later gathers his grapes in "*zakībatayn (ayy juwālaqayn)*" (two sacks) (*QRK*, 54, 66, 110). In each set of parentheses, the translator offers Arabic alternatives for the item in question, a move that not only highlights the difficulty of making the two texts commensurable but also demonstrates the lexicographical richness of Ottoman-era Arabic. The first several examples highlight the linguistic diversity of its loan words: *damnajānāt* (sing. *damnajāna*, variation of *damajāna*) was in circulation in nineteenth-century Arabic, according to Buṭrus al-Bustānī's *Muḥīṭ al-muḥīṭ*, but it is derived from Persian, while *parkalīn* (sing. *parkal*) is derived from Turkish (a variation of *bīkārīn*, derived from Persian).[90] And the last two demonstrate Arabic's regional diversity: *Darābīn* (sing. *durbīn*) and *zakībatayn* (sing. *zakība*) were both current in the Egyptian dialect at the time of translation.[91] By asking the readers to read among the etymological and regional variations of Ottoman-era Arabic in these synonyms, the translator draws attention to his role in mediating the text. What is more, and more essential, is that he asks his readers themselves to translate in order to understand its meaning. By making clear the extent to which multiple languages are implicated not only in a text but in a single language, *Kurūzī* draws attention to the central role of translation in Ottoman society, where Ottoman subjects performed quotidian acts of translation even when speaking the same language.

The opening line implicates more than one of those acts. Specifying that Kurūzī was born "in the Christian year 1632" refers to the religiously diverse Ottoman Empire and to the simple fact that people in the eastern Mediterranean were often required to translate between several calendars. These included not only the Gregorian and Islamic, or *hijrī*, calendars but also the Ottoman fiscal (*mālī*) calendar, the Julian calendar (used among Eastern Christians in the Levant), and the Coptic calendar (used by Coptic Christians in Egypt). In early periodicals, two dates would often appear at the masthead, but their alignment was not consistently calibrated. Mismatches in calendar dates occurred, and attempts to harmonize calendars did not always succeed, exposing the "fragility of an ostensibly seamless temporal grid," as On Barak argues.[92] The Ottoman fiscal calendar could only keep its tax years in line with the *hijrī* calendar by omitting one year for every thirty-three, but even this system broke down (as it did in 1287 AH, or 1870–1871 CE).[93] Translating this English text into Arabic was more than a matter of finding equivalent words and also more than moving from one cultural context to another (what some scholars call "cultural translation"): it was a matter of situating *Crusoe* in a context in which the translation between systems of knowledge was already a given.

Instead of advocating for an interpretation of the world solely according to Christian Protestant interpretive mechanisms that will bring about a future global Kingdom of Christ, *Kurūzī*'s translator displays a routine acknowledgment of multiple modes of understanding. The use of the "Christian year" is a minor and implicit acknowledgment of the Islamic calendar, but more explicit references to Islam occur throughout. In addition to Kurūzī's frequent quotation of biblical passages, he also makes reference to non-Christian examples of what he calls "Arab learning" that are not present in the English original.[94] When, during Crusoe's first "successful Adventure," for example, his friend and mentor, the unnamed Captain, dies, the Arabic translation embellishes the scene with a popular quotation from *Sūrat al-Baqara* ("The Cow," Qur'an 2:156): "when I heard the bad news, pain and sadness clouded upon me, and from an excess of grief I swallowed my fate and said, 'I am God's and to him do we all return'" (*QRK*, 17). Instead of purifying the language of its association with Islam or initiating the reader into a mode of reading that uses only Christian scriptures as interpretive authorities, the translator constructs a more inclusive frame of interpretive reference.

Invoking less a worldview in which "no accommodation with other religions could be long tolerated" than one that acknowledges and even seeks to engage in a dialogue with other religious scriptural traditions, *Kurūzī* does not interest itself in the religious domestication and political stewardship of all of its spaces or their subjection to one religious and cultural order.[95] Later, when Kurūzī journeys into the island and finds an abundance of fruit trees, he praises God as the unseen hand that planted them and refers to himself as the "slave" (*al-ʿabd*) who labors in God's garden and who has only the right to the surplus he himself produces. This is a theme of the previously quoted *Sūrat al-Baqara*, but the wording derives from Qur'anic interpretation (*tafsīr*) and is a direct quotation of the Qur'anic interpreter al-Qurṭubī: "al-ʿabd la ya'kulu illā rizq nafsihi" (*QRK*, 98).[96] While Crusoe uses the language of "discovery" in both Defoe's version and the abridgement and refers to his home as his "castle," Kurūzī employs a Qur'anic argument explicitly negating Crusoe's claim to sovereignty.[97] For, as the verse on which al-Qurṭubī comments and to which *Kurūzī* therefore makes an oblique reference makes clear, "There is no moving creature on earth but its sustenance depends on God."[98] Kurūzī does not claim the land so much as he negotiates his presence on it as a borrowed home, tending it "*as if it were* [his] own garden" (*QRK*, 97). Instead of a fantasy of property ownership and political sovereignty (his "kingdom," as it is frequently called in the abridgement), Kurūzī insists on his lack of claim on the island.

Unlike Crusoe, then, Kurūzī serves as only a mediocre model for the missionary overseas. The pedagogical and social hierarchy that is inscribed in the English version and that most likely attracted the attention of the CMS in the first place becomes unstable at best. While Crusoe teaches Friday to speak, to cook, to hunt, and even to dress like "we do" in England, Jumʿa (Friday) does not look like Kurūzī when fitted with his belt and hatchet; "the result was the Jumʿa looked like [the pre-Islamic hero] ʿAntar ibn Shaddād rushing toward a hundred men and felling them" (*QRK*, 203). While Crusoe seems to have much to teach but little to learn from Friday or Xury (even though, as Peter Hulme points out, Crusoe educates Friday in "European ways" by "instructing him" in two skills—grilling meat and navigation—that happen to both be aspects of Carib technology), Kisār (Xury) and Jumʿa (Friday) are sites of strength and even potential authority.[99] Kisār makes reasoned and eloquent arguments: "Night is unknown but day is a riddle" (*al-laylu majhūlun wa al-nihāru maḥzūrun*), he tells Kurūzī when he advocates for waiting until daybreak to go ashore, "for if someone came upon you during the day, when you could see him, you could aim and shoot him where he stood, . . . while at night, you are in danger" (*QRK*, 27–28). Complete with rhyming elements, Kisār's speech has at least the same rhetorical authority as Kurūzī's—a fact that Kurūzī acknowledges: "I found his opinion estimable, and considered him to be correct, and so I obeyed" (*QRK*, 28). Friday, similarly, uses language that is indistinguishable from Kurūzī's in register or diction. Friday reaches a point where he is not only fluent but "eloquent" (*bāligh*); in *Kurūzī*, furthermore, and unlike in *Crusoe*, Friday learns to read—giving him an opportunity, one imagines, to engage with the scriptures without Crusoe's pedagogical intercession (*QRK*, 203).

Kurūzī offers the reader not just one source of doctrinal or linguistic authority but multiple interlocutors from which he learns, multiple holy texts from which he draws wisdom, multiple calendars by which he organizes his days, and multiple languages among which he represents his reality. In doing so, it stands in direct contradistinction with the translation strategies authorized by the CMS, which wanted its translations to appear to be untranslated Arabic originals, and even the product of fixed boundaries around discrete cultures and languages. While the CMS established processes that enforced the homogeneity of a linguistic community, the translator of *Crusoe* emphasized its heterogeneity.[100] *Kurūzī* poses enlightenment as the product of multiple acts of translation—making it less an example of missionary translation than a product of the kinds of heterolingual interactions and reading practices that were essential to life in the Ottoman Empire during the *nahḍa*. The Arabic novel, in this context, could perhaps not but be read in translation.

Reading the Novel in Translation

The first novel in Arabic is not only published in translation but initiates the reader into the practice of reading "in translation," both cultural and linguistic—among and against multiple frames of reference, voices of authority, languages, and intertexts. This mode of translation allows for potential equivalences and instances of untranslatability, spaces where reading communities overlap and part. As with the alternative definitions in parenthesis, it shows the work that translators must perform in order to make texts and languages equivalent and opens up the specter of incommunicability, the potential for a part the audience not to understand unless an alternative is suggested or a parallel religious tradition invoked. Translation, as Benjamin writes, can only be a "provisional way of coming to terms with the foreignness of languages," a temporary and provisional solution to the problem of plurality and heterolingualism.[101] Kurūzī, his "home" no more than borrowed, his word no more than one among his companions, and his religion one of several, is no longer the sovereign interpreter of *Crusoe*: he is the impure transmitter, the translator, himself.

To read in translation is to recognize translation that occurs within a single language. This is to read against a model of translation that Naoki Sakai has called "homolingual" and that rests on the discourse of the nation-state and the discrete boundaries of its imagined communities. These are the assumptions of the missionary societies (which were interested in preserving the "nationality of feeling") as well as many studies of transnational reception, which assume translation to take place among an international economy of autonomous national literatures with correlating national languages and print cultures.[102] In this international model, the original work is understood to emerge from an autonomous national context and address a homogeneous national audience, only to later "travel" to another autonomous national context and address a second homogeneous national audience.[103] In that model of a work's reception, what travels is the English book (to borrow a phrase), and what receives it is a representative of a second national community. As Franco Moretti quotes Edward Said, "at some point writers in Arabic became aware of European novels and began to write works like them."[104] Translation, in this understanding, only shores up the purported autonomous origins of genres and movements, which are either resisted or accepted by readers of the receiving, "target," or in some cases "dominated" language when they "become aware" of the original.

This is an image of the literary work as solitary adventurer, sailing across the seas to colonize a new territory (and rarely to be turned back, like Napoleon was in Egypt).[105] It is not unlike canonical interpretations of Crusoe himself, which have seen Defoe's novel as erecting an ideology (or "myth") of individualism and self-sufficiency, where a self-made man tells the story of himself "Written by Himself."[106] In a fantasy of sovereignty extended to language, Crusoe's imagined solitude allows him to produce his self-composition; he turns "the randomly varied world" into "a self-expressive structure," as John Richetti argues.[107] Or as Peter Hulme offers, *Crusoe* is the story of a protagonist who sees himself as a "practical man of the world who operates entirely in a realm of trial and error": his self is composed away from the mediation of outside interference, through a direct and unmediated relationship to the world around him.[108] Just as he makes a "plain earthenware pot" with "no Notion of Kiln" but through "experimentation," that is, Crusoe fashions himself and the world around him (*RC*, 88). As he writes, "Tho' I miscarried so much in my Design for large Pots, yet I made several smaller things with better Success, such as little round Pots, flat Dishes, Pitchers, and Pipkins, and any things my Hand turn'd to" (*RC*, 88) This is why, for Virginia Woolf, the solitude and solidity of the single pot is the central organizing figure of the novel. It stands in the foreground like the solitary hero who is "in all his sublimity standing against a background of broken mountains and tumbling oceans," as Woolf finishes her essay.[109]

For postcolonial critics, this solitude itself marks the text as a colonial fantasy, as it allows Crusoe to be posed as "the fully-fledged colonial adventurer, self-composed, ready for action."[110] Seeing Crusoe as embedded in transnational relationships of commerce and imperial competition as both an agent and a victim of power, critics have highlighted the way that Crusoe's myth of self-sufficiency obscures the colonial underpinnings of Crusoe's island adventure: for Lydia Liu and Robert Markley, for example, it hides European dependence on East Asian trade and technology, while for Hulme, it masks the colonial dependence on the South Seas islands.[111] As Liu argues in an essay that revisits both Woolf's argument and the historicity of the earthenware pot itself, Defoe transforms rivalries among economies and civilizations into "a tale of (white) man's *solitary survival in nature*," where "the experiment with earthenware is symptomatic of . . . the poetics of colonial disavowal" that suppresses not only international economic rivalries but also "transcultural meanings."[112]

Yet, if in *Crusoe* the single, solid pot and the solitude of its maker stand almost as one in the foreground and deny "material connections and transcultural meanings," in *Kurūzī* the foreground is crowded:[113] "Then I brought more clay, and I mixed it and kneaded it, and formed with it stewing dishes [*ṭawājin*], pitchers [*bawāṭī*], soup tureens [*sulṭāniyāt*], bowls [*zabādī*], washbasins [*injānāt*], watering pitchers [*marākin*], milk jugs [*ḥawālīb*], flagons [*qilal*], tankards [*kīzān*], carafes [*dawāriq*], kettles [*qidr*], pots [*buram*], and all that is related to the potter's craft [*ṣan'at al-fākhūrī*]" (*QRK*, 122). Instead of a single pot or even the several smaller "Earthen-ware vessels" ("Pots, flat Dishes, Pitchers, and Pipkins") that he later succeeds in firing, the Arabic version lists no fewer than twelve different varieties of clay vessel: stewing dishes, pitchers, soup tureens, bowls, washbowls, watering pitchers, milk jugs, flagons, tankards, carafes, kettles, and pots.[114] Since each is listed in the plural, which in Arabic indicates at least three of any object, this amounts to at least thirty-six different pieces of earthenware—enough to fill a small potter's workshop, a locale the text evokes in relating these objects to *ṣan'at al-fākhūrī* (the craft of the potter). Instead of highlighting the solidity of the finished product—the pots that are "dry and hard" and "hard as stone" and that "did not crack at all" (*RC*, 88), as Defoe insists—the Arabic version focuses on the process, the *ṣan'a*: highlighting the clay and its mutability, it insists on how Kurūzī "mixed it, kneaded it, and formed [his objects] with it" (*QRK*, 122). Molding and remolding, Kurūzī fires multiple vessels that are all differentiated, each with a specific shape and function that is not interchangeable in either appearance or usage.[115] Indeed, the generic term "earthen pots" that Defoe uses seems inadequate to describe the variety of objects that *Kurūzī* enumerates; this list overloads the word "pot" and threatens to collapse it under the weight of the proliferating specificity. The Arabic does not try to reproduce the pot at all, offering only the multiplying list in the place of any generic word for "vessel." Commensurability in translation, either between English and Arabic or within Arabic itself, is put at stake. As Samuel Gobat so lamented of al-Shidyāq's translation practices (which may well be on display here), rendering one word with "four or five so called synonyms" means that the reader "cannot rely upon the decided meaning of the individual expressions, and will be tempted to seek for a difference of meaning in the different synonymous words."[116] Instead of offering single, solid meanings to the reader, the text "tempts" us to read in translation, or among the nonsynonymous synonyms that form dissimilar fragments of language.

Neither a replication of an original nor an independent literary production but a divergence and a multiple, *Kurūzī* is a reading of and with *Crusoe*. Equipped now not with Woolf's image of the pot's solidity and solitude but with the anonymous creator of *Kurūzī*'s sense of the overwhelming proliferation and mutability of the craft of pot making, we are able to read *Crusoe* in translation to see that the stability of the term "pot" was in danger of collapse even in English. The adaptation of *Crusoe* already emphasizes the ambiguity of the clay, "the awkward ways" that Crusoe used it, and the "ugly misshapen things" he made. The process produces a crisis in naming: the products were "awkward things," "clumsy things," or even "any thing[s]" that were merely "in imitation of earthen jars."[117] Yet the original makes this crisis even more apparent. Defoe writes, "After this Experiment, I need not say that I wanted no sort of Earthen Ware for my Use; but I must needs say, as to the Shapes of them, they were very indifferent, as any one may suppose, when I had no way of making them, but as the Children make Dirt-Pies, or as a Woman would make Pies, that never learn'd to raise Past" (*RC*, 89). Instead of the solid, single pot that Woolf conjures in her essay, the results of the experiment that Defoe offers here are far vaguer; he makes a "sort of Earthen Ware" suitable, simply, for "Use." As in the adaptation, Defoe gives us a series of indefinite and unmodified nouns, "indifferent" in shape but also encased in a language riddled with negatives: "I need not say that I wanted no sort," "I had no way of making them," or "a woman that never learn'd." The negative verbs seem to dissolve the very solidity of his product with every word. What the reader is left with is of indifferent shape, indeed.

Defoe produces an object that can only take shape in the reader's imagination with the help of readerly inference and interpretation. As scholars of the English eighteenth century have increasingly pointed out, the relationship between word and thing (as well as person and thing) in *Crusoe* was neither as direct nor as certain as earlier Defoe scholars had hypothesized; it was not an example of "epistemological naïveté" that used "denotative language" to bring "particular objects" home concretely to the reader but exemplified the struggle to bring objects to the minds of readers using hermeneutical and descriptive processes.[118] As Lynn Festa points out, Crusoe often has a problem naming objects. Crusoe sees a bird but "know[s] not what to call it"; he builds objects but cannot settle whether they are "Chests or Boxes" (*RC*, 54). This continues throughout the journal, where he finds a tree of Iron Wood "or like it," makes an object "in the Form of a Shovel or Spade," builds a "Room or Cave" to use as a "Warehouse or Magazin," in his larger "Cave or Vault" (*RC*, 54–55). Description and analogy emerge as ways of resolving this crisis, producing "jury-rigged approximations," as Festa writes, and descriptive borrowings: he finds "catlike" creatures, creatures that look "like a Hare, but different in Colour" (*RC*, 67), and "Fowl like a Hawk" (*RC*, 224). Crusoe's objects, Festa argues, are not just there to be seen; they must be brought into being, with language "*making* the object."[119]

What bears further examination is how Crusoe does so through linguistic borrowing, approximation, and analogy; we might call that making "translation," as bringing things into language more often means finding a name for it, rather than creating one from whole cloth.[120] That word and thing fit awkwardly together shows that the process of assemblage can only be provisional. For Benjamin, who also uses the image of a clay vessel to describe translation, it amounts to "an echo of the original": like "fragments of a vessel which are to be glued together," they "must match each other in the smallest details, although they need not be like one another."[121] Nor can they be. Translation can never be a reproduction. Errors must be repaired.

Crusoe's is an island of misfit words in English as in Arabic; both novels, in this sense, rely on translation. Translation, though, as scholars have long noted, has underwritten *Crusoe*'s own history of composition, though the impacts of its presence have yet to fully be explored. The origins of Defoe's sources are as wide ranging as his protagonist's travels and include French utopian novels, Dutch and French stories of marooning, and at least two Arabic sources: Ibn Ṭufayl's twelfth-century philosophical narrative *Ḥayy Ibn Yaqẓān* (The Life of Ibn Yaqẓān), which was translated into English three times by 1719, and "The Story of Sindbad the Sailor," which had appeared in at least five extremely popular printings by the time of *Crusoe*'s publication.[122] Defoe was not immune to the wave of popular interest in the East that had followed the first 1705 Grub Street publication of the *Arabian Nights*. Two years before *Crusoe* appeared, in 1717, Defoe published a religious polemic in the Oriental style, *The Conduct of Christians Made the Sport of Infidels, in a Letter from a Turkish Merchant at Amsterdam to the Grand Mufti at Constantinople*, and he is the likely author of another Oriental-style work appearing a year later, a ninth volume to Marana's *L'Espion Turc*, entitled *A Continuation of Letters Written by a Turkish Spy at Paris*. *Robinson Crusoe*, written in the style of "Himself," comes at the heels of pseudotranslations that claim to be written "in the Stile of the Original [Oriental author]," which preserves the author's "surprising Turns of Wit, and Flights of Fancy."[123] Authentic narrative might also require translation.

Written as if in translation and using mock-Oriental phrasing that combines several of the time's popular notions of Islam and the Ottoman Empire, these works simultaneously (and sometimes contradictorily) evoked an image of religious severity, uncontrollable sexual urges, unquestioning loyalty, and despotic tyranny. "I bow my Head to the Dust under thy venerable Feet, O thou divine Image of heavenly Wisdom," the fictional Kara Selym Oglan writes to the "Mufti at Constantinople," for example, "beseeching thee to inflame my Soul with an Ardour becoming a true Mussul-Man."[124] His repeated assertions of loyalty, "translated" from Arabic, have their echoes in *Crusoe*; just as Oglan swears loyalty "by the hoary Head of my Father and Grandfather, by the grey Hairs now encreasing on my Face," and later by "laying my Hands upon my Beard,"[125] Crusoe asks his Muslim fellow slave Xury, "stroak your Face to be true to me" (*RC*, 19). He elaborates: *"that is, swear by* Mahomet *and his Father's Beard"* (*RC*, 19).[126] Actual and fictional translations from Middle Eastern languages are part of *Crusoe*'s very text.

Translation and transmission, that is, are as integral to the origins of the purported English original as they are to its Arabic translation. In this sense, while the Arabic translation of *Crusoe* might have seemingly arbitrarily Arabized some details of the protagonist's life, it could also be argued that the translator was merely amplifying connections that were already in place in the original, re-Orientalizing what was already, in small ways, occupied with the East. Thus the supranational imaginary world of this novel is composed not just of a believed-to-be-deserted Caribbean island but also of South America, West Africa, North Africa, and Turkey—as before Crusoe is shipwrecked, he owns a plantation, trades in slaves, is kidnapped by Turkish pirates, and has a Moorish traveling companion on what was known as the Barbary coast of North Africa. What we see, in the first novel to be translated into Arabic, is the translation of a global imaginary in which the Middle East was already a key component. It is just as Mikhā'īl ʿAwrā hypothesized: English authors, having encountered and appreciated Arabic narrative via dubious translations, "followed their example."[127]

Crusoe is not an exception. We must remind ourselves that nation-bound theories of the novel itself, which assume a homolingual address or homogeneous and monolingual public or print culture, are relatively recent phenomena. Like early Arabic histories of the genre, early English and French histories of narrative fiction suggested its extranational origins; Abbé Huet (1670) traced the *roman* from ancient Egypt, Persia, and Syria to western Europe, while Clara Reeve (1785) explained that "progress of romance" was westward, having been "communicated to the Western world by the Crusades."[128] For these historians of the novel, the history of the form was always one of translation and transmission, putting it, as Srinivas Aravamudan argues, in the context of a "horizontally integrative 'geography' of transcultural influence and exchange, rather than the more familiar vertical and genealogical 'history' of the national model."[129]

Canonical theoretical formulations of the genre similarly foreground horizontal frameworks and can be profitably mined for their extranational investments. For Georg Lukács, the novel is the consequence of a conception of the world as infinitely large and heterogeneous, the result of the "fragmentary nature of the world's structure" being carried "into the world of forms."[130] For Mikhail Bakhtin, the form itself carries the traces of heterogeneity: the novel is defined by its heteroglossia, the internal heterogeneity of languages and national literatures. "Every novel," he writes, "is a dialogized system made up of the images of 'languages,' styles and consciousnesses" that cannot be unified, as words themselves are not a "direct expression" of an object or of "its own unitary and singular language."[131] Meaning, in the novel as in language—and in the novel as an image of language itself—can only arise between an utterance and an "alien word about the same object," where it "take[s] on the nature of an internal polemic."[132] Crusoe's island of misfit words and things is not the exception but the rule; in the novel, Bakhtin writes, the "direct and unmediated intention of a word presents itself as something impermissibly naïve," and meaning instead emerges between and among languages, or in the "Tower-of-Babel mixing of languages."[133] Novelistic meaning-making, that is, occurs in translation.

As Derrida reminds us, the Tower of Babel "does not merely figure the irreducible multiplicity of tongues; it exhibits an incompletion, the impossibility of finishing, of totalizing."[134] All that the novel can do is translate among the divergences and multiplicities within languages as among them; it can assemble the fragments into a provisional unity, until they are disassembled again. Or, as Lukács writes, "The composition of the novel is the paradoxical fusion of heterogeneous and discrete components into an organic whole which is then abolished over and over again."[135] Stewing dishes, pitchers, soup tureens, bowls, washbasins, milk jugs, flagons, tankards, carafes, kettles, and pots can only provisionally be unified as a "vessel," but so too can "chest or box" and "shovel or spade" be made equivalent only by "jury-rigged approximations." Translation is constitutive and problematic in all cases.

To read *Kurūzī* in translation is not only to identify the novel as an effect of the context of a transregional, heterolingual, and multifaith network of encounters that made up the nineteenth-century Mediterranean but also to see it as a mode of critical reading that posits a relationship to Europe and European literature that is more than a lateral movement from language A to language B. *Kurūzī* comments on and rereads its purported original, highlighting the submerged traces of an earlier interaction between Europe and the Middle East and situating *Crusoe* in its own origins in translation. By focusing on the work of the native translators themselves, and not just the ideologies of the institutions that employed them, we see how the Translation Movement opens by producing neither an imitation nor an independent creation but a translation of a translation, an unending "internal polemic" that recognizes difference as occurring not just between two discrete languages as they marked bounded territories or cultural entities but as multiplicities found within them. That the literary form that emerges from this movement and becomes dominant in literary modernity would be the novel must not surprise us, but not because the novel was an inevitable product of cultural hegemony. The "true" Arabic novel did not develop over time from its "protonovelistic" translated beginnings; it emerged in translation and marked translation as a constitutive element in it. As a translation of a translation, *Kurūzī* might be its purest expression of form.

Chapter 2

Stranger Publics

The Structural Translation of the Print Sphere

> Journals are among the greatest means for civilizing the public and increasing the number of readers, if used properly.
>
> —Buṭrus al-Bustānī, "Speech on the Literature of the Arabs," 1859

> If anyone should find [linguistic simplification] presumptuous and insulting to the Arab intelligence, let him take the trouble of translating a speech by a British Parliament member or, better still, render in Arabic the proceedings of a session, an article on European theater, a political study, a commercial report, and the like. Surely he would find himself facing an abyss with every single sentence. He might not transcend it without seriously complicating the language, leaving his readers in disconcertment and doubt.
>
> —Khalīl al-Khūrī, "On Periodical Writing," *Ḥadīqat al-Akhbār*, 1858

Qiṣṣat Rūbinṣun Kurūzī and the other Church Missionary Society publications were printed annually in small quantities and distributed by agents of the church by hand, and *Al-Sāq*—available only in its first Paris-printed edition until the twentieth century—was destined for an elite audience of scholars and educated readers.[1] The forms of Arabic literary circulation that existed when al-Shidyāq began his career in print were mainly restricted to religious and government publications, which were focused on liturgical and scientific texts, and only occasionally produced editions of poetry or narrative fiction.[2] And even literary societies—of which there were several in Lebanon—served smaller and more selective audiences still. The Syrian Society for Arts and Sciences (al-Jamʿīyya al-sūriyya li al-ʿulūm wa al-funūn, 1847–1852) met to collect books and newspapers "especially in the Arabic language" as well as to exchange and discuss literary information through papers and debates, but with the exception of occasional public speeches, its meetings and library were accessible only to its fifty-five members, all of whom were Christian.[3] The Oriental Society of Beirut (al-Jamʿīyya al-sharqīyya fī Bayrūt, 1850–1852) focused on "the acquisition of useful books in Arabic and foreign languages," ostensibly "for the benefit of the masses," but was sponsored by the Jesuit Fathers and held its meetings in French.[4] The Syrian Scientific Society (al-Jamʿīyya al-ʿilmīyya al-Sūrīyya, 1857–1860, 1868–1869) made the most concerted effort to reach a larger audience, aiming to "disseminate the sciences and arts among Arabic speakers" by "composing . . . useful speeches to be read to those present and later printed and distributed," but its library was only available for the "use and enjoyment" of a select few.[5] Those "disconnected" peoples that al-Shidyāq imagined connecting via the printing press would have been limited to a small group of readers, indeed. As Buṭrus al-Bustānī complains in his address to the Syrian Scientific Society in 1859, although there existed many private libraries in Lebanon, they were "locked with iron doors" and left to accumulate worms and dust. "What is the benefit of so many books," he asks, "if there is no one to read them?"[6]

Al-Bustānī's "Khuṭba," addressed to those very elites whom he described as "stingy" with their access to learning, culminated in a comprehensive plan for the renovation of the Arabic letters and sciences that hinged on the creation of a reading public. He called for reforming Arabic lexicography through the elimination of "dead words" "weighing down" Arab authors, increasing literacy through the founding and funding of schools, and above all investing in print.[7] "Journals," as he writes, "are among the greatest means for civilizing the public [*li tamaddun al-jamhūr*] and increasing the number of readers, if used properly."[8] Al-Bustānī's speech as well as a later one ("Discourse on the Social Structure") that called even more forcefully for publications "appropriate to the spirit of the age" that would "instill a desire for education among the illiterate," sparked a conversation that would engulf the region, as private citizens opened printing presses and periodicals with explicitly stated missions to educate and advance Arab society.[9] Beirut journals like Khalīl al-Khūrī's *Ḥadīqat al-akhbār* and al-Bustānī's *Al-Jinān* aimed to be a "lantern of improvement" and a "garden of morals and useful news" for their readers by spreading "knowledge and arts" among them, and once government regulations allowed, private Egyptian journals followed suit.[10] These featured debates about how to draw in and shape a robust readership, including how to simplify and clarify Arabic for all readers to participate in the emerging public sphere. As al-Bustānī and other journal producers repeatedly explained, this took effort on their part as well as on the part of the reader. It was only, as he wrote, if print was "used properly" that it was of benefit. At the center of the drive to cultural reform was the creation of the reading subject and the public sphere as a community of "proper readers" of Arabic, a category—as we shall see—that might never have entirely emerged. Reading competencies, techniques, and values, periodical writers worried, were simply too diverse. Reading print required too much translation, as al-Khūrī put it: writing for the public was not only *like* translation but *entailed* translation. It was, for him, not a sphere but an "abyss." The modern reader, and that institution of literary modernity the public sphere, emerged as a problem of translation.

A Public of Strangers

Unlike the members of scientific and literary societies, who produced speeches and tracts for smaller and more circumscribed audiences, periodical writers addressed an explicitly nonspecialist audience, the *'umūm*, or public.[11] Derived from *al-'āmma*, a category indicating a social class without access to education (as opposed to the elite, *al- khāṣṣa*), the pluralized *'umūm*, and eventually *jumhūr*, took on an expanded meaning in the nineteenth century to refer to the general public, both literate and illiterate, all of whom could be addressed as potential readers.[12] If the New Age was to be brought about, these periodicals claimed, it would be through wider access to education and literacy, a goal that they promoted by publishing articles advocating general education or women's education, by announcing the opening of new schools and the printing of textbooks, and by advertising and reporting on schools' annual examinations and end-of-year spectacles. But even more attention was paid to inculcating the habit of reading itself: journals urged their audiences to develop the habit of periodical reading, which they argued would facilitate the acquisition of general knowledge and "enlighten the minds of the people and lead them to a high degree of innovation and artistic achievement," as al-Khūrī writes in an article simply titled "Reading."[13] Variations of this ambition echoed in the introductory statements of many of the periodicals that began their print runs in the boom years of commercial presses in the 1860s and '70s. Their goal, as Buṭrus al-Bustānī writes in the first issue of *Al-Jinān*, was to participate in the greater project of the *nahḍa* that "extends cultivation [*al-tamaddun*] and widens its circle little by little in the East"—enveloping all within it as readers or potential readers.[14]

What these journals make explicit is that enlightened modernity was to be achieved above all by increasing the number of readers in society and producing *al-'umūm*. As Fransīs al-Marrāsh argues in *Al-Jinān*, the single innovation that is most responsible for the nineteenth-century improvements in intellectual development is not the printing press or even general education or "freedom of thought" (about which he writes elsewhere) but the writing and "publishing of newspapers" specifically *"for the general public"*: "We do not say that newspapers were unknown before this century but that they were not widespread until then. . . . The only means to improve the intellect [*nawāl al-ma'qūlāt*] is through education, and education is only possible through the reading of books. And when there were no books with general information benefiting the general public, attaining education was tiresome and difficult. Newspapers began to make the road to that exertion easier by simplifying those benefits for them. . . . And so the many [*'umūm*] were enriched by the select few [*khuṣūṣ*]."[15] This is true for Buṭrus al-Bustānī, too, whose "Khuṭba" ends with a section describing "the means to achieve civilization" that lists libraries, presses, and schools as those institutions that will benefit "the public in general" (*al-jamhūr al-'umūm*) by delivering culture to it.[16] Periodical publishers saw themselves as part of this project, framing the consumption of their own journals as advancing a collective goal. Al-Khūrī makes this clear in multiple articles in *Ḥadīqat al-akhbār*, promoting his own newspaper as participating in the circulation of knowledge to a general audience, even criticizing publications that fall short of this goal.[17]

These prominent writers were not alone. Descriptions of and references to periodical culture and its benefits were plentiful in the early Arabic press from in its early years in Lebanon through the height of Egyptian turn-of-the-century periodical production.[18] Articles enumerating the number of journals published in foreign countries or the ratio of citizens to journals regularly appeared in these contemplations of cultural revival, as did references to periodical reading in articles and fictional narratives. As Elizabeth Holt argues, it was through instructing the readership in the "useful role" of reading that periodicals attempted to produce a modern public in print—a goal that was not exclusive to Arab periodicals or even to non-European ones. The first English weeklies were where, as Jürgen Habermas has argued, "the public held up a mirror to itself, . . . entering itself into literature as an object."[19] Similarly, *nahḍa* journals, as Holt writes, "invited bourgeois readers to imagine and participate in local models of proper reading habits and intellectual comportment" and therefore produced, and were produced by, "a newly emerging public."[20] The *kātib 'āmm*, a new term for a periodical writer that translates to "public writer," did not serve a ready-made *'umūm* but produced it by modeling and managing the reading practices of its new and expanding "general" audience.

Habermas's model, critics have noted, can take too general a view on its general audience. As Habermas explains in *The Structural Transformation of the*

Public Sphere, an audience became a reading public through the periodical's ability to be a means for conducting rational critical debate among people who do not know each other and yet have interests in common. He writes, "However exclusive the public might be in any given instance, it could never close itself off entirely and become consolidated as a clique; for it always understood itself and found itself immersed within a more inclusive public of all private people, persons who—insofar as they were propertied and educated—as readers, listeners, and spectators could avail themselves via the market of the objects that were subject to discussion. The issues discussed became 'general' not merely in their significance, but also in their accessibility: everyone had to *be able* to participate."[21] A reading public, for Habermas, works by virtue of its inclusivity or potential to be inclusive, which itself relies on the accessibility of the print object in which public discourse appears. In other words, a *kātib ʿāmm* is only a public writer to the extent that his writing appears in a form that is *in principle* accessible to anyone who can obtain it. Yet it is precisely this principle that has attracted criticism: scholars writing from feminist, queer studies, critical race, transnational, and Marxist perspectives have all shown how his rhetoric of accessibility rests on structural exclusions. Habermas's caveat itself points to this. It is only "insofar as they were propertied and educated"—and, in the mid-nineteenth century Middle East, insofar as they were also male, urban, and of the *efendiyya* class—that persons could participate in the print public sphere.[22] Even then, however, the ability of a reader to do so was far from certain. These periodicals' calls for increased readership were often accompanied by cautionary caveats. "Journals are among the greatest means for civilizing the public and increasing the number of readers, *if used properly*," al-Bustānī warns. The general public, they explained, must first learn *how* to participate in the public sphere in order to for periodicals to be culturally effective.

It is in the public sphere model's limitations and caveats, then, that we might best understand the emerging category of the *ʿumūm*. These journals as well as the novels serialized inside them were not produced by or even for a popular audience; for that we would have to seek out other literary forms like oral epic narratives, shadow plays, or vernacular poetry.[23] Instead, they were produced by the literary elite (*khuṣūṣ*) for the masses (*ʿumūm*) in order to improve them. As Yūsuf al-Shalfūn writes in the introduction of weekly *Al-Zahra*, part of the goal of his publication is "the enticement of people of this country, and especially *al-ʿumūm*, to enjoy reading and instill in them the desire to acquire scientific and literary works."[24] Elite authors sought to produce and manage new literary agents and forms, to guide the way in which the public entered itself into literature as a disciplinary object. That the Arabic public sphere imagined by these elites could exist only if certain conditions of proper use were met, or if certain people were disciplined into it, defines the ambivalent attitudes of these reformers toward their audience and its untrained reading habits.

Reading across the journals of the 1860s and 1870s, the qualifications and even accusations abound. Nearly as often as periodical editors and writers invoked or modeled a reading public, they voiced their uncertainty that their readers *did* use journals—consumed them, circulated them, read them—"properly" or that they had or even sought access to them. Marrāsh's "Newspapers" transforms quickly into a plea: "So come, oh sons of the nation, and buy these newspapers that extend to you the arts of literature and improvement and deliver to you the spirit of learning and knowledge of your earth . . . and know that buying newspapers is a duty to everyone who has an attachment to his world and what it contains."[25] The wide circulation of knowledge depended on a form of material circulation—individual accumulation—that seems to have only rarely occurred. And when readers did subscribe, journals appeared to have trouble convincing them to conform to subscription rules. *Al-Jinān* and *Al-Bashīr* (the Jesuit-run Beirut weekly) ran periodic "announcements" reminding their audience to resubscribe for the following year, and *Al-Jawā'ib* and *Ḥadīqat al-akhbār* frequently admonished their current subscribers to pay their fees. On several occasions, *Ḥadīqat al-akhbār* went so far as to threaten to list delinquent subscribers individually by name.[26] Payment problems, indeed, continued well into the twentieth century in all of the major publishing centers. In this early period, these problems account for the large rate of turnover in privately owned journals, many of which lasted only a year or two before closing.[27] The existence of a stable consuming public was itself tenuous.

The caveats and qualifications in describing the value of periodicals to progress were echoed in almost every periodical of the period, and often on the front page, above the lead article. These appeared in the form of announcements, advertisements, and even sets of instructions for readers. *Al-Bashīr*, which regularly printed readers' correspondence, published a series of corrective guidelines to manage the practice of letter writing to the journal: readers who wanted their letters published, the guidelines explained, should make sure that their letters are of "clear script" and are "easy to read"; in particular, they should be sure to use dots to distinguish between the letters of their signatures so as to avoid misattribution.[28] In addition to asking readers to write more clearly, *Al-Bashīr* requested that readers include specific information about the subjects of their letters, especially when their purpose is to praise leaders for admirable deeds. *Al-Jinān* and *Al-Jawā'ib* printed similar instructions, asking their readers to include their names with their letters and to write in "clear and legible script."[29] Yet, though these journals took pains to reduce "ambiguity and error," uncertainties still arose, and newspapers printed corrections to their correspondence section.[30]

These announcements were concerned not only with the way that the journal audience wrote but also with how they read. The first issue of *Al-Muqtaṭaf*, for example, was prefaced with explicit instructions for proper reading:

> [If] you read it as you would read a story, then you will not benefit from it a bit, and if you pore over a part of a subject while ignoring another part of it, you will only gain a partial benefit and perhaps even a corrupted one. . . . So reflect on what you are reading and do not leave a sentence without having understood it well and concentrated upon it, for "a little understood well is better than much understood poorly." And neither should you rely on your memory alone. . . . And if you tire of a subject or reach the limits of your concentration, then take a break and return to it so that it may become clearer to you and easier to retain and more difficult to forget.[31]

These instructions continue for two full pages in a twenty-four-page issue, outlining in detail not only step-by-step instructions for reading but also the merits of acquiring broad general knowledge, the importance of the sciences to civilization, and the right general attitude to take toward knowledge. The editors of *Al-Muqtaṭaf* considered none of this to be common knowledge. They phrased their instructions as corrections of the status quo.

Direct communications like these to readers show the extent to which unsanctioned uses of periodicals ruled the day, revealing points of tension between producers and consumers about what constituted the "proper" use of print culture. Instructions about reading were not an indication of how people actually read or of how the public was actually formed but evidence of a debate about how people *should* read. As Stephen Sheehi so urgently warns, when trying to understand nineteenth-century discourses of reform, we must not confuse reformers' social analysis with historical fact and should instead see reformers' "articulations as effects of the disjuncture between shifts in material culture and social practices that otherwise negotiated society in the past."[32] These announcements and articles do not describe existing practices or delineate an existing sociocultural category of the reading public but register the aftereffects of the collapse of the monopoly of elite communities over the production of religious and secular knowledge. Like other emergent reform discourses, *al-ʿumūm* is one of "the visible effects of epistemological and material ruptures" that presents an imaginary relationship between people and their real social conditions.[33] It functions much like the qualifications and caveats in the evocation of the reading public: they conjure a proper public only "if" certain criteria are met, while simultaneously pointing to the fact that this was not quite the case. As such, these paratexts signal a reformist ideology as well as the contradictions that this ideology attempted to reconcile; they mark the "public" not only as a disciplinary mechanism but also as its failure.

Above all, what this discourse of proper reading signaled was that these periodicals—from the outset—circulated by errant means and to errant readers. Though some had subscriber lists containing a narrow and largely uniform audience of literate male city dwellers from the bourgeois classes, their audience was far less knowable and their reading practices far more varied. This is part of Marrāsh's complaint: low subscription rates did not indicate that few people were consuming periodicals, only that few people were consuming them *in the way he had hoped*. He lists the causes of low subscription rosters in a series of imaginary readers' responses: "Why should I buy *Al-Jawā'ib* and *Al-Jinān* when my neighbor buys them and I can borrow them?" "Every day I hear the telegraph correspondent pass by, so why should I pay for news?"[34] People were reading periodicals, not purchasing them. At the end of al-Khūrī's article "Reading," he makes a similar complaint to his readers, asking them to buy his newspaper. As he admonishes, one of the signs that "we have not raised our heads from our slumber" is that people prefer not to spend their money on circulating papers. "*Ḥadīqat al-akhbār* is in its sixth year and is still on the edge of extinction due to a paucity of subscribers, and yet it has conquered many a reader who hastens to gather to read it."[35] Instead of buying the newspaper in a yearly or half-yearly subscription, or even buying single issues, readers were accused of improperly using them by "gathering" to read: they borrowed, read communally, and even listened to newspapers.

Though newspapers and journals were purchased by only the small percentage of the population that was literate and had enough disposable income to afford an item that could cost the equivalent of a pound of rice, a much wider population consumed them.[36] Men and the fewer women who were literate indeed did gather to read periodicals; they also shared subscriptions and borrowed each other's copies. Periodicals were also available in coffeehouses, shops, and reading rooms that began to open in the last quarter of the nineteenth century in Egyptian and Lebanese towns; later they could be found in railway stations and marketplaces, where they could be read for the price of a cup of tea or coffee.[37] Communal oral-reading practices also enlarged the demographic variety of print users. Contemporary accounts describe paid readers and ordinary consumers reading newspapers aloud in places such as "a workshop, low class café, or carriage/transportation stop" to diverse crowds that included those who would not have been able to afford a subscription: "servants, donkey breeders, and others who cannot read."[38] Circulation, that is, did not only take place in print, nor did rational-critical debate. As Ziad Fahmy documents in the case of the Egyptian periodical *Abu Naḍḍāra*, reading aloud was also an occasion when consumers "debated, digested, and discussed" the issues of the day.[39]

The new "general readers" whose numbers swelled in this period were not a single, bourgeois public that read and debated about itself solely in print. New consumers were clearly reading but in multiple and often improvised ways that were not approved by the producers themselves. Scholarly estimates have calculated that these alternative reading and circulation practices increased the number of consumers by as much as 500 percent and considerably expanded the demographic range of the readers the periodicals reached—a fact that journal producers lamented. An editorial in *Al-Jinān* looking forward to its third year of publication notes that not only does the audience include "those who are interested in political matters and so ignore the rest [of the paper] . . . and those who are interested in scientific matters above all else" and those "who prefer small print and [those] who prefer large," but more importantly there are numerous "sects, interest groups, and parties" that proliferate and make their views known to the journal. An article praising someone, as the editorial explains, will raise alarms from those who oppose him, and an article blaming another person will be contradicted by those who support him. For *Al-Jinān*, these divisions account for the greatest "difficulties" of the publisher and are even the "greatest reason for the delay in the success of journals."[40] Similarly, for al-Khūrī, they impede the journalist's very purpose, his ability to simply "uncover the truth." Divisions within the audience instead make the journalist "a target for the archers' arrows": "for perhaps what one condemns another will approve, which makes everything he says a cause for some to assail him and others to praise him, depending on the difference in their tastes and opinions."[41] He blames the vast variety of "interest groups" for his journal's financial difficulties: the readership is too diverse, contains too many strangers, to form a general public.

These complaints support Nancy Fraser's claim that "virtually contemporaneous with the bourgeois public there arose a host of competing counterpublics," which were there "from the start" and not just in its later development, as Habermas has implied.[42] As Michael Warner has emphasized, "A public is always in excess of its known social basis. It must be more than a list of one's friends. It must include strangers."[43] During the *nahḍa*, multiple publics and counterpublics were not segregated from each other but folded into what was called *al-ʿumūm*, making the inclusion of strangers "a condition of possibility" for public discourse.[44] Strangers and strange reading practices might have been seen as a hindrance to forming a general public, but they were integral to its very formation. Their traces are the way that it registers debates about the shifts in epistemological and social categories. They help identify the ruptures in any easy consensus about what constituted knowledge and who is qualified to produce or receive it.

Earlier in the publication run of *Ḥadīqat al-akhbār*, al-Khūrī demonstrates precisely this point. In the thirty-first issue of the first year, he was compelled to print a "Request for Forgiveness" for having likened the telegraph to gossiping women. As the article explains, after he used an infelicitous turn of phrase, he unexpectedly received a number of impassioned protests, and from sources he likewise did not anticipate: "In our previous issue we had described the new invention of the telegraph as having the speed of diffusion faster than that of a secret between women. We did not mean anything by that other than a humorous phrase, but it was a phrase that has echoed from province to province and against which voices of the fair sex have been raised."[45] After a brief defense of his article—which includes explaining that the expression was not the author's invention but taken from an English newspaper—he prints the text of one of the letters from his dissatisfied female readers. In eloquent rhyming prose, she expresses her displeasure at her gender being maligned and points out the irony that the analogy was made by a "writer of journals, whose business it is to disseminate and broadcast secrets, . . . while most women in this region spend their entire lives as if in prison, so little news do they hear." She then ends the letter with an appeal to her fellow women readers to do as she has done and write in when necessary to make their recriminations heard, so as not to let such accusations stand in print when they find them. "These sorts of *general* accusations [*tuhma ʿumūmiyya*]," she explains, "should not be recorded in the pages of newspapers."[46]

In pointing out the ways that access to information is gendered and in calling for redress from the journal and action from fellow female readers, this letter writer makes it clear that the reading public is not composed solely of bourgeois men but also unknown and even unexpected readers such as herself. In this letter, the very subject of reform discourse—the new reader—actively contests the very terms of her instruction into a social category that might be called the reading public. She shows how the author's ability to make the analogy of telegraphs to gossiping women in the first place relies on the exclusion of women's voices from print and the assumption of their absence from the audience. While journal producers saw the multiplicity of the audience as a problem to be solved by instructing readers in the proper usage of print, this female journal reader urges readers to make that multiplicity visible, to highlight the fact that the social makeup of the public sphere includes unknown readers—strangers—such as herself. In doing so, she demonstrates how the articulations of this journalist ("public writer," *kātib ʿāmm*) about what constitutes general knowledge and a general readership are not statements of historical fact but "the visible effect of epistemological and material ruptures."

Indeed, the letter writer's use of *ʿumūmiyya* to describe the charges levied specifically against women opens up a space of contestation around the ability of the word "public" to signify a truly general category into which she is able to enter. Instead of following *Ḥadīqat al-akhbār*'s model for the "useful role" of print—articles about which it regularly published—she urges female readers to use print for their own purposes, in order to prevent such "accusations" from being published. She encourages them to inscribe themselves in print but to enter themselves into literature as objects that mark their *partial estrangement* from it, objects that express their social and ideological difference within the public. Indeed, she encourages women readers to use print to educate its producers. Errant reading practices in the *nahḍa* are critical reading practices, which produce theorizations of their own institutions, including print.

Strange Lexicons

The stranger sociability of the public sphere was visible to any readers who encountered the editor's announcements or their fellow readers' disagreements, but it was above all visible in its linguistic effects. Debates about the appropriate language of the newspaper preoccupied authors well into the twentieth century, highlighting again the disciplinary problem that this public of strangers raised. In 1895, for example, the Egyptian biweekly *Al-Hilāl* ran a series of retrospective articles aimed at describing the history, art, and "obligations" of periodical writing that stressed the importance of language choice for this diverse audience: "We have seen in some of these newspapers . . . vocabulary that would embarrass a man of letters if he read it aloud, much less an innocent young woman. For newspapers are exchanged among people of various ranks and ages, and among them are merchants, artisans, priests, and teachers, as well as young men and women."[47] Periodical writers, the author argues, must be mindful of their obligations to these different groups of readers, the "people of knowledge, regardless of their station of life."[48] Similarly, Ibrāhīm al-Yāzijī, perhaps the best-known commentator on the subject, prefaced his *Lughat al-jarāʾid* (The language of newspapers)—itself a compilation of essays he wrote on the subject for *Al-Ḍiyāʾ* magazine—with an explanation of the importance of correct language use in periodicals. He cites their great "influence on [the people's] views, taste, manners, language, and the rest of their habits" as the motivation for his inquiry, "especially considering how many and how widespread they are in our current age—thousands are published every day and distributed among the readers, each one of whom consumes them according to his own ability and preparation."[49] The ability of periodicals to reach segments of society previously excluded from knowledge production required authors to monitor and alter the language they used in print.[50]

Reformed reading required reforming writing, and journals aimed to "revive the language and improve it and preserve its consistency among its speakers," both the *khāṣṣ* and the *ʿāmm*.[51] Variations of this ambition abounded, as periodical writers and language scholars debated the proper use of language in journalism, from the selection of vocabulary and correct use of grammar to its ability to transmit sound moral values. As Marrāsh explained in his 1871 article "Newspapers" in *Al-Jinān*, the intellectual improvement of the public was only really possible once newspapers began "simplifying" style for them.[52] Fāris Nimr and Yaʿqūb Ṣarrūf, editors of *Al-Muqtaṭaf* agreed: they stated the purpose of their literary-scientific journal as "provoking a desire for knowledge" among its audience by "making the arrival to knowledge easier," likening the act of reading their article-length introductions to scientific subjects to sampling new foods.[53] In order to create a new public, editors and authors of periodicals such as these ones self-consciously avoided rare vocabulary, stylistic embellishments, and syntactical complexity and streamlined the content of their articles, using what Salāma Mūsā (1887–1958), the reformist journalist and intellectual, would later call "telegraphic style":

> To *al-Muqtaṭaf*, then, I am certainly indebted for the scientific inclination that remained with me all my life; and I am equally indebted to it for the "telegraphic style" which I use in my writings, and which many readers believe to have been invented by myself. Dr. Yaʿqūb Ṣarrūf was averse to the use of ornaments of style. In general he did not like at all eloquently arranged sentences, subtly chosen words, or brilliantly figured expressions and most of all he scorned the puerile trivialities that were, until shortly before the first great war, so exclusively cultivated by our authors.[54]

Elsewhere, in an essay entitled "Style in the Press," Mūsā widens the circle of attribution from *Al-Muqtaṭaf* to writers in the nineteenth-century press at large for this stylistic innovation. The "simple Arabic style" that reigned after the *nahḍa* "should not be credited to school teachers, or even to the literary elite but to the press," whose members were tasked with educating readers who otherwise were "not exposed to world affairs."[55] To do so, he argues, they developed a style that was neither colloquial nor elevated and that could transmit information—in the form of "the informational article"—quickly and directly to a wide readership. Yet, as Mūsā's description makes clear, simple style was not easy to execute. This language had to be easy to understand and yet "transmit profound meaning"; it required "year after year" of effort on the part of newspaper editors; and it entailed more than simply "lower[ing] literary writing" to the level of the masses but rather required them to "raise" newspaper language to the standards of the people.[56] As al-Khūrī quips in an article about a fictional journalist who is having trouble filling the pages of his column, "he had not even time to simplify his style, especially on such a hot day."[57] The initiation of the public into proper modes of readership required work on the part of the elite to make knowledge accessible and even palatable to the masses. More precisely, it required *translation*, a fact to which editors were well attuned.

As the editors of *Al-Jinān* announced at the end of their first year, though they had avoided employing complex vocabulary up to that point, in their second year they would begin to introduce it for the improvement of the readers' minds. "Please forgive us," the announcement states, "if you have to use a dictionary."[58] Writing for the public required the kind of work and even the kinds of paratexts—dictionaries, glossaries, interlineal explanations—that were common in interlingual translations. This was not limited to the production of new literary forms. Even the preservation of literary and linguistic tradition necessitated a complex array of intralingual translation devices. In an advertisement for a new edition of the *Maqāmāt* of al-Ḥarīrī (1874), for example, the editor glosses almost every term, combining visual elements of both premodern scribal traditions like marginalia and new European ones like the footnote (figure 2.1).

Many journals made use of such devices, including definitions of specialist terms, rare vocabulary, or foreign words, and acknowledged them as forms of translation.[59] In doing so, editors acknowledged through their practices the fact that translation was an unavoidable aspect of print culture necessitated by the diversity of the reading public. As al-Khūrī writes in another article about the simplification of language in newspapers, "If anybody should find [linguistic simplification] presumptuous and insulting to the Arab intelligence, let him take the trouble of translating a speech by a British Parliament member or, better still, render in Arabic the proceedings of a session, an article on European theater, a political study, a commercial report, and the like. Surely he would find himself facing an abyss with every single sentence. He might not transcend it without seriously complicating the language, leaving his readers

ان كتاب مقامات الحريري الذي اعلنا عنه قبلاً قد ناهز طبعه الانجاز وجاء بحوله تعالى
حسن كالمرغوب في طبعه واتقانه وضبطه ومن الاطلاع على الوجه المطبوع ادناه يتحقق ذلك اما

المقامة السنجارية ١٧٦

ربح * أو يكهن بها سطيح * أو ينم عليها برق مليح * فما اتفق لوشك
الحظ النجوس * ونكد الطالع المنحوس * أن انطقتني
بوصفها حميا المدام * عند الجار النمام * ثم ثاب الفهم *
بعد أن صرد السهم * فأحسست الخبال * والوبال * وضيعة
ما أودع ذلك النربال * بيد أني عاهدته * على عكم ما
لفظته * وأن يحفظ السر ولو أحفظته * فزعم أنه يخزن الاسرار *
كما يخزن اللئيم الدينار * وأنه لا يهتك الاستار * ولو عرض
لأن يلج النار * فما إن غبر على ذلك الزمان * إلا يوم أو يومان *

١ يخبر ٢ كاهن مشهور كان يخبر بالمغيبات وانما سمي بذلك لانه كان دائماً مستلقياً
لا يقدر على القعود والقيام واخباره مشهورة منها انه اخبر بظهوره صلى الله عليه وسلم لما
جاء اليه ابن اخته عبد المسيح وقد حضرته الوفاة وكان قد ارسله اليه كسرى حين انشق
ايوانه ليلة ولادته عليه السلام ٣ يظهر ويخبر ٤ بالضم متلألئ
٥ لسرعة زوال وفي نسخة وهي الاصوب لوشل واصله الماء القليل والمراد به هنا القلة
والنقصان ٦ البخت والنصيب ٧ المنقوص ٨ اي تعسر ومشقة البخت وفي
نسخة وكدّ الطالع ٩ ضدّ المسعود ١٠ وفي نسخة انطقني ١١ اي حدّة
الخمر وسطوتها ١٢ الذي ينقل الكلام على وجه الافساد ١٣ رجع وفي نسخة ثاب اليّ
١٤ العقل ١٥ اي بعد ان خرج من قوسه يعني بعد ان اصاب سهم الكلام
هدف اذن النمام ١٦ استشعرت وعلمت ١٧ اراد به الفساد والنقصان
١٨ سوء العاقبة ١٩ اؤتمن عليه ٢٠ شبه به النمام لانه لا يمسك ما جُعل فيه
٢١ غيراني ٢٢ حالفته ٢٣ يعني حفظ وصيانة واصله الشد والربط
٢٤ تكلمت به ٢٥ اغضبته ٢٦ بضم الزاي من باب قتل ٢٧ لا يخرق
٢٨ وفي نسخة الاسرار ٢٩ يدخل ٣٠ ان زائدة وفي نسخة فما غبر بحذفها
وغبر بالغين المعجمة يستعمل في الماضي والمستقبل ومعناه هنا مضى وفي لغة عبر بالمهملة للماضي

الاشتراك به وقيمته سبعة فرنكات فيبقى مفتوحاً الى ٥ اذار القادم وهي مدة انتهاء طبعه ومن ثم يسد بابه ويتعين ثمن النسخة تسعة فرنكات مع ان اجرتها الآن سبعة فرنكات

FIGURE 2.1. An example of the necessity of intralingual translation for preserving the classical literary tradition: this advertisement for a new edition of the *Maqāmāt* of al-Ḥarīrī (1874) glosses almost every term and combines visual elements of both premodern scribal traditions (marginalia) and new European ones (footnotes). It appeared in *Al-Jinān* as an advertising supplement to the January 1874 edition. (*Al-Jinān* 5, no. 2 [January 1874]: n.p.) (Yale University Library)

in disconcertment and doubt."[60] Stylistic simplification, as he understood it, not only was made necessary by the amount of translation required to publish a newspaper but was *produced by* those acts of translation. Newspaper writers were central actors in a complex and deliberate process that made use of non-Arabic vocabularies. Not only did these authors transform syntax—shortening sentences and clarifying meaning without the use of case markers, for example—but they employed new vocabularies with borrowed, Arabized terms (*taʿrīb*) as well as neologisms derived from existing Arabic roots (through various forms of *ishtiqāq*).[61] None of this, as any of these authors indicates, was simply a matter of letting language settle into a simpler state. It was a process of translation that always entailed the possibility of mistranslation; even after the author-translator suffers to produce a text appropriate for the diverse public, his end product might still not be understood by his readers. For al-Khūrī, to write for a public was to risk being unreadable.

Not only was newspaper language developed with a special attention to the practice of translation as a metaphor for linguistic modernization, but the newspaper itself was composed of literal translations. *Nahḍa* thinkers who wished to reform modes of writing and reading and who strove toward the creation of a modern Arab public were necessarily in the business of translation. Indeed, much of the content of early periodicals was a kind of translation *bricolage*, composed of excerpts from and analyses of foreign news reports. Each of the periodicals surveyed that were published in the 1860s and '70s (and, indeed, beyond) contained translated and summarized news items from European periodicals as well as translated or adapted short anecdotes (*nawādir*), and many included serialized translated fictional narratives or historical works as well (as chapter 3 discusses). The early header for *Al-Jawāʾib* makes translation explicit as one of the routine but essential facts of its production: "*Al-Jawāʾib* is published once a week translated from foreign languages, and its annual price in Istanbul is 150 *qirsh*."[62] Foreign news sections included not only the country of a news item's origin but its original publication site and often the date of its publication. Phrases like "we read in the *Times* of London" or "it was reported in *Le Moniteur* of Paris" began many articles, alerting their readers to the fact that they were encountering translated documents. In a single issue, one could read news items attributed to newspapers in Paris, Berlin, and New York as well as from European-language newspapers published in Beirut or Alexandria and telegrams from any number of cable-networked European cities (often from Naples, Lisbon, Madrid).

Nearly every aspect of journal production required an act of translation: editors or authors needed to translate from European newspapers in order to include foreign news items; correspondents needed foreign-language skills to investigate and report on events and matters of commerce in foreign cities; translators with literary skills were needed to render novels into Arabic. Even news items from Egypt and Syria were often translated from English- and French-language sources like the *Levant Herald* (published daily in Istanbul in English and French). And with the increasing use of the telegraph, which operated in the Ottoman Empire from 1855, translators were needed in order to read international messages—which were received in French or (more rarely) in Turkish—and to publish them in designated "Telegraph News" sections.[63] Indeed, telegraph offices, like later news agencies (which began selling bulletins to Egyptian newspapers in 1865), were in reality "vast translation agencies," as Esperança Bielsa and Susan Bassnet put it.[64] In the Egyptian and Ottoman cases, this is explicitly so, as the Egyptian and central Ottoman telegraph offices were manned by staff recruited from translation schools and bureaus.[65] As noted in 1861 in *Ḥadīqat al-akhbār*, even cables to Beirut from nearby Damascus required a Turkish-Arabic interpreter.[66]

This was not, for these journal producers, a special problem of the Arabic periodical. They considered translation to be one of the essential roles of the newspaper itself, whether in Arabic or otherwise, which was—as *Al-Jinān*'s introductory essay explains—to inform the public about "foreign and domestic events," the benefit of which is a "stimulation of general knowledge and . . . its exchange between peoples."[67] This was indeed the case: English news pamphlets in the sixteenth century, as Andrew Pettegree explains, were verbatim translations from French or Dutch sources, and the first English-language newspaper was published in Amsterdam, not England.[68] Newspapers, whether in Beirut, Cairo, or London, as *Al-Jinān* was aware, were in the business of "connecting" people through translated news content. These Arabic periodicals were not the only ones in the business of translation, and they made it clear to their readers by enumerating the acts of translation that occurred even before an item entered into Arabic. "The following was mentioned in the *Moniteur universelle*, translated from *Delakru*, the newspaper aligned with the Count du Bismark," or "A news item from *Le Soir* translated from *The Standard* in London" were common sights.[69]

Some editors even considered translation to be one of the essential roles of the newspaper itself. Salīm al-Ḥamawī, founder and editor of the Alexandrian daily *Al-Kawkab al-sharqī*, named publishing the work of "skilled translators" as one of the paper's primary goals.[70] And *Al-Najāḥ* also marked translation's centrality in an announcement at the beginning of its third year in print:

> This year we are following through with our promise to improve the journal. . . . We will continue to publish news from the most famous of

> European newspapers and to verify it. We have also appointed correspondents in various places to report on important events and matters of commerce. And as the benefits of understanding history cannot be denied, nor can our country's propensity toward its knowledge, we will be including in each issue four pages of a historical narrative translated from the French language and written by the most trusted and famous authors, Monsieur Dūrwī, the well-known historian. We will also be publishing the aforementioned pages in a volume that can be bound separately.[71]

The emerging *nahḍa* reading public that the newspapers created was one that read overwhelmingly and knowingly in translation. The popularity and predominance of translated fiction in new *nahḍa* reading habits, then, were neither exceptional nor a consequence of the relative "weakness" of modern Arabic literature in the literary polysphere or world of letters.[72] It was, rather, the logical consequence of the pedagogical reform project that sought to bring the whole world of knowledge to the wider Arab public. Or, as al-Khūrī phrased it in his introductory statement to his newspaper, it is "the publishing of news in many languages" that has served as "the lantern of improvement in all countries that have achieved a high level of civilization."[73] Al-Khūrī's translation project is not one that seeks to absorb the learning available in an "original" that he locates elsewhere but one that instead seeks to join those other "advanced" publishers in the practice of translation in which they are *also* engaged.

In some cases, the translators were named in bylines. Yet even in cases when they remained anonymous, their work was visible in other ways: translators not only self-consciously delineated source texts but also outlined their translation processes, with periodicals devoting space to discussions of translation methodology and queries. *Al-Muqtaṭaf*'s scientific articles were so replete with translations of specialist terms that readers wrote in to request a list of translated words that had appeared thus far in their issues.[74] Translation concerns were a common theme of *Al-Muqtaṭaf*'s correspondence, too, as readers wrote in to its "Questions and Answers" forum asking for translation advice and for definitions of English or French natural and scientific terms, and the journal regularly advertised bi- and trilingual dictionaries called *turjumān*, or "translators."[75]

Translators themselves at times prefaced their articles with clarifications of their techniques or wrote in to explain their methodology. Jurjī Jibrā'īl Balīṭ al-Ḥalabī, a translator writing in *Al-Jinān*, for example, explained that it was for "the benefit of those who do not read texts in a foreign language" that he undertook a literal translation of the "strange" news item "Riwāyat rajul dhī imra'tayn" (The narrative of a man with two wives). In order to do this, as he specifies, he developed specific techniques: "I have left its sentences in their foreign order not because it is preferable to the order of our own noble language but out of a desire to show this order to those who are not familiar to it."[76] Many translators followed a model similar to al-Ḥalabī's and chose to preserve foreign sentence structures and even words, which they transliterated into Arabic script.[77] Yet others chose to accommodate the source material to Arabic vocabulary and syntax. Just weeks before al-Ḥalabī's translation and prefatory remarks appeared, ʿAbd al-Qādir Afandī al-Mu'ayd, translator of the official Damascus weekly *Jarīdat Sūriyya*, offered an entire article devoted to his own translation philosophy, which directly contradicted al-Ḥalabī's. In it, he offers six axioms for translation designed to urge translators to "pour [the original material] into the mold of the Arabic language," rather than use a more literal technique, and to avoid European punctuation, sentence structures, and transliterated vocabulary. "Foreign terms," he writes, "like *kūmīsur* [*commissaire* or commissioner] and *ūfuqātū* [*avocat* or lawyer] and *dīblūmāt* [diplomat] . . . and the like are used frequently in the journals of the empire and add difficulty to difficulty, requiring one who is learning Turkish to also acquire French in addition to Arabic and Persian."[78]

Al-Ḥalabī's comments elucidate the linguistic diversity of what we have been calling "Arabic print culture" and also its unique power dynamics. Despite voicing a resistance to the inclusion of European words in the newspaper, al-Ḥalabī does not imagine his beleaguered readers to be monolingual: they are in the process of learning Turkish and already speak Persian and Arabic. Far from describing a monolingual print culture, he acknowledges that members of the public were already reading in multiple languages, as they encountered foreign words both Arabized, transliterated, or even in Roman script. What is more, he acknowledges the fact that the nature of this multilingualism was changing in the context of increased European cultural hegemony. Many bi- and trilingual periodicals addressed multilingual audiences, and those that included a European language far outnumbered bilingual Arabic–Ottoman Turkish or Arabic-Persian (or even Arabic-Persian-Urdu). Commercial journals like *Al-Naḥla* (Beirut, then London) and *Barjīs Bārīs* (Paris) were published in Arabic and English and in Arabic and French, for example, and official Ottoman journals—including *Jurnāl al-khidiw* and *Al-Waqā'iʿ al-Miṣriyyh*—frequently appeared in Arabic and Turkish.[79] In order to join the global network of print, producers and readers must now learn a European language. Multilingualism in Arabic, Turkish, and Persian would no longer suffice in the New Age. The question was not *if* to incorporate European languages—that was unavoidable—but *how*.

١٦٦ معجم المعرَّبات

معجم المعرَّبات

تابع لما قبله

اكسي كلوريد الرصاص (Oxychloride of lead) يوجد على شكلين مختلفي التركيب احدهما ابيض ويُسمّى ايضًا ابيض يتيصن والثاني اصفر ويُسمى اصفر ترنر وهما مستعملان في صناعة الادهان

الألبَستَر (Albâtre, Alabaster) نوع من المرمر شفاف قليلاً مادتهُ كبريتات الكلس مع قليل من كربونات الكلس ومنهُ نوع اسمهُ الالبستر الشرقي مادتهُ كربونات الكلس

الالبيومن (Albumen) مركَّبٌ آليٌّ يوجد في النبات والحيوان وهو القسم الاكبر من زلال البيض ويكثر في الدم والمصل وعصار النبات وبزوره. ويشبههُ في تركيبهِ الكيماوي الفبرينُ والكاسينُ فتُسمى هذه الثلاثة المركَّبات الالبيومينية. والعناصر الداخلة في تركيبهِ هي الكربون والنيتروجين والاكسجين مع قليل من الفصفور والكبريت. وكبريتهُ هو الذي يسوّد ملاعق الفضة اذا لمست البيض ومنهُ تتولد رائحة البيض المنتنة عندما يفسد اي من الهيدروجين المكبرت المتولد منهُ. والالبيومن يذوب في الماء ثم اذا سخن الماء الذي أُذيب فيهِ الى درجة بين ١٤٠ و١٦٠ يجمد ولا يعود يذوب في الماء وذلك معروف من جمود زلال البيض عندما يسخن. ويجمد ايضًا بالسليماني (بي كلوريد الزئبق) والشب الازرق (كبريتات النحاس) وحجر جهنم (نيترات الفضة) فيُستعمَل ترياقًا لها

الالدهيد (Aldehyde) سائل طيَّار يتولَّد من تاكسد الالكحول ونحوهِ من المركَّبات الآلية

الالكحول (Alcohol) سائل معروف يُستحضَر الخفيف منهُ وهو المسمّى بالسبيرتو او روح الخمر باستقطار الاشربة الروحية. ويستحضر الالكحول الثقيل من الخفيف باستقطارهِ بعد اضافة كربونات البوتاسا مثلاً اليهِ ولهم طرق كثيرة لاستحضارهِ

الالومينا (Alumina) هو اكسيد الالومينيوم الآتي ذكرهُ ويوجد في الطبيعة على انواع كثيرة من الحجارة الكريمة كالكرَنْد والسنباذج والياقوت والصفير والزمرد

الالومينيوم (Aluminium) معدن ابيض كالفضة خفيف جدًّا ثقلهُ النوعي ٢،٥ فقط وهو موجود بكثرة مركَّبًا ولكن استخراجهُ صعب كثير النفقة

الاليزارين (Alizarine) خلاصة الفوة وهي اما طبيعية وتستخرج من جذور الفوة واما صناعية وتستخرج من الانثراسين الذي هو جزء من قطران الفحم

الامفيسيما (Emphysema) "تجمع الهواء بزيادة في الرئتين او في قسم منهما"

Figure 2.2. "Muʿjam al-muʿarabāt: al-hamza" (A glossary of translated terms: Letter A), a continuing series of definitions of scientific terms. (*Al-Muqtaṭaf* 8, no. 3 [January 1883]: 166)

These periodicals, as the print historian Jūzīf Iliyās makes clear in his study of the Syrian press, were multilingual even in their Arabic sections—a feature he considers a fault. As he argues, these periodicals contained so many foreign words and expressions (and contained so many grammatical and orthographic mistakes in Arabic) that their editors must surely have been "either Turks or illiterates who were ignorant of the Arabic language." These periodicals, he lamented, constituted "a school of linguistic barbarism" in their multilingualism, which was then imitated by Arabic-only journals.[80] Indeed, if one looks at the statistics on *nahḍa* periodicals' publishing languages, a monolingual Arabic print public sphere—however wished for by contemporaries or later critics—simply did not exist.[81] Instead, it was a translated public sphere: it occurred in multiple languages or as translated from foreign-language periodicals published abroad or within the Arabic-speaking regions. It was composed of readers of varying competencies not only in Arabic but in foreign languages, constituting what detractors considered a sphere of Babel—an impediment to the civilizational goals of enlightenment.

Scholarship on print culture and the public sphere, however, has tended to think in monolingual and monocultural modes. Not only has public sphere theory, as Fraser argues, "been implicitly informed by a Westphalian political imaginary" that assumes "the frame of a bounded political community with its own territorial state," but it has also assumed a basis in monolingual national print culture.[82] Though Habermas's later works have theorized the postnational structure of the twenty-first-century public sphere, for him the public sphere has its origins in national political problems.[83] And though he argues that the public arose elsewhere (France, Germany) soon after, these events are treated as separate phenomena; British coffeehouses, French salons, and German table societies, for Habermas, shared certain elements but did not intercommunicate. Their focus, instead, was on "the native tongue, now interpreted as the medium of communication and understanding between people in their common quality as human beings."[84] What is common to the public, even the seeming supranational quality of being human, is mediated by the national vernacular alone.

The monolingualism implicit in Habermas's work forms the basis of subsequent theories of print culture, which have minimized the role that foreign languages have played and instead emphasized their monolingual and monocultural dimensions as explanatory mechanisms for print culture's ability to cultivate a community of readers.[85] Anderson's *Imagined Communities*, which stands as the founding text of this line of inquiry, links the newspaper to the nation by way of print vernaculars, which "laid the bases for national consciousnesses" by creating unified fields of exchange and communication and giving "a new fixity to language" in print.[86] Or, as Timothy Brennan formulates this argument, newspapers objectified the "'one, yet many' of national life . . . by helping to standardize language, encourage literacy, and remove mutual incomprehensibility" among a people.[87] Print capitalism, that is, is imagined to be monolingual: it "created monoglot mass reading publics" and eventually national print languages, largely along state borders, eroding the transnational vectors of dynastic or imperial languages.[88] Even later studies of multilingual contexts have described the multiple languages of print as forming discrete print cultures, reading publics, and identities. They follow Anderson in his understanding that these newspapers "refract" world events into a "specific imagined world of vernacular readers."[89] Newspapers, they argue, created Anglophone and Hispanophone print culture*s* in the Americas, for example, even when readers themselves were bi- and multilingual and helped to construct audiences that defined themselves in relation to a single language of publication in polyglot South Asia.[90] However multilingual a print *public* was, the print that it produced and consumed has been understood as being organized into linguistically bound print cultures. Monoglossia remains a defining feature and perhaps even precondition of "print culture," many times in opposition to the multilingual objects (periodicals, novels, lexicons) that circulate within it.

In the case of the *nahḍa* periodical, on the other hand, the language for representing the world was never homogeneous, nor was it the result of an "unself-conscious standardization of vocabulary," as Anderson later asserts.[91] Linguistic modernization, as we have seen, was eminently self-conscious and often the result of deliberate and even acrimonious debates in the shadow of European encroachment and threats of cultural dissolution. Authors not only discussed translation techniques but also critiqued translations that appeared elsewhere. Al-Mu'ayd prefaces his article on translation in *Al-Jinān*, for example, with the assertion that many translations "in this age" are weak. Similarly, several articles in *Ḥadīqat al-akhbār* focus on the quality of translations in other newspapers. In fact, an assessment of *Barjīs Bārīs*, a bilingual French-Arabic newspaper published in Paris, appeared on the front page of the journal, where the editors quipped that "the public is obliged to read both of its [facing] pages regardless of the differences between them": "we could not understand the meaning or intention of [the Arabic] terms without recourse to the French page." They added, "we cannot tell which is the original and which the translation."[92] And *Al-Bashīr* ran a series of articles on the 1865 Protestant translation of the Bible that included "How the Evangelicals of Beirut Distorted the Verses of the Holy Bible" and "On the Distortions of the Protestant Bible Published in Beirut," which questioned the translation of specific words and phrases from the Greek.[93] These articles detailed all of the points at which, they argued, the translators "not only took liberties with the meaning [of certain verses] but also omitted from and added to its textual content."[94]

Translation disputes highlight the extent to which language instability and heterogeneity, rather than standardization and homogeneity, characterize this period of print production; Jaroslav Stetkevych describes language modernization in the *nahḍa* as "unorganized, individual, and sporadic," and Ami Ayalon describes it as "a problematic development whose stages and underlying motivations are hard to trace." Both of their studies deal with "the fluctuating meaning of words" or "a vocabulary in transition" that is in evidence well into the twentieth century.[95] Ayalon, in fact, devotes an entire chapter to the terms used for different rulers, which were never entirely standardized in the nineteenth century. In the early decades of the century, especially, such terms were extremely unstable. Napoleon Bonaparte, for example, was variously referred to as "the French *sulṭān* in Egypt," "*malik* [king] of the Franks," "al-malik Nābūlyūn qayṣar" (king Napoleon the emperor), and "imbarāṭūr al-Fransīs" (emperor of France)—applying preexisting terms to a contemporary political entity.[96] Yet even after the birth of the press, when designations began to become more uniform, writers still differed as to their usage: while *qayṣar* and *imbarāṭūr* became the most common ways to refer to European emperors, some used *qayṣar* to refer to the czar and *imbarāṭūr* to all other emperors; still others used them interchangeably. And at no point were these terms applied to domestic rulers, who retained their hierarchical designations as conferred under the Ottoman Empire: The Ottoman *khalīfa* and his lesser representatives may have ruled over territory just as the *qayṣar* of Russia and the German *imbarāṭūr* did, but they were not represented as belonging to the same generic series.

Instead of international news delivered as refracted through domesticating translations or interpretive lenses of local interests, readers found international news *marked as in translation*, with journals citing their original sources and methods of translation, many of which retained their foreignness both linguistically and in their external markers. Direct translations of political speeches made in France or Germany, for example, which appeared regularly in *nahḍa* periodicals, address Arabic readers *as French ones*. Victor Hugo's March 1, 1871, address to the National Assembly about the actions of "our beloved nation" (*waṭanunā al-maḥbūb*) appeared two months later in *Al-Najāḥ* in a full and literal translation that included audience reactions in parenthetical asides, translated from the session's official transcription.[97] *Al-Najāḥ*'s Arabophone readership, then, received this speech as its secondary or even tertiary readers, as Arab spectators of a French assembly whose primary target audience they observed in great detail. But these readers were also—by virtue of the speech's being a translation and not a reportage—rhetorically enfolded within its virtual primary address, the "we" of the nation that happened to be a foreign one. Readers of this speech, addressed like the National Assembly as "ayuhā al-sādāt al-kirām" (dear honorable sirs), were able to imagine themselves among other, French, "sirs" as well as among their fellow Arabic-readers. These translations invited members of the public to imagine themselves as part of multiple communities at once, both local and international: they were readers not only of *Al-Najāḥ* or *Al-Jinān* but also simultaneously of *La Moniteur universelle*, the *Times of London*, and *Le Soir*. These rhetorical modes of identification did not erase the power distribution that distinguished the text's European reader from its reader-in-translation but sought to momentarily redress it.

Composed of translations from different languages and reports from various source texts and locations, which were themselves conveyed in a number of translation styles, newspapers of the *nahḍa* presented readers with a daily experience of linguistic and stylistic multiplicity. These periodicals were not only "space-time landscape[s] of many times, many places, given as a single experience," as Marshall McLuhan described the newspaper, but also landscapes of many *languages* presented in many modes of translation.[98] One could argue that periodicals are themselves a mode of translation:[99] they offer an everyday version of what Antoine Berman—after Martin Heidegger—has called "the experience of the foreign," or the metaphysical and ethical challenge of translation.[100] By presenting the juxtaposition of these languages as a single experience, the periodical requires the reader to negotiate multiple near-simultaneous *épreuves de l'étranger*. It makes an experience with something other than "us" and that "goes against us" a daily occurrence, interrupting the simple coherence of an imagined reading public and again highlighting its central attribute: its stranger sociability. This public of strangers, however, was not just composed of unknown fellow countrymen; *nahḍa* periodicals often made their audiences aware that they were the secondary readers of translated news items originally published elsewhere.

This was not simply the case of Arab readers being made aware of how their newspapers were copies of European originals but of them identifying translation as central and necessary to the way newspapers themselves work. Rather than entering a narrowly defined sphere of regional or protonational print influence, then, editors and translators of these periodicals framed reading as joining a networked public sphere—composed of readers not just of *Al-Jinān* or *Al-Jawā'ib* but of the European newspapers translated within them—that relied on translation at each node. The special case of the Ottoman Empire, whose international news came from Europe, from this perspective, seems less special. Marking even how those original readers read some of the same items elsewhere, the translated *nahḍa* periodical figures all newspaper readers as readers in translation.

Reporting on the world in these periodicals not only required a new vocabulary but required one of the many multilingual lexicons advertised in their pages. There was no linguistic remedy for the disunity of the reading public; translation was disunity's cause and its cure. Rather than forming a public through the employment of uniform vocabularies and homogeneous forms of address, which effectively standardized and stabilized national languages, print culture was read primarily "in translation"—through modes of reading that emphasized inter- and intralingual heteroglossia. Foreignness was at all times visible in these periodicals, in the discrepancies in designations for rulers, territories, and systems of government; in disagreements over methods of simplification; in the discussions of translation techniques and debates over the proper translation of foreign words. To see translation as a fundamental condition of the reading public is to highlight these strange currents that run through the periodicals.

Almost as often as the new category of the public was invoked, its unruliness was emphasized—periodical authors and editors simultaneously conjured it as a single entity and one whose integrity was on the verge of collapse. This would not be the only time that publishers included dissenting voices within their pages, responding to criticism or defending themselves and even printing multiple rounds of exchanges.[101] The public sphere, as Michael McKeon has shown in the case of seventeenth-century England, was "by definition an explicit exercise in conflict," a space of adjudication "between an indefinite number of inherently legitimate interests."[102] Far from an easy unity, these periodical writers make it clear that they understood the emerging public as a space of conflict between "sects, interest groups, and parties," unstable vocabularies, and audiences in translation that could never be fully accounted for given their diverse modes of reading.

Chapter 3

Errant Readers

The Serialized Novel's Modern Subject

The Arabic novel made its own proper entry into the Arabic print sphere at this moment as a part of the uncertain reform project of print culture. Buṭrus al-Bustānī's son Salīm cofounded *Al-Jinān* and wrote nine original novels for it, which are listed as the first entries in Ḥamdī Sakkūt's bibliography of the Arabic novel and which are sometimes identified as the "beginning of modern Arabic fiction."[1] Yet these novels were published after and alongside a larger body of serialized translated novels that in fact occupied the greater part of the new audience's leisure reading habits. Over the course of the first decades of commercial print from the late 1850s to the late 1870s, serialized translated novels appeared in almost every type of Arabic periodical; for many readers, the word "novel" itself probably referred to these works and not the few original ones produced to compete with them.

It was not just news translation that was central to the development of Arabic print culture; the translated novel, which appeared first and most prominently in serialized form, was often identified as part of periodicals' reform projects. The editors of *Al-Jinān* introduced a translation of *Gil Blas* as beneficial to those who can "reap fruit" from the "garden of [his] book" and "benefit from the customs and morals of the [different] nations."[2] Similarly, *Ḥadīqat al-akhbār* published its first translation, an excerpt from *Les Confidences et causeries de Mlle Mars*, as an example of a "morally beneficial" genre (*rūmāntīk*) that—like the newspaper itself—"aims to describe the social situation."[3] Even the Jesuit-produced *Al-Bashīr*, considered a champion of Catholic religious causes in the East, describes the first of its translated novels, *Wardat al-Maghrib* [Rose of the West] as an example of "stories that aim not merely to amuse . . . but also to educate [the reader] in accordance with the commands of the Merciful One."[4]

At the same time that editors embraced translated fiction as a vehicle for their messages, however, their claim that these works served serious moral purposes was by no means indisputable. One wonders, in fact, how it could have been so, considering the number of sensationalist and melodramatic elements that many of the plots contained: murder, kidnapping, disguise, secret kinships, and false denouements abounded, and often in rapid succession. These novels' excesses were not always containable by the moral intentions of journal editors, who sometimes resorted to qualifications and elaborate interpretations in order to justify their publication. Indeed, the editors of *Al-Bashīr* took great pains to explain to their readers that though the "rose" (*ward*) of the title is a symbol of love, *Wardat al-Maghrib* focuses on forms of love that are not immoral—filial love and a love for one's enemies—as "blame would be upon a religion and those that hold its reins if they did not teach these lessons."[5] The single-edition printing of this work elaborated further on this notice, expanding it into a four-page preface that claimed the novel's exceptional status and warned of the many other kinds of "fables [*asāṭīr*] that excite deviant tendencies" and represent "thorns of corrupted learning" on the rose-strewn path to righteousness.[6]

Print's civilizing reform mission, as uncertain as it was, had a primary object: the modern reading subject. Transforming the public into a reading public, and one that read *properly*, was the goal of many magazine producers who outlined ideal reading practices and modeled them through novels. And it was likewise a goal with an uncertain outcome. Reading novels in the early years of Arabic print culture reveals the reading subject as an ambivalent one, walking on rose-strewn paths that were also filled with thorns. Like print itself, the reading subject was produced through pedagogical and (internal) civilizing discourses that were always on the brink of failure.

And as in print itself, the translated text took central stage. The translated novel served as a negative example for articles promoting proper reading but also a model for original reform novels whose protagonists demonstrated good reading habits. It therefore served as a repository for attitudes—both proper and improper—about modern reading. Al-Khūrī's description of news translation as an abyss in fact was an echo of the foreword to his periodical's first installment of serialized fiction, *Riwāyat al-Markīz dī Fūntānj* (M. le Marquis de Fontanges), which had appeared in the previous edition just four days earlier.

Written by either al-Khūrī or the work's translator, Salīm dī Nawfal, the foreword explains the "difficulty of translation" with an aphorism attributed to Voltaire: "every translation in respect to its original is like the back of a cloth to its face."[7] For al-Khūrī and others, these two projects—the creation of a reformed reading public and the development of the novel—were both translation projects that shared similar goals *and* anxieties. Editors claimed to interpolate the translated novels into their educational mission even as their thrill-granting and entertainment-driven plots threatened to undermine it, with their "strange" plots leading their audiences to adopt improper reading habits. Translated novels, that is, were not just the cause of debate but an active participant in it; their styles, tropes, and attitudes toward reading lived on in the very reform novels that repudiated them and that have since overshadowed them in the literary canon. As this chapter shows, they also shared linguistic styles, narrative tropes, and even plots, which themselves revolved around (unresolved) issues of circulation, communication, and translatability. In these serialized novels, readers encounter not only protagonists who model proper reading but modes of improper or illicit circulation: books are stolen, misinformation circulated, and letters intercepted, causing misinterpretation and misadventure similar to that which editors warned against in their articles and prefaces. These translated novels were neither marginal nor aberrant but a necessary component of the *nahḍa*'s reform project and a locus of uncertainty within it; they constituted its public sphere both *despite* and *through* translation's "abyss."

The Novel's Improper Uses

That the field of novel studies should no longer assume the primacy of self-representation in the genre is one of the major arguments of this book. By looking at the field of print culture studies in particular, we can see that the novel—in contradistinction to the romance or the epic—has been seen as primarily concerning itself with the everyday goings-on of a single public, a readership identifiable as coterminal with a defined geographic and linguistic milieu. The novel, as Habermas argued, is where the public, "by communicating with itself, gained clarity about *itself*" and not about others that might exist either within the public's midst or elsewhere.[8]

This assumption overlooks narratives that represent foreign places and people, as well as translations from other people's self-representations. Looking at scholarship of the print sphere in particular, we can see that this bias against foreign-oriented fiction rests not only on an institutional bias toward national literatures but on a homology between how the reading public consumes novels and what is represented in them. What Habermas posits as the novel's social function—allowing a reader to read *about oneself* in order to gain clarity about oneself—Benedict Anderson further specifies as one dependent on a "sociological fixity that fuses the world inside the novel with the world outside."[9] In his account, the social imaginary that the novel creates has a horizon that is "clearly bounded," providing readers with a "succession of plurals" that creates a unified readership who would recognize those plurals in the world outside the text. The image of reading that emerges—"exact replicas" of texts being read by a single, mass readership that understands that "the imagined world is rooted in everyday life"—underlies even later, more nuanced accounts, which posit that the novel did not begin as a national genre but became so over time.[10] In a classic version of this argument, Clifford Siskin argued that the hegemony of the novel form in England was achieved through its domestication, with writers casting "early and other forms of writing as foreign . . . and warn[ing] against the foreign as uncontrolled . . . and therefore, potentially uncontrollable."[11] It was through the simultaneous management of content and reading practices that not only the nationalization of the novel could be achieved but also the nationalization of English culture at large: "under the rubric of the newly triumphant novel, writing was domesticated at the same time as that society whose coherence was, in important ways, dependent on it," he writes.[12] This centrifugal theory of the novel, by which both its form and readership increase in coherence and uniformity, however, depends on a particular understanding of print circulation: one that theorizes public discourse as "discussion among already co-present interlocutors," a group that most likely shares a physical space and language, rather than among much wider and more diverse circles of readers.[13] Acts of reading, generalized from this imagined group of interlocutors, are "understood to be replicable and uniform," a succession of pluralized encounters with the same text.[14] Print theories of the novel too often imagine a uniform experience of reading because they think of it as an extension of print itself, which they imagine as standardized and replicable content that travels along regular and predictable routes.

The circulation and consumption of early Arabic periodicals, as we have shown, did not conform to this image, even if *nahḍa* reformers attempted to make it do so through promoting "proper" reading practices. That it was in those same pages that the novel itself began to gain currency should already prompt a new look at the role of print culture in the rise of the Arabic novel. What is more, the rise of the commercial periodical press and the novel coincided chronologically: according to Sakkūt's bibliography of original Arabic novels, which takes into account works appearing in only one periodical, *Al-Jinān*, nearly half of the works published in the first fifteen years of the Arabic novel's history (1865–1879) were serialized ones. If one were to add to that list the original novels serialized in other publications, the proportion would be higher than 50 percent; if one were to also add translated novels published both serially and in single editions, we would find that close to two-thirds of the novels published in this early period were serialized, or first serialized, in the press. In fact, a good number of the single editions of translated novels were reprintings of formerly serialized texts by the press that produced the periodical of origin. This practice was even institutionalized by al-Khūrī, who began serializing novels in *Ḥadīqat al-akhbār* using the same printing plates that would later be used by his Syrian Press for the single edition. Subscribers could cut these pages from the newspaper and compose a stand-alone version for themselves—a practice of self-collation that itself encouraged a second and undocumented round of circulation for the same printed object. (Serializations in *Ḥadīqat al-akhbār* were paginated in such a way as to be easily legible only once collated but out of order as they appeared in the newspaper.) Any analysis of the Arabic novel must be performed inside the history of print circulation and consumption and alongside an understanding not only of print's idealized functions but also its diverse methods of readership.

Readers did not just read about the ordinary experiences of their own everyday lives. Novels that appeared in the Arabic press registered the participation of strangers and their unpredictable modes of consumption and interpretation and overwhelmingly represented foreign places and people, as well as unusual circumstances. Because of this, the novel—as a new literary form without an established set of norms for its interpretation—stood as both the quintessential cause of concerns about the reading public and the best possible mode for representing them. The link between novels and improper reading, in fact, seemed to be so strong in the minds of literary producers that already in 1873 Salīm al-Bustānī felt the need to begin his serialized novel *Asmā'* with a defense of the genre that relied on a call for the public to properly read and interpret it. In the preface, al-Bustānī explains that it is the genre of the novel itself that many elites considered to be improper reading material for the *nahḍa* reader precisely because they do not represent characters or events that are "rooted in everyday life." "There will be those who say that novels contain unbelievable coincidences," he writes, and that "what leads an author to compose one is [an interest in] strangeness [*gharāba*]." As he continues, "And by strangeness I mean coincidences and events that are out of the ordinary, and by novels I mean imaginative narratives full of youthful exaggerations and miraculous tales. Yet it is probable that no less than two thousand novels are published each year, and if we said that the population of the world was one thousand million, then we should not be surprised if we heard that two out of each two million had experienced something strange."[15] Rather than dispute the description of the novel as a narrative of strange events, al-Bustānī recognizes the prominence of such events. It is despite its focus on strangeness and its recalcitrant insistence on entertainment, improbability, and even counterfactuality that the novel should be embraced by reform-minded readers. "It is ignorance to say that literary novels are harmful," he writes.[16] By his account, as he continues in the conclusion, they have a place in the enlightenment project in their ability to "guide one on the path of love" and "plant morals in their readers."[17] But there is one caveat: the audience must have "enough wisdom to differentiate between the lean and the fat."[18] They must be able to read and appropriately interpret these stories in order to extract their true value. Al-Bustānī sought to integrate the novel within *nahḍa* reform discourse, but its integration relied on the ability of the reading public to use the form properly.

Yet it was precisely this ability that al-Bustānī seemed least assured of, as he also explains that he has changed names of people and places in the novel in order to prevent readers from launching spurious interpretations: he warns that "ignorant people and those with motives" might analyze the novel so as to "produce explanations appropriate to their ignorance and motives."[19] The public of strangers, whose education al-Bustānī here considers suspect, may interpret according to their own ultimately unknowable motives, and they may even, by attributing the fictional action to identifiable persons, turn a didactic novel into mere gossip. The participation of strangers is thus inscribed into the novel *as a problem*.[20] The plot of *Asmā'* then proceeds to address this problem through representing the reading habits of its main characters: Asmā' and her brother, Jalīl, eschew rumor and seek out reading that promotes self-improvement: the second chapter begins with Asmā' reading a history of ancient Greece, while we are first introduced to Jalīl as he reads a newspaper alone in the greeting room (figure 3.1). Later, both pointedly retreat from communal gossip sessions to silently peruse written materials. And instead of entertaining their guests with small talk or card games, Asmā' offers to read to them from beneficial works, such as an article "she had read last night about women's intelligence."[21] Over the course of the novel, Asmā''s reading practices show how she discerns the lean from the fat, as she chooses "useful information" and learning over mere entertainment, which appears in the form of rumor and gossip, those other forms of circulating information that—unlike print—are unstandardized and subject to modification in their transmission. *Asmā'*, in the end, is a lesson in the value not just of reading but of reading

أسما
(من قلم سليم افندي البستاني تابع الاجزاء السابقة)

FIGURE 3.1. Illustration of Jalīl reading properly, appearing with Asmāʾ. (*Al-Jinān* 4, no. 20 [October 15, 1873]: 713) (Yale University Library)

properly: beneficial works, in print, that are consumed silently and alone and then perhaps shared with a group. It is a lesson in the value of standardized and replicable content and in how to read it.

Al-Bustānī's allegory of proper reading does admit novels as part of its project. Yet even this inclusion is qualified: In *Bint al-ʿaṣr* [The girl of the era, 1875], readers are admonished not to read "entertaining novels" (*al-riwāyāt al-tankītīyya*) only for the plot ("what happens to the lovers, and nothing else") but to pay close attention to the moral qualities of the characters.[22] Asmāʾ reads historical works and "literary novels" rather than the "empty stories" enjoyed by the children of her father's colleague and, more importantly, reads in order to understand the underlying social message of narratives rather than to enjoy "the simple parts about the lover and the beloved."[23] In the end, it is her reading skills—discerning truth from rumor—that prevent her from marrying the superficial and criminal Badīʿ, despite the fact that her father had promised her to him, and that allow her instead to choose the stranger she meets at the beginning of the novel, a Baghdadi merchant named Karīm. They are also what allow the reader—in a parallel plot—to determine that another "stranger," a European named Richard attempting to woo a rich woman, Nabīḥa, is not a nobleman but a dangerous grifter. In each case, the identity and morality of the traveling stranger is bound up with written texts and oral narratives that also travel and whose circulation is tracked in detail: half-truths about Asmāʾ's preference of Karīm over Badīʿ spiral into outright falsehood over several pages; letters are sent and messages passed; telegrams are written, exchanged, and received.[24] In *Bint al-ʿaṣr*, characters choose between "periodicals and the published dispatches in the newspaper" and games of cards, over which they circulate (untrue) rumors.[25] At each turn, model readers as well as the periodical readers themselves are asked to differentiate between the lean and the fat, separating rumor and fact, "literary novels" from gossip, and narratives with social messages from those "empty stories" that aim solely to surprise and delight.

But how does one distinguish an "empty story" from a valuable one? This is a very old question in the history of Arabic literature, in which fictional narrative has since at least the Abbasid period occupied a contested place in the canon of Arabic belles-lettres. *Adab*, which "became literary" during the *nahḍa* and indeed now translates simply to "literature," encompassed in earlier times the general moral and intellectual (though not strictly religious) knowledge deemed necessary for the education of the cultivated man, or *adīb*.[26] *Adab* itself in this context can therefore refer to a body of texts that the *adīb* should have knowledge of—largely narrative, many anecdotal, and emphasizing rhetorical mastery—or the more general training in social and ethical values. *Adab* could be entertaining, that is, but its entertainment is subordinated to its usefulness, to "the transmission and renewal of cultural values and information," as Hilary Kirkpatrick puts it.[27] In this sense, narrative fiction has always held an ambiguous place in the Arabic literary canon and has long needed justification.[28] Even the preface to the oldest extant version of *The Thousand and One Nights*, full of improbable events and clearly fictional personae, asserted its ability to educate the listener: it "abounds with highly edifying histories and excellent lessons for the people of distinction."[29]

Al-Bustānī, who interrupts his narrative in *Asmāʾ* at several points in order to expound on the potential value of novel reading, makes use of these classical modes of legitimation for this modern genre. Novels can be "of benefit to the mind" and value to society only if readers choose the proper kinds of works to read, which entertain in the service of moral education. "Oh how nice it would be," he writes in the novel's postscript, "if human nature could stand to choose bodily restraint and read literary educational books" rather than those that merely "give pleasure": "stories of love and the unusual circumstances that leads to it."[30] These are the attributes that give the novel its poor reputation to begin with, but they also echo the historical concerns with the dangers of fiction and warn of its depiction of "events that are out of the ordinary," its "fictitious narratives" and "miraculous tales." In order to bring the public into being as the audience for *his novel*, that is, he had to first differentiate it from other, unenlightened fictions. He moreover aligns it with the edifying literature of the premodern period; *adab* remains both literary and moral. His work, as he maintains, offers inspiration for the mind rather than merely the senses; it comments on "social structures" rather than reporting "imaginary anecdotes" and portrays events "gathered from the world" rather than "wondrous fables" like those found in *The Thousand and One Nights* or even those that the fake European nobleman makes Nabīḥa believe.[31]

In making this last distinction, al-Bustānī makes sly reference to a very modern phenomenon and what had by that time become a significant literary trend in Beirut: the publication of adventure-romances, many of them outlandish and sensational and the vast majority of them translated from French source texts. Novels that had appeared in the press until that point (as well as afterward) featured episodic narratives that strung together chains of improbable occurrences and "strange coincidences" that either prevent or cause a couple's happy union. *Al-Zahra* (1870–1872) and *Al-Shirāka al-shahriyya fī Bayrūt* (1866), two of Yūsuf al-Shalfūn's short-lived serials, serialized translated and original novels that featured adventure-romance plots, as did *Al-Naḥla* (1870–1877) before abruptly abandoning the project.[32] *Al-Bashīr* (1870–1947), which serialized three of the Christian didactic works of Christoph Schmid between 1870 and 1873, transposed the romance to a filial context but retained a focus on strange events; Schmid's robinsonade *Gottfried der junge Einsiedler* (Gottfried, the little hermit, translated from a French version) was translated as *Gharā'ib al-waqā'i li-Ghūdfrīd al-ḍā'i'* (The strange occurrences of Gottfried, the lost boy). *Al-Jinān*'s first fictional publication—a translated story called "Idwār wa Sīlfā" (1870)—begins with a shipwreck in a "strange land."[33] Unlike *Asmā'*, these translations often emphasized their entertainment value, even when they claimed to also transmit beneficial content—advertising a pious parable as a marvelous tale or inserting moralizing commentary alongside episodes of improbable fantasy.

Yet none published these translations more consistently or prolifically than *Ḥadīqat al-akhbār*, the first periodical to establish a regular fiction. The extant copies of *Ḥadīqat al-akhbār* show that during its first ten years of publication, between 1858 and 1868, it serialized one original novel (Khūrī's *Wayy . . . Idhan lastu bi-ifranjī*) and twelve works of translated fiction: one "poëme en prose" (François Fénelon's *Les Aventures de Télémaque*), four short stories, and seven novels, all of which were taken from collections of French sentimental fiction and gothic romances—subgenres that laid an emphasis on surprising turns of events. Of the seven novels published, five were taken from collections of popular sentimental narratives: La Comtesse Dash (Gabrielle Anna Cisternes, Mme. du Poilloüe Vicomtesse de Saint-Mars, 1804–1872)[34] published *Une Saison à Baden* (*Faṣl fī Bādīn*) in her 1842 collection of novellas, *Les Bals masqués*, Madame Charles Reybaud (Henriette Étiennette Fanny [Arnaud], 1802–1871) first published *La Mademoiselle de Malepeire* (*Madamuzīl Mālābyār*) in the December 1854 issue of *La Revue des deux mondes*, Mademoiselle Mars's (Léocadie Aimée [Doze] de Beauvoir, 1822–1859) *Monsieur le Marquis de Fontanges* (*Al-Markīz dī Fūntānj*) and *Les Deux Georges* (*Al-Jirjisayn*) both appeared in her best-known collection, *Les Confidences de Mademoiselle Mars* (1855), and Alberic Sécond's (1817–1887) *À quoi tient l'amour*, which was translated as the unfinished *Natījat al-ʿishq* (The result of love), appeared in the eponymous collection of "fantaisies parisiennes" (1856). The two remaining were popular gothic romances: *Yamīn al-armala*, a truncated version of Emmanuel Gonzalès's (1815–1887) *Le Serment de la veuve* (1861), and *Būlīna Mūlyān*, a heavily condensed translation of Alexandre Dumas *père*'s (1802–1870) *Pauline de Meulien* (1838).

In selecting translations exclusively from these two genres, al-Khūrī prioritized precisely the kinds of narratives that al-Bustānī derided: they were all "stories of love and the unusual circumstances that lead to it." Despite their belonging to what we now recognize as subgenres with wildly diverging social settings and atmospheric conditions (they ranged from aristocratic balls to highway robbers and from manicured Parisian gardens to ruined abbeys), they were strikingly similar in their narrative construction, turning on recognizable romance conventions: the physical separation of lovers, threatened or real assaults on female protagonists, disguised or mistaken identities, and the revelation of true identities. What unites these novels, even across subgenres, is not only that they take place in the "elsewhere" of Europe but also that they focus on extraordinary events. They are relentless in their exposure of their protagonists to the vicissitudes of chance and random occurrence, what more than one translator refers to as the *ṣudfa mustaghraba* (surprising coincidence).[35] Their stories are all "strange," the characters "unusual," and the events that befall them "singular" and unexpected—whether they are a noblewoman whose improper choice of husband leads to a life in domestic servitude or a kidnapped wife of a murderer who has been left for dead.[36]

While all of the *Ḥadīqat al-akhbār* novels include sentimental plots in which female protagonists are forced to make difficult social choices, the narratives themselves did not unambiguously serve a higher social or aesthetic purpose. The genres chosen by translators to represent the novel to its readers, in fact, had decades beforehand come under fire in the French press, when the novel underwent what Margaret Cohen describes as a cultural transvaluation from trivial entertainment into "ambitious social analysis" and a "historically accurate panorama of . . . social life." French literary commentators of the 1830s and 1840s, some writing in the very publications in which *Ḥadīqat al-akhbār*'s source texts first appeared, criticized both gothic and sentimental novels alike for their lack of realism: their dearth of descriptive detail, their subordination of social truths to sentiment, and their reliance on outlandish plot devices.[37] Contemporary detractors, much like al-Bustānī, complained of the sentimental novelists' preference for "stag[ing] bizarre adventures with an emphatic style" and what Stendhal dismissed as "extraordinary scenes that completely dissolve [the reader] in tears."[38] More simply put, these novels provide the wrong kinds of pleasure to the wrong kinds of readers—Stendhal names women, the uneducated, "chambermaids," and the petit bourgeoisie—who themselves read improperly. "Provincial petty bourgeoises ask the author only for extraordinary scenes that put them in tears," he complains.[39] Yet rather than selecting texts from what had become the preferred mode for analyzing social problems, the realist novel, al-Khūrī and his translators selected precisely those texts that critics argued offered improper sorts of pleasures—what al-Bustānī called "bodily pleasure" rather than texts that benefit the mind.[40]

This is not to argue that al-Khūrī did not understand the novel, or literature at large, to be part of the enlightenment project but that he did not frame its inclusion as a choice between affective pleasure and civilizational advancement. Instead, he proposed affective response as a tool for progress: as he argues in an article on theater, the purpose of plays (also referred to as *riwāyāt* at this time) "is not only to include what surprises the audience" but also to include scenes that provide negative examples for them, portraying "ugly traits" on the stage so as to provoke disgust in the audience and "inspire them to do the opposite."[41] Indeed, when the translator Salīm dī Nawfal prefaces the first translated novel to appear in the journal, *Al-Markīz dī Fūntānj* (*Le Marquis de Fontanges*), he introduces the new form as one that provides readers with both pleasure and social benefit: "We found this book to be simple in its expression, and in a lively style very different from the styles of the Arabic language. And so we wanted to translate something from it as an example . . . of the art known as *rūmāntīk* or poetic stories that aim to describe the social situation [*hay'a ijtamā'iyya*] in a way that pleases the reader and provokes his emotions . . . and aims at the improvement of morals and the softening of temperaments."[42] While Nawfal introduces the new form by emphasizing its aesthetic and entertainment value as equally important as its moral one, the translators that followed in *Ḥadīqat al-akhbār* ascribed less value to the novel's social benefits. The introduction to Nawfal's second translation, *Al-Jirjisayn*, simply states that the newspaper "presents another novel no less pleasing from the translator [of *Al-Markīz dī Fūntānj*],"[43] while those of *Faṣl fī Bādīn* (*Une Saison à Baden*) and *Riwāyat Būlīna Mūlyān* (*Pauline de Meulien*) respectively promise "pleasing writings . . . of strange events" and "stories . . . invented by his wondrous mind," and both are offered "for the amusement [*fukāha*] of the audience."[44] No mention is made of the moral, social, or educational benefit of novel reading after the appearance of that first translation. Of all of the fiction to appear in the periodical, it is only Rifāʿa Rāfiʿ al-Ṭahṭāwī's translation of *Télémaque* that is advertised as edifying literature, which he explains provides "instruction" (*taʿlīm*) for both students and rulers (it was undertaken, as al-Ṭahṭāwī explains, while he was in exile in Khartoum). Yet al-Ṭahṭāwī refrains from referring to *Tīlmāk* as a novel, instead calling it "a book" written by "a poet."[45] The label "novel," which appears in every installment of the other long narrative works, never appears in *Tīlmāk*'s headings. *Tīlmāk* was even set apart from the other novels typographically, appearing in the regular columned sections of the newspaper rather than in the facing-page format in which the remainder of the narrative fiction appeared. Al-Ṭahṭāwī's translation may have fulfilled the instructional function that al-Khūrī envisioned for literature, uniting it with *adab* even, but it did so by performing its distance from the novel.

By the time the seventh novel, *Yamīn al-armala*, was serialized in 1861, the prioritization of the form's entertainment value was unmistakable. Readers would have read the early installments of the edifying *Tīlmāk* alongside Iskandar Tuwaynī's *Yamīn al-armala* and would have noticed the dissimilarities between the two. Instead of the moral and political education of a young ruler, readers of Tuwaynī's translation followed a gothic work of sensation fiction that featured murderous brigands, imprisonment, revenge, and the shocking revelation of identities. They would have found no pretense of "civilizing" purpose in this novel, no appeals to the reader's sound taste and judgment, no reproach to unseemly actions. *Yamīn al-armala* ends with the female protagonist attempting to stab her lover's murderer in his sleep ("my passion for the late Andrea is my best and only weapon," she explains), and yet she still ends up in a happy marriage.[46] Nor did Tuwaynī design it for a moral purpose. In his introduction to the translation, he is forthright about the novel's goal of entertainment as entertainment, as well its plot's improbability. Instead, he prefaces the translation by poking fun at the kind of argument that al-Bustānī would later make and that others—it seems—had already begun to present. Mocking the introductory trope of authors excusing their novels to the readers, he writes, "introductions are but . . . efforts to convince the reader of the novel's veracity, that they are not like the rest of those *Sindbad*-like stories" (*al-qiṣaṣ al-sindibādiyya*).[47] As he does not wish to excuse his novel, he explains, he will abstain from an introduction entirely. Instead of distancing his translation from accusations of improper reading, he presents the attempt to discipline the novel and its readers as an object of derision.

Anxieties of Circulation in *Ḥadīqat al-akhbār*

That Tuwaynī uses *qiṣaṣ sindibadiyya* to describe the deficiencies of the modern European novel may seem ironic to today's reader. Yet its use here points to historical congruities and transnational literary-critical affinities. At the debut of the English novel in the eighteenth century, after all, commentators like the third Earl of Shaftesbury complained of the seductive effects of novel reading in similarly "Eastern" terms, warning that a "love of strange narrations" and "Moorish fancy" would lead to the creation of "a thousand Desdemonas" who would meet a morally tragic end.[48] In both cases, *Sindbad* and its folkloric ilk stood as shorthand for the kind of improper reading that the novel engenders. More than pointing to a set of recognizable tropes or literary styles, in making reference to *The Thousand and One Nights* and to folkloric literature in general Tuwaynī signals *nahḍa* concerns about the tastes and reading practices of the newly imagined public. Jurjī Zaydān, in the fourth volume of his *Tārikh adāb al-lugha al-ʿarabiyya* (History of literature in the Arabic language), itself an in-depth history of the *nahḍa* and its literary producers (himself included), attributes the early success of translated novels—and the novel form in general—to the preference of a marginally educated audience for oral epics. As he argues, translated novels had become popular among "men of reason"—by which he meant, as Badr explains, "those who could read and write but who had not developed enough awareness to make them aware of the real problems in their countries."[49] Readers of questionable taste and values read not for "social or historical or other benefit," as Zaydān argues, but for "entertainment," turning to novels when before they would have listened to folk epics or storytelling cycles "and in particular the ancient stories such as *ʿAnṭar* and *The Thousand and One Nights*."[50] The link that Zaydān makes between translated novels and oral narratives has little to do with their content—that case would be made by Badr half a century later—but rather with *how* they were read. Novels, as Zaydān writes, not only were primarily used as entertainment but also "took the place of these stories that were widespread [*shā'i'a*] among the masses": they replaced them in the economy of literary circulation, in their ability to spread (*shā'a*) among an audience he considered insufficiently prepared to receive them.[51]

Instead of the translators of *Ḥadīqat al-akhbār*'s novels framing their works in order to excuse this concern or manage their audience's reception, however, they embraced this affinity. They used translation techniques that enhanced the novel's resemblance to oral narrative, expanding the very category of literature—*adab*—itself. The stories selected unapologetically drop the reader into small-talk sessions and chains of gossip transmission, where listeners gather in salons, parties, and inns to hear interesting and unverifiable tales. *Al-Mārkīz dī Fūntānj*, *Al-Jirjisayn*, and *Faṣl fī Bādīn* are all excerpted from collections whose central conceit is that the stories were narrated firsthand to the author-character; these all begin with the author-character "retelling" the story to the reader, as does *Būlīna Mulyān*, a fact that is emphasized by the translator's addition of "*qāla* [so said] Iskandar Dīmās" to the beginning of the novel, inserting a marker of oral culture reminiscent of the *qāla al-rāwī* (the reciter said) that appears throughout *The Thousand and One Nights*.[52] In doing so, translators chose texts that bore structural resemblances to the very Arabic oral narratives that al-Bustānī, Zaydān, and Badr impugned and featured embedded narrators and listeners and often several layers of framed narratives: "even stranger stories to come." *Būlīna Mulyān* is a relatively simple example of such a structure; it proceeds as a single enframed story, which is told to the narrator at a gathering of friends. Meanwhile, *Mādmwāzīl Mālābyār* is composed of a series of secondhand narratives told to the fictional narrator by guests of his uncle; listeners gather around a fireplace to hear their telling and even ask the servant to bring them coffee so that they can settle in for the evening. And *Faṣl fī Bādīn* is composed of thirdhand narratives told at successive parties, which are then retold to a primary embedded reader, who also sits by her fire waiting to be entertained by visitors. The translator adds narrative breaks between the levels of narration similar to those found in manuscripts of oral performance; in an added section in the Arabic version, she tells her visitor, "Tell me the story," and the narrator tells the reader, "And so our friend the poet tells us what happened to him, saying [*fa-qāla*] . . ."[53] The translator's additions interpolate the reader into the scene of storytelling, creating a community of readers who imagine themselves as a community of second- and thirdhand listeners.

The advertising of these novels as containing strange stories, then, was also a performative stoking of the reader's curiosity for ever more curious narratives, where the promise of "*Sindbad*-like stories" stood as a trope of circulation itself. In *Faṣl fī Bādīn*, the unnamed translator begins by announcing it not only as a novel about "the strange goings-on at masquerade balls" but also as one in which characters "dance together without knowing who the other is, passing between them stories and light anecdotes [*nuwādir*]."[54] The circulation of strange stories is bound up with the circulation of unknown listeners and tellers, even metonymically standing in for them. In the translated version, the protagonist's description is almost entirely omitted, replaced by the repeated reference to the "curiousness" of her story, which is remarked on no fewer than four times in the first page and a half. Description in *Faṣl* is so condensed by its translator, in fact, that the word *gharīb* stands in for descriptive detail, replacing entire passages. While the French source contains robust descriptions of the ball and its guests, with an analysis of their fashions and a comparison to those of the ancien régime, the translation notes only that people wear "unusual dress" (*al-milābis al-mustaghraba*).[55] And the protagonist, who is introduced in the French as "being scrupulously masqueraded from head to foot, enveloped in a vast cape, her hands covered with irreproachably white gloves, and her feet in black satin shoes with light, silk stockings," is described in Arabic with a single, three-word phrase: she is "disguised with great care."[56] Strangeness serves as a metonymic placeholder for these details, as a promise of description yet to be transmitted, deferred until the next installment or indefinitely, in a manner similar to the metonymic structure of enframed storytelling.[57] Readers are led along by this promise: they wait to read the "strange anecdote" (*ḥadīth gharīb*) that will constitute the novel, which will be told to the narrator by a poet prone to "strange feelings" (*iḥsāsāt gharība*), who had himself heard it from a young woman who confessed her "strange story" (*qiṣatī . . . gharība*) to him. It is a narrative chain of strange narrations that formed the structure of the story itself.

In contrast to *Asmā*'s protagonists' distaste for rumor and idle storytelling and their eschewal for more stable modes of print circulation, *Ḥadīqat al-akhbār*'s serializations do not disdain these forms of unmanaged narrative transmission. Instead, far from avoiding unusual narratives, it was strangeness itself that justified the appearance of the novel in print in the first place: the narrator herself found the story curious (*mustaghrab*) enough to relate to her audience in the form of the printed novel the reader holds.[58] Rumor is both a trope and a central structural feature of the *Ḥadīqat al-akhbār* novels, the stories of which are presented not as pretexts for moralizing but as ways for embedded fictional readers to pass idle hours or to satisfy curiosity. These novels are then transmitted to the newspaper reader through translation to serve the same purposes. As the anonymous translator of *Faṣl fī Bādīn* explains, "One of the most famous female French writers named al-Qūntīsa Dāsh has written some of the most pleasing writings . . . [and] we have singled out one of them for translation here for the enjoyment [*fukāha*] of our readers."[59] Instead of engaging in rumor trading at characters' explicit peril, rumors serve as amoral plot devices, which can both harm and preserve characters. The rumors that circulate in *Faṣl fī Bādīn* both are "pleasing" narratives and cause the injury of a main character, yet neither the original novel nor the translation offers any warnings about rumormongering. The central character, abandoned first by her husband and then by her lover when their affair stirs gossip, commits suicide after eavesdropping on her lover at the masked ball; and yet when the author's voice intervenes at the end to distill a moral, she has nothing to say about the spreading of rumors or the dangers of believing gossip but warns only of the "madness" of love and the "baffling" nature of women.[60] Rumor, like oral storytelling, is unpredictable in its manner of circulation, yet it is the single most important mode of information transmission in these serialized novels. It is a mode of reading.

Scenes of reading, then, appear more frequently than books do in these novels. More often than not, they are scenes of reading that occur independently of print or that work to highlight the anxieties of print consumption and circulation. As in the scene of eavesdropping that forms the denouement of *Faṣl fī Bādīn*, narratives are represented as texts that can circulate outside their expected routes and to unintended audiences; they have a tendency to be misread or read by strangers with bad intentions, and they have the potential to transmit false or falsified information. In Nawfal's second translation, *Al-Jirjisayn* (The two Georges), the plot turns on several scenes of misreading, or what the translator refers to as "the strangeness of a mistake."[61] A young woman named Louise is unknowingly courted by a friend of her father's, a duke named Georges, who tutors her in music, reforms her tastes, and improves her mind. Like Asmā', she acquires beneficial knowledge in the domain of *al-funūn wa al-ma'ārif*, the arts and learning, but unlike with Asmā', it does not allow her to make an appropriate romantic choice. Indeed, she is unable to even correctly understand the choice presented to her: at the same time as she is being tutored by the Duke, she has fallen in love with another Georges, the young son of another friend of her father's, who instead of art and music speaks to her of "things related to love."[62] And so, when her father brings her the proposal to marry the older Georges, she agrees, thinking it is the young Georges whom she is to marry.

This strange mistake, which leads to Louise's unhappy marriage, occurs amid the circulation of substantial amounts of text—sheet music and books are exchanged among the Duke and Louise, and letters are sent between Louise and the younger Georges, as well as between Georges's father and Louise's father. Misinterpreted actions are narrated and reported as true facts, and instructions are given but not enacted. Later, more narratives circulate to unintended audiences, causing more confusion and ultimately tragedy: Louise again misinterprets a narrative when she overhears a conversation between her husband and an admirer. After he tells the woman the story of his unhappy marriage (it would make a "very good novel," she remarks), Louise becomes unjustifiably jealous. The Duke then "reads what is in her heart"[63] and interprets her mood as lovesickness for the younger Georges, imagining that she has received news of him that has caused her pain. Neither the Duke nor Louise learns of the other's true feelings for the other, as the Duke commits suicide beforehand; it is only by reading his suicide note that Louise realizes that he loved her despite her ambivalence toward him.

The scenes of reading and interpretation that drive the plot in this sentimental romance are translated into a familiar *nahḍa* vocabulary of enlightened knowledge acquisition but still yield tragic results. With the Duke, Louise finds herself compelled to "stroll through the domains of learning" much like readers of the journal itself were invited to enter "the field of civilization" and Buṭrus al-Bustānī's listeners were exhorted to "wander in the fields of knowledge."[64] They have conversations about literature, art, and music, in which Louise learns to appreciate "the pleasures of the mind" rather than the physical attraction that her younger suitor offered her, an education of both her morals and her taste that echoed essays on "civilizational progress" that appeared in *Ḥadīqat al-akhbār* and elsewhere.[65] An editorial article in *Ḥadīqat al-akhbār*, for example, which preceded *Al-Jirjisayn* by mere months, used similar language to advocate the simultaneous spread of knowledge and "personal, familial, and social habits that govern proper taste" as ways to produce a desire for "the pleasures of civilization."[66] Discussions of "proper taste," as Toufoul Abou-Hodeib shows, emerged in the late nineteenth century as part of an expanded discourse of enlightened domesticity, in which women were enlisted into the production of not only the home but also a space for an "idealized middle class whose cultural habits were distinct from both the upper classes and what they perceived as European influences."[67] Louise's marriage to the Duke promises to interlace education and domesticity into the *nahḍa* project through practices of proper reading. Yet even as the activity of reading is translated into the language of enlightened sentimental education, the circulation of narratives prevents that reading from yielding the knowledge that will promote the success of this enlightened union. What circulates are statements that are either untrue or invalid, are improperly interpreted and contextualized, or are simply nonexistent. In the end, the only text that both makes it into the hands of its intended reader and contains a message that is successfully transmitted is the Duke's suicide note, which demands that Louise marry her true love. If any reform-minded moral can be perceived in her marriage to the cultivated and cultivating Duke, it is minimized by her eventual pairing with his uncultivated romantic rival. In this case, not even proper reading can ensure the appropriate romantic choice.

It is not just oral storytelling and letter writing that undergo strange circulations in these novels; print appears as no more stable a medium. The anonymous translation of Alexandre Dumas's *Pauline* is framed by the question of print's reliability—it omits the source's first chapter to begin with a traveler asking for details of local crimes so he can publish "strange stories." And then he is offered an "even stranger" tale by one of his fellow travelers, of his rescuing a young woman from her brigand husband and his gang, his forging a passport for her, and his escaping with her to England, where she tells him her own "strange story." This story is itself peppered with scenes of illicit reading that yield illicit knowledge: a book that hides a secret passageway leads to her discovery that her husband is a murderer; a newspaper left carelessly on a table reveals that her suitor has murdered her husband in a duel. These scenes describe the unpredictable results of text's ability to reach anyone, as Pauline is not the intended audience for either printed item, the reading of which causes grave consequences: in the former instance, her husband poisons her for having acquired that knowledge, and in the latter, the knowledge causes her health to deteriorate. Eventually Pauline's identity will become tied up with that of a circulating text, albeit a forged one: her suitor forges a name for her onto his passport, allowing them to leave France. The falsified passport becomes the perfect metonym for the stranger public: a text that is designed to provide certainty instead unfixes an identity. It is then, on their passage to exile and with Pauline having become a stranger living under an assumed name, that the narrator muses about the events that have befallen him, "contemplating, bewilderedly, these strange events."[68] The public of strangers appears not as an enlightenment community of proper readers but as an agent of gothic epistemology, overturning previously certain truths and exposing their inadequacy.

"But Foreigners Never Lie!"

By the time *Ḥadīqat al-akhbār*'s first decade had ended, the popularity and narrative expectations for foreign fiction had become firmly established. Yūsuf Al-Shalfūn, al-Khūrī's former printer and primary competitor in the private publishing market, had begun to devote a substantial portion of the output of his press, al-Maṭbaʿa al-ʿUmūmiyya (Public press, founded 1861), to foreign translations, as did Khalīl Sarkīs with the press he cofounded with Buṭrus al-Bustānī, Maṭbaʿat al-Maʿārif (Educational press, founded 1868).[69] These works had become so popular that al-Shalfūn introduced the serialization of *The Count of Monte Cristo* in his monthly subscription series, *Al-Shirāka al-shahriyya fī Bayrūt*, with an explicit reference to them, admitting that he hopes to capitalize on what he called the readers' "thirst" for translated novels:

> So said Yūsuf bin Fāris al-Shalfūn: When I saw the larger part of the young audience of our great country, sons of the New Age, had been very much ignited by reading *al-rumān*, or literary stories, and that their desire for them, especially those in French, had increased, I decided to follow their thirst and translate this venerated novel known as *Amīr Jazīrat Mūntū Krīstū* LE COMTE DE MONTE-CRISTO written by Monsieur Alexandre Dumas and famous for its eloquent phrases, entertaining *maʿānī* and beautiful construction that includes the life story of a young sailor named Edmond Dantès who was at first in poor circumstances . . . and becomes a great prince who takes revenge upon those who wronged him, only after he has suffered excessive scorn and dreadful toil.
>
> This novel is very long and has historical events and details that will give the reader pleasure in reading it and attest to its author's great abilities, talents and intellect. I have heard that he has achieved high standing and wide praise from one of the greats for having succeeded in rendering [the story] in a manner suitable to every taste. For it [the novel] at times breaks the heart with its sad events and affecting phrases, and other times it cheers us and enlivens our thoughts with happy news and wondrous coincidences. And it, in any case, is not bereft of any excellent benefits for those who pay attention to the intentions behind it.[70]

As al-Shalfūn's preface shows, foreign fiction and "unusual stories" were often one in the same in the minds of readers, who were driven to read them less by their pursuit of knowledge than their "desire" and "thirst" for fictional stories, *especially the French*. By March 1866, when this issue was published, literary producers had noted the popularity of foreign fiction whose primary characteristics were not only its laudable aesthetic properties ("eloquent phrases") but more importantly its emotional effects ("breaking the heart") and improbable plots ("wondrous coincidences"). The "excellent benefits" are relegated to the end of the introduction, listed as present as a matter of course but only of interest to "those who pay attention." Al-Shalfūn expected the majority of his readers to pay less attention to the novel's social benefit than to its entertainment value, its "happy news and wondrous coincidences."

To read translated fiction, this preface suggests, was to read for entertainment, for unusual stories and wondrous coincidences. The prefaces to translations published by al-Shalfūn's and Sarkīs's presses—which alongside al-Khūrī's al-Maṭbaʿa al-sūriyya were the most prolific commercial presses in operation in Beirut at the time[71]—are particularly illustrative of this fact: Salīm Ṣaʿb introduces his translation of Camille Bodin's (the pseudonym of Jenny Bastide) *Le Monstre, Riwāyat al-ʿajāʾib wa al-gharāʾib* (1865), as "a novel of wondrous [*ʿajība*] anecdotes of unusual [*mustaghrabāt*] behaviors, and containing a dreadful tale of sad occurrences," which he offers "as entertainment to the youth of our country,"[72] while Ḥunayn Khūrī dedicates his translation of Eugène Sue's *Le Morne au Diable, Kitāb ra's ṣakhrat al-shaiṭān* (1874), to his father for him to enjoy in his old age.[73] And Salīm al-Ḥalyānī explains that he undertook his translation of Elie Berthet's *Le Mine d'or, Riwāyat maʿdan al-dhahab* (1868), because he found it to be "an amusing novel with a wondrous [*ʿajība*] and pleasant story."[74] Even didactic source material could be assimilated to this category; al-Shalfūn took out an advertisement in *Ḥadīqat al-akhbār* promoting *Al-ʿAjāʾib wa al-gharāʾib*, comparing it to Bernardin de Saint-Pierre's *Paul et Virginie* (*Riwāyat Būl wa Firjīnī*), also translated by Ṣaʿb. Both are advertised as similarly "entertaining" and "stylistically innovative."[75] Their status as foreign fiction—and therefore primarily pleasurable rather than instructive—here trumps any differences one might find between them, even in the case of a canonical eighteenth-century novel of moral sentiments and a largely forgotten popular gothic novel that sensationalized violent criminality.[76]

By contrast, in Yūsuf al-Shalfūn's preface to his own original novel, *Ḥifẓ al-widād* (The preservation of affection, 1866), he makes no reference to a strange plot but instead explains that while he wrote it after seeing the popularity of French novels, he "did not write it in order to invent like the rest of them but took [the story] from what had occurred in reality."[77] Foreign fiction, that is, offers unusual events, while domestic fiction more often purports to offer "reality." Novels like *Ḥifẓ al-widād* constituted what critics have seen as a competing novelistic trend, the didactic novel exemplified by Salīm al-Bustānī's novels in *Al-Jinān*. As opposed to the entertainment novel, which was produced by nonprofessional writers and "deferred to the uneducated taste of readers," the didactic novel was written by the professional intellectual class who "expressed their feelings about the environment in which they lived and their desires to reform that environment," educating their readership rather than entertaining them.[78] The performance of this distinction between popular, foreign, unrealistic novels, on the one hand, and elite-educated, domestic, realistic ones, on the other, is, according to Samah Selim, what helped recuperate the novel for social, and in particular national, uses. "When Arab critics use the word 'reality' to talk about Arabic fiction," she writes, "they mean 'national reality,' a term that raises the specter of a whole set of specific historical and social issues . . . as well as the real and imagined social composition of the national community."[79] The novel, that is, was considered by reformers to be one of the mechanisms by which the properly reformed public, in the form of an imagined community of the nation, was created: by the disciplining of literary taste and subjective understanding or by the disciplining of how the public "entered itself into literature as an object." As Badr explains, Egyptian critics first in the late nineteenth century (he cites the al-Bustānīs as examples of a similar phenomenon in Lebanon), then at the beginning of the twentieth century, and finally in the 1920s sought to domesticate the novel as a vehicle for educating readers' tastes and values.

Yet, as Selim notes, "highbrow authors" like Ṭaha Ḥusayn (1889–1973), Maḥmūd Taymūr (1894–1973), and Tawfīq al-Ḥakīm (1898–1987) complained well into the twentieth century about the "scandalous but nonetheless fierce competition offered by the popular serialized fiction of the day, condemning it as yet another sign of the lamentable state of Egyptian culture."[80] Like Badr writing in 1963 and Buṭrus al-Bustānī writing in 1870, they were ambivalent toward the reading habits of the *ʿumūm*, which were scandalous because of their inclination toward translations. Elites, in fact, continually called for the reformation of the Arabic novel, and did so at least four specific historical moments within the span of a century. These multiple calls to reform the public, whether it be a reading one or a national one, cannot be understood as proof of the *existence* of such a public. Instead, in demonstrating a *need* for a reading public, they may more strongly indicate its *nonexistence.* Calls for reform thus point simultaneously to the idea of the public being a disciplinary mechanism and its failure.

The distinction between foreign, unrealistic fictions and domestic, realistic ones that critics hoped would produce a proper reading public was continuously performed by reinscribing impropriety within purportedly "proper" narratives. *Ḥifẓ al-widād,* which al-Shalfūn offered as a story taken from reality to those "sons of the nation who have good taste," is framed—much like the *Ḥadīqat al-akhbār* novels—as the true story being related to a friend. A man whom the narrator had not seen in many years and who had just returned from Europe tells him his story in the hopes that the narrator "might find it agreeable and write it down." Yet even that faithful act of the representation of reality, specified as a Lebanese one that occurs in 1858, is conditional. The narrator must transcribe it accurately, "without changing a thing."[81] Even in a novel that claims to be taken faithfully from reality, the very task of portraying a true story is cast with doubt. These first pages set up a parable of reading designed to educate the novel's readers, helping them to identify their own task with the protagonist. Similar to how al-Bustānī characterized the readership at the time, reader are insufficiently prepared, "spending the bulk of [their] time in the perusal [*muṭālaʿa*, unconcentrated reading] of learned books though [they] knew nothing of the affairs of the world"; as a result, they become embroiled in "a love story concerned with strange matters."[82]

In al-Bustānī's description of his story as such—"qiṣṣa gharāmiyya dhāt umūr gharība"—he uses a phrase that would not be out of place as the subtitle for a translated novel. In performing the distinction between improper and proper reading, al-Shalfūn quite literally inscribes a fantastic romance within it. So too does al-Bustānī: in *Asmāʾ*, the seduction of Nabīḥa by the man posing as a French nobleman is only possible because she is a bad reader who values all things foreign for the sake of their foreignness. Her fantasy of marrying a foreign prince—which could also be described as a "a love story concerned with strange matters"—turns into a disappointing reality, in which she is abandoned by a foreign thief. A similar plot occurs in al-Khūrī's original *Wayy . . . idhan lastu bi-ifranjī*, in which the protagonist's daughter is seduced by a Frenchman who charms her with stories of the "rarities [*gharāʾib*] of his country and the great adventures that befell him."[83] As the protagonist—whose main flaws include his not owning a single book "and not even a copy of *Ḥadīqat al-akhbār*"—ironically exclaims, "but foreigners never lie!"[84] Translated romances were refigured as the "lies" of foreigners.

Just as in the translated *Ḥadīqat al-akhbār* novels, the circulation of texts—often marked as foreign ones or narratives told by circulating foreigners—occurs along irregular routes, produces acts of reading that are not replicable or uniform, and creates unreliable knowledge. It prevents predictable reading outcomes and leaves the reader in what al-Khūrī called "disconcertment and doubt."[85] *Ḥifẓ al-widād* presents the reader with the possibility that the events "taken from reality" are in fact mistranscribed oral narrative. And *Asmāʾ* offers Nabīḥa as an object lesson in bad reading; she reads and quotes newspaper articles but without fully understanding them: "her thoughts resembled many newspaper editorials in that they used important words like 'progress, success, and decline' without pausing to think about their underlying social and political issues or their relationship to people's living conditions," the narrator explains. "It is thus that [newspapers] can praise something that the day before they had condemned."[86] Even the reading of proper materials like newspaper editorials can be done improperly, as it is circulation itself that is uncontrollable. As with oral narratives, the veracity of the written and printed word is not guaranteed: telegrams transmit false and true information; police reports can be falsified as well as truthful. In the end, *Asmā'*'s project of modeling proper reading methods is only ambiguously successful. Amid the dueling rumors and unreliable written material, Asmā' is only saved by evidence that she can see with her own eyes—experiences that are not reproducible and that are far removed from the written word.

The anxieties of circulation represented by and within translated novels were not exorcized by *nahḍa* authors' aspirations for literary reform but were rearticulated within their original novels as a potential source of misreading. Translation's abyss, the uncertain transmission of messages that al-Khūrī described as the essential problematic of the print sphere, also formed the foundation of the novels that were published in journal and newspaper pages, where those novels expressed the ambivalent attitudes of the literary elite toward the public they hoped to create. If it was in these novels that the public entered literature as an object, then it entered itself in translation. Instead of a public that "by communicating with itself, gained clarity about itself," we see a public that problematized communication and doubted any clarify about itself—establishing narrative techniques and theoretical questions that were to last into the contemporary Arabic novel and literary criticism. Original novels did not resolve these questions any more than they supplanted the translations that inspired them. Instead, they were read alongside those translations—both literally and figuratively. These early original novels, too, were read "in translation," with the same narrative expectations that translated novels established.

Part Two

The Transnational Imagination

> The English want a rail road, which would confine the use of Egypt to themselves. The French desire a canal that would admit the hardy cruisers of the Mediterranean into the Red Sea. The cosmopolite will hope that both projects may be carried out.
>
> —Richard Burton, *Travels in Arabia and Africa*, 1866

> What an excellent thing is the railway! How many a bottom
> on its seats spreads wide, while breasts there quiver galore!
> If that alone were all it did for us—never mind its forward dashing—
> one couldn't think to ask for more
>
> —Aḥmad Fāris al-Shidyāq, *Leg over Leg*, 1855

The newspaper was but one of the long-range technologies that connected the nineteenth-century Mediterranean to the rest of the world. The steamship and the railway, as al-Shidyāq remarked in *Al-Sāq 'alā al-sāq*, were innovations that distinguished the New Age, "connecting the disconnected." At the time when print culture was networking the Arabophone regions, long-distance communications and transportation technologies began their work of integrating the whole world into a single unit. As early as 1854, telegraph cables that would "wire the world" connected Algeria and then Alexandria and Istanbul to Europe.[1] By 1871, according to the British consul in Cairo, "every town or village of importance in Lower Egypt ha[d] a telegraph station."[2] In 1866, with the laying of the transatlantic cable, a telegram could theoretically be sent around the entire world. Meanwhile, the connected world had become part of Arabic readers' everyday experiences, even when staying home. Railways brought mail and periodicals to people's homes, and cables brought news from wire agencies like Reuters to coffee-shop walls, where customers could peruse them for the price of a cup of tea. By midcentury, periodicals were announcing the opening of railways that spanned much of the continent of Eurasia and all of North America, and steam technology allowed larger ships to run on smaller amounts of coal, allowing more classes of travelers aboard. More travelers than ever before were circulating into and out of eastern Mediterranean harbors, and more readers were learning about that circulation than ever before.[3]

These technologies facilitated al-Shidyāq's own mobility. He described them as "like the lines on the palm of your hand: via them the traveler can go wherever he wants—up or down, east or west."[4] This was one of many visual metaphors that authors used to describe the new experience of connectivity: Buṭrus al-Bustānī conjured the image of "a great global chain" linked "by means of the steamship, telegraph, and other things,"[5] while Khalīl al-Khūrī celebrated the ability of the telegraph to cause the major cities of the world to be "interwoven" (*mushtabaka*), linked with "Europe, India, and other places in the East and West."[6] These images point to the ways that these new technologies created more possibilities for imagining the region or even the globe as a single, traversable or visible entity: lines converging on a hand, a single chain spanning the circumference of the globe, or a net (*shabaka*) encompassing the whole world.

In this, these authors joined writers, lyricists, and poets elsewhere who, in response to these technologies, imagined similar scenes of progress and global unity. Popular verses like A. Talexy's "Atlantic Telegraph Polka" (1858) pictured telegraph lines forming "a loving girdle 'round the earth," while Rudyard Kipling sang "the Song o' Steam!" and Lord Tennyson gave readers a "Vision of the world" in which the railroad rushed civilization "Forward, forward."[7] The celebratory tone of many of these works echoed the imagery used by the producers of technology themselves, which extolled the virtues of what Simone Müller has called "wiring the world." As Müller writes, "The new technology's avowal of a peaceful and civilized modernity entailed an imagined global unity that reached far beyond the telegraphs' actual means of point-to-point communication . . . produc[ing] not only a unified market of goods but a unified market of morality." These works promised "an electric union, universal peace, and the telegraphs' civilizing mission."[8] As Rifāʿa Rāfiʿ al-Tahṭāwī explained in his philosophical inquiry into Egyptian social progress, *Al-Manāhij al-albāb al-Miṣriyya fī mabāhij al-adab al-ʿaṣriyya* (*The Paths of Egyptian Minds towards the Delights of Modern Culture*, 1869), transportation and communications technology are among the drivers of global harmony: steam power and telegraphs make "travel easier and news travel faster," as he writes, and by this means, "people can realize their own ideas and exchange ideas and products," thus linking them into perfect agreement.[9]

When *nahḍa* authors wrote about global interconnection, they did not do so as receivers of globality. Just like their European counterparts (indeed, often simultaneously with them thanks to the incorporation of telegraph news in the Arabic press), Arabic readers learned about telegraph cables being laid and railways being opened; they saw maps showing steamship routes, railway tracks, and telegraph cables crisscrossing the globe; and they could check the schedules and fares of trains and steamships or track international currency rates in weekly conversion tables. They did so as participants in a worldwide reimagining of what constituted "the worldwide."

With sharply increasing frequency, they could also read translated novels about characters from or events taking place elsewhere. During the 1870s and 1880s, the production of novels in translation at least tripled from the output of the previous two decades, making distinctly different parts of the globe become important parts of the Arabic literary imagination. In the 1890s and early 1900s, the increase was exponential, saturating the print market. Novels such as *Zawāj Jartrūda* (Gertrude's marriage, 1871), *Qiṣṣat al-bārisiyya al-ḥasnā'* [The story of the beautiful Parisian women, 1884), or *Matīlda* (Matilda, 1885) announced their foreignness in their very titles, worrying commentators. An entire subgenre, as we will see in chapter 6, portrayed the lives of foreign women in often sensationalist ways: their strange lives were portrayed as especially foreign to the reading public. Their translators, as commentators worried, turn away and even "flee" from the local environment and its social problems, preferring to produce what ʿAbd al-Muḥsin Ṭaha Badr called "novels of entertainment": "For this reason," as he writes, "they presented entertainment novels to the public that resembled those in the West, resulting in the entertainment novel having no direct connection to Arabic and Islamic narrative heritage."[10] In other words, foreign literature circulated in Arabic with such prevalence that critics considered it a literary and social problem.

More importantly, not only did the last decades of the nineteenth century see a marked increase in the circulation of foreign novels in the Arabic print sphere; it saw an increase in particular of novels *about* circulation. It was then that two of the most well-known authors to imagine mobility on a transnational scale, Alexandre Dumas *père* and Jules Verne, made their first lasting impressions on Arabic readers. Among the hundreds of Dumas's novels, at least thirty-three novels listing Dumas *père* or *fils* as original author appeared in Arabic translation, in at least forty-one separate editions, of which eight were editions of three separate translations of *The Count of Monte Cristo*.

Translations listing Alexandre Dumas, *père* and *fils*, as original author, 1859–1919

1. Anonymous, *Būlīna Mūlyān* [*Pauline*], serialized in *Ḥadīqat al-akhbār*, 1859; single volume, Al-Maṭbaʿa al-ʿUmūmiyya, January 1865, "Under the supervision of Yūsuf al-Shalfūn"
2. Salīm Ṣaʿb, *Amīr jazīrat Mūntū Krīstū* [*Le Comte de Monte-Cristo*], serialized in *Al-Shirāka al-shahriyya* (Beirut: al-Maṭbaʿa al-ʿUmūmiyya, 1866)
3. Naṣrallah Misk, *Riwāyat Amīr Mūntī Krīstū* [*Le Comte de Monte Cristo*], serialized in *Al-Najāḥ*, 1870–1873
4. Ibrahīm Ḥakīm, *Al-Sāltiyādūr* [*Le Gentilhomme de la Montagne*] (Beirut: Maṭbaʿa ʿUmūmiyya, 1870)
5. Bishāra Shadīd, *Qiṣṣat al-Kūnt dū Muntū Krīstū* [*Le Comte de Monte-Cristo*] (Cairo: Maṭbaʿat Wādī al-Nīl, 1871)
6. Nakhlah Ṣāliḥ, *Riwāyat al-Daryāq fī Aḥwāl al-ʿushāq* [*La Dame aux Camélias*] (Beirut, 1875)
7. Qayṣar Zīniyya, *A-Kūnt dī Mūnqūmīrī* [*Le Comte de Montgomery*], serialized in *Al-Ahrām*, 1881; single volume, Alexandria: M. Jirjī Gharghūrī, 1907
8. Nakhlah Qilfāṭ, *Qiṣṣat al-Kūnt dī Mūntū Krīstū* [*Le Comte de Monte-Cristo*] (Beirut, 1883)
9. Sāmī Quṣayrī, *Al-Ikhtifāʾ al-gharīb* (Beirut, 1887; 2nd printing, Alexandria, 1902; 3rd printing, 1910)
10. Najīb Ḥaddād, *Al-Fursān al-thalātha* [*Les Trois mousquetaires*] (Cairo, 1888, 1899, 1913)
11. Najīb Ḥaddād, *Fursān al-layl*
12. Shukrī Yūsuf al-Khūrī, *Murūʾ al-ghāniyāt* (Alexandria, 1889)
13. Najīb Ḥaddād, *ʿŪd ʿalā badʾ* [*Le Vicomte de Bragelonne*], serialized in *Al-Ahrām*, 1891–1893; single volume published 1904
14. Tawfīq Dūbray, *Riwāyat Margharīt* [*La Dame aux Camélias*], serialized in *Al-Silsila al-durriyya fī al-fukāhāt al-tārīkhiyya*, n.d.; single volume, Cairo: Maṭbaʿat al-Taʾlīf, 1892
15. Najīb Ḥaddād, *Fursān al-layl* (Alexandria, 1895, 1903)
16. Anonymous [Ḥāfiẓ ʿAwwaḍ?], *Fātina Bārīs* (Cairo, 1898, 1899)
17. Najīb Ḥaddād, *Faḍīḥat al-ʿushāq* (Alexandria, 1898)
18. Tāniyūs ʿAbduh, *Al-Burj al-hāʾil* [*Tour de Nesle*], 1899
19. Tāniyūs ʿAbduh, *Shaqāʾ al-gharām* [*La Dame de Montsoreau*], 1899
20. Najīb al-Ḥaddād, *Al-ʿAshiqa al-mutanakkira* (Cairo, n.d. but before 1899); advertised in *Hilāl* 7, no. 19 (July 1, 1899): 607

21. Faraḥ Anṭūn, *Nahḍat al-asad*, ca. 1900
22. Sāmī Quṣayrī, *Al-Kūnt dī Mūnghūmīrī*, ca. 1900
23. Nasīb Mash'alānī, *Al-Qā'idīn* [*Le Capitaine Richard* (Cairo, 1903)
24. Najīb Marguṣ, *Al-Hanā' ba'd al-'anā aw Mādām di Shamblāy* (Cairo, 1904)
25. Faraḥ Anṭūn, *Al-Burj al-ha'il* [*Le Tour de Nesle*], 1904
26. Najīb Ḥaddād, *Ḥadīth Layla* (Alexandria, 1904)
27. Ḥāfiẓ Awwaḍ, *Mādām dī Kāmīlyā*, ca. 1904
28. Anonymous, *Maṭāmi' Nābuliyūn* (Cairo, 1905)
29. Ṣāliḥ Jūdat, *Sirr al-i'tirāf*, serialized in *Musāmarāt al-sha'b*, 1905
30. Ṣāliḥ Jūdat, *Ḍaḥāyā al-'ifāf*, serialized in *Musāmarāt al-sha'b*, 1906
31. Ṣāliḥ Jūdat, *Al-Yad al-athīma*, 1906
32. Ṭāniyūs 'Abduh, *La Dame aux Camélias* (1906)
33. Najīb Ibrāhīm Ṭarād, *Ḥadāthat Hanrī al-Rābi' malak Faransā* (Alexandria, 1906–1907).
34. Nīqūlā Rizq Allah, *Alf khayāl wa khayāl*, serialized in *Musāmarāt al-sha'b*, 1910
35. S., *Mayyitat al-aḥyā'*, serialized in *Musāmarāt al-sha'b*, 1910
36. Nīqūlā Ḥaddād, *'Iqd al-mālika* [*Le Collier de la Reine*], serialized in *Musāmarāt al-sha'b*, 1911
37. Najīb Ḥaddād, *Raj' mā Inqaṭa'* (Cairo: Maṭba'at al-Hilāl, 1913)
38. Muṣṭafā Luṭfī al-Manfalūṭī, *Al-Ḍaḥiya* and *Mudhakkirāt Margarīt* [*La Dame aux Camélias*], in *Al-'Abarat*, 1915, 1920, 1929
39. M. A. 'Inān, *Gharā'im Nābūlī aw al-Jarīma wa al-intiqām* (Cairo: Maṭba'at Muḥammad Muḥammad Maṭar, 1916)
40. Ṭāniyūs 'Abduh, *Dhāt al-zahra al-bayḍa'* [*La Came aux Camélias*] (Cairo, 1918, 1927)

Several are listed in bibliographies without dates:

41. Kāmil 'Abd al-'Azīz, *Al-Ḥubb wa al-ḥurriyya aw Fursān al-malika* (Cairo, n.d.)
42. Tāniyūs 'Abduh, *Saltiyādūr* [*Le Gentilhomme de la Montagne*] (Alexandria, n.d.)
43. Ḥabīb Fahmī, *Al-Qābitān Būl* [*Le Capitaine Paul*] (Cairo, n.d.)
44. Najīb al-Ḥaddād, *Raj' mā inqata' ba'd 'ishrīn sana* [*Vingt ans après*] (Cairo, n.d.)
45. Ḥanā As'ad Fahmī, *Kurat al-talj*, serialized in *Al-Riwātāt al-shahriyya*, n.d.

By the end of the century, it was sufficient to write that a novel was "written in the style of Alexandre Dumas" to recommend it to readers; he was, as a reviewer in *Al-Hilāl* explained in 1899, "more famous than can be mentioned," as was his main character, Edmond Dantès, who crisscrossed Europe and the Mediterranean at alarming speeds and demonstrated his extraordinary power by gathering goods "from all four corners of the world."[11] Meanwhile, the novels of Jules Verne provided a fantasy of global mobility and transnational communicability for readers that propelled him to international fame, with four of his novels (*Voyage en ballon*, *Le Tour du monde en quatre-vingt jours*, *Voyage au centre de la terre*, and *Voyage au pole nord*) appearing in Arabic in at least nine editions between 1875 and 1894. Both Dumas and Verne produced characters that stand as avatars of hypermobility and communicability. They presented a new model for the modern man, who was not bound by his locality or language but was a man of the world, helping to make the world as a single unit available for contemplation. Even the marriage plot, in turn-of-the-century popular translations, took place on multiple continents. Readers encountered the New Woman question as a transnational one, comparing foreign women's situations to their own and placing seemingly local issues on a global scale.

Yet even *this* phenomenon was not unique to the Arabic case. In India, China, Latin America, and Europe, these transnational fictions were objects of marked transnational circulation.[12] According to Franco Moretti's *Atlas of the European Novel*, Dumas's novels thoroughly "saturated" the nineteenth-century European markets and were those most commonly held in European circulating libraries.[13] Priya Joshi similarly cites melodrama as one of the most translated genres on the Indian continent in the nineteenth century. And Jules Verne's *Extraordinary Journeys* (1863–1905) *continue* to saturate literary markets, constituting a global sensation the likes of which are difficult to overstate. According to UNESCO's *Index Translationum*, Verne is still the second-most-translated author in the world, after Agatha Christie but before Shakespeare.[14]

In the case of many of these novels, their internationalization occurred virtually simultaneously across the globe. Whereas a century passed between the original publication of French sentimental novels and their translation in *Ḥadīqat al-akhbār*, only twelve years separated Verne's *Voyage en ballon* (1863) and Yūsuf Sarkīs's *Al-Riḥla al-jawwiyya fī al-markaba al-hawā'iyya* (1875), roughly the same amount of time that separated its French and English publications. Its reprinting and those of the three other *Extraordinary Journeys* translated into Arabic in this period all appeared at the height of Verne's European popularization via the *Boy's Own* magazine and multiple English, Spanish, and

German editions.[15] Similarly, Labība Hāshim's translation of the sensationalist best-seller *Called Back* closely followed the novel's transnational popularization; it was published nearly contemporaneously with French, German, Danish, Czech, Swedish, Italian, and Spanish versions, making the novel—which features protagonists on long-distance train rides—a global best-seller. Arabic translations of these novels of circulation allowed their readers to join readers in Europe, Asia, and the Americas in imagining a world connected by transportation networks.

These facts point to the transnational importance of the transnational imagination in the constitution of global literary modernity, at the very moment that audiences were experiencing the globe's interconnectivity. Yet neither modernity nor globality were equalizing forces. The inequalities built into the systems of colonialism and its enabling technologies powerfully shaped what Mariano Siskind calls the "globalization of the novel" and the "novelization of the global" (the transnational circulation of the novel form beyond western Europe and the narration of processes of globalization in the novel for these various audiences).[16] Those very poets and novelists who celebrated transportation technologies for their ability to connect the world often also celebrated their role in colonial exploitation. When Tennyson and Kipling pictured railroads and steamships, they also imagined them as a means to harvest natural resources and sexual services. "I will take some savage woman," Tennyson writes in "Locksley Hall," mincing no words.[17] Verne makes this no less explicit: in *Around the World in Eighty Days*, Phileas Fogg stares out the window of the Great Peninsular Railway and wonders not at the Indian countryside but at British imperial power. "The locomotive, directed by the arms of an English engineer and burning English coal, cast its smoke out over the cotton plantations," he muses.[18] The celebration of world unification is in fact a celebration of the mobility of European capital.

In point of fact, the bulk of these popular translations appeared in Egypt, and only after the turn to direct colonial rule. Some, like *Around the World in Eighty Days* and *Journey to the Center of the Earth*, were translated by employees of the colonial transportation and communication networks and dedicated to British administrative superiors. These translators surely knew, as did their readers, that only the privileged few could afford the luxuries of pure mobility and communicability and that mobility came at the expense of others' immobility. The celebrated railroad that transported tourists and delivered periodicals to bourgeois readers was largely built by forced labor under the *corvée* system, and the steamships that brought imported goods and delivered journals came more frequently by virtue of another indentured project, the Suez Canal.[19] The telegraph, itself established via Ottoman-British imperial cooperation, was never a neutral relay; during the 1882 ʿUrabi revolt, the Eastern Associated Telegraph Company helped the British stay in touch with London by disconnecting the Alexandria line and putting the severed end of the cable on a British naval ship.[20] Empire, as Bernhard Siegert writes in his literary history of the postal system, is "just a word for chains of command," the "site of transmission."[21] Derived from the Latin *imperare*, "to give an order," empire is first and foremost a network of communication for giving and receiving orders. The telegraph, like the postal system, was developed not for public communication but for imperial control.

The irony that these systems of fantastic mobility were established through the forced immobility of several hundred thousand conscripted workers could not have been lost on residents who were asked to marvel at the "perfect agreement" between peoples brought by the railway or steam. A European "cosmopolite" like Richard Burton might hope for the completion of the Suez project for the opportunities of worldwide mobility it would offer him. Conscripted workers, meanwhile—treated as "unindividualized, interchangeable objects of a new machinery of power," as Zachary Lockman argues—were forced into routinized patterns of mobility and immobility, as they were ordered by the Egyptian state in groups of one thousand to board trains to Suez and remain there until the term of their conscription had ended.[22] Meanwhile, women—as the anonymous female critic in *Ḥadīqat al-akhbār* pointed out so early in Arabic print's history—were afforded far fewer opportunities to travel and communicate than their male peers were. Arab, especially Egyptian, readers in the *nahḍa* were well aware that world imaginings relied on connections forged by economic, political, and social power. It is no wonder that translators explored the "woman question" against the backdrop of international transportation. The experience of the global that transnational adventure fiction captured brought the imagined possibility of admittance to a worldwide contemporaneity but also incorporation into a world system whose "world" is imagined by empire and male-dominated lawmaking.

Only in this complex context of connection *and* disconnection do fantasies of global mobility make sense as some of the most widely circulated narratives in late nineteenth-century Arabic print. Readers understood that no easy isomorphism brought together the imagined world of mobility and the immobile world they transited. Reading the globe in translation meant reading discrepant worlds overlaid on each other. The wonder of hypermobility in *Monte Cristo* gives ways to the banality of travel and communication, and the confidence in a traversable world in Verne's fictions gives way to an emphasis on faulty connections and near misses. The world that the source texts imagined was a seamless totality; the world of Arab readers was one that acknowledged its breaks. We can see, then, why the original travel fiction that distinguishes this period—ʿAli Mubarak's *ʿAlam al-Dīn* (The sign of religion, 1882) and Muḥammad al-Muwayliḥī's *What ʿIsā ibn Hishām Told Us* (1898–1902), for example—features protagonists who never arrive at their intended destinations. Mubārak's fifteen-hundred-page text contains chapters centered on modes of connectivity ("Railroads," "Steamships," and "The Post") and features characters traveling to England to translate an Arabic dictionary for an Orientalist and yet ends abruptly in France.[23] ʿIsā ibn Hishām, who intends to travel to Paris to visit the *exposition universelle*, never makes it farther than Cairo (though when al-Muwayliḥī revises the text in 1927 as a textbook, he adds the Paris episodes).[24] In this text, new modes of transportation are ridden, discussed, and even tripped over.[25] Local bodies, economies, and languages get in the way. Here, globalization raised its most important question, one that remains important in our day: What was the relation between technologies imagined as disembodied, rational, and inevitable and the vulnerable, precarious local entities whose access to those technologies was not guaranteed?

Chapter 4

Fictions of Connectivity

Dumas's World in Translation

Fittingly, Edmond Dantès, the protagonist of one of the nineteenth century's most well-traveled texts, sailed into the minds of readers on a vessel of transnational circulation. Helming a trading ship named the *Pharaon*, which had just returned from "Smyrna, Trieste, and Naples," Dantès directs the boat in an uneventful arrival at the port of Marseille. The usual crowd of onlookers watches the approach of a common sight, the arrival of a ship being "always an important event in Marseille, especially when the ship, like the *Pharaon*, had been built, rigged, and laden at the old docks of Phocée, and belonged to one of the city's own ship-owners."[1] *Monte Cristo* thus begins with an apparently routine scene of Franco-Ottoman commerce, referencing one of the most commonly used Mediterranean shipping routes of the early nineteenth century, when the novel is set. And not only does *Monte Cristo* begin with East-West movement and economic relations, but it continues to make them an engine of the plot: Dantès, wrongly imprisoned, escapes with the help of a coprisoner, an Italian abbé, and then seeks out the abbé's hidden island treasure; having enriched himself, he gathers goods in the East and poses as an Ottoman merchant who calls himself Sindbad the Sailor, before taking on the identity of the Count of Monte Cristo and exacting his revenge on those who wronged him. Trade with the eastern Mediterranean provides him with the raw materials to construct his powerful image and enact his dramatic revenge, which itself requires him to cross and recross the Mediterranean at great speeds.

The novel provides a complex image of these transnational connections from the French perspective. Dantès helms a shipped named "The Pharaoh": its owner, Monsieur Morrel, trades with the Ottoman Empire under the figurative guise of a controller of another Eastern empire. And the name of the port in which it was rigged, the Phocée, conjures a historical memory of Marseille's own Eastern origins, it being the name both of a city on the coast of the Ottoman Empire (Phocée, Phocaea, or Foça, located fifty miles from Smyrna) and of the people who historically settled that port (the Phocaeans, who hailed from western Anatolia). These markers confound the very separation of that sea into "eastern" and "western" coasts, as they locate Phocée not only as an Ottoman port to which a ship may travel but also as a port *inside* France, just as it locates "The Pharaoh" in the House of Morell and Son, the ships owners. In this Mediterranean, capitalist accumulation compresses trade routes into proximity, and Dumas imagines Smyrna, Phocée, and even Egyptian pharaohs as enfolded within the sphere of French domination: the Mediterranean made small. Furthermore, Dantès travels not only *to* the East but *as* the East, posing as the Count of Monte Cristo who often poses as Sindbad the Sailor, a mysterious merchant who claims to have acquired his fortune from a silver mine he discovered in Thessaly. His power, too, is signified by his accumulation of Eastern goods and capital—and even a slave, Haydée, whose father was an Ottoman governor—that he uses to decorate his island cave and later Roman and Parisian apartments. "Turkey carpets," "Arabian swords," a "Nubian" servant, and an Albanian slave all locate the Ottoman Empire in the European interior instead of on the opposite shore of the Mediterranean.

French readers encountering the first serialization of *Monte Cristo* from 1844 to 1846 would have found little surprising here—they had grown accustomed, by this time, to seeing Eastern signifiers circulating at home in France. They would have not been surprised to learn, just a few chapters after the opening scene, that the *Pharaon* was laden with cotton from Alexandria or that the Count and others expressed their economic status by wearing "Turkish silk," garters "worked with a thousand arabesques," or other textiles marked as having Eastern origins.[2] Elite French consumers wore clothing made from textiles dyed in Turkey (in particular, *le rouge de Turquie*, or "Adrianapolis," which was vibrant and fast) and silk spun in Mount Lebanon, perfumed themselves with Egyptian and Arabian oils, ate *sherbets* and drank *café turque*, while middle and urban working classes bought cheaper "populuxe" products, Eastern-style goods manufactured in Europe.[3]

Published on the heels of the 1830 Algerian conquest, *Cristo's* images of Eastern trade would have also been folded into a specifically colonial craze for North African products and most notably textiles. The new access to Eastern markets through Napoleon's Egyptian and Algerian campaigns precipitated what Walter Benjamin and others have called "cashmere fever": a craze for expensive and handwoven Eastern textiles and later their mass-manufactured imitations.[4] The Count's impressive "Tunisian costume" that he wears while taking on the persona of Sindbad the Sailor, for example, features elaborately embroidered and woven textiles that seem to pile one on top of the other: he wears "a red cap with a long tassel of blue silk, a vest of black cloth embroidered with gold, trousers the color of ox-blood, large and full spats of the same color, embroidered with gold like the vest, and yellow *babouches*," as well as "a magnificent cashmere around his waist," which held "a small *cangiar*, sharp and curved."[5] More than merely signifying wealth or exotic narrative potential, this costume would have been read—by readers embedded in this Mediterranean history—as one that conjured specific scenes of conquest. Indeed, it would have evoked the very image that Frank Ames argues precipitated the cashmere craze itself. As he notes in his history of the Kashmir shawl, "When Napoléon returned from Egypt, the generals and officers who had served under him brought back mementoes of the Orient. Among these were Kashmir shawls which they wore wrapped around their waists as belts, and which had been plundered from the Mamelukes, the soldiers of the Egyptian army."[6] Edmund Dantès of Nantes, projecting economic power by dressing as the wealthy merchant named Sinbad the Sailor, projects imperial power by simultaneously dressing as a conquering French soldier. The Mediterranean circulations of the Count are signified through Eastern goods that themselves circulated as figures of conquest. They "brought the empire home," as Catherine Hall and Sonya Rose put it, inscribing empire as part of everyday life that required people "to think imperially, not in the sense of political affiliations for or against empire, but simply assuming it was there, part of the given world that had made them who they were."[7]

But what of Arabic readers, reading translations of this text in 1866, 1871, and 1883, for whom transnational trade signified yet other modes of interconnection? As Elizabeth Holt has argued, the manufacturing trade—especially that driven by textile production—was formative in the development of the early original Arabic novel, because of its importance not only as a local industry but as an element of the *global* economy.[8] Integration into global markets, she argues, meant hope for economic progress at times, disillusionment at others, and an overall skepticism toward speculation and credit, as well as toward the fictions—economic and social—that attended them.[9] When the first translation was begun in 1866 in Yūsuf al-Shalfūn's *Al-Shirāka al-shahriyya fī Bayrūt* [The Beirut monthly subscription], the US Civil War had created a demand for Egyptian cotton, and a silkworm epidemic had prompted European factories to invest in Lebanese and Syrian silk. By the time the final translation was published in 1883, newspapers were reporting losses, as speculative practices had resulted in private and public bankruptcies.[10] The Ottoman Empire itself had declared bankruptcy and turned over the administration of its debt (and much of its taxation) to European banks, and Khedive Isma'īl had borrowed so much capital that Great Britain had assumed total control of Egypt's financial affairs. Global trade, for those who were living in these times of uncertainty, could not simply be figured as unfettered mobility, as capital was experienced as something channeled, controlled, and sometimes stalled.[11]

The Arabic translations of *Cristo* demonstrate that what Holt calls the "thick nexus of global finance and Arabic fiction" manifests itself above all as a problem of translation. Scenes of exchange necessarily invoke problems of translation, which in the context of *nahḍa* debates about the relative benefits of Arab and European cultures and economies puts special emphasis on what Lydia Liu has called "the meaning-value" of the sign.[12] Especially in systems of exchange like global markets and literary translations, neither meaning nor value are intrinsic but are what Gayatri Spivak has called textual, in that they have no adequate literal referent. Value, as Spivak writes, is a "contentless differential" that "can never appear on its own."[13] It is produced in exchange and circulation, where it is always on the move, in a state of constant deferral that—like translation—opens a gap within "identity-as-adequation."[14] As she quotes Karl Marx, "You may turn and toss an ounce of gold in any way you like, and it will never weigh ten ounces. But here in the process of circulation one ounce practically does weigh ten ounces."[15] Circulation requires translation, just as translation implies circulation. Especially in the context of Ottoman-European relations, when monetary crises caused by debt, the debasement of the *kurush*, and the introduction of paper money—when for a time ten *kurush* did equal one—representations of global relations required a discussion of translation that problematized equivalence.[16]

Fictions of connectivity like *Monte Cristo*, which focus on the global mobility of capital and bodies, are ideal places to see this instability in meaning-value. The Count is never only the Count, even in French. He is a vanishing semblance, always appearing in translation: Dantès, an English lord, and Sindbad the Sailor—himself an avatar of circulation—too.[17] Global trade, from the perspective of France in 1846, was not as stable as it seems in the novel. Between 1798 and 1814, Napoleon—Dantès's shadow twin—had built an empire that at its peak spanned from Madrid to the Ottoman Empire's Balkan border, but it was dismantled after his defeat at Waterloo in 1815. In the intervening years, too, his campaigns were by no means a string of military successes. In 1801, the short-lived conquest of Egypt ended with the last of Napoleon's troops having been removed by British warships; in 1804, a slave revolt in the former colony of Saint Domingue led to its declaring its dependence as the new country of Haiti; in 1808, Napoleon's westward European campaign was halted in a surrender; and in 1813, Russia expelled his surrogates from central Europe. Waterloo was only Napoleon's last and most lasting defeat, as the ensuing Congress of Vienna would put structures in place to prevent a new continental European empire and ensure British maritime control of the Mediterranean for the next century.[18] That opening scene of transnational circulation can thus be read as figuring the closing of France's global economic horizons, time-stamped as it was to less than four months before Napoleon's defeat at Waterloo. It was when Napoleon went from being "sovereign of half of the world" to being "king of the Island of Elba," *Cristo*'s narrator recounts.[19] The Count's extraordinary mobility is a recuperative fantasy of imperial might. In this light, his posing later as Sindbad with a belt once worn by a defeated Egyptian soldier can also be read as a figure of defeat, as standing in for the vanquished soldier himself, the slave (*mamlūk*) that made up the military class of Ottoman Egypt. As a token of exchange in an uneven global market, the scarf has no stable meaning. To paraphrase Marx, here in the process of circulation, a symbol of conquest does also signify defeat. The formerly imprisoned Dantès masters the imperial circuits of the sea by posing as one of empire's (Ottoman) imperial victims. Circulation—aided by transportation networks, empire, and translation—is tied not only to conquest but to imprisonment and defeat.

That *Monte Cristo* is a novel-length exploration of transnational circulation explains its singular popularity during the *nahḍa*'s own world-making projects. The translations of *Monte Cristo* embed the economics of their literary relation with Europe into their techniques. In 1866, Yūsuf al-Shalfūn published a first installment of *Amīr jazīrat Mūntū Krīstū* (The Prince of Monte Cristo Island) in his subscription series, *Al-Shirāka al-shahriyya fī Bayrūt*, translated by Salīm Ṣaʿb and "supervised and Arabized" by al-Shalfūn himself.[20] Yet, as al-Shalfūn found the work "too large" to complete quickly, it was also the last installment to appear. Then, in 1871, when he began publishing the Beirut bi-weekly *Al-Najāḥ* with Luwīs Ṣābūnjī, he restarted the translation with the help of at least one new translator, Naṣrallah Misk, under the title *Amīr Mūntī Krīstū* (The Prince of Monte Cristo).[21] This version not only strove for adequation, translating the text almost word for word, but posed a relationship of virtual equality between French and Arabic readers and seamless transfer.

This was not the case for the other two versions, which raised skeptical questions about the possibility or even desirability of equivalence and the conditions under which circulation occurs. Also in 1871, Wādī al-Nīl Press in Cairo published a single-volume edition of a new translation by Bishāra Shadīd, a Lebanese emigré to Alexandria, under the title *Qiṣṣat al-Kūnt dū Mūntū Krīstū* (Story of the Count of Monte Cristo).[22] As he claimed that it was the first translation of *Monte Cristo* to appear in Arabic, he had probably not encountered either the Shalfūn/Ṣaʿb or the Shalfūn/Misk translation, but it is clear that *his* text traveled: it is the obvious yet unacknowledged source of Nakhla Qalfāṭ's *Qiṣṣat al-Kūnt dī Mūntū Krīstū* (Story of the Count of Monte Cristo), which was published in Beirut in 1883. Though Shadīd's is rendered in rhyming prose (*sajʿ*) and Qalfāṭ's in unrhymed prose, Qalfāṭ follows Shadīd's condensed narrative organization, omitting many of the same portions and even preserving some of Shadīd's additions. These versions, as objects of circulation as well as meditations on it, raise questions of economic and literary value as problems of translation in a global network of exchange.

An Economy of Literary Relations

The earliest translation of *Monte Cristo*, begun in 1866 in *Al-Shirāka al-shahriyya fī Bayrūt* and completed in 1873 in *Al-Najāḥ*, appeared at a time when bourgeois readers in Beirut were experiencing changes in world economic relations in their daily lives. Since the 1820s, agricultural exports and especially silk had bound the economies of the Mediterranean and were essential factors driving the economic and social changes within Lebanese society. As Roger Owen explains, "the central role of silk in the economic and social life of [Mount Lebanon] is difficult to exaggerate."[23] At the trade's peak, silk thread constituted nearly half of Beirut's exports by value, and silkworm-feeding mulberry trees covered half the cultivated lands in the mountain. This concentration of a commercial crop had wide-ranging consequences for the greater Syrian region: it promoted the exchange of goods for money rather than kind, which in turn increased the need for intraregional trade and infrastructure projects like railways and carriage routes; it created a market for women weavers and pickers who became family wage earners; and it drove local and international investment in factories and therefore the Beirut banking industry. With one-third of silk directly exported to France and most silk factories partially or fully financed by French-protected entrepreneurs and French capitalists, the production and export of silk integrated the region into France's economic and strategic interests—so much so that after the 1860 crisis in Mount Lebanon, French troops rebuilt Christian-owned factories and workshops that had been destroyed and French charitable organizations provided money to purchase new spinning and weaving equipment.[24] People outside the area of silk cultivation were equally impacted, though in different ways: "men of capital" from across the region invested in the mountain-area production and anticipated its profits, and the increasing value of silk exports produced an increase in port activity and a boom in its related industries and helped finance an overall increase in the consumption of imported goods.[25] As a result, French products and people circulated with new visibility in Lebanon and Syria, and public debate ensued about how to properly engage or consume them.[26] Foreign styles, goods, and languages entered everyday social and intellectual life for a growing segment of society, a new pattern of consumption that was itself fueled by wealth produced in maritime trade with Europe.

Simply put, Beirutis increasingly understood their lifeways and livelihoods as inextricably linked to structures of value and taste that came from elsewhere. What is more, they saw these structures of value as ones in which they could participate and from which they could profit. Unlike other foreign-dominated urban economies of the North African and Ottoman Mediterranean, local Beirutis themselves steered Beirut's balance of trade and shared in profits that seemed almost guaranteed.[27] Elizabeth Holt, Jens Hanssen, and others describe a period of confident participation in the local economy and commercial press. As Toufoul Abou-Hodeib explains, the economic environment of the mid- to late nineteenth century created a new class, "those of middling means" (*mutawassiṭ al-ḥāl*) who were "invested in an upward social mobility and the promises of political equality enabled by state reforms" and whose purchase power allowed them to "assert their presence in public spaces and in political and intellectual life."[28] This period was one of simultaneous participation in the local *and* the transnational economy: the promise of upward mobility was often expressed with the anticipation of continued consumption of European goods. Meanwhile, the middling classes could scrupulously track their purchasing power on the international market by reading political and economic news, following currency prices, and checking the import and export valuation tables that often appeared on the back pages of local periodicals. And while this period saw the conditions for economic dependency being laid, as the Ottoman Empire took on ever more loans that would eventually ruin the empire while competition from East Asian silk producers depressed prices and European manufacturers moved their centers of operation to industrialized factories in England and France, its effects were not yet widely felt. Lebanese and Syrian residents were, if for a brief window of time, able to imagine that they participated in a transnational economy on mutually advantageous terms of exchange. They could imagine a world made up of rational and equitable relations.

Indeed, in the 1866 preface to *Amīr jazīrat Mūntū Krīstū*, al-Shalfūn offers the translation itself to his readers as an optimistic example of cultural and linguistic exchange: it is a "noble text that has received wide praise" and that he offers to "those sons of the New Age who possess correct taste."[29] Following *nahḍa* reformist conventions that we explored in chapter 3, he presents the text as a type of "lantern of improvement" but also one that he hopes meets the standards of the discerning consumer public of the current age, who demand quality products: it is an exchange of an object whose value is determined both by its originators (it received wide praise in France) and by its receivers (its new Arab readers). As he continues, "I have striven myself to Arabize and improve [the translation]—knowing that every language has its own merits and particular usages that cannot be overcome—and have divided it into sections according to its narrative order [*tartīb*]. I therefore ask my learned and observant readers to excuse its deficiencies and errors, whether in its translation [*tarjama*] or its Arabization [*taʿrīb*]."[30] Rather than locating value exclusively in an original that might be degraded by an imperfect translation, al-Shalfūn presents the text as both a translation and an Arabization, the result of a two-stage process generated by two different people and adhering to two different sources of value. Error can arise in Ṣaʿb's translation, that is to say, in its attempt to transmit the original meaning, a fact detectable according to the standard of the French source text. But it can also arise in its Arabization, or its attempt to create meaning in Arabic, a fact measurable by the standard of Arabic stylistic norms. The success of translation is negotiated between French *tartīb* and Arabic *taʿrīb*.

As such, translation itself is articulated as what Lydia Liu describes as the circulation of "meaning as value" that places translation "within the political economy of the sign."[31] As she argues, the linguistic and the economic are not merely analogous but "have long evoked and inhabited each other," with both acquiring meaning and value (and meaning as value) through circulation, when a sign or commodity is exchanged with something foreign to itself (whether that is, following Saussure, another sign within the same language or a sign in another language). Much like the valuation tables that appeared alongside the translation in *Al-Najāḥ* and that gave the equivalent value of local and international currencies, al-Shalfūn presents translation as the encounter between two economies of signs, where value is determined between the meaning of the text in French *and* the meaning as it appears in Arabic, two "competing universalisms" that both "hypothesize equivalence."[32] This system—itself a world relation—forgoes the existence of a universal, French meaning or value and a particular, Arabic one in favor of a negotiation of value between the French source and imagined Arab readers. "I have striven myself to Arabize," al-Shalfūn explains, "knowing that every language has its own merits and particular usages that cannot be overcome."[33] Both French and Arabic, that is, are structures of value ("merit") and meaning ("usage") that are complete in and of themselves and between which he is free to negotiate, to make independent choices according to his particular priorities. In the *Al-Shirāka* version of the preface, he makes this explicit, explaining those priorities with this addition: "for my goal was to make [the text] Arab rather than foreignized [*mutafarnaj*]."[34] Al-Shalfūn declares himself free to negotiate between systems of value that he imagines as equal.

The text that al-Shalfūn publishes in both *Al-Shirāka* and *Al-Najāḥ* displays translation techniques that are similarly grounded in a hypothesis of equivalence. Unlike later versions, both adhere closely to the French source, accounting for nearly every line of Dumas's text, including easily condensable dialogue, and follow each of the many chapter breaks—producing, as al-Shalfūn described it in his preface to *Ḥifẓ al-widād*, "a very long novel."[35] These practices, in fact, led to publishing difficulties: he delayed the second monthly installment in *Al-Shirāka* because the text was "too large" and found continuing the project in *Al-Najāḥ* to be so cumbersome that he enlisted at least one other translator to "lighten his workload."[36] Then, in August 1871, al-Shalfūn's co-owner, Lūwīs Ṣābūnjī, announced his resignation from the journal, citing the translation as the primary reason for his exit. In an advertisement Ṣābūnjī took out in *Al-Bashīr*, he announced that he would no longer be participating in the production of the journal or in the translation of *The Count of Monte Cristo*: "We had taken upon ourselves the responsibility of translating [the novel] from French to Arabic while correcting those impolitenesses that transgress religion. In order to lift all responsibility from ourselves for the journal *Al-Najāḥ* as well as responsibility for the impolite language in the novel *Monte Cristo*, the reading of which is forbidden to all Catholics by Rome due to its excessive crudeness against religion, we have issued this announcement without delay, written the 16th of August in the year 1871."[37] While Ṣābūnjī did not in fact leave *Al-Najāḥ* of his own volition but was pressured to do so by the Ottoman *vali* (provincial governor) for reasons unrelated to the ones he cites, his resignation announcement nonetheless points to a conflict he saw between preserving French *tartīb* and his own morals.[38] Notably, his objections are not framed as an indigenous conservative reaction to foreign immorality but as a transnational Catholic one, citing "Rome"—and probably the Catholic Church's *Index Librorum Prohibitorum*, or list of prohibited books, on which Dumas's works had appeared—as the source of his objection. The authority to produce this translation was not attributable to either "French" or "Arabic" systems of valuation narrowly circumscribed but to a *relationship* between these systems. The texts produced are not literal translations but complex negotiations among French narrative order, Arab stylistic norms, religious mores determined by a supranational spiritual body, *and* local social norms.

Some of that impolite language, for example, had been preserved in the *Al-Shirāka* translation but edited from the *Al-Najāḥ* version. The insinuation that Mercédès, a beautiful woman (*jamilāt al-ṣūra*), was "surrounded by young men" in Dantès's absence, for example, is omitted in the latter version; instead, their union is under threat by those who were jealous of a girl of "such fine morals" (*ḥasanat al-akhlāq*).[39] The result is a text that resists easy characterization as either foreignizing or domesticating, as it preserves the French formal characteristics while using sentence structures conventional to *nahḍa*-era prose and selectively Arabizing aspects of its content. It is a negotiation between stylistic and social norms that is often characterized as a negative feature of belated novelistic discourses, where dominant literatures impose conventions that are at odds with local realities and social norms. These "cracks," as Franco Moretti calls them, or "faultline[s] running between story and discourse, world and worldview," throw structure "off balance."[40] Yet whereas Ṣābūnjī saw a crack between world and worldview that prevented him from continuing to work on the translation, al-Shalfūn apparently saw none. *Krīstū* continued to be serialized until at least 1873.[41] Instead of an inconsistency signaling an underlying dysfunction, itself identifiable only if we measure the text against an original standard, we can see a translation ideology of choice and negotiation that sees no contradiction between following foreign *tartīb* and producing an "Arabized" text.

Both the translation ideology and content of the al-Shalfūn publications allow the reader to imagine an international field of free exchange. Like Dumas's version, the translated version is peppered with scenes of unproblematic translation, intercultural communication, and travel. Characters communicate in multiple languages—Cristo himself speaks French, English, Italian, and Arabic—without so much as a misunderstanding, let alone the intercession of a translator. And the Count appears and reappears in far-flung locations without an intervening explication of the means of his travel. Yet, far from translating readers into a fantasy of extraordinary imperial power, al-Shalfūn's translation renders these feats as ordinary. Multilingualism and cultural pluralism are described as familiar, rather than exotic, features of Mediterranean life. The Catalan community of Dantès's lover, which in French is described as "une colonie mystérieuse [qui] arrivait on ne savait d'où et parlait une langue inconnue" (a mysterious colony that arrived from no one knows where and spoke an unknown language), for example, is instead quickly explained as an unremarkable minority community living in France: the Catalans are described as "a group of Spanish people who long ago arrived in France [and who] preserved the customs [*iṣṭalaḥāt*] and language of their country."[42] Addressing readers receiving the text in Ottoman Syria and to whom linguistic, religious, and ethnic diversity would have been legible, or even everyday, experiences, al-Shalfūn registers the differences between this minority community and the French majority as matters of fact. He even describes their houses, which in French are "moitié maure" (half Moorish) and therefore "bizarre et pittoresque," as nothing more than "houses that look like those in their country."[43] The exoticism deriving from their foreign origins is simply edited out. Al-Shalfūn makes such plurality an ordinary fact of life, not the result of extraordinary feats of power or "bizarre" migrations.

In the *Al-Najāḥ* continuation, similarly, the disbelief that Dantès feels when his prison mentor explains his multilingual reading abilities is not because Abbé Faria's faculties are "presque surnaturelles" (almost supernatural) but because Dantès suspects the Abbé of exaggerating: "Dantès looked at him with surprise and disbelief after hearing this untruth, and the Abbé saw signs of his doubt."[44] For *Al-Najāḥ*'s Dantès, such multilingualism is not fantastic so much as it is merely unlikely, as is the Abbé's method for language learning: memorizing a key of one thousand words in five languages that he "arranged, combined, turned, and returned" until he could express himself in each.[45] Using a method that works through data compression and extrapolation, the Abbé teaches Dantès techniques for language learning that minimize linguistic particularity and cultural difference.[46] His techniques resemble forms of machine translation, in which words are correlated with the use of multilingual dictionaries, a technique of word-by-word substitution that Lisa Parks has described as "linguistic liquidity," allowing users "to seamlessly permeate language barriers and access forms of cultural consciousness that were previously inaccessible," effectively "effac[ing] the foreign language environment and the challenge of navigating through it" as if through water.[47] Dantès, after escaping from prison, uses that same methodology to navigate the Mediterranean and its social environments. His first social act after his rescue at sea, in fact, is to pose as a Maltese sailor, an act made possible because he "knew nearly all the languages spoken around this large lake they call the Mediterranean, from the Arabic to the Provençal."[48] He could combine and remix these languages to approximate Maltese, a language to which Karla Malette assigns the characteristic of "fluidity," as Maltese speakers "are able to select between the Arabic and Romance lexemes [in the language] with relative ease."[49] In this way, Dantès was able to communicate *fluidly* without interpreters, "who were always troublesome and often indiscreet."[50] In al-Shalfūn's version, Dantès's ability to master transportation and communication derives from a linguistic ideology that poses all languages as perfectly exchangeable, a fluent system that reflects a belief in an equal field of intercultural exchange in which he and his contemporaries could participate. In this field, multilingualism saturates every cultural actor to such an extent that translation itself becomes superfluous. Dantès, the merchant-mariner turned multilingual smuggler and international man of mystery, stands as the perfect avatar for the translator in the boom period of Mediterranean exchange, who could imagine himself as circulating and trading in a context of liquid fungibility, seemingly unconstrained by systems of power or stable regimes of difference.

Colonial Connectivity

If the *Al-Shirāka / Al-Najāḥ* translation of *Monte Cristo* imagines the Mediterranean economy of the sign as a liberal one that renders the global exchange of ideas and languages accessible to ordinary residents, Shadīd's 1871 translation and its 1883 retranslation by Nakhla Qalfāṭ in Beirut made visible the power structures that enabled and constrained these transnational flows. Around the same time that al-Shalfūn planned to restart *Amīr Krīstū* in *Al-Najāḥ*, a Lebanese emigré in Alexandria, Bishāra Shadīd, began work on his own translation of the text, *Qiṣṣat al-Kūnt dū Mūntū Krīstū*. Contemporaneous and yet a world away, his text introduces a literary relation more vexed than the simple negotiation among equal forms and styles. Apparently having never seen the lone *Al-Shirāka* episode, he explains in his introduction that he "regretted that it was not to be found in Arabic libraries or mentioned in any of our literary texts" and so began the "considerable effort" it took to condense it and make a "riwāya ʿarabiyya" (Arabic novel) of the French source. Shadīd highlights the scholarly "effort" it took to "pour the text into an Arabic mold," the class politics of his language choice (he uses "ordinary language," as he states), and the structures of literary authority that govern the conferral of value on the text (its mention in "literary texts") and even the text's authenticity. He went as far as to seek permission from Dumas himself before beginning his work (though he does not mention if he received it): unlike al-Shalfūn, Shadīd did not consider himself to have unfettered freedom of choice.

Twelve years later in Beirut, Nakhla Qalfāṭ, perhaps via the bookshop he owned at the time, Maktabat Sūriyā, had clearly obtained a copy of Shadīd's translation. His version follows Shadīd's abridgement and organization, uses the same twelve chapter breaks, and maintains its added scenes. Though in places his text clearly shows that he had recourse to the French source, we might think of his version, which prosifies Shadīd's *saj'*, as an intralingual translation of Shadīd's text. As Qalfāṭ carefully words it on the title page, he had "translated from the French language" and "arranged [literally, "cast in an Arabic mold"] and corrected" the text. His translation was doubly constrained, by the original text and the precedent translation. Qalfāṭ, perhaps as a result, places an even stronger emphasis on authority and convention, which he identifies as limitations on his translation choices:

> May God be praised for leading me to this story and for the knowledge he gave me and the understanding he bestowed to my mind. By his power, it will be accepted by the *khāṣ* and the *'āmm* for the easiness of its expression. . . . I did not attempt to amend or correct it more than what is in my ability to do so and have cast it into an Arabic mold knowing that the general opinion of readers of novels and stories is an inclination toward a style that they can read easily, understanding [the text] from inside out and outside in.[51] I therefore ask forgiveness from every dignified cultured [reader] and do not ask about the blameworthy censures.[52]

For Qalfāṭ and Shadīd, translation is not a choice between equally compelling literary conventions but a compromised act dictated by different publics, the "general opinion" of readers, the original author, and God. Both figure translation as pouring the French into an Arabic mold, a well-known but not frequently used expression for translating. They saw their role as shaping the text into a *preexisting* form, according to rules established outside their own tastes and inclinations. They acknowledge those unequal structures of power that enable and constrain global flows.

While the constraining force of law, the market, and literary convention structure both of these later translations, they do not yield postures of inferiority in relation to French literary values. The Qalfāṭ and Shadīd versions begin, for example, not with the arrival of the protagonist or his ship but—in a significant and telling departure from the source text—with Napoleon, described as "the valiant hero, he of might and magnanimity" whose return "the people of France were awaiting . . . with their hearts full of affection and compassion."[53] Readers with an eye to colonial history might be surprised to learn that these translations portray Napoleon in a positive light, adding praising epithets to his name and interjecting new paragraphs describing him as a beloved leader and man "of the people" (*al-sha'b*).[54] Yet this was not uncommon. Imagining themselves to be *like the French*, who were themselves like "people" the world over who aspired to a society of equals under the law,

Arabic readers appropriated Napoleon as a symbol of that aspiration that belonged equally to them. (Indeed, in a biography of Napoleon translated in 1868 and later distributed to Egyptian soldiers, he is described as "the greatest *kāmūkrātū*," or democrat, in Europe.)[55] If Dumas's earlier translators hypothesized equality between Arabic and French meaning-value structures, here we see the formation of equivalences from structures that are contextualized within an unequal politics. Napoleon—whose colonizing troops invaded the very port where Shadīd currently resides—stands, ironically, as a universal symbol of freedom. Here we see evidence that, as Shaden Tageldin notes, "the very *ground of competition itself* is not neutral under (post)colonial conditions."[56] Like the *Al-Shiraka/Al-Najāḥ* translations, these texts propose their translation as an exchange of equivalents, but they do so by showing us the condition of unequal exchange that structures colonial translations.[57] The Arabic text is not naturally or automatically equivalent to the French but must be made as such.

Qalfāṭ and Shadīd only mention the *Pharaon*, in fact, halfway through both texts' first page, as merely "one of the ships" that illegally passed near the island of Elba during Napoleon's imprisonment. Shadīd adds "600 guards" who stood watch over the imprisoned emperor, and in Qalfāṭ's translation, they passed by Elba "despite the warnings and surveillance of the current government."[58] Thus, both translators create a pointedly political frame around the scene of the ship's arrival and indeed around Dantès's story as a whole. The arrival becomes an act of illicit circulation, in which the political institutions that structure Mediterranean mobility move from context to text. In part, we might ascribe this move to the fact that residents of Cairo in 1871 and Beirut in 1883 perceived these structures more acutely than did Beirutis during the silk boom of the 1860s. In Egypt, where Wādī al-Nīl Press published Bishāra Shadīd's *Qiṣṣat al-Kūnt dū Muntū Krīstū*, the Mediterranean mobility of Cristo that Dumas and al-Shalfūn idealized was beyond the reach of most Egyptians. While the successive khedives removed restrictions on the movement of goods and capital, authorizing development projects with European financing and technical expertise and creating legal structures that enticed European immigration and investment, they restricted the movement of vast numbers of Egyptians. In fact, the very projects that today signify increased mobility for regional people and products—railways, commercial steamships, and the mass production of consumer goods—were sites of immobility for vast numbers of Egyptians. Forced labor (*corvée*) and debt defined the lives of hundreds of thousands of conscripts building railways and farming cotton fields—Egypt's main export crop.[59] Large prisons, such as the *liman* of Alexandria, the arsenal established to produce Muḥammad ʿAlī's naval and commercial fleet, functioned effectively as labor camps for "all kinds of people the authorities had declared 'outlaws.'"[60] And European-managed factories forcibly recruited workers from nearby villages, tattooing their arms with the names of their factories to prevent desertion.[61] The worldwide mobility achieved in this period, culminating in the Suez Canal's opening in 1869 as the "nodal point and lynchpin of . . . global interconnection" that resulted in great wealth for European institutions and citizens, was produced by the heavy regulation and restriction of Egyptians' movements.[62]

Beirut, too, the site of the other later translation, saw an increased European dominance of Mediterranean trade at the expense of Ottoman sovereignty and economic health. Both Egypt and the Ottoman Empire took on increasing debt to cover large-scale infrastructure projects. Over the course of the 1870s, the khedive's trade deals and loans allowed European powers to establish control over Egypt's finances, effectively taking control of the state itself. In Lebanon, meanwhile, the intervening years between al-Shalfūn's first installment of *Al-Shirāka* and Qalfāṭ's 1883 *Qiṣṣat al-Kūnt dī Mūntū Krīstū* saw the Levantine provinces enter a similarly dependent relationship with Europe and mainly France. The 1870s brought increased competition from East Asian silk producers, as well as the devastating blows of silkworm disease and failures in local egg cultivation, which resulted in factories relying on eggs imported by the same French silk traders who then bought their finished products at more favorable rates.[63] At the same time, the number of European factory-made goods (often mimicking local styles) going to the Levantine provinces dramatically increased, nearly tripling by the 1870s. By 1883, Ottoman provinces were importing more than they were exporting, as cheap, European-made textiles put pressure on local manufacturers. What Buṭrus al-Bustānī called "the global chain"[64] integrated Aleppans, Beirutis, and Damascenes on terms set by European manufacturing powers.

Dumas's translators would have been acutely aware of the institutions that shaped the movement and valuation of circulating goods, as they had both in their lives been subject to the financial, political, and religious structures that govern movement on the Mediterranean. The translator of the Cairo edition, Shadīd, who an 1859 newspaper listed as one of the founding members of the Syrian Scientific Society in Beirut, was by August 1869 living in Alexandria, where he was trying to make a name for himself as an *adīb*.[65] He was one of the many Syro-Lebanese immigrants to Egypt who made up the center of Egyptian literary and journalistic production (and are often claimed as Egyptian in national literary accounts) but yet have been excluded from accounts of Alexandrian cosmopolitanism that lie at the heart of scholarly understanding of Egypt's literary efflorescence.[66] Such images of Alexandria—those of Lawrence Durrell, E. M. Forster, and C. P. Cavafy—focus mainly on the city's

European elites, many of them foreign merchants, who enjoyed freedom of trade, exemption from taxation, and trials in separate consular courts. Arabophone foreigners like Shadīd, however, circulated in the Mediterranean without such exceptional status and often immigrated out of necessity rather than choice—they were compelled to mobility by the exigencies arising from civil war and economic depression. In the case of Nakhla Qalfāṭ (1851–1905), the translator of the 1883 Beirut edition, those exigencies also included governmental pressures. Qalfāṭ, a well-known author, publisher, and translator from Persian, Turkish, and French, made his living from the circulation of texts under the increasing censorship of the Ottoman state. After having been convicted of "provoking discord among the people" and losing all his assets because of the activities of his Beirut journal *Silsilat al-fukāhāt fī aṭāyib al-riwāyāt* (Series of entertainments found in the most amusing novels), he emigrated to Egypt, only to move back in 1901 when he received permission to open another bookshop in Beirut. Authorities again arrested him three years later for selling proscribed books, and they sentenced him to three years of prison with hard labor.[67] This last sentence ended his life; he was released after one year in failing health and died just days afterward.

These translators experienced nineteenth-century transportation networks in ways that undermined the fantasy of travel in Dumas's source text. The Count is distinguished by his extraordinary mobility—his ability to seemingly be anywhere at any moment he chooses—and therefore extraordinary power. As David Bell notes in his study of speed in nineteenth-century fiction, the Count's wealth—which he finds buried on an uninhabited island and therefore outside the social and economic orders that usually structure identity and mobility—allow him to operate outside the structures of time and place that seem to govern other characters. He moves faster and farther not only than the other characters in the novel but also than "anyone—fictional or nonfictional—in the period."[68] Dumas stages elaborate scenes of overland travel in which Cristo seems to fly in coaches so expensive that "not even a king could afford them" and can obtain information with his own private relay system that "not only outpaces the railroad" but "moves faster than the telegraph."[69] In doing so, Dumas helped his readers participate not only in a fantasy of power and wealth but also in the pleasures of world-making that power provides: as scholars in technology studies have repeatedly argued, these fictional representations of spatiotemporal compression joined contemporaneous efforts to standardize global time, itself a tool of territorial conquest.[70] Dumas's novel is therefore not only one of the first nineteenth-century portraits of empire but one of the first portraits of a specifically imperial mode of globality. It shows how empire, itself a communications and transportation network, "brought together far-reaching and disparate regions of the globe under the controlling power of nation-states."[71]

The two later translations, however, treat international mobility with more circumspection than did Dumas's text or even al-Shalfūn's translation. Both Shadīd and Qalfāṭ circumscribe or regulate the extraordinary freedom with which the Count circulates. In order to explain his ability to pose as "Lord Wilmore," for example (or "the Englishman," as in *Al-Najāḥ*), Shadīd adds that the Count uses "an English passport," a fact that occurs much later and more incidentally in the French source; Qalfāṭ augments the scene even more, emphasizing the illegality of the act by changing this to "he bought a passport from an Englishman."[72] Instead of an extraordinary ability to travel seemingly without regard for boundaries or law, the Count is subject to the same limits that bind the rest of the characters, who must obtain and present their passports when they travel.[73] Even in one of the best-known scenes, when the Count bribes the telegraph operator into transmitting false information that causes the financial ruin of an enemy, Qalfāṭ adds legal consequences (though not for the Count) to the act. The authorities, instead of attributing the operator's "error" to fog, as they do in Dumas's text, find him criminally negligent and sentence him to a few days in prison.[74] In each case, Shadīd and Qalfāṭ reorient the Count's movements.

Shadīd and Qalfāṭ also transform the Count into a character who must grapple with the mundane logistics of travel and translation. Whereas French readers delighted in the sudden appearance of the Count in a new location or wondered at the speed and ease with which he traveled, Shadīd's and Qalfāṭ's readers were treated to demystifying explanations of the protagonist's surprise appearances. When Dantès appears as the Italian priest and as an English lord, Qalfāṭ gives away his identity to the reader almost immediately, introducing him in the latter case as "the Englishman who was really Edmund."[75] Similarly, when Dantès makes a clandestine appearance in Marseille to repair his previous benefactor's finances and is at first described in French only as a man "with his face half-covered by a black beard," Shadīd and Qalfāṭ not only immediately reveal that "this man was Edmund our hero" but insert an explanation of how Dantès came to be able to perform such a feat, as well as how he achieved his transformation from Edmund to the Count.[76] "I will now explain to you [the reader] in great detail," Shadīd explains in his rhyming prose, filling in gaps in the narrative:

> After he parted toward Jacopo he went * and both toward Italy bent * then to "Sublime Gate" * and the Levantine states * for Edmund, after he had sold his jewels * in the city of Istanbul * could not enter Europe

> with so much capital and so to the Eastern provinces he was conveyed * where for a period of time he stayed * and then to Italy with its known illustriousness * and there bought the Island of Monte Cristo from the government * and named himself its Count * and stayed on that island after he had refurbished the cave in that mount * in which he found his fortune * and furnished it with the finest of provisions * silk furnishings and shining dishes * and then decorated it * and returning over time to improve it * though he never stayed in a fixed place after then * as he was continually searching for his enemies to bring them to their end * to the extent that in his rage he could not sleep * thinking of how he would treat those to blame * And the rest will follow * so you will permit us [to continue] now, oh generous [readers].[77]

To this, Qalfāṭ adds additional details:

> After he left Muriel he headed toward his companion Jacopo in his boat, and they sailed toward Italy, where he spent a few days, and then on to Constantinople, where he sold all the gems he had acquired [from the Island of Monte Cristo]. As he was not able to enter Europe with so much capital, he sailed to the Eastern provinces, where he stayed a long time before returning to Italy to purchase the Island of Monte Cristo. He resided there for a time, to renovate the cave where he had found his treasure and then ready it with household items, carpets, and furniture he had brought with him from the Levant [*al-mashriq*], so that it looked as if it were the grandest of castles. From that moment he called himself the Count of Monte Cristo and began traveling the cities and seas, searching for his enemies and returning to his beloved island. This was his tireless pursuit for a long time.[78]

Giving away the central mystery of the text—which lingered over many installments in the French source text—we learn in these two versions about Dantès's sojourn in Italy, the sale of his treasure in Istanbul, his purchase of the island, and his renaming of himself as the Count. Much of this explanatory information is gleaned from details that are stated in or hinted at in the French text but that never appear together as a unit of narrative—French readers would have instead pieced them together over the chapters to come. Arabic readers, by contrast, not only learn information for which their French counterparts would have had to wait but also receive details that appear nowhere in the original text: while Edmund certainly had spent time in Istanbul (that is where he bought his slave, Haydée), there is no mention of his having sold his jewels there. Nor is there a mention of a limitation on the transfer of currency; in the French text, the treasure includes coins as well as jewels, which he conveys without incident directly to Marseille. It is yet another example of the addition of legal obstacles to Cristo's movements—exchange, whether of currency or language, is subject to regulation.

By inserting this passage, the translators override Dumas's signature narrative device of transitioning abruptly from one scene to the next (usually via a chapter break), making Cristo appear unexpectedly in places far from where the reader last encountered him.[79] Indeed, in French, this chapter ends just after Edmund alights on the yacht, and the next chapter begins in Italy eight years later. When the French reader next encounters Edmund, he is already installed as the Count in his underground palace. Yet instead of delighting in the Count's quasi-supernatural ability to defy spatiotemporal constraints, the Arabic reader follows his itinerary step by step and finds that his mobility is limited by international maritime regulations and motivated by such mundane projects as home furnishing. In doing so, Shadīd and Qalfāṭ add information that prepares their readers for unexpected scenes to come and blunts some of their mystery: a sojourn in *al-bilād al-sharqiyya* (the Levantine provinces) explains why we next encounter the Count in his strange guise as Sindbad the Sailor as well as why he lives in an exotically furnished cave, and the addition of the details of his journeys to and from the island and his many sleepless nights prepare the reader for the unanticipated amount of time that will pass between the chapters.[80]

In these and other passages, Shadīd and Qalfāṭ emphasize the passage of time rather than its marvelous compression, whether it is in the Count's "returning over time" to remodel the cave or in his "continual searching" for his enemies or—as in Qalfāṭ—in his "tireless pursuit" of revenge that lasted "a long time." If, as scholars of technological modernity have argued, the innovations in communication and transport that arose in the nineteenth century allowed for an imaginative participation in empire's compression of space and time, these translations offer an alternative model of temporality that *de*compresses space and time, filling it with excessive details of the Count's travels and projects, marking the repetitive passage of time with sleep and relays to and from the island. Shadīd and Qalfāṭ leave no narrative gap unfilled, inserting explanatory details, flagging aspects of the text so that "the intelligent reader will have noticed" them, and adding seemingly superfluous information that one could characterize as spoiling the reader's surprise.[81]

Though Shadīd and Qalfāṭ condensed Dumas's sprawling prose considerably (squeezing over 1,000 French pages into 230 and 150 pages, respectively), these and other techniques nonetheless created a slower experience of reading. They omit long sections of dialogue and combine chapters but also add elements that open digressions, make intertextual references, or otherwise lead the reader away from the events of the plot. Shadīd translated in the rhyming prose (*sajʿ*) common in both the *maqāmāt* of the twelfth century and contemporary neoclassical compositions and omitted all punctuation save asterisks that separated each rhyming phrase (which I have attempted to reproduce in the preceding quotation); Qalfāṭ, while he did not translate into *sajʿ*, used unpunctuated prose, in which Arabic dialogue markers such a *qāla* (he said) are substituted for the line breaks that appear in the French. Both also used strategies common in oral narration, inserting lines of poetry to demonstrate emotional states, embedding narratives to explain character's stories, and using epithets to assign character traits (referring to Dantès's nemesis, Danglars, as "Danklār al-Khā'in dhū al-Khibātha," Danglars the Traitor the Malicious One).[82] At several points, the translations even make explicit reference to those oral narrations, such as after a young nobleman encounters Dantès in the guise of Sindbad, when the translations add that he awakes the next morning in his own bed "like Abu Hasan al-Saʿīd with the Sultan Hārūn al-Rashīd."[83] These translation techniques create what Tzvetan Todorov called "narrative men" of Dumas's characters, which themselves extend narratives into seemingly endless chains of supplementation. "Such is the incessant proliferation of narratives in this marvelous story-machine," he writes of *The Arabian Nights*.[84] Like Spivak's description of value, there is no logical end to the supplementary mode. It is always on the move, in a state of constant deferral.

Translation itself, as it is represented in the novel, transforms from an immediate process to a lengthy one whose intermediaries are visible and multiple. The Count of Shadīd and Qulfāṭ is regularly in need of interpreters, whereas the French Count was not: he receives a note via a translator rather than from his servant directly; he speaks French mixed with Spanish (or simply in Spanish, in Qalfāṭ's version) rather than Italian-accented French when he appears as an Italian priest; and when he appears as Lord Wilmore, he speaks "in translation" rather than simply in English.[85] Coupled with more stylized linguistic techniques—rhyming prose in the case of Shadīd—these versions make linguistic difference manifest. It is only fitting, then, that the last and most emotional denouement appears after a prolonged multichapter narrative that relies on representations of translation. After having been paralyzed by a stroke, an ally of the Count, Monsieur Noirtier, communicates with his granddaughter by moving his eyes in code; whereas in the French version, she simply "understands his language," in both Shadīd and Qalfāṭ, she "translates" for him.[86] Along multiple performances of linguistic interpretation, at times with the aid of a dictionary, she helps her grandfather cause the downfall of Dantès's most hated enemy. Rather than seemingly fantastic displays of seamless intersemiotic communication—with the Count simply understanding and being understood in the language of his convenience—these translators highlight the negotiations, false starts, and even labor that such communication often requires.

These translation techniques guide uninitiated readers through plot elements or through the workings of the *feuilleton*'s narrative suspense, but they also create a new experience of reading Dumas that prioritizes description over surprise—a prioritization that itself points to important differences in the political unconscious described by the two texts. French readers would have experienced Cristo's "miraculous rapidity" as a form of literary pleasure that delights in the novel's suspense but also in its fantastic aesthetic recuperation of imperial power over time and space and its imagination of a Mediterranean still dominated by French financial and military power. Rather than invoking the magical power of a character from *The Thousand and One Nights*, for example, "Arabian" decorations (in fact, several references to the *Nights* are omitted) are described according to their specific origins and means of acquisition: in the passage quoted earlier, the reader learns that the furniture is brought back over many years from the Levant; later, in the description of Sindbad's cave, we learn that his carpets are Persian, his chairs Syrian, his *tarbūsh* Moroccan, and his girdle Egyptian.[87] Instead of a fantasy of quasi-supernatural imperial power over a broadly identified "East," we see the banality of commerce from individual locations. We are invited to imagine Cristo shuttling between his island and the ports of the eastern Mediterranean, picking out dishes, testing chairs and tables, considering the shine of fabrics. As a shopper, rather than a mysterious adventurer, Sindbad does not transcend or control the Mediterranean economy but merely participates in it.

The additions and reformulations of Shadīd and Qalfāṭ might have seemed unremarkable to their readers, as what they emphasize above all are the borders—both geographic and linguistic—that ordinary people would have had to negotiate in order to travel among and even reside in Mediterranean port cities. Contrary to the image created in a dominant strain of the "oceanic turn" in literary studies, which sees the water as borderless alternative to the violence of national and imperial boundaries on land, Shadīd's and Qalfāṭ's translations represent no movement without the negotiation of political boundaries, the law, or the threat of violence. Even the son of Morrel, a character whose life the Count works secretly to improve, is described not just as a "war hero" but as one who in Shadīd "had killed Algerians."[88] Here, even a sympathetic character is implicated in imperial violence; in reminding the readers that the hidden context of this scene is the Algerian conquest, Shadīd constructs a setting in which there is no imagined escape from political realities and in which mobility itself relies on empire, which governs the Mediterranean's flows. Instead of a "trackless" sea that offered "freedom of movement . . . available to anyone on the globe," those waters as well as the port towns of its shores were the sites of the proliferation of borders and differences.[89] As Julia Clancy-Smith shows in her research on the port activity of Tunis, "the growing cosmopolitanism of Tunis (and Alexandria, Beirut, and Istanbul, to name only a few) was both cause and consequence of the legal-political imbroglios unleashed by people on the move, who crossed borders as they called into existence new kinds of borders."[90] The "multilingual street" found in these port cities or in the multilingual crews of ships like the smugglers' boat that Cristo boards was never seamless or without conflict: legal disputes, violent brawls, and jurisdictional conflicts characterized and even shaped the particular cosmopolitanism of the nineteenth-century Mediterranean. Similarly, Shadīd's and Qalfāṭ's translations show that (as a historian of the Ottoman Empire puts it) "that sea is indelibly fragmented into ports, islands, coasts, and their attendant interiors" but more importantly that traversing this fragmented space required the negotiation of political boundaries and local laws and held the potential for violence.[91]

At stake in these variations is no less than the world itself. As the Count tells one of his enemies,

> Kingdoms are bounded, either by mountains, rivers, or a difference in practices or in a mutation of language. My own kingdom is as vast as the world, for I am neither an Italian, nor a Frenchman, nor a Hindu, nor an American, nor a Spaniard: I am a cosmopolitan. . . . I adopt all customs, speak all languages. You believe me to be a Frenchman, don't you, for I speak French with the same facility and purity as yourself. Well! Ali, my Nubian, thinks I am Arab; Bertuccio, my steward, a Roman; Haydée, my slave, thinks me a Greek. So you understand, that as I am of no country, ask protection from no government, recognize no man as my brother, that not one of the scruples that restrain the powerful, nor the obstacles that paralyze the weak, paralyze or restrain me.[92]

In Qalfāt and Shadīd, instead of a "cosmopolitan" whose kingdom's limits are only the world itself, he is merely "not like other men." Shadīd's abbreviated translation, which is almost identical to Qalfāṭ's, reads, "My servant Artīchū believes me to be from his country of Corsica, and my servant Ali believes me to be from the Arab countries; I have a *rūmī* daughter named ʿĀ'ida who thinks I am from her own country and speaks to me in her language."[93] Neither makes reference to the world or to an unbounded kingdom of power but only to the more mundane issues of the Count's particular transnational grudges. None of his companions, the Arabic Count adds, "knows the truth of my condition," but this is not that he is a world citizen but that he marshals these impressive skills and resources to search for a group of men who wronged him, in order to "take revenge upon them one by one."[94] The reference to "the world" and the cosmopolitan, in fact, is omitted in all of the four Arabic translations: there may be transnational connections, communications, and mobility, but they do not merge into a single world-picture.

Rather, they do not merge into Dumas's world picture. As Pheng Cheah reminds us, world citizenship is not a claim that can be proved empirically. Because one cannot *see* the entire world, "the cosmopolitan optic is not one of perceptual experience" but is "given to us by the imagination."[95] Dumas's Count here does not so much enumerate the actual conditions of his world citizenship but claim a *particular* imaginative relationship to the world, one that correlates to a form of power that places him above the law, bounded not by earthly dominions and their rulers but by the limitless boundaries of the globe itself. Or, as Eric Hayot argues, novels both "have certain *kinds* of worlds" and propose a certain "idea of the world."[96] To paraphrase Martin Heidegger, on whom both Cheah and Hayot rely, the work *worlds*. It proposes a system of meaning, whether that totality is called empire, globalization, or a world system, that governs relationships between the parts within the whole. Here, in the process of circulation, it is the world itself that is a vanishing semblance. It has no stable, intrinsic meaning but is made by putting together disparate parts of the globe and making them communicate—the globe itself is a set of relations, of necessary but inadequate translations. When a work is translated, it does not just engage a new worldly context but "worlds the world" anew, proposing new sets of relationships between the parts within the whole that not only reflect economic and power relationships but also seek to correct or realign them. By stressing the logistics of travel and portraying the Count as in need of a passport or an interpreter, Shadīd and Qalfāṭ enact a translation strategy that reimagines the world, worlds the world anew.

Chapter 5

The Novel in the Age of the Comparative World Picture

Jules Verne's Colonial Worlds

The popularity of *The Count of Monte Cristo* came at the leading edge of a much larger Arabophone imaginative interest in transnational communications and transportation networks. *Nahḍa* readers regularly encountered advertisements for foreign-produced publications, overseas letter and package delivery services, and foreign distribution of local periodicals; notices announcing the construction of telegraph cables and the establishment of postal systems; and articles following the opening of steamship and railway lines. *Al-Najāḥ* and *Al-Bashīr*, for example, regularly featured announcements alerting readers to the names of the international steamships docked in the Beirut harbor, while the Egyptian journals *Al-Hilāl* and *Al-Muqtaṭaf* published articles detailing the number of telegraphs sent or miles of cable laid in various parts of the world. Nor was this interest confined to the Arabophone reading public. The opening of the Suez Canal was itself an international media event: Arab newspapers—like their European and American counterparts—covered the 1866 connection of the American continent to Europe by telegraphic cables, the 1869 linking of the Union and Central Pacific Railroads to span the coasts of the United States, and the 1870 incorporation of the Indian railways that allowed travel from Bombay to Calcutta.

By the last quarter of the century, the world itself had become a common unit of analysis. Articles quantifying the "railroads of the world" or "newspapers of the world" appeared with increasing frequency,[1] as did those explaining modes of travel "around the world" and comparative essays that explained differences between "areas of the world."[2] Readers could understand themselves as living in the same world as people far away. They had a railroad *too*, that is: the Egyptian, Syrian, or Iraqi railroad was one of the "railroads of the world"; it was understood as belonging to a larger global series of railroads. The translations of *Monte Cristo* and other fictions of connectivity joined these reports of connectivity to allow readers to participate in the worldwide reimagination of the worldwide.

In January 1872, in fact, readers in Beirut learned that they themselves could circle the entire globe. Between other news of transnational circulations—an account of a mobile haunting in which spirits followed a French family to multiple locations ("it is the truth, though inexplicable") and an update on international prices for coffee, sugar, and rice—readers of the Catholic weekly *Al-Bashīr* encountered a news item entitled "A Trip that Takes the Traveler around the World." "It was reported in the *Trade Gazette*," this notice began, "that one can see, hanging on the walls of the city of San Francisco in America, a notice advertising a trip around the globe in the span of 82 days." After enumerating the itinerary and distance of each leg ("Hong Kong to Calcutta, 3,500 miles"), the author explains that the reader can make the same trip even more quickly and with more convenience: "Circling the globe in just forty minutes," he explains, would soon be possible with the telegraph, once the line between America and Japan is completed.[3] Members of the *nahḍa* reading public could read about a connected world, as well as travel it, metaphorically and literally. Communications and transportations networks acted as both figure and ground to the global imaginings of this readership.

Indeed, in the case of representing the world, the material and the imaginary were often, and often necessarily, fused. In September 1874, two years after the advertisement for a trip around the world appeared in *Al-Bashīr*, the same readers learned of another journey, entitled *Al-Riḥla al-jawwiyya fī al-markaba al-huwāʾiyya al-maʿrūfa bi al-bālūn* (Air voyage in the flying vessel known as the ballon), which was "summarized" from Jules Verne's *Cinq semaines en ballon* (1863).[4] Serialized until November of the next year, this translation appeared alongside factual accounts of long-distance travel and was even ambiguously presented as one. Though it appeared below the bar in the section previously devoted to narrative fiction, it was not labeled as a *qiṣṣa* (a fictional narrative) as the previous serialized narratives were.[5] Instead, it was simply described more generally as a *kitāb*, or book, about "a voyage from East to West Africa" in a balloon. Compounding this ambiguity was the fact that it was interrupted by several long factual articles about travel and exploration: "Research in Geography and Cartography" and "British Expedition to the

Kerguelen Islands" replace the narrative for an issue, while "The Benefits of English Scientific Exploration to the North Pole" interrupts it for three consecutive weeks.[6] The voyage recounted in this *kitāb* could have taken place in the real world or a fictional one.

This fusing of the imaginative and the material worlds is no sign of epistemological naiveté. Journal producers did not interpose these genres because they mistook fiction for fact. They did so because they participated in the central ideological project of late nineteenth-century globality: the transformation of all of the diverse areas and peoples of the world into a single, legible, and interconnected entity. "The fundamental event of the modern age," as Martin Heidegger argued, "is the conquest of the world as picture," which is itself "the world conceived and grasped as a picture . . . in its entirety."[7] Far from a solely empirical process, that is, the making of globality was also a procedure of the imagination and one that required new techniques, aesthetics, and forms. Literary and cultural studies scholarship has excavated many of these, showing how the adventure novel, the urban realist novel, the sketch, the panorama, and the world's fairs were all late nineteenth-century forms that reflected and shaped this "new global consciousness."[8] And because the world until the Apollo 8 mission in 1968 presented a representational problem—it was a totality that could never wholly be visible—even scientific representations of it required the work of the imagination. World maps, globes, and atlases, all of which gained in popularity in Europe as explorers mapped what they saw as the last remaining undiscovered spaces, were manufactured using what a literary scholar might call figurative means: extrapolations, abstractions, and projections. Indeed, though the global is often assumed to refer to an objective empirical object, it should actually be seen as a mode of thought, or what Sanjay Krishnan calls "thematization."[9] More than individual methods of representation, it is "an instituted perspective" for bringing the whole diverse world into view.[10] Or, as Heidegger remarked, globality is the institutionalization of a "world-view."[11]

The thematization of the world, what literary scholars currently call "worlding," was precisely the work that Jules Verne's novels performed. As Verne himself described the fifty-four novels that constitute his *Voyages Extraordinaires*, their very task was "to portray the entire earth, the entire world, under the form of the novel," using what his publisher, Pierre-Jules Hetzel, described as the "knowledge . . . amassed by modern science."[12] It is this facet of his writing—the "recycling of facts, figures, and statistics" that "incorporate and perforate the modern"—that has prompted Verne scholars to describe his novels as emblematic of modernity itself.[13] It was the means by which Verne produced his worldview, which, as Heidegger argues, allows man to mark the realm of human action as "a domain given over to measuring and executing, for the purpose of gaining mastery over that which *is* as a whole."[14] World-picturing and world-conquest, as chapter 4 argued, were commingled in both fact and fiction. What Verne's fiction shows us is that the very mingling of fiction and fact was a technique of both.[15]

Translations of Verne's fiction made the world available to their readers as a single discursive unit, during a decade (largely from the mid-1880s to the mid-1890s) in which the material conditions of globality were not only economic and physical precarity but increased government involvement in bodily and family autonomy and movement, as well as direct colonial rule. Starting with a *Al-Riḥla al-jawwiyya*, which was reprinted at least once in 1884, eight editions of four works attributed to Verne were published before the turn of the century. And all but one of these—*Al-Riḥla al-jawwiyya*—was published in colonial Egypt: translations of both *Voyage au centre de la terre* (*Al-Riḥla al-ʿilmiyya fī qalb al-kura al-arḍiyya*; Scientific journey to the center of the globe or *Journey to the Center of the Earth*) and *Le Tour du monde en quatre-vingts jours* (*Riwāyat al-Ṭawwāf ḥawl al-arḍ fī thamānīn yawm*; Circling the Earth in eighty days or *Around the World in 80 Days*) appeared first as serializations in *Al-Maḥrūsa* in 1885 and then as standalone editions, with *Le Tour du* monde reprinted again in 1889; and *Voyage au pole nord* (*Al-Riḥla al-shitawiyya fī al-jihāt al-thaljiyya*; The winter voyage in the icy regions or *Journey to the North Pole*) was published as a single edition in 1894.[16] The translations of *Around the World in Eighty Days* and *Journey to the North Pole* were listed as available for purchase in *Al-Hilāl*'s very successful bookshop as late as 1897 and so may have gone through even more printings.[17]

And yet globalization did not *come* to Arab readers via Verne and other modern novelists. Instead, it was the translators and Arab publishers of Verne's novels that joined Verne in the transnational project of thematizing the global, which was a project—like colonialism itself—that required the fusion of fact and fiction. Verne's process of creation was not very far off from the ambiguous way that Arabic readers had received his novels in translation. It was probably that very same translated notice about actual world travel, which had also appeared in French and English papers, that inspired *Around the World in Eighty Days*.[18] Verne based his narrative on newspaper accounts of transportation innovations, updating each new edition as new information and routes became available. And his most famous fictional traveler, Phileas Fogg, began his own global circumnavigation after reading about the opening of the Indian Peninsular Railway in the *Morning Chronicle*, a real but anachronistic English periodical.[19] Later, Verne's novels would themselves become the bases for actual journeys and factual representations of the world, many of which were reported in the Arabic press. In 1889, Nellie Bly began her well-publicized trip following Fogg's route, and the world's fair in Paris that same year displayed exhibits in which visitors could travel virtually around the world or venture twenty thousand leagues under the sea.[20] Arabic newspaper audiences reading Verne's novels in translation would have thus encountered a rich web of global references: in addition to installments of Verne's novels, which appeared in *Al-Bashīr* and the Cairo daily *Al-Maḥrūsa*, they would have encountered notices about the publication of Verne's fictional account, descriptions of world's fairs, and articles about actual journeys around the world.[21] In the simple act of reading the newspaper, these readers participated in the thematization of the world.

Arabic translations of Verne's novels are not simply a result of the globalization of the novel but are ambivalent participants in that process. These Arabic versions helped establish his fiction as a worldwide phenomenon. By his death in 1905, Verne's novels had been published in at least thirty-six languages, including five Middle Eastern ones.[22] What is more, they became some of the most translated of all literary texts worldwide: his first novel, *Cinq semaines en ballon*, was published in French in 1863 and appeared in translation beginning six years later in 1869; at the end of his career, translations were published almost simultaneously with their original publication, with work probably begun as soon as the source texts began serialization.[23] Verne's novels, that is to say, not only depicted the world but traveled the world. They were both the subject and the object of the novel's globalization. In reading Verne in translation, Arabic readers imagined themselves as part of global modernity while also partaking in transnational circuits of media, which they also pictured as global.

"There Can Only Be One World"

Though we may speak of "literary worlds," even global fictions do not reflect the actual world. That the world and some literary worlds *appear* to be the same thing, in fact, is the result of techniques of representation, techniques that Verne himself pioneered. The abundant appearance of worldly details, the incorporation of actual works of geographical or scientific reference describing the globe, and the gestures toward the representation of social plenitude all give the appearance of a complete fusion of world and work, the striving toward an accurate and complete representation of the real world. As Roland Barthes explains, Verne "had an obsession for plenitude," striving always toward realizing the "fullness" of the world. "[Verne's] tendency is exactly that of an eighteenth-century encyclopedist or of a Dutch painter," he writes: "The world is finite, the world is full of numerable and contiguous objects. The artist can have no other task than to make catalogues, inventories, and to watch out for small unfilled corners in order to conjure up there, in close ranks, the creations and the instruments of man."[24] His novels aim to fill out those corners, to populate them with color and character, but do so using only information that is already known. The novel's audiences—both original and translated—encountered only technology that was already in use, travel routes that were already well established, and geographical information that was already widely available. The world and the work, Verne's oeuvre announces, are one and the same.

Given this encyclopedic tendency, it is fitting that Verne's first translator was also an encyclopedist. Yūsuf Ilyān Sarkīs (1856–1932) translated *Cinq semaines en ballon* when he was just eighteen and still a student at the Jesuit seminary in Ghazīr, where *Al-Bashīr* was also edited and published.[25] Later, in 1912, he moved to Cairo and became a well-known bookseller and printer, but according to his entry in his own bibliography, he was above all a polymath, researching and publishing in the fields of numismatics, geography, history, and archaeology.[26] He would be best known by his bibliography, *Muʿjam al-maṭbūʿāt al-ʿarabīyya wa al-muʿarraba* (A bibliography of Arabic and translated publications), published between 1928 and 1930, which was itself encyclopedic. As he explains in its introduction, its aim was to catalogue "every Arabic book published in the civilized regions from the establishment of the printing press until today," as well as to provide biographical information on each of its authors—a lengthy task that took sixteen years of reading and researching.[27]

In this, *Ballon* and the *Muʿjam* have a project in common. Sarkīs explains in the introduction to his bibliography that he aimed for it to be "exhaustive and complete," a "trustworthy guide to knowledge about authors ancient and modern, Eastern and Western."[28] *Ballon*, similarly, proposes to "connect [*relier*] the efforts of [previous] travelers and complete [*compléter*] the series of African discoveries."[29] The novel does not strive toward newness, that is, but *wholeness*. Its plot is to follow a well-known geographer, Dr. Samuel Ferguson, as he confirms the information of previous African travelers, conjoining and triangulating their journeys by using a faster means of transportation, a balloon. Like the rest of Verne's novels, all of *Ballon*'s measurements, descriptions, and calculations come from previously published geographical works, and many include precise references, nearly all of which are preserved in Sarkīs's translation. When the explorers reach the Mandara mountains in what is currently the eastern part of Nigeria, for example, Ferguson recounts in detail the journeys of Captain Dixon Denham (undertaken 1822–1824), Captain Hugh

Clapperton, Dr. Walter Oudney (1823), Eduard Vogel, and Dr. Heinrich Barth (1854–1856), who had all died or nearly died in the vicinity.[30] *Ballon*'s journey, like Sarkīs's literary encyclopedia, completes, connects, and orders the knowledge produced by others.

Ballon's journey emphatically yields no *new* knowledge. Sarkīs even goes a step further than the source text in emphasizing this. In Arabic, the first chapter is omitted, and the novel begins by emphasizing the journey's precedents; it does not mention the protagonist's name, in fact, until the fourth paragraph.[31] At other times, Sarkīs adds missing or supplementary information: while Ferguson mentions that there are conflicting accounts of the origin of the Nile's name, for example, Sarkīs adds a footnote to resolve the issue; later, when the travelers fear they will be attacked by "fallatahs" (which refers to Arab farmers encountered on their route), the translation is corrected to *falāḥīn* (peasants).[32] Explanatory footnotes and parenthetical references, too, so typical of the translations we have seen, are peppered throughout and work in service of preserving and even emphasizing the novel's primary drive toward totality.

The world, both texts reassure their audiences, is a mappable, and indeed a fully mapped, object. Furthermore, they demonstrate that this map is both accurate and stable: the doctor "consulted the excellent map that served as his guide," the French reads; the Arabic adds, "it was most detailed and precise."[33] "The doctor, map in hand, recognized the kingdom of Damerghou," both texts read; "the doctor consulted his map and recognized the village of Tagelel."[34] The world, they seem to argue, is the same one found in maps and books; indeed, the world can be experienced *like* a map or book. As such, one can imagine how this text—of all of Verne's geographical novels—attracted Sarkīs the encyclopedist. Looking down from the balloon, its passengers and the readers see the terrain at a scale that simulates cartography: people are the size of ants, houses are barely distinguishable, and fields resemble a book of fabric samples. Like the panorama and the world's fair, the perspective rendered from the balloon is a representational technique that provides a picture of the world in the age of the world-picture. It is part of a regime of totalizing vision that Heidegger argues sets up a world as singular and stable and that relies on "the certainty of the knowable," a belief in facts that seem to exist independent of humans' participation in their creation.[35] The world is the world, these pictures tell us. One has but to write it down.

This, Eric Hayot explains, is itself is the project of modernity as conceived in European centers of power: the ideological assertion that there can only be one world, which is both singular and universal. Or, as he quotes Descartes, "There cannot be a plurality of worlds."[36] The Arabic versions of Verne's novels test this premise, presenting and complicating images of a single world newly connected and traversable in a common era called the modern age, *al-ʿaṣr al-jadīd*. They leave open, however, important questions about that world's construction: What world, exactly, exists? Who, precisely, has connected it? And who is permitted to traverse it? Fictions of global connectivity served as means to explore the scientific, cultural, and ethical ramifications of interconnection.

Colonial World-Making in the Air

As we know from postcolonial scholarship, realist and encyclopedic representational regimes were part of a larger project of imperialist knowledge production about and territorial acquisition of the former regions of the Ottoman Empire.[37] Yet world's fairs, panoramas, and even atlases and globes produced more than the geopolitical entity called "the Orient."[38] In the imperialist era, cultural forms such as these employed what the geographer David Harvey calls a "cartographic imagination," one that combined geographical science with the exercise of political and economic power to produce "spatial orders" that were potential sites of capitalist accumulation, efficient colonial administration, and resource allocation.[39] They produced such spaces as colonies, states, and regions as defined through their relationship—potential or actual—to a colonizing European power.[40] This included, importantly, "the world" itself, that set of total relations that Verne took as his "task" to represent.

Verne's genre of the adventure / travel narrative holds a special place among these spatializing forms. These fictions were produced at a moment when the capacity for global circumnavigation coincided with the drive toward comprehensive categorical descriptions of natural life (and therefore natural resources), which themselves produced "the world" as an entity available for European exploitation. This process, the development of what Mary Louis Pratt calls "planetary consciousness," marked a change in "European elite's understanding of themselves and their relations to the rest of the globe" and made modern Eurocentrism an integral part of global visions and scales.[41] As one of Verne's contemporary critics puts it, in reading his novels, "you become a citizen of the world in the literal sense of the term. Before you unrolls the scenery of the whole universe. We [readers] take possession of the whole earth, the whole firmament."[42] Verne's planetary consciousness submits all it depicts—the scenery of the whole universe—to the interpretive mechanisms of the center, rhetorically producing a world that is single, traversable, conquerable, and commodifiable. As these readers imagine, Verne's representation of the world allows them to imagine that they "possess" it, all of it, at once. That there cannot be a plurality of worlds is a central enabling claim of world-possession, or empire.

As I have argued elsewhere in this book, singularity and universality of the "world" is not a neutral fact, but one that had to be manufactured, and this manufacturing was often the task of the novel as a genre. This was the work that Verne performed for his French readers, which is perfectly illustrated by the balloon itself. Separating European observers from those African inhabitants they observe, it sets up a physical analogue of what Pratt calls "objectivist discovery rhetoric": a monologic, self-contained system of knowledge produced by setting up the explorer as the sovereign knowledge producer and potential colonizer, "the monarch-of-all-I-survey."[43] In the hot-air balloon, ground exploration is rare and often treacherous; the explorers spend most of their time in the air, far removed from the scenery they explore, which they observe according to their maps and charts—organizing the terrain. Indeed, this perspective turns everything they see *into* terrain, into objects of nature that are categorizable and potentially (yet never fully) containable and that may be submitted to the cartographic imagination of the reader. The inhabitants of Zanzibar "appeared like insects" from the balloon; further west, the explorers could not distinguish between serpents and "sauvages" (savages), and multiple times they mistake apes for Africans and Africans for apes.[44] All turn into geographic information, data to be collected from a distance.

These descriptions assert, violently, that there is only one world, a European-authored one seen and organized from far above. Yet, if the world is European authored, how can Arabs place themselves within its civilizational hierarchy? This is the question that *Al-Riḥla al-jawwiyya* poses, even as it does so largely via Africa and Africans. The explicit aim of the explorers, after all, is to "open avenues to modern civilization" (*chemins à la civilisation moderne*) in the African continent, a goal that Sarkīs translates as "planting the flag of *tamaddun* in those regions where now the wings of darkness and ignorance still flutter."[45] Merging the civilizing mission with the familiar *nahḍa* language of *tamaddun*, this translation draws Arab readers into a conversation about progress and enlightenment. It asks, Where does modern civilization come from? When these characters aim to bring *tamaddun* to Africa, is it *civilisation moderne* in its exclusively European definition? Or in translating the term into Arabic, is the concept Arabized, too?[46] To rephrase the question in the idiom that Sarkīs himself sets up, Are the Arabs like the explorers who "plant the flag" of modernity, or are they—like the fictional African inhabitants—its receivers?

The French version, of course, provides an unequivocal answer: "the Arabs," the name given to several groups encountered in the course of the journey, are a category of people in need of civilizational instruction. They appear as slave traders, ferocious warriors, and at best, "less savage" merchants.[47] In the Arabic version, not surprisingly, these are the passages that least adhere to the source text. Consider, for example, those Arab merchants. In French, Ferguson muses, "In Kazeh we should find some Arab merchants who are more educated and less savage" (*plus instruits, moins sauvages*) than the Africans in front of him.[48] In Arabic, however, subtle changes raise the status of these merchants: "The city of Kazeh has no shortage of traders or Arabs, who are educated and cultured" (*al-muthaqaffīn wa al-mutamaddanīn*).[49] There is no mention of any amount of savagery and no equivocation about their education status. Similarly, when the explorers encounter a group of rowdy and threatening "sorcerers" (*saḥra*) in Kazeh, the Arabophone chief is described far more favorably in Sarkīs's text: rather than an "abundant and florid harangue" (*une abondante harangue, très fleurie*), the Arabic describes his speech as a "long and elegant discourse" (*khaṭaba . . . khiṭāban ṭawīlan anīqan*).[50] The Arabic language is not described as in need of improvement; in fact, it seems to be a *source* of eloquence for an otherwise uneducated group.

Readers of this book who hope to learn about an anti-imperialist Verne in Arabic, however, will be disappointed. The translation often takes up colonial attitudes toward Africa and Africans, interpellating Arabic readers into the colonial perspective of the "monarch-of-all-I-survey." Sarkīs's version reproduces many of Verne's racist tropes, reinscribing the differences between the reader and Africans and minimizing the differences between the reader and the European colonizers. This includes retaining comparisons between Africans and animals as well as descriptions of Africans as unintelligible, barbarous, and savage.[51] At times, the translation even enhances those differences: when the French text mentions the "ceremonies" of Zanzibaris, for example, the Arabic describes them as "laughable" and their songs as "without rhythm or coordination."[52] And in relating a story about an anticolonial movement in Senegal, the text replicates a negative description of the followers of al-Ḥajj ʿUmar Tal as "hordes de fanatiques" (*al-qawm al-raffāḍ*) and a positive description of the "valiant" (*ṣandīd*) French colonial leaders who defeated him.[53] Readers therefore join the explorers in the balloon—rather than the natives on the ground—as observers of the landscapes and people below. Sarkīs makes it possible for his Arabophone readers to distinguish themselves from those who are ignorant and in need of improvement and even to participate in their being made "civilized."

This civilization, however, does not originate solely in Europe, for Sarkīs. He uses both these fictional Africans and the novel at large to assert the centrality of Arab learning in the world-scale project of the civilizing mission.

When Verne describes civilization progressing from "L'Asie . . . première nourrice du monde" (Asia, the world's first wet nurse) to Europe, Sarkis changes the itinerary. *Tamaddun* originates in "*al-mashriq* [the Levant], the cradle of the human race," before moving to *al-maghrib* (North Africa).[54] And while in French Ferguson goes on to speculate that the future of the human race is in America, in Arabic it is specifically "al-aqwām al-ifranjiyya" (the Frankish peoples) who "are leaving their countries and escaping in droves to the Americas."[55] *Al-Riḥla al-jawwiyya* retains the hierarchical structure of *Ballon*'s civilizational geography but questions Europe's place at its peak. Here, Europe is depicted as but a way station on progress's worldwide itinerary. Elsewhere, it is sidelined altogether: in a passage describing the African slave trade, Sarkīs inserts a footnote rebuking the practice, explaining that "people of moral quality have been working to abolish this horrible trade, which anyone with a sound heart rejects," and reminding the reader that the Ottoman Empire had already outlawed slave trading and established severe punishments for transgressors.[56] Translating the civilizing narratives of Verne meant translating the Arabic reader into a hierarchical worldview, but one whose center—geographic or moral—is not in Europe but in the Middle East.

Not just receivers of improvement, then, Arabs and Arabophones are depicted as sources of knowledge and moral authority, especially as it relates to the geographical picture of the world. When the narrator cites "the tales of the Arabs" as a possible resource for information about the sources of the Nile, the Arabic elevates them into a legitimate source of knowledge: rather than "great storytellers" that are even "too great," as in the French, the Arabs recount a great many "reports and pieces of information" (*akhbār wa aḥādīth*)—genres of oral transmission that are largely reliable and have scientific merit. In Sarkīs's translation, the genre of recital itself is recast; instead of deriving from unreliable and likely fictional sources (*récits de conteurs*), Arab geography enters the vocabulary of the Arab sciences, *ʿilm al-ʿarab*. These sources, as the Arabic continues, were compiled into a "package of papers" from which Arab geographers "extracted measurements and various methodologies" that had a kernel (*jawhar*; literally "gem") of "soundness." The passage ends with an explicit move to rehabilitate their narratives as sources of valid information: "you can see now," Ferguson tells Kennedy in an interesting addition, "that their stories [*ḥikāyāt*] about the sources of the Nile were true, even if before they were not previously taken to be credible."[57] In Arabic, the information provided by these Arab travelers did not just happen to be true in its broad strokes; it was the source of measurements and methods. That is, more than just providing raw material for European geographers to use in their theories, the Arab travelers also contributed geographic methodologies.

These are significant moments not the least because the Arab travelers in question formed the basis of the factual expeditions on which Verne relies. The expedition that most informs *Cinq semaine*'s itinerary, Speke and Burton's East African Expedition of 1856–1859, was itself plotted using the well-developed Arab-Nyamwezi caravan routes and other "native" sources, and contemporary geographers' maps were produced using classical Arabic texts.[58] Like Speke and Burton did, however, Verne's explorers minimize and devalue these sources. In *Ballon*, geographical knowledge derived from Arab sources is rendered as "tales" delivered by overly loquacious "storytellers" and as neither systematized nor entirely reliable: a "jumble of notions," as one English translation interprets; records that were "slapped together," for another.[59] These tales turn out to be accurate, or even more equivocally "not wrong," only by chance. *Al-Riḥla al-jawwiyya*, through such subtle translation choices, restores the Arab sources effaced by imperial geographical sciences.

Reading these two versions of geographical epistemology side by side re-engages the question of whether there can be only one world, a question that Heidegger himself left open. As Heidegger explains, the world-picture only exists "to the extent that it is set up by man, who represents and sets forth."[60] Readers of Arabic journals during this period were often reminded of this: in 1870, for example, the Beirut journal *Al-Zahra* ran a multipart series entitled "The Division of the World According to European Geographers."[61] Articles like this lead the reader to imagine the possibility of other articles describing the division of the world according to Arab, Chinese, or Indian geographers. The organization of the "whole world" was not always assumed to be singular or an a priori entity. It is, as articles such as this suggest, man-made and even the result of a process of translation. Indeed, articles on geography appearing in the press often began with a meditation on the foreign origins of the discipline itself (signaled in its very name, *jughrāfiyā*, which authors frequently explained to be borrowed from the Greek) and continued to recount its path—via translation—into the Islamic sciences.[62]

Consider even the small changes made to the explanatory subtitle of the novel. *Voyage de découvertes en Afrique par trois Anglais* (Voyage of discovery in Africa undertaken by three Englishmen) becomes *Riḥla min sharqay ifrīqiyā ilā gharbihā qad bāsharahā thalātha rijāl inkalīz qāṣidan fī iktishāf al-amākin al-majhūla* (A journey from eastern Africa to its west, which three Englishmen undertook with the purpose of discovering unknown spaces). In translation, we see a noun transformed into a verbal clause ("*Voyage de découvertes*" / "A voyage of discovery" becomes "a voyage . . . with the purpose of discovering"), and a passive verb rendered as an active one ("*par trois Anglais*" / "by three Englishmen" transforms to "a voyage . . . which three Englishmen undertook").

The translation presents these characters as active producers of knowledge, asking readers to focus on the work performed to produce it ("discover*ing*") rather than presenting that knowledge as universal, settled fact ("discovery"). This is reemphasized in small ways throughout the translation. The information presented by the explorers is often relativized, with units being given in multiple systems, for example, along with advice for the reader about how to manage the conversion.[63] At other times, it is qualified, with the objectivity-creating "master-of-all-I-survey" perspective rendered instead as if from particular human ones or with the presentation of settled facts translated instead as the recitation of individual narratives.[64] When Ferguson presents the findings of the expedition at a public meeting of the Royal Geographic Society, his *récit* is rendered not as a *riwāya* (which would be the literal equivalent) but as a *qiṣṣa*—a "tale" or even "novel."[65]

World-making, *Al-Riḥla al-jawwiyya* makes clear, is a fundamentally *comparative* endeavor. Heidegger's analysis concurs: in producing the world as an image of totality, "man contends for the position in which he can be that particular being who gives the measure and draws up the guidelines for everything that is."[66] A worldview is never fully singular. It is, "in its decisive unfolding, a confrontation of world views."[67] The world map was not simply one drawn by "European geographers," that is, but one that writes over and competes with other maps. Through selective translation and minute amendments, *Al-Riḥla al-jawwiyya* produces a cartographic imagination that highlights the process of mapmaking itself, dramatizing the production of geographic knowledge as multisited and contingent. It asserts that the Arab sciences were the conveyers, not recipients, of civilization. Sarkis's translation marks the world-making properties of the novel as comparative and even coauthored.

Fictions of Disconnection

Like Sarkīs, who imagines the beneficial results of connecting the African continent with other parts of the world, many contemporary reflections on the steamship, railway, and telegraph were optimistic about the more unified world these technologies would bring about. Elites the world over seemed to agree: telegraph cables would, as Samuel Morse put it, "bring mankind into a common brotherhood," or as other writers echoed, it would bring about the "universal brotherhood" of "universal man."[68] Arabophone elites held similar hopes. Rifāʿa Rāfiʿ al-Tahṭāwī, in his philosophical inquiry into Egyptian social progress, *Al-Manāhij al-albāb al-Miṣriyya fī mabāhij al-adab al-ʿaṣriyya (The Paths of Egyptian Minds towards the Delights of Modern Culture*, 1869), figured transportation and communications technology as drivers of global harmony, explaining that steam power and telegraphs make "travel easier and news travel faster" and that, by this means, "people can realize their own ideas and exchange ideas and products," thus linking them into perfect agreement.[69] The sentiment was repeated often especially in the late-century Egyptian press, where news items tracked the boom in transportation and communications projects there and commentaries contemplated their cultural or economic consequences. Not surprisingly, *Al-Muqtaṭaf*, the monthly "scientific and industrial journal" that moved to Cairo in 1882, was a particularly lively venue for these discussions, which also included poems musing on the greater significance of interconnection. In response to another reader's invitation to write poetry about the inventions of the current age, Amīn Shumayyal submitted "Kanz al-munā," which depicts the telegraph as a line connecting two hearts and scientific progress as a communal project of global history ("India, and elsewhere"), in which "some prefer to work at its beginning, and others at its completion."[70] In another poem the following year, As'ad Dāghir (d. 1935), a prolific translator himself, lists steamships, trains, and hot-air balloons as manifestations of progress that pull even the peasant toward "the shores of civilization [*tamaddun*]."[71] As natural as the tides in these poems, interconnectivity was portrayed as universal, inevitable, and positive.

Yet, just as often as readers consumed news of triumphant feats of global connectivity, they saw evidence that the promise of interconnection was not always beneficial. Integration into the world market, from the context of Ottoman-French relations, for example, was often reported as increased debt and depressed earnings. The international textile trade in particular, that engine of nineteenth-century global financial integration, had by the 1880s destabilized dreams of progress with poor stock-market returns, an unsteady foreign market, and capital flight.[72] And the same steamships that allowed faster transportation of goods and people also transported pathogens that caused the century's many global pandemics. The serialization of *Al-Riḥla al-jawwiyya* in *Al-Bashīr*, in fact, coincided with an outbreak of cholera in Syria and Lebanon that was believed to have arrived by sea; news of the disease's travels appeared simultaneously with the narrative of Ferguson's, at times on the same page.[73] In Egypt, returning pilgrims carried both cholera and the plague from the hajj, from which it was believed to have spread to southern Europe (with especially widespread outbreaks occurring in 1883 and 1893–1895). As Eric Tagliacozzo writes, "the prospect of contagion traveling on the wings of the hajj became one of the great health issues of the late nineteenth and early twentieth centuries."[74] For residents of the Mediterranean basin during these periods, global connectivity also meant fears of immigrants, travelers, and imported goods, as well as experiences of quarantines and new and invasive sanitary regimes.[75]

Translations of Verne's explicitly global fictions—in particular, *Riwāyat al-Ṭawwāf ḥawl al-arḍ fī thamānīn yawm* (*Around the World in Eighty Days*) and *Al-Riḥla al-ʿilmiyya fī qalb al-kura al-arḍiyya* (*Journey to the Center of the Earth*)—helped readers mediate their understandings and experiences of globality at a moment when its promises of greater prosperity were pierced by experiences of economic and physical precarity along with increased government involvement in bodily and family autonomy and movement. During the period between 1885 and 1895 in which these translations were produced, readers saw their own movements regulated by regimes that were themselves managed and restricted by outside forces—via direct and indirect colonial rule. At the same time that these novels depicted sovereign-seeming bodies moving autonomously and unobstructedly through space and even time, their translations contained traces of those experiences of restriction.

The dangers of circulation were no abstract fact to the producers of these novels. Every one of the networks of print actors involved in their production, including their translators, the press owners, the periodical founders, and the owners of the bookshops that sold them, was a Syro-Lebanese immigrant to Egypt, a member of the *mahjar*. The translators Yūsuf ʿAṣṣāf and Iskandar ʿAmmūn were born in Mount Lebanon, while the publisher Salīm Khalīl al-Naqqāsh (1850–1884), who founded *Al-Maḥrūsa*, and Jurjī Zaydān, who founded *Al-Hilāl*, were both born in Beirut; all had emigrated to Egypt between 1875 and 1885. What that means is that they, like over a third of the population of Mount Lebanon, had been displaced by civil war, government oppression, or economic pressures.[76] What is more, all of the translators had direct ties to colonial regimes. Tawfīq Dūbariyah Ibn Yūsuf Bey, translator of *Voyage au pole nord*, was the grandson of Alexandre Debray, a member of a contingent of medical scholars invited to Egypt by Mehmet ʿAlī and led by Clot Bey.[77] And both Yūsuf ʿAṣṣāf and Iskandar Anṭūn ʿAmmūn were employed by the British colonial administration at the time they published their translations. ʿAṣṣāf is identified on the title page of *Ṭawwāf* as "Commissioner of the Egyptian Post in al-ʿAṭf," and ʿAmmūn is listed as the "Khedival Representative on the National Court of First Instance," one of the new "native" courts that just two years earlier had replaced Ottoman *sharīʿa* ones and that Samera Esmeir describes as the outcome of "the colonial legal conquest of Egypt."[78] Thus enmeshed in institutions of colonization at the very moment of their inception, these translators produced works and worldviews that were inextricable from coloniality. Indeed, ʿAṣṣāf even makes this inextricability explicit: he dedicates his translation to his British superior, "Hāltūn Bey," or William Fox Halton Pasha, who was then the postmaster general of Egypt and chief of the colonial railway administration.[79] "Your zeal for the arts and sciences inspired me to translate this work," he explains in the Arabic dedication. In his English-language dedication that follows, he adds some extra emphasis, explaining that the work was "translated by me in the express end to be presented to your Excellency."[80] He presents the translation itself as a token of exchange in the colonial economy of power and influence.

These novels, moreover, are the ideal texts to explore such complex experiences of globality that were shaped by empire. As Verne scholars have repeatedly argued, his works present utopias of mobility: they are "epics of circulation" in which he puts "mobility [of capital as well as humans] and its liberating effects on stage."[81] In *Around the World*, Phileas Fogg traverses the globe via explicitly imperial routes, passing through British colonies or economic protectorates and often in a vehicle "driven by the arms of a British engineer and burning British coal," and is pursued by a British detective, Fix, whose jurisdiction is, effectively, worldwide. Empire knows no limits; it is coterminal with the world itself.[82] When Professor Lidenbrock leads a team of scientists to an Icelandic volcano in *Journey to the Center of the Earth*, he does so with the help of government agents; their handshakes, letters of introduction, and permits smooth his way. Along the way, they find several sources of power—heat, electrical current, vast coal deposits—to supplement the coal that Verne writes "will be exhausted by excessive consumption in less than three centuries."[83] As a source of power for "les peoples industriels," the Earth itself is at empire's disposal.[84] The cartographic imagination constructed by these novels was, specifically, a colonial globality.

As I have argued with regard to *Al-Riḥla al-jawwiyya*, while Verne's texts set out to demonstrate that the world is synchronous, single, and traversable, the Arabic translations instead note that global unification was an effect of the imperial project. These two translations offer complex pictures of nineteenth-century globality and are far more than utopian images of global harmony. Detective Fix, who pursues Fogg in *Around the World*, for example, is not portrayed as a singular phenomenon, a sole detective obsessed with a man he believes to be a notorious bank thief, but as part of a larger apparatus of power. He is introduced as but one of many figures of colonial authority, an "English policeman who had come in the name of his government to the Suez Canal in order to surveil all those going to India."[85] The world that the reader encounters in *Around the World* is one that is connected not by universal brotherhood but by Big Brother—by surveillance that exceeds territorial bounds and empire that reaches around the world. In fact, the celebratory portrayals of connectivity that pepper the French source are often absent in *Al-Ṭawwāf*. Praise for the North American railroad as "an instrument of progress and civilization thrown across the desert, designed to link towns and cities," for example, is simply omitted.[86] Instead, just pages later, that railroad is described as an explicitly colonial enterprise. As in Verne, the train is attacked by Sioux horsemen—who are described as monkeys in the French but not in Arabic—an attack that the Arabic portrays as justified by the violence of the railway's construction. The Sioux, as ʻAṣṣāf's Arabic remarks, had, "since the establishment of the railway on their lands," "made it their business" to attack the trains: this was no unthinking attack or mercenary act but calculated anticolonial violence whose "business" was liberation.[87] In *Al-Kura al-arḍiyya*, when Professor Lidenbrock pays the guide's weekly salary, it is no comic punctuation to the tense story but itself an event worthy of commentary and expansion. In the Arabic version, the scientist had, for the entirety of the journey, kept a record not only of the entire history of the world but of his servant's salary. The history of the globe, this addition reminds the reader, cannot be written without servitude.[88]

What these scenes make clear is that global unification—itself an effect of coloniality—was unevenly experienced. From the perspective of middle-American townspeople, the railway was a way to feel linked to the rest of the world, while for the Sioux, it cut them off from even their own land. In this, the translation adds emphasis to elements in the French source text that also make this point: Fogg and company travel on railroads that are fully operational in Europe but that are incomplete or vulnerable to attack in India and the United States. In the case of the Indian railway, the protagonists are the only travelers to have not made alternative travel plans when they reach the incomplete stretch of rail. "But the newspapers had announced the complete opening of the railway!" the French and Arabic texts read. "The newspapers got it wrong," reads the French. "It appears to be an inadvertent omission; they must not have known," reads the Arabic, more generously.[89] The subtle change from an accusation of error to an inadvertent omission exposes a rift in the expectations for global circulation: in Arabic, only Fogg and his companions expect the news to circulate perfectly from Allahabad to London.

Just like the fictional conductor who is nonplussed at the knowledge of transportation breakdown, Arabic translators and their readers knew that these technologies brought not only connectivity but disconnection. In 1858, after all, a railway accident had brought a crisis of succession: the car float carrying Khedive Ibrahim's nephew and heir, Ahmad Rifaʻt Pasha, overturned, drowning all aboard. The *nahḍa*'s audiences would have read about not only new breakthroughs in communications and travel but also their accidents and breakdowns. Announcements of delays in steamship arrivals frequented the front pages, often just below the masthead, and notices of delays in printing or distribution often accompanied them. Early journals in particular often announced the late arrival of steamships and their impact on publication and delivery schedules. In 1866, for example, delays became so frequent that *Ḥadīqat al-akhbār* changed its publication schedule in order to ensure that its overseas customers received their issues on time.[90] In 1873, *Al-Jinān* noted a similar problem; it announced that it would be switching from Ottoman steamships to European ones in order to ensure timely deliver to its Egyptian readers.[91] The wreck of a steamship carrying mail was even central to the plot of one of *Al-Jinān*'s translated serials.[92]

Telegraphs, too, the inclusion of which had become a regular feature of journals by the 1870s, were mentioned in the context of service interruptions as well as their proper functioning. The undersea Mediterranean cable was especially prone to interruption, but even overland cables were vulnerable to environmental and human interference. Provincial rulers who did not want to be monitored by the capital derailed construction and approval at every chance, and farmers would move telegraph poles out of the way of their crops. To many people, the telegraph was most valuable for its material properties: residents in Ottoman Turkey stripped wires off poles to make heel ropes for horses; farmers harvested their wood to use as fuel; others removed their porcelain insulators to use for target practice or their copper wires to make bracelets.[93] For these neighbors of the telegraph lines, they were more useful when they were interrupted than when they transmitted information. Yet even when they were in use, they were not always reliable. Records show that Ottoman, Persian, and Indian telegraph agencies' translation offices, essential to the transmission of international news, were often short staffed or insufficiently trained. As one British report bemoans, "ignorant and untrained native officers are alone obtainable."[94]

Problems like these were so common that they were central to Arabic print itself. Funding problems, distribution-chain glitches, and government censorship and embargoes all interrupted circulation.[95] As I argued in chapter 2, not even the printing press—long understood to offer modern readers a homogenization of diverse regions—guaranteed smooth communication among Arabic readers, as journals' different typefaces or language use were criticized as illegible to consumers outside their immediate market. As *Ḥadīqat al-akhbār* notes of a new official journal opened in Tripoli, "As we know, the goal is to make journals available and ensure that they reach from one country to another; yet this goal will not be reached by the paper of West Tripoli because of its obscure type."[96] Though Benedict Anderson and other theorists of world literary circulation have understood print journalism as "stretching out across, and seamlessly mapping, a singular world," it was not experienced as guaranteeing smooth transfers of information.[97] The seams were at all times visible in the form of missed connections, incomplete circuits, and faulty nodes.

Steamships, railways, telegraphs, and periodicals brought more and more territory under their purview with each year, creating a single planetary unit, but it was one that was formed not despite of *but through* its glitches and faulty connections, its operator and user errors. They were a part of its everyday functioning for *nahḍa* readers, the front-page material that framed their reception of their news and their world. This was the vision of circulation that made its way into these global fictions of connectivity—one that highlighted the cofunctioning of disconnection in the creation of the global. Most crucially, in these translations of fictions of globality, the visible seams of world connectivity were not identified as located solely in Europe's peripheries. In *Al-Ṭawwāf*, ʿAṣṣāf makes a significant change to a discussion of the feasibility of a trip around the world in just eighty days. In order to accomplish this goal, Fogg must make every connection—whether by rail, steam, or donkey—on time, a difficult feat. A character comments in Verne's French text, "In Europe . . . one can count on the arrival of trains at their appointed times; but when they take three days to cross India or seven to cross the United States, how can we rely on their exactitude?"[98] In Arabic, however, the problem of rail regularity is recast as universal: "If in Europe one cannot count on the trains to arrive at their appointed times," the same character asks, "how can they do so in India?"[99] It recalls a similar moment in *The Count of Monte Cristo*, when the veracity of news items is characterized as a universal problem: the Count and another character debate the veracity of a news story but cannot settle their argument. In the French source text, they ask themselves a rhetorical question, "But how can you verify what is in the newspaper?" In two of the Arabic translations, an answer is posed: more articles should be published. The narrator intervenes to add, "this is the way that newspapers work."[100]

This is the way that newspapers (and trains and telegraphs and steamships) work. The reader will notice that the narrator does not say, "this is how *our* newspapers work," nor does ʿAṣṣāf's narrator identify non-Western trains as the only late ones. These Arabic additions comment on communications and transportation technologies from their local perspective but take as their object their existence as *global* institutions. They narrate what On Barak has called "countertempos" to the contraction of space and time and regimes of punctuality that social scientists conventionally argue to be markers of modernity. "Egyptian time," he writes, as opposed to Western time, exposes the colonial machine as "a poorly tuned and dysfunctional engine." It "unwinds and exposes the otherwise tightly coiled spring that makes the modern world smoothly operative."[101] Here, though, in these global fictions, translators locate those countertempos in the heart of the metropole as well as in the peripheries. European trains, *like Indian ones*, do not run on time, and French newspapers, *like all newspapers*, circulate false stories. Unpunctuality, miscommunication, and gaps in circulation are *worldwide* phenomena. Errors constitute globality, everywhere.

What these fictions of connectivity offer is not resistance to globality but a competing conception of it. Technological modernity can only offer a broken totality, they show, and not wholeness. This explains why, more often than not, the word "world" itself is omitted in these translations; wholeness is withheld. Yet, importantly, it is not annulled but merely reconfigured. In *Al-Riḥla al-jawwiyya*, that wholeness is withheld until the very end, when—after omitting at least four references to the world, earth, or globe—Sarkīs adds a globally minded summary lesson that was entirely absent in Verne's French. While Verne ends his text by explaining that the narrative's significance is in the geographical knowledge about Africa that it provides, Sarkīs widens the scope of the text's importance, summing up with much-larger geographical and moral claims. Instead of simply providing information about a circumscribed area, "that vast region comprised between the fourteenth and thirty-third degrees of longitude," Sarkīs adds that the travels "made a large part of *the earth* no longer unknown to those who possess knowledge, as it had unfortunately been in previous days to its inhabitants who had before been separated from the rest of *humanity* as if they were not of the same [human] race and had no brothers."[102] The whole that is imagined is that of the "human race" and its brotherhood. These changes result in a significant shift in what Heidegger called a work of art's "world": its "measure which guides us along." The world, for Heidegger, is above all a relation—a way of placing an object in relation to all other entities—and thus giving its viewers (or readers, in this case) an "outlook on themselves."[103] This is the most striking difference between these translations and their source material, as each of their translators add moral language and analysis. 'Aṣṣāf, for example, portrays Fogg not as "mechanistic," "unfeeling," or "amoral" but as having sound principles and good intentions; 'Ammūn similarly gives his Professor Lidenbrock additional empathic moments. This is why Pheng Cheah argues that the literary work does not simply reflect global forces or reactively respond to them but has what he calls a "normative force . . . in the world."[104] A novel does not show the reader what the world *is* but makes an argument about what it *should* be: "it fight[s] the fight in which the disclosure of beings as a whole—truth—is won," Heidegger explains.[105] As Sam Weber explains, "there are no secure places" in Heidegger's worldview.[106]

These translations of Verne's global fictions highlight the gap between the world and worldview, what Heidegger calls the "openness" of works of art—by which he means not simply their ability to create meaning in multiple and conflicting ways but their ability to create multiple *frames* of meaning.[107] When Fogg sees a young woman about to be immolated on her husband's funeral pyre, Verne's description frames it within the British Empire's civilizing worldview: "How, when the British have spread civilization to all of India, does this barbarous practice persist?" a companion asks. "There are places where our power has not reached," Fogg muses. In Arabic, ʿAṣṣāf adjusts the frame: as the empire itself has not succeeded in saving her, Fogg decides, in yet another addition, that he must do so himself—"to defend humanity [*al-insāniyya*]."[108] Later, when translating the scene of Fogg rallying a group of men to defend the train against the Sioux raiders, ʿAṣṣāf adds a similar cry: "who among you will defend humanity [*al-insāniyya*] with his life?"[109] Fogg's circumnavigation of the globe reveals the gaps in the British Empire's global project where colonial authority and law cannot reach. In ʿAṣṣāf's version, global power is replaced by a moral order of a larger magnitude still: a defense of *insāniyya*, or humankind.

Both *Al-Riḥla al-jawwiyya* and *Al-Ṭawwāf* add "worldly ethics" to otherwise-materialist accounts of globalization to produce a competing version of the world.[110] Verne's source texts as well as their translations display a "yearning for totality," as Verne critics have argued; the translations transform the mode of that yearning from bourgeois accumulation into moral universalism.[111] Translating the world as "humanity" produces a competing globality to the colonial one. It imagines a world connected not just by colonial power but by moral good, which is imagined as truly universally available.

Locating the Center in Translation

Thinking the whole world, all of these authors and translators understood, meant reading in translation. In *Cinq semaines en ballon* and *Le Tour du monde*, dangerous moments are avoided or navigated by understanding or speaking foreign languages—the protagonists would not have survived the journey were it not for translation. In *Le Comte de Monte-Cristo*, Dantès's transformation into the Count is facilitated by his learning of languages; they are the source of knowledge, power, mobility, and wealth. Jules Verne's *Voyage au centre de la terre* does even better, as the voyage begins with a four-chapter-long scene of translation: the protagonist's uncle, a venerated geologist, had discovered a twelfth-century Icelandic manuscript written in cryptic, runic characters. As if that were not enough deciphering, a parchment—also bearing runes but this time also in code—falls out and demands to be read. Over fifteen pages in French and twenty-three pages in Arabic, the professor and his nephew attempt to decode the document, combining and recombining characters, organizing them in columns, assigning number values to them, until they finally determine the key and read the message backward to reveal a secret route to the center of the Earth (figure 5.1). The key to the world itself—its history, its energy, its hidden mysteries—is translation.

So too was translation the key to the technologies that propelled these fictional circulations. Just like print journalism, the other technologies of global circulation—steamships, railroads, the postal system, and the telegraph—all relied on translation in their daily functioning. In the case of the Egyptian State Railroad (ESR), as archival research implies, this circulation required regular acts of translation, on the part of both railway workers (European and Egyptian workers made the ESR the largest permanent workforce in Egypt) and railway users. Arabic, English, and French were used in railway signs, schedules, and public notices and were even the subject of public debate. As On Barak notes, "a 1905 article expressed popular frustration with the fact that the departure and arrival times of the Alexandria light railways were written only in French and English."[112] The region's telegraph offices, similarly, relied on translation. When telegraph news items became a staple in global journalism, wires would be transmitted in a single house language (French for Havas, English for Reuters) and then translated into local languages at their point of destination—requiring every receiver to employ multilingual telegraph staff.[113] This was the case even when those wires were transmitted regionally. Telegrams in the Ottoman system, whether domestic or international in destination, were transmitted in French; later, even when transmission in Turkish became more common, they were transmitted in transliterated Turkish.[114]

Of course, the importance of translation in these technologies was not restricted to the Middle East or even to locations outside Europe. Bureau Havas, the first wire news agency, began as a translation service to deliver foreign news to France, and those receiving either its wires of Reuters ones would have to translate them from English or French.[115] As Esperança Bielsa and Susan Bassnett explain, describing not particular cases but the "global news," "news agencies can be viewed as vast translation agencies, structurally designed to achieve fast and reliable translations of large amounts of information."[116] This was especially the case if, as Buṭrus al-Bustānī puts it, the purpose of newspapers was to serve those "who want to know what is happening *in the world*."[117]

Worlding is a process, this chapter has attempted to show, that requires translation: it brings together things, people, and places that were used to be

١٩

بدون انتباه وافكاره مشتغلة بحل كتابة الرقعة فحمدت الله الذي حوّل غضبه عني واثنيت على كاتب الرقعة التي شغلته ونسيت اني لولا تلك الرقعة لما فرط مني ما فرط وكان عمي لا يزال يردد تلك الكلمات ثم نظر اليّ وقال

ان صح ذلك فلنستعمل هذه الطريقة لحل الرقعة السرية

فقلت في نفسي ان كان حل الرقعة موقوفًا على صحة محبتي لغريبة فبشر الاستاذ بفوز قريب

ثم اخذ يسرد عليّ حروف الرقعة السرية بحسب الطريقة التي وضعناها فانعكست حروفها بالكيفية الاتية

م ي س و ن ك
س ن ر ا ا ن
ا ا ه ت ك ل
س ق ي ر ط ض
ر ل ا ب ل
ق ي ل ا و ي
ن و ي ر ه ش
ر خ ا و ا ي
ف س ي ر ت ر
ك س ا ا ه ل
ل ظ ي ي ث ل
ا ل ف ي ن س
ا ن ا ك ر ب
ه ه و ف ن م

FIGURE 5.1. Decoding the inscription in Iskandar ʿAmmūn's version of *Voyage au centre de la terre*, *Al-Riḥla al-ʿilmiyya fī qalb al-kura al-arḍiyya* (Alexandria: Maṭbaʿat al-jarīda al-Maḥrūsa, 1885), 18. (Bibliothèque nationale de France)

thought of as separate and posits a relationship between them. But what that translation looks like—what connections it yields, what equivalences it posits, what world it creates—is what the translators put to question. Just as Verne imagined it, a journey to understand the history of the *whole world* begins with a single act of translation. This is why he dramatized the struggle, the despair, the exhaustion, and the triumph of translating the tiniest scrap of Icelandic script. Professor Lidenbrock's eyes "were throwing lightning bolts through his glasses" as he attempted to decipher the text; "his hands trembled." "Who would win," the translator or the original source? And the narrator also suffers during the process. As he explains, "I was having a sort of hallucination; I was suffocating."[118] In ʿAmmūn's Arabic, too, these two translators suffer from "exhaustion and watery eyes"; they see the letters of the text "buzz around like meteors or phosphorescent traces."[119] In this version, however, the translators discover that the angular, detached, rune-like characters are not Icelandic but ancient Arabian; the message is in Arabic, scrambled and written in Himyaritic (a pre-Islamic Semitic language) script. But "why would a twelfth-century Icelandic scientist write the secret of the world in Arabic?" the narrator incredulously asks. His uncle, the learned professor, however, is not surprised: "All languages have a limited lifespan, . . . but Arabic," he explains, "it will not change over time because God transmitted his book in it, and so long as there is a single Muslim left on Earth, it [Arabic] will yet exist."[120] The fictional Icelandic author has chosen Arabic because it is globally important, and globally available, accessible to all Muslims "on Earth." Transhistoric and transnational, Arabic is the key—literally—to the mysteries of the whole world.

The mysterious script only resembles runes, but they are not exact matches. So do these global fictions present a world that resembles that of the sources but not exactly so. World-making, to recapitulate Heidegger, is a comparative process—a worldview establishes itself by competing with other ones. World-making is always plural, "a confrontation of worldviews," a process that not only requires translation but presupposes it. And it does so in the service of establishing competing globalities, universals that are centered on Arabic, and not European, histories and perspectives. This, too, is the project of translation. Comparative scholars seeking to place Arabic in the world of letters would do well to attend to ʿAmmūn's inquiry into the nature of world-making and his version of Verne's search for the center of the world.

Chapter 6

The Melodramatic State

Popular Translation and the Erring Nation

Iskandar ʿAmmūn's imaginative recentering of Arabic language took place as Arabic-speaking countries' political status itself became further marginalized. He was, in fact, a direct witness to this event, as he published his translation of *Voyage au centre de la terre* just two years after the British restructured the Egyptian court system, and he lists himself as a representative on one of the colonial native courts. The politics of translating European literature registered beyond legal domains, however, as social commentators described the print market itself as a site of colonization: an 1898 article in *Al-Mashriq* describes the Egyptian literary market as a colonization both literary and sentimental: "these writings that had overthrown the desires of the Europeans had been sent to this country in cheap editions to be purchased and then—if enjoyed—passed to a friend and then to an acquaintance, and thus from reader to reader without the exchange of a single coin."[1] Books of educational, literary, or historical value, the writer laments, sat untouched on shelves, while these literary "shams" circulated with a singular power, seducing the reader with unrealistic and unseemly events.

European and European-style fiction, and especially "romantic novels," as *Al-Muqtaṭaf* warned, for example, had a detrimental effect on Egyptian youth by encouraging foreign practices like mixed-gendered socializing, early courtship, and "laziness."[2] Other commentators at the time agreed: Jurjī Zaydān, founding editor of the cultural stalwart *Al-Hilāl*, warned in 1897 of foreign novels that "damage the social structure."[3] His series of twenty-two historical novels that covered events from the Muslim conquests to the Young Turk revolution of 1908 were an explicit Arabizing response to the danger of foreign reading habits.

Concern about the moral influence of reading novels, as we saw in chapter 3, was not new at this moment. By the turn of the century, however, these concerns had fused with anticolonial political ones. The author of the *Al-Mashriq* article, a Jesuit named Amīdī Lūryūl, adds to the list of negative consequences of novel reading the erosion of "love for country," and Zaydān warns that allowing foreign languages too great an influence on cultural production could halt cultural progress in the same way that colonialism had halted national progress: "having traveled so far in our Arabic *nahḍa*, it would be as if the wheels of our carriage had suddenly stumbled over the British occupation and stopped short."[4] Still other commentators worried that popular novels reinforced these readers' preference for "incredible and unbelievable" stories rather than cultivating a taste for novels that "depict events that happened or could have happened."[5] The locus of concern was readers' preference for foreign unreality rather than "national reality."[6] Print's role as a medium of social and national reform was again in danger of failure, its potential thwarted by users with no heed for proper modes of reading and circulation.

The historical record confirms these commentators' fears. At the turn of the century, it was certainly not high-minded literary works that predominated in the Arabic literary marketplace. Rather, the market privileged thrilling and emotional works, the vast majority of which were in translation and which prioritized titillation and "scandal" over moral, civic, or religious progress. Most of these hewed to the same system of subgenres that organized the European market of the hour: domestic dramas, sentimental tear-jerkers, *policiers*, Penny Dreadfuls, and *feuilletons*—what nineteenth-century French critics derisively called *la littérature industrielle*.[7] Literature for the mass market and not the cultivated mind, it suffered like the scandals themselves from unchecked circulation: untrained authors, as French critics warned at the *feuilleton*'s debut, "invaded" and "infested" the literary field.[8] In both cases, a new corpus of authors arose. After Dumas, the original *feuilletoniste*, the most frequently named are the crime and detective novelists Ponson du Terrail, Maurice Leblanc, Émile Gaboriau, and Arthur Conan Doyle; the cloak-and-dagger specialists Michel Zévaco and Xavier de Montépin; the sentimental moralists Émile Richebourg, Jules Mary, Georges Ohnet, and G. W. M. Reynolds; and urban sensationalists like Eugène Sue.

Contrary to world-systems translation theory models, in which "weak" target cultures become "strong" ones through the selective translation of canonized literature, we see a marked absence of canonical authors and many that—though they also constituted the bulk of the European market at the time—have been forgotten by literary history. Muḥammad al-Sibāʿī translated Charles Dickens, as part of his attempt to plant "seeds of superiority" into "this grave that people call 'Egypt,'" but this was two decades after this popular corpus had taken hold. His earlier translation of Wilkie Collins's sensation classic *The Woman in White* was more in keeping with the spirit of the age.[9] Walter Scott's historical methods were often cited in defenses of the novel's pedagogical purpose, but only three of his novels were translated; articles about Émile Zola were common in the press, but his works—like those of other great realists like Honoré de Balzac and George Elliott—are almost entirely absent from the record. The foreign literary influx brought a steady march of criminals, outlaws, fallen women, and oppressive fathers into the minds and homes of Egypt's readers. The market was saturated with titles like *Al-Rajul al-jahanamī* (The man from hell, 1893], *Faḍīḥat al-ʿushāq* (The lovers' scandal, 1892), and *Al-Burj al-hāʾil* (The tower of horror, 1899), which proudly announced their entertainment value while skirting the issue of self-improvement that had guided the public domestication of the form in previous decades.

Yet the new popular novels were accused of more than just portraying unrealistic foreign situations; more dangerously, they were seen as promoting unhealthy reading practices and cultivating excessive, nonrational emotions. Readers, as *Al-Mashriq* lamented, could waste hours on such novels as if in "a haze of narcotic smoke," figuring their influence as an almost involuntary response.[10] Indeed, for many commentators, the foreign content of the novels was inextricable from their promotion of excess emotions. As Tawfiq al-Hakim writes in the 1930s, "the difference between literature [*al-adab*] and fiction [*al-qiṣṣa*] is like the difference between the higher regions of the body and all the rest."[11] Critics worried that reading them could lead people to emulate the immoral behaviors of foreign protagonists, promoting "envy, impudence, revenge, and shamelessness."[12] Provoking emotions rather than rational thought and promoting foreign rather than domestic values, these novels led the error-prone reader astray.

In other words, to borrow a phrase from Samah Selim, these commentators worried about the prominent place of "bad books for bad readers" in the national literary market.[13] They identified categories of especially vulnerable readers, young people, the newly literate, the popular classes, as those who were likely to be led astray by this seductive reading and who engaged in difficult-to-control circulation practices. It was no longer a question of *if* people other than the *efendiyya* should read but *what* they should read and often how they should do so.[14] Novel reading, journals claimed, caused young people to neglect their household duties, disobey their parents, and engage in early courtship, while also leading those of the "inferior classes" to neglect their work.[15]

But bad readers were above all figured as women readers: this is not surprising, when women were central figures in the allegorization of the nation, whether that be as "mothers of the nation" who were responsible for the moral character of Egypt's children or as the "New Woman" whose education and sophistication personified the rational progress of the modern Egyptian nation-state. Novel reading, it was feared, would distract women from their serious business—whether that be domestic duties or education—that was newly coded as *national*, that it would promote intemperate emotions and nonrational responses to literature, and that it would encourage behaviors that sat outside the new gender roles that nationalists sought to delineate. Romantic novels were singled out as particular dangers: "They plot a thousand and one ruses for violating the virginity of a girl and to take her chastity," as a writer for *Al-Jawā'ib al-miṣriyya* wrote.[16] They "have the effect of an electric cable," another author writes, "for we see her shedding tears at times or emitting ululations of joy at others."[17] Rather than the studied exercise of the moral imagination, women's reading provoked untrained physical responses and uncontrolled emotions.

Bad books spoke to and—more frequently—*about* women. The two largest subgenres of the end of the century often focused on women's lives. Sentimental romantic novels often centered around a single female protagonist and her marriage decisions, and crime fiction in many cases explored similar themes. In fact, the border between these two subgenres was often blurred: romantic plots were often simultaneously legal ones, bound up with marriage and inheritance law, labor disputes, political conspiracies, revolutions, and war; meanwhile, legal and criminal fictions contained prominent sentimental plots. Indeed, criminal plots were often *translated into* a sentimental register, making melodrama the dominant turn-of-the-century literary mode. Critics rejected both as detrimental to national progress, characterizing their emotional excesses and sensationalist plots as "clownish."[18]

Bad books aimed at bad readers *seem* to be evidence of a counter-enlightenment—anti-*nahḍa* texts—but that was not necessarily the case. Foreign novels were sometimes figured as positive conduits for social values and national consciousness. Writing in 1899 in *Al-Ḍiyā'*, which featured many translated novels, Salīm al-Khūrī held up Najīb Ḥaddād's translation of Sir Walter Scott's *The Talisman* (*Ṣalāḥ al-Dīn al-Ayyūbī*) as an example of the genre's ability to "enlighten the mind and educate the morals" of readers, just as it had in Europe. There is no reason to dismiss novel reading or theatergoing in the name of "politics," al-Khūrī argues, when "wise men, *'ulumā'*, and statesmen" of Europe agree on its benefits.[19] Novels offered pathways to national improvement, rather than obstacles to greatness. Zaydān admits as much in that 1897 article: "We used to think that there was no benefit to reading novels and other literary books, . . . but we found after research and experience that a person in need of literary knowledge could [through novels] strengthen his mind, refine his emotions, educate his morals, and widen the circle of his experience."[20] Such benefits relied on the translator's discernment in selecting texts to translate. Zaydān recalls reading *Riwāyat Janafyāf* (one of Christoph Schmid's moral tales) with "our tears falling" but finds himself embarrassed for the translator, who wasted his effort producing *Al-Intiqām al-ʿādil* (A just revenge, trans. Salīm ʿAnḥūrī).[21] In fact, Scott provided the explicit model for Zaydān's historical novels, and some readers even mistook his original novels for European translations.[22] The national canon was itself unthinkable without translation.

The translators of such works saw themselves as actors in the formation of national novelistic discourse. Their prefaces to their own publications and their works in the press promoted the value of their work to civic and social consciousness. Faraḥ Anṭūn (1874–1922), the Lebanese emigrant journalist, author, and political thinker whose writings on secularism and socialism influenced Egyptian national thought, also translated and authored at least five novels. In the preface to his original novel *Ūrūshalīm al-jadīd* (*The New Jerusalem*, 1904), he argued that novels—especially historical novels such as those he wrote—inculcate a triumvirate of civic virtues in readers, by honing their sensibilities for beauty, goodness, and truth. "We hope," he wrote, "that these three sentiments will develop in our beloved countries, because they are the foundation of all refinement, honesty, and virtue and the source of all greatness. The nations that are not founded on this tripartite base strive and build in vain."[23] Similarly, Khalīl Baydas (1875–1949), a translator of Russian literature who is credited with introducing Pushkin and Tolstoy into Arabic, begins his journal, *Al-Nafāʾis al-ʿaṣriyya*, with a nation-centered definition of the novel and its reading community: "Novels describe the conditions of different nations and the lessons of history," he explains; "the novel shifts and transforms, until it captures the interest of the majority in each nation."[24] In his distinction between the "true" or "artistic" novel from the "commercial" or "counterfeit" one, the translated novel occupies an ambivalent role. Even if some were "feeble, superficial novels of the kind that fling their reader into an abyss of wrongdoing," he argues, authors learned from them, such that they could eventually "rise up and rival their Western counterparts in composing literary and nationalistic [*waṭaniyya*] novels."[25]

Some of these defenses came from translators of those "clownish" *feuilleton*. Niqūlā Rizqallah, the translator of more than a dozen crime and popular sentimental novels (including works by Xavier de Montépin, Michel Zévaco, Maurice Leblanc, and Jules Mary), argued for the literary and social usefulness of translated novels. Arab authors who wanted to write their own excellent literature, he argued in *Al-Amāl*, should first translate European novels, whose benefits include displaying "the morals of nations, the histories of countries, and the distinction between good and bad deeds."[26] Shākir Shuqayr (1850–1896), the author or translator of at least thirty works with titles like *The Lover in Disguise* (*Al-ʿĀshiq al-mutanakkir*, ca. 1900) and *The Ruses of Men* (*Makāyid al-rijāl*, 1886), similarly extolled the "benefits" of the genre: "literary amorous novels" (*al-riwāyāt al-gharāmiyya al-adabiyya*) make up an important part of his journal's purpose, which was to "announce to every region Egypt's progress in knowledge."[27] This was common in those journals that serialized popular novels; *Al-Rāwī* (The narrator, 1893), *Al-Mawsūʿāt* (1898), *Al-Laṭāʾif* (1886), and *Al-Ḍiyāʾ* (1898) all framed their incorporation of translated fiction as a "service to the nation."[28] "What are newspapers but a nation's educator?" asks an article in *Al-Laṭāʾif*, a monthly journal that focused on publishing novels, many of them sensational and scandalous stories of foreign noble and other plots that turned away from what would later be called "national reality."[29] Even those translators who pleaded to readers to avoid the "vice" of popular translated literature participated in that trend. Alongside Tolstoy and Pushkin, Khalīl Baydas translated the swashbuckling fiction of the sensationalist Emilio Salgari, and both he and Anṭūn capitalized on the popularity of scandalous fiction, giving their works titles that bear a striking resemblance to the sordid works they disparaged: Baydas entitled his translation of Tolstoy's historical novel *Prince Serebrenni* as "The horrors of despotism" (*Ahwāl al-istibdād*, 1909), and Anṭūn gave his translation of Dumas's *La Tour de Nesle* the title *Al-Burj al-hāʾil* (1899), or "The tower of horror."[30] Such translated novels—even popular ones—were not counterexamples to nationalist discourse but participants in it.

These translations' participation has been difficult to track because it has been written in registers that nationalist reformers dismissed as unserious. Translations of sentimental fiction and crime novels shared an employment of the melodramatic mode—a mode that, as Peter Brooks argues, is not *anti*-realist but rather in *excess* of realism: "The essential point may be that melodrama, even when it starts from the everyday, . . . refuses to content itself with the repressions, the tonings-down, the half-articulations, the accommodations, and the disappointments of the real. Melodrama's relationship to realism is always oblique—it is tensed toward an exploitation of expression beyond. It insists that the ordinary may be the place for the instauration of significance. It tells us that in the right mirror, with the right degree of convexity, our lives matter."[31] The question of which lives *matter* was, then as now, the essential question of politics in the context of national formation, consolidation, and crisis. Events later derided as arbitrary and unrealistic—a poor father debating selling his daughter rather than let her starve, a woman wrongly accused of arson—opened for readers real questions about the social function of power as well as the emotional lives of the powerless. It elevated everyday emotions and events and unlikely or underrepresented characters into social symbols and presented readers with characters whose lives are suffused with moral and political meaning. These melodramatic novels did not necessarily turn away from the nation; their oppressive fathers, fallen women, and corrupt police gave readers a means of confronting questions of power and justice in an unjust society. It asked who—the working class, the poor, and above all, women—should be included in an ideal society's domain of rights, justice, and freedom.

As this chapter shows, translations redeploy excess popular emotion as political, and they do so in such a way as to test gendered national discourses, complicating some of the very New Woman ideas that elite writers were putting forth. Though women were often at the center of national allegories, as Beth Baron has shown, even elite women were excluded from many of the rights that their nationalist male counterparts fought to hold. "The irony persists," Baron writes, "that although a woman symbolized the nation, women were pushed aside in national politics." In elite publications, they were often spoken *about* but not *to*—making "women's inclusion in the nation . . . a question."[32] Popular translations, on the other hand, spoke to—or at least their critics worried they did—women as well as men. Not only that, but these popular translations also framed those very questions in comparative and transnational contexts. Cross-continental criminal plots and investigations as well as sentimental novels about women from elsewhere—Japanese virgins, English maidens, Venetian damsels—set national issues inside much-larger questions of justice. These novels' participation in nationalist discourse, therefore, was always ambivalent. They enlarged the circle of sympathy and fellow feeling beyond the properly national, to a transnational affective community of women victims but also to a greater variety of classes and kinds of people within the nation. This chapter reinserts these popular translated novels and their major figures—the oppressed wife, the bad female example, and the good criminal—into the national conversation and shows how they make social and political claims. These melodramas, hardly trivial distractions from matters of national import, engaged readers in significant conversations about justice, freedom, and community, and they did so by provoking tears and chills.

The New Marriage Plot

In a climactic scene, appearing in Salim Ṣaʿb's translation of Camille Bodin's 1864 *Le Monstre*, translated as *Riwāyat al-ʿAjāʾib wa al-gharāʾib* (Strange and wondrous events, 1865), a central mystery is resolved: Louisa, unbeknownst to her, was the product of adultery, and her father has turned out to be none other than the head of a band of criminals, in whose home she had taken refuge after her own had burned down. The terrifying and yet romance-driven scene unfolds, fittingly, in the most chilling location: a cemetery. Ṣaʿb translates:

> The two men brought me to a church and threw me onto the graves. I saw a cross hanging on one of its walls, and a lit candle in front of it, so I immediately fell to my knees and began to pray to the Almighty to have mercy and save me. Suddenly the Prince's voice rang in my ears, ordering me to stand. He screamed:
>
> "Get up, you wretched weakling who wanted to help a woman flee her husband's home. What punishment do you request from me, who has treated you with favor and goodness, while you repaid me with ugliness."
>
> Then he turned to the crowd [*al-jamhūr*] of his companions who had arrived, saying, "What does this accursed woman deserve?"
>
> And the crowd [*al-jamhūr*] replied, "Murder, murder." And I saw daggers flashing in all of their hands.
>
> "Listen, you traitor . . . ," then he said, "she deserves more than that, but I will forgive her because I am her father."
>
> "You are her father?" the crowd [*al-jamhūr*] screamed.
>
> "Who is my father?" I screamed, and I fell to the ground.[33]

Al-ʿAjāʾib wa al-gharāʾib is a novel of international criminal networks, murder, and aristocratic sexual intrigue that its translator described as "dreadful [*mahūla*]" and "full of sad matters."[34] And yet, despite its body count, it is no thriller. Its larger story is about marriage practice, inheritance, and domestic order: the French female protagonist, who is in love with her young French cousin, is pressured into marrying an older, wealthy friend of her father's—this same criminal leader who poses as a German prince living in Sicily. He mistreats, abuses, and imprisons her until she is rescued by her true love, only to be recaptured by her husband and unjustly tried, imprisoned, and executed by the state. A sentimental social novel, scandalous but not anomalous, *Le Monstre*'s sensational elements perform what Margaret Cohen identifies as one of sensational novels' core functions: they "heighten [their protagonists'] 'interesting' status as victims of unjust codes."[35] Bodin was a virtuosa of this subgenre, pitting virtue against social mores, where the warp of sensational and melodramatic rhetoric tensed against the weft of conventional social grammar. Together, these elements formed a literary fabric woven throughout the nineteenth-century Arabic novel, culminating in turn-of-the-century Egypt, where elements of this plot repeated themselves in seemingly endless variations in hundreds of popular novels.[36] The sentimental novel bent toward crime as much as the crime novel bent toward sentiment.

Ṣaʿb's translation is an early example of this dynamic but a telling one. The issues it explores, including arranged marriage, romantic or companionate couplings, and unequal access to justice, would become, in the 1890s and early twentieth century, the dominant themes of translated and original novels alike. And the language in which it explores these themes—what Brooks calls "melodramatic rhetoric"—would become the era's dominant literary mode. Even in the preceding passage, we can see the figures that "evidence a refusal of nuance and the insistence on dealing in pure, integral concepts" including hyperbole: Louisa is not just "wretched" but a "wretched weakling"; there is not one knife but many.[37] A conventional moral antithesis structures the struggle between the two characters: they signify the contrast between pure concepts and nothing less than between good and evil. The evil prince calls her cursed or blameworthy (*malʿūna*) and describes himself as treating her with goodness (*khayr*). The narrative, in this tableau, counterpoises her piety with his murderous rage.[38]

These literary techniques, designed to provoke excitement, fear, and desire, were exactly what caused literary historians to dismiss novels such as this and what critics associated with women. A plot driven by adventure and romance, ʿAbd al-Muḥsin Ṭaha Badr writes, "reduces the activities of reason, and crowns sentiment as its ruler, turning over leadership to the heart."[39] In doing so, translations like *Al-ʿAjāʾib wa al-gharāʾib* are unrecognized participants in the debates about the New Woman, embedding issues like partner choice in entertainment reading. Indeed, we have already seen examples of a dramatic expansion in scholarship regarding what constitutes women's texts and writing about women. As Baron argues, though Qāsim Amīn is often referred to as "the father of Arab feminism," his *Taḥrīr al-marʾa* (The emancipation of women, 1899) and *Al-Marʾa al-jadīda* (The new woman, 1900) in fact trailed a decade of debates in which women writers and readers were key participants.[40] If we take translated novels into account, we can date these very same debates as early as the 1860s.

Like other translators, Ṣaʿb declined to recognize a strict distinction between these improper readerly responses and proper ones. As he put it in his translator's preface, the "extraordinary" events described in the novel were designed to provoke *hawl* (terror or shock) and *ḥuzn* (sadness), and yet he thought "their perusal would not be without benefit to the reader."[41] That is, he grounded his claim to having translated a "useful" work in his ability to provoke physical and emotional sensation. Ṣaʿb, as the reader will recall from chapter 4, produced a partial translation of *The Count of Monte Cristo*, but he also translated Bernadin de Saint Pierre's monument to readerly virtue, *Paul et Virginie* (*Būl wa Firjīnī*, 1864). While specialists of French literature might be keen to distinguish between the adventure novel, the salacious sentimental novel, and the novel of moral philosophy, Arabic translators and readers grouped them as part of the same subgenre. An advertisement in *Ḥadīqat al-akhbār* makes this explicit, describing *Al-ʿAjāʾib wa al-gharāʾib* as "a charming tale in the same style as Ṣaʿb's previous translation, *Paul et Virginie*."[42] Melodrama predominated not only because translators chose source texts that featured it but also because they *transformed* their source texts into it.

Part of the print public sphere from its very beginning, melodramatic sentimental novels put women's family, work, and emotional lives at their center, as participants discussed women's access to public space (including the space of the page), education, and wage labor; her proper role inside the home, which was newly imagined as that of the "mother of tomorrow" who undertook rational household management and oversaw the rearing of ideal modern citizens; and her contribution to forming and sustaining ideal marriages. The problem of marriage-partner choice drove more than just popular plots; it became one of the prominent issues driving public conversation during the *nahḍa*.[43] Romantic *ẓulm* is one of the most—if not *the* most—common themes of turn-of-the-century literary production.[44] In Najīb Gharghūr's *Hilāna*, an overbearing father promises his daughter to an older bachelor in exchange for a prestigious political position, and in another of his translations, *Gharāʾib al-tadwīn* (The strangest of recorded events, 1882), a father forbids a love match, inspiring multiple speeches condemning arranged marriage.[45] Forced marriage also featured in many of the novels serialized in *Al-Laṭāʾif*, including the appropriately titled *Al-Markīz al-ẓālim* (The oppressive marquis, 1896), as well as in a good number of sentimental translations, including Alexandra Avierino's *Shaqāʾ al-ummahāt* (The Severest of mothers, 1900) and Yūsuf ʿAṣṣāf's *Dhāt al-niqāb* (The veiled woman, 1886). Though the source of oppression is commonly the father, it is not always the case. In *Ghādat Fanīs* (The maiden of Venice, 1904), parents support their daughter's refusal of her cousin's proposal, but he kidnaps her anyway.[46] And in Labība Hāshim's *Al-Ghāda al-Ingiliziyya* (The English maiden, 1895), it is an uncle who marries the "maiden" of the title without her full consent.

Hāshim's translation of the English sensation novel *Called Back* (Hugh Conway, 1883) might be one of the most distilled examinations of the problem of marriage without female consent. The narrator describes Pauline as having a child's mind in a woman's body and as having lost even the ability to read. Docile and unlettered, she is described by the translation as *adība* (polite) in the same passage where her husband discovers her to be illiterate (and therefore not *adība*, or learned). In an addition not found in the source text, the husband (and narrator) wonders, "How could a woman like her be forbidden from education?"[47] Thinking that she is merely meek, the husband interprets her silence as consent and marries her with the help of an uncle, only to learn later that she lost her cognitive abilities when she witnessed her brother's murder. The husband turns out to be an oppressor, albeit an unwitting one; he is transformed into one by the patriarchal structure of courtship and marriage itself, which demands obedience from brides and gives them few official avenues to refuse a match.

Far from being irrelevant, *Al-Ghāda al-Ingiliziyya* appeared at a time when debates about marriage were roiling the women's and general press. Authors and intellectuals—both women and men—proposed and debated a modern vision of marriage and the family, including revised ideas about companionate marriage, coerced or arranged marriage, minimum age requirements for betrothal, a bride's ideal education and her understanding of household management, women's political participation, and women's work outside the home. As even the most liberal among these writers divided social life into gendered spheres of experience—and with woman's sphere imagined as the domestic one—marriage became the central conduit for all aspects of gendered reform. Since the home and family were imagined as the privileged sphere of women's experience, authority, and expertise, to modernize marriage was to modernize women's role in society at large. Simply put, marriage *was* women's politics.

The author, translator, and professor Labība Hāshim (ca. 1880–1947) wrote extensively about marriage practices, both in her journal articles and in her university lectures (she was the first Arab woman to be appointed lecturer in an Egyptian university, as well as the first woman to hold a government post in Syria). She argued for the value of companionate marriage among social and economic equals, promoted an ideal of the wife as a rational household manager, and expounded on women's role as the educator of future citizens. In this new ideology of marriage and domestic organization, Hāshim saw education as central. A "superficial education," Hāshim argued in a 1911 lecture, will not sufficiently prepare a young wife for the rigors and sacrifices of married life or give her the resources she needs to support her husband or educate her children.[48] Though Hāshim was one of the era's more liberal thinkers, having lobbied governments for the right to vote, her ideas about marriage were by no means outside the mainstream of the greater marriage debate. As Kenneth Cuno has shown, the new family ideology took the conjugal unit as the primary locus of reform and saw its stability as a social and even national good.[49] A woman's autonomy in maintaining that stability—from her informed consent in betrothal to her excellence in child rearing—is a central aspect of what was generally depicted as modern domestic progress. Even conservative writers on gendered issues saw women as the locus of civilizational progress. As one prominent essayist, Hanā Kasbānī Kūrānī (1870–1898), wrote, though women should by no means invade men's "field of action," the woman is nonetheless the "manager of the human world, tasked with the matter of progress and decline, for she is the mistress of homes."[50] For liberal writers like Hāshim, conservative commentators like Kūrānī, or Islamist critics like Malak Hifnī Nāṣif, the ideal wife and mother is educated for the purpose of domestic duties and marital stability and therefore national progress. Marriage, even companionate marriage based on shared romantic love, was by no means an exclusively domestic matter but had clear national (and nationalist) political implications. As Hanan Kholoussy writes, "marriage was a site of contested national identity formation that attracted the growing social attention of the middle-class press and the legal attention of the Egyptian administration under British rule."[51] Marriage politics *was* politics.

Though now dispatched to the margins of literary history, Hugh Conway's *Called Back* would not have been a surprising choice for a young translator in the 1890s.[52] Published in 1883 in *Arrowsmith's Christmas Annual*, a shilling literature series, it was an unprecedented success. It sold over 350,000 copies by 1897 and became one of the best-selling works of English fiction of the late nineteenth century, establishing the cheap "railway reading" series itself as a viable cultural form.[53] Indeed, by the time Hāshim picked it up, it had been translated into French, German, Danish, Czech, Swedish, Italian, and, most notably, Spanish, by the Cuban nationalist José Martí.[54] Emily Dickinson had read and praised it; not only did she compose a poem, "Called Back," on its theme, but the words "Called Back May 15, 1886" appear on her gravestone. Categorized variously as a thriller, a proto-detective novel (Arthur Conan Doyle's debut would be in the next year's *Christmas Annual*), and a late sensation novel, critics have emphasized its legal and political aspects and especially its description of a Siberian penal colony that "adds a pang of pity" to the tale, as the Scottish novelist Margaret Oliphant explained.[55] This is probably the case because the source text also emphasizes these aspects: told in the first person from the perspective of the male protagonist, it explains how he once witnessed a murder by walking into the wrong home. Having been himself severely visually impaired at the time, he only heard the event, but years later he coincidentally marries the only other witness—Pauline—who had fallen into a trance-like state ever afterward. In order to solve the murder and understand the source of her trauma (and thereby repair the psychological damage that resulted), the protagonist must travel to Italy and then Siberia. In Siberia, he learns that the victim was Pauline's brother, who was killed as part of an Italian nationalist plot. The protagonist solves the mystery of the crime and thereby aids in the recovery of his wife's memory, allowing them to at last begin a life of marital happiness.

In English, an international political conspiracy dominates the idiosyncratic personal mystery. In Arabic, Hāshim emphasizes the marriage plot above others. Though still narrated in the first person, the novel is focused—as the title suggests—on Pauline, "the English maiden." The sentimental and political plots are presented as one and the same. The language of justice, judgment, and law permeates political and amorous scenes alike: in English, the narrator wants to save Pauline from "danger"; in Arabic, she is "waiting for justice."[56] In English, the protagonist's goal is to learn what happened to her brother; in Arabic, it is to learn what happens to *her*. *Al-Ghāda al-Ingiliziyya* foregrounds not only the marriage plot but those aspects of courtship and marriage that make up an ideal modern marriage, one that will bring the couple "sure happiness," as Hāshim's text ends.[57] Both the translation and the source text end the story with the protagonist repairing Pauline's ability to consent to their marriage once she has regained her cognitive abilities, by his wooing her and proposing marriage a second time. In Arabic, however, Hāshim adds a political subtext: "I will submit myself to a judgment from her lips," the protagonist tells the reader, "as love is the only power that can compel her to stay with me."[58] Her freely given answer is rendered law, a power capable of legitimizing or voiding their legal marriage, at least morally speaking. Rather than subordinating the marriage plot to international politics, as the English does, Hāshim casts marriage itself *as* politics. She casts companionate romantic marriage between educated, consenting parties as a moral and even legal standard.

Al-Ghāda al-Ingiliziyya asserts—as Hāshim herself and others did in the press—that marriage without the bride's active and informed consent is a form of injustice. And it puts that injustice on equal footing with international political events. Pauline's tormenter, and her brother's murderer, is also an enemy of the state and not one of the republican *muḥibī al-waṭan* (lovers of the nation) like her pitiable uncle. In English, the novel ends with this villain escorted away by French soldiers after the fall of the Paris Commune, years after Pauline regains her memory. In Arabic, Hāshim not only sets this event to coincide with their honeymoon but adds a crowd (*jamhūr*) that gathers to jeer the "corrupt hooligans."[59] Private marital happiness coincides with an emphatically public political resolution.

By adding the *jamhūr*, Hāshim employs a term that had recently experienced a significant evolution, as Wael Abu-ʿUksa explains. While eighteenth-century common usage of the term meant simply "crowd" or "public," it was "increasingly politicized with the emergence of the popular masses as a force in politics."[60] During the nineteenth century, it began to be employed as a translation of "republic" and was used in the phrase *qiyām al-jamhūr*, or "popular uprising," to indicate revolution (what would later be called *thawra*). Like *al-ḥurriyya*, or "freedom," it is a word that translators added to often-romantic texts and that brought with it significant political connotations. Hāshim uses it to add political resolution to her marriage plot: Pauline's long-awaited "justice" is achieved simultaneously by her honeymoon and the apprehension of this criminal in front of The People.

Hāshim's use of *jamhūr* also echoes, probably unwittingly, Ṣaʿb's addition to Bodin's sensational *Le Monstre*. In the scene with which I opened this section, when the villainous Prince accuses Louisa of being a "traitor" (*khā'ina*), he does so in front of a jeering, knife-wielding "crowd." This, like Hāshim's *jamhūr*, is an addition and one that is repeated three times over the course of the scene. Bodin refers to this group merely as "those that accompanied the Prince," but Ṣaʿb repeatedly names them *al-jamhūr*, or the public. Louisa's mock trial takes place in front of this audience (another translation for *jamhūr*), turning the private shame of her parentage, and the private scandal of her friend's forced marriage, into a matter of public concern. The emotionally charged spectacle, far from providing a distraction from social issues, is actually the *locus* of those issues. Here, as well as in the legal trial and public execution that follow, the novel produces political commentary—about justice, marriage, and even "freedom"—through the suffering bodies of female characters. Melodramatic scenes such as this one, dismissed though they might be by literary historians, demonstrate what Lauren Berlant has called "the place of painful feeling in the making of political worlds," where models of citizenship include not just dutiful wives or productive workers but suffering bodies that, with their pain, demonstrate their value as citizens.[61] Melodrama's inquiry into the moral legibility of society, in front of fictional and actual publics, marks it as a political mode, albeit a tear-soaked one.

Melodrama registers tears, particularly women's tears, as political objects. Women's suffering, as an object of both polemical writing and fictional narrative, transported melodrama's political modes into nonfictional political discourse as well. Books and biographical articles about "female worthies," one of the central genres of nonfictional writing about women, are saturated with depictions of women's psychic and physical suffering in the pursuit of their "'atypical' careers" and exceptionality.[62] In both women's journals and general ones, articles and stories highlighting women's suffering helped make the case for expanded education and rights for women. Stories of child brides committing suicide argued for raising the minimum age of marriage, for example.[63] At least one periodical, Rūz Anṭūn's *Majallat al-sayyidāt wa al-banāt* (Ladies and girls' revue, 1903), ran a regular "Wronged Woman Column," in which "oppressed women" (*nisā' maẓlūmāt*) wrote in to narrate their complaints to a national community of women readers. As Booth writes in her pioneering study of these biographies, "invocations of female authorship and readership" in columns like "Wronged Women" and other reporting of female complaint "include a reference to 'we Easterners.'"[64] Narratives of women's suffering, far from being depicted as inchoate experience or "prelapsarian knowledge,"[65] as Berlant writes, are a form of ideology.

Indeed, the declaration of personhood, or what Samera Esmeir has called "juridical humanity" (the declaration of humanity as the basis for legal rights),[66] was itself an important dimension of women's rights discourse at the time, and it takes a central position in Qāsim Amīn's nationalist argument. While "despotic governments" oppress women, Amīn argues in *The Liberation of Women*, modern women "believe that they are human beings and that they deserve freedom, and they are therefore striving for freedom and demanding every human right." For Amīn, it is the personhood of women—their education, the elevation of their status within the family, and the conferral of their rights according to Islam—that eventually determines "the development or underdevelopment of a country."[67] This was an argument "that was mobilized in the effort to redeem Egypt and deliver it from backwardness, as well as to signal the advancement of Egyptian men," who Amīn argues should, if they are themselves "sensitive and refined," recognize "that a woman is a human being, too."[68] Melodramatic narratives performed multifaceted political work—creating modern women whose tears demand "justice," as well as modern men whose tears recognize the political import of women's suffering, thereby signifying their own enlightened status. Novels about women's suffering were not only written for a female audience but also aimed to produce morally educated male readers in order to reform the political community at large. The original works of 'A'isha Taymūr (1840–1902) and Zaynab Fawwāz, as Booth writes, make exactly such an argument: "Successful masculine political leadership must be based on responsible, respectful interaction with others, notably women as speaking members of the political community"—or, more specifically, with women as *weeping members* of the political community.[69] The New Man was one who "weeps with the poor, sympathizes with the wrongly charged innocent, and rejoices for any good that befalls others," as Amīn writes.[70] Through melodramatic rhetoric, which aligns moral opposition with extreme emotion, politics is rendered not through representational modes but through affective ones.[71] Through the feeling of being scared *for* someone or sad *with* them, melodrama—those events that Ṣaʿb describes as *mustaghraba* (shocking) and *muhawwala* (terror provoking)—produce a political community, a *jamhūr*.

Characterizing the romantic plot (*al-riwāya al-gharāmiyya*, as many authors and translators subtitled their own novels) as unpolitical or unrealistic is one of the critical biases that has helped to marginalize these translations in the Arabic canon. Ahmad al-Zayyāt, in 1928, described this prerevolutionary period as one characterized by "the literature of essence, in which people sought . . . stories that describe sorrow and depict vices."[72] Though the titles and subtitles of these works categorized them as romantic novels, however, it would be a mistake to see their political commentary as incidental or part of the setting or to see their marriage plots as simply the sugar coating the pill of more serious subjects. Hāshim's fiction is a good example; critics have predominantly praised her work for its insights into "a woman's heart," as one contemporary reader put it, rather than her analysis of moments of political turmoil.[73] Similarly, *al-Ghāda al-Ingiliziyya*'s title invites readers to characterize it as a light romance, but its plot fuses a political crime plot and a marriage plot. It invites us to read beyond the (often misleading) titles to discover the political content of women's suffering and the essential link between political events and women's domestic and emotional lives. As the narrator of Ḥanā Ṣāwa's *Ḍaḥiyat al-gharām* (The victim of romance, 1905) explains, these novels often chart "the effect . . . on love" of the nation's political events.[74]

Some translators, like Ṣāwa, seemed to choose their source texts for their political relevance. On the title page, he explains that the work translated is "a romantic historical novel based on real events that occurred during the French Revolution." Other translators, however, translated romantic source texts *into* a political register. In Adīb Isḥāq's translation of La Comtesse Dash's *La Belle Parisienne* (*Al-Bārisiyya al-ḥasnā'*, 1884), which was popular (and presumably socially relevant) enough to warrant two reprintings before 1902, female characters assert their "rights" and debate the true meaning of "freedom," signaling a larger political conversation by adding phrases with the keywords of national liberation movements, *ḥuriyya* (freedom) and *istiqlāl* (independence).[75] Isḥāq, in fact, frames the entire novel as a meditation on marriage and women's suffering. He detaches part of the source text to use as an "introduction," transforming it by translating it into the language of justice and social reform: "This is the fate of women much of the time in this day and age, and yet they are accused and judged by every tongue. Ah, if only the *manṣifūn* [righteous] knew what you suffer, if only the just [*ʿādilūn*] saw what miseries you endure, and if only the people of truth [*ahl al-ḥaqq*] saw what trials of injustice you combat, then they would grant you mercy and compassion rather than blame and censure."[76] The French source text does not share the Arabic's ideological ambitions. It does not mention righteousness, justice, or injustice; while Dash describes women as enduring "sorrows and battles" (*souffrances* and *combats*), these are sorrows that are particular to them. "Si l'on se rendait compte de *leurs* souffrances . . . *leurs* combats," she writes: if we were aware of *their* sorrows, *their* battles.[77] In Arabic, women's suffering is instead made relevant to larger questions of truth and justice—proving what scholars of women's issues have been arguing for over two decades, that gender politics was central to debates about modernity.[78] In *Riwāyat al-qulūb al-kasīra* (Novel of the shattered hearts, 1896–1897), when the protagonist learns that the object of his affection will be forced to marry an older (and hunchbacked) man, he asks, "How can this be possible in our age of freedom?"[79] Melodramatic rhetoric in these novels is a type of political discourse, one that does not turn away from social and national concerns but is rather the very means used to interrogate them. These translators, then, translated these texts into two registers simultaneously: a melodramatic *and* a sociopolitical one. They figure scenes that attract the "lower faculties" and the heart as matters of *public and legal order*.

Women's Freedom in Mistranslation

> "Dear Madams,
>
> Permit me to present my English Maiden, dressed in Arab garb and circulating among you heedless of disdain or contempt . . . not because she claims infallibility; but because she desires your understanding. How could she not when the kinder sex of the eminent station has judged her, could she not then afterward fear blame or rebuke?"[80]

Marriage, in these texts, was not simply a women's issue but a larger social one whose repercussions reverberated outward into the largest umbrella of political conversation, as questions of justice and freedom, and whose politics were not exclusively radical. The beautiful Parisian of Isḥāq's title, after all, claims to be "completely free" at the moment of her scandalous attempted suicide.[81] And the titular "bad wife" of Ḥanā Asʿad Fahmī's *Qarīnat al-sūʾ* (The bad wife, 1904) is described as a "model of those young women who ask for complete freedom (*ḥuriyya*) of behavior.[82] Her "freedom" takes the form of abandoning her working-class fiancé to become the kept woman of a wealthy man and results in her mother's death and her own ruin. And in yet another novel about marriage choice, Najīb Jirjis ʿAbd Allah's *Ḥasnā' Niyū Yurk* (The belle of New York, 1905), the titular belle declares herself "free" the moment she pushes her captor and legal husband off a bridge.[83] A woman's ability to choose her partner not only was a central debate about women's domestic lives but was framed as a marker of their greater "freedom," itself a watchword of anticolonialist national debates. As a conservative character in Murqus Fahmī's 1894 play *Al-Mar'a fī al-sharq* (The woman in the East), puts it, "If we permit the woman to choose her husband, we'd also have to allow her free movement and the opportunity to meet men in order to find someone she likes. . . . This would harm society morally and materially."[84] Freedom to choose a spouse is connected, in a chain of interlocking and ever-widening freedoms, to the largest structures of society and, ultimately, for some, to national liberation itself.[85]

Like many of the translated novels of the period, *Al-Mar'a fī al-sharq* tells the story of a young woman coerced into marriage despite being in love with another man and ends with typical melodramatic pathos, with her killing her husband and herself. Again, not only private happiness but public matters of criminality and injustice are the result of this woman's unfreedom. As Margot Badran explains, Fahmī's play was an important touchstone for the debate about women's issues and was an unacknowledged source for Qāsim Amīn's *Liberation of Women*. Amīn, in fact, devotes the bulk of his section on the family in *The Liberation of Women* to issues of marriage choice, advocating for the right of women to meet their intended before an engagement and to be consulted on their choice. Marriage in its present state, both Fahmī and Amīn contend, is a form of tyranny that is echoed in state oppression.[86] "When the status of a nation is low," Amīn writes, "the status of women is also low, and when the status of a nation is elevated, reflecting the progress and civilization of that nation, the status of women in that country is also elevated." If reformed, however, marriage "will become the natural means for fulfilling the dreams of both men and women."[87] Like many thinkers after him, he links marriage reform and women's freedom to national reform.

Fahmī's play was based on actual events that occurred in his delta hometown, but a great many of these marriage plots were to be found in translated novels whose action took place elsewhere. Rather than "women of the East," their titles highlighted their focus on foreign women who were frequently the protagonists in the typical sentimental "double bind" that unearths contradictions in issues of domestic morality.[88] Many translations were titled solely with the names of this foreign protagonist, like *Matīlda* (trans. Sāmī Quṣayrī,

1885), *Blānsh Fūbārūn* (trans. Yūsuf Ṭawwa, 1902), *Margarīt* (trans. Tawfīq Dubrīy, 1892; and Aḥmad Zakī, 1914); some of these female protagonists were royal ones, like *Amīrat Anjal* (1886) and *Waqā'i' al-Malika Kātrīn* (trans. Ibrāhīm Ṭarād, 1898); and some were identified only by their nationality, like Hāshim's *Al-Ghāda al-Ingiliziyya* or Isḥāq's *Al-Bārisiyya al-ḥasnā'*. Indeed this final category could itself be seen as an important subgenre of Arabic novel at the turn of the century. The appetite for narratives of young women from elsewhere seemed to have been insatiable: there were maidens from Paris (*Fātinat Bārīs*, 1892), Venice (*Ghādat Fanīs*, 1903), and Berlin (*Ghādat Birlīn*, 1906), beauties from New York (*Ḥasnā' Niyū Yūrk*, 1905), princesses from England (*Amīrat Inglatarā*, 1907) and Greece (*Al-Amīra al-Yūnāniyya*, 1907), and virgins from Japan (*'Udhrā' al-Yābān*, 1906).[89] The genre, in fact, seemed to be established enough by the end of the nineteenth century that authors were creating original novels with similar foreign-sounding titles.[90] The editors of *Al-Jāmi'a* even took exception to that fact; they were skeptical that Ḥassan Riyāḍ's *Al-Fatāh al-yābāniyya* (The Japanese maiden, 1903), published in *Musāmārāt al-sha'b*, was an original novel as the author claimed, rather than the translation that it seemed to be. "If the esteemed author truly did compose this work without relying on a foreign novel, then it would have been easier to write it about an Egyptian maiden rather than a Japanese one," they write.[91] The question of marriage reform was a national question yet one narrated through the stories of foreign women confronting their own local marriage issues.

The marriage plot, that is, was part of a larger discussion that was both transnational and national: it explored notions of "freedom" for Arab or Muslim women in conversation with and in comparison to women elsewhere, which was a discussion that was folded (and sometimes uncomfortably so) into a discussion of freedom for the nation, itself a political concept that required the translation of purportedly universal concepts into local political vernacular. Tracking the history of the use of the word "freedom," as Wael Abu-'Uksa has done in *Freedom in the Arab World: Concepts and Ideologies in Arabic Thought in the Nineteenth Century*, highlights the extent to which its mutation occurred in tandem with processes of translation. The abstract verbal noun first came into use, he tells us, in the translation of Napoleonic proclamations after the invasion of Egypt in 1798, when about four thousand copies of a translated French address were distributed among the Egyptian population. The chronicler 'Abd al-Raḥmān al-Jabartī (d. 1825 or 1826) records its text as proclaiming that "the French [state] that is built on the basis of freedom [*ḥurriya*]" declares "all people are equal in the eyes of God" and that "from now on no Egyptian shall worry about not being able to take part in high positions [of the state]."[92] It is a claim that al-Jabartī finds preposterous. He describes the entire document riddled with "incoherent words and vulgar constructions" resulting from bad translations, with "liberty" being an especially egregious example. Defining "their term 'liberty' [*ḥurriya*]" as "mean[ing] that they are not slaves," he ridicules the statement as "a lie and stupidity," for "how can this be when God has made some superior to others"?[93] It is also, as he continues, hypocritical: "They follow this rule: great and small, high and low, male and female are all equal. [Yet] sometimes they break this rule according to their whims and inclinations and reasoning."[94] Two decades later, the Lebanese chronicler Niqūlā al-Turk (d. 1828) also provided an analysis of this proclamation but differed as to his translation of *ḥurriya*, which he understood according to the political status of Christians in the Ottoman Empire: "the principle of Freedom," he explained, was freedom of worship, which also implied "collective emancipation from social and legal constraints."[95] Even before the association of freedom with national sovereignty, its definition was manufactured in conversation with representations of European politics, with "proponents of freedom" (*ahl al-ḥurriya*) understood first as exclusive to western European political movements, then by the 1850s to "all proponents of the idea of progress," and in the 1870s to constitutional movements in the Ottoman Empire.[96] The production of this central political category of *nahḍa* sociopolitical thought was a history of translation that included both bad translations and their critiques.

Although Abu-ʿUksa remarks that "the evolving discourse on politics was associated mainly with men, not women," several of his examples use women's behavior as an index of the word's semantic evolution.[97] Al-Jabartī, as he notes, folds a critique of French-Egyptian intermarriage into his inquiry into political concepts, and accounts contemporary to al-Turk's writing record freedom's effects on social norms and particularly on women.[98] Yet if Abu-ʿUksa had ventured into the women's press, he would have found a robust discussion about *ḥurriya* and its interpretation. Over the course of two decades, both in response to Amīn's publications and extending well beyond them, articles on "freedom of thought," "freedom of action," and simply "freedom" appeared regularly in the women's press. And male and female thinkers in the religious and secular press alike debated the value and even the meaning of freedom and "free choice" for women. "Freedom for women," an author in *Al-Hilāl* laments in a common argument, causes them "to forget their duties as mothers . . . in the pursuit of the rights of men."[99] Still other writers rejected this notion, arguing—as an author in *Al-Ḍiyāʾ* did—that the gradual increase in women's freedom will bring the nation "out of ignorance."[100] For Amīn, this difference in opinion was nothing more than a misunderstanding of the *meaning* of freedom, which for him "means a person's independence of thought, will, and action, as long as this does not exceed legal limits and maintains the moral standards of society."[101] "If they [readers] understood the *meaning* of freedom," he writes, "they would share my opinion."[102]

Women authors, however, disagreed. They were divided on the issue of women's freedom precisely because they *did not* agree on its meaning. They launched a robust inquiry into the meaning of women's freedom in both the secular and the religious press, and it was principally a comparative inquiry. Lamenting social ills among women in Britain like adultery and gambling, an author in *Fatāt al-sharq* (Woman of the east) magazine writes, "This freedom with which women of the West are so pleased does not always bring happiness and pride to women."[103]

What freedom is there, asked Fāṭima Rashīd, the editor of the Islamic revivalist woman's magazine *Tarqiyat al-Mar'a* (Women's progress, 1908), "in coming and going, working with man shoulder to shoulder," like European women do?[104] Malak Ḥifnī Nāṣif, writing under her pseudonym Bāḥithat al-Bādiya (Researcher from the oasis), published an entire essay in this vein in her "Women's Issues" (*Nisā'iyāt*) column in *Al-Manār* (The lighthouse). She identified "women's freedom" as a modern Islamic value, writing,

> Some Muslim women wish to resemble Western women in their clothing and manner of living, thinking that freedom has cast its anchor with them alone and is legally forbidden to Muslim women. Yet if they were to properly manage the affairs of their religion and look carefully into the laws that the West follows, then they would see that their own share of *true freedom* was larger than that of Western women. They must not confuse the clothes of the Western woman or how many of them stroll the streets, for this freedom of hers is like someone giving you a dirham only to ask you for a dinār.[105]

Defining freedom, in the women's press as well as in larger political discourse, involved a process of translation. In Nāṣif's effort to define "true freedom" and distinguish it from what she later will call a "superficial" definition, she employs—as she does in much of her writing—at least two contrasting vocabularies. Islamic discourse frames many of her ideas, even those that her fellow reformers found shocking, as she describes women's social roles in the language of *sharī'a* and *turāth*. Yet so too did she employ the terminology of what she calls the "laws of the West," including *al-ḥuqūq al-madaniyya* (civil rights) and *qawmiyya* (nationhood), just paragraphs later.[106] She uses the word "freedom" repeatedly in this piece, and at each instance its valences shift. Some permutations are written with implied quotation marks around them, and some are qualified (e.g., "true" freedom, "this freedom"); but none are rendered as neutral or stable entries in her lexicon of liberation. The debate, even this short passage demonstrates, was less about *if* freedom is appropriate for women than what freedom *means* and what that meaning in turn signifies for society, religion, and the nation.

More precisely, Nāṣif employs each vocabulary to translate the other. Her "true freedom" emerges from the mutual questioning of *ḥuriyya* and *liberté*, in which freedom is neither solely the province of Western women nor—as she continues—found in isolating women from the West's influence.[107] Instead, as we have seen in the *nahḍa*'s mode of reading in translation, it arose through mutual critique, what Naoki Sakai calls the "being-with" of translation. As Sakai explains in the case of Japan, national culture and literature emerge as a process of mutual mediation: "It takes the form of 'I am conscious of you,'" he writes, but "in this case, the act of seeing you is already prescribed by your act of seeing. . . . Hence, my consciousness of you *is interwoven in your consciousness of me*."[108] *Ḥuriyya*, that is, is neither separate from *liberté* nor solely determined by it; for Nāṣif, it is most properly defined by a woman who sees her "freedom" with the eye of Western expectations but who also understands her rights under Islamic law.

Shaden Tageldin translates Sakai's insights into an Egyptian context: "Egypt learned to recognize itself . . . in the translational mirror of the universal: the imperial universal of the modern West."[109] Egyptian intellectuals debating national liberation after the turn of the century, as she argues, called for reforms that would be "recognizable to the European" as attributes of a modern nation, which would allow these reformers to "re-recognize themselves in the mirror of European recognition."[110] Yet, unlike the male intellectuals that she argues engaged in a "willed forgetting of the inequality of the putatively 'universal' ground," writers like Nāṣif and her fellow feminists (both Islamist and non-Islamist) were well aware of the way that Orientalists had portrayed their purported unfreedom. This was because their bodies and romantic autonomy were not translational figures but the very sites of inequality that grounded both Orientalist and nationalist writings. Amīn's apologist reply to the French Duc d'Harcourt's indictment of Egyptian gender practices, *Les Égyptiens: Réponse à M. le Duc d'Harcourt*, had already drawn vigorous debate, leading the Egyptian princess Nazli Fazil to invite Amīn to her influential salon to hear counterarguments.[111] And Fatme ʿAliya, the prolific Ottoman Turkish novelist, columnist, and translator whom Zaynab Fawwāz called a "source of pride for the secluded women of Islam,"[112] frames her own lauded *Women of Islam* as a correction to the mistaken way Muslims, and especially Muslim women, had been characterized by European authors. As she writes, "These foreigners stay in Hotel Bey or Hotel Ghalī and attempt to describe the lives of those about whom they know nothing, asking uninformed questions in order to attain information. And in order to respond, [the subjects of these inquiries] are forced to reply with meaningless speech. They [the writers] are praised for what they do not understand, while our affairs become the subject of fiction."[113] 'Aliya, who was herself a translator of French sentimental fiction and whose own work was translated into French, sees women's issues in the refracted mirror of mutual translation. The garbled responses of Orientalists' native informants are in response to uninformed questions, and the resulting publications—though lauded in France—are no better than fiction, perhaps even the sensationalist fiction that female readers are accused of overconsuming. As she corrects a European woman guest who characterizes Muslim women as overly obedient, "if you wanted to sell some of your investments, you require the permission of a man; as for us, we are free and independent in selling and investing what we own."[114] Freedom's meaning emerges through a process of mutual *mis*translation. 'Aliya prompts us to revise Sakai's hypothesis: it is not mutual recognition that underpins the formation of national culture but mutual misunderstanding. As 'Aliya continues, reprising her anecdote later in her text, "when we read their books we imagine that we are reading about some other country that we don't recognize."[115] There is no universal ground, no perfect original, but only proliferating examples and counterexamples. *Liberté*, one might conclude, may in fact be a bad translation of *ḥurriya*.

Women's writing and writing about women at the turn of the century are saturated with similar comparative impulses. The women's press contained articles that compared the lives, habits, and education of Eastern and Western women, reported on international women's association meetings, and staged fictional "conversations between Eastern and Western women." In the process, these writers returned, again and again, to the issue of freedom. "The Eastern woman," a contributor to *Al-Ḥasnā'* (The beauty) writes, "does not lag behind the Western one in intellectual, emotional, or spiritual talent . . . for she is no doubt her equal.—And what Turkish women have done in the service of *ḥurriya* before the constitutional revolution and afterward strengthens our hopes [in that equality]."[116] Translators and biographers alike put, as Hāshim wrote, foreign women like her English maiden into "Arab dress," translating European women into Arabic and Arab women into transnational definitions of political concepts.[117]

Yet the exemplarity of Western women held a contradictory place in women's discourse: if, on the one hand, readers were admonished not to become bad translations of their European counterparts—copying the outward trappings of freedom while ignoring its true meaning—they were also given repeated positive examples to contemplate and follow. The Western role model was a regular feature of women's biographical articles and compendiums, in which authors told the life stories of exemplary women and drew out pedagogical insights and moral lessons. While these writers did not see their commitments as derivative of Western feminism, they did translate them into local nationalist imagery and compare various "women's *nahḍas*" in international history. They were also often articles themselves translated from French and English texts. If narratives of women's lives formed a "complex narrative of modernity that put female heroines at the center," as Booth writes, the predominance of Western women's lives should remind us that it is a translational narrative of modernity conceived of as transnational.[118]

Good Criminals

It is no small wonder that translated fictions that put Western women's lives at their center constituted such a large part of the novel market during this period. They were an important conduit for understanding and debating women's agency and its morality and one that brought the New Woman debate and its focus on marriage law into the living rooms of a wide range of middle-class families. But they also brought new and sometimes problematic models of exemplary femininity in their incorporation of this rhetoric of "freedom." As Hāshim's dedication to *Al-Ghāda al-Ingiliziyya* makes clear, these were not ideal models of feminine agency. Instead, they demonstrate another kind of exemplarity. They were portraits of fallible, vulnerable women whose search for freedom in an unfree system of gender relations brought them shame or ruin and who demanded a mode of engagement from their readers beyond imitation or rejection. Instead, they asked for sympathy, reflection, and understanding: an affective response that is itself a form of critique and an essential one, according to Tarek El-Ariss. Emotional responses to romantic literature transformed the body—in this case, the female one—into what he calls "sites of transformation and new meanings" that emerged "in and between Europe and the Arab world, the literary text and political discourse."[119] Nonexemplary examples struck a melodramatic mode of debating modernity in which tears, "electric" tremors, and joyous ululations put modernity and the modern woman on trial.[120]

Putting the modern woman on "trial" was a process both metaphorical and literal in these novels: their references to "freedom" and "justice" placed women's issues within structures that were marked as explicitly political. The cry, "I am innocent," so often heard in these narratives, did more than elicit tears of sympathy for a virtuous protagonist who has been wrongfully accused.

It fused sentimental and legal issues in a single moral-affective vocabulary. Even the most cursory of surveys of Arabic sentimental romances yields a storehouse of tropes that simultaneously exercise readers' legal and romantic imaginations: kidnapped brides, romantic outlaws, violent attacks on women's "virtue," infanticide, wrongful imprisonment, virtuous criminals, corrupt policemen, mistaken identities, and heroines in disguise were the popular translator's stock-in-trade. Their ubiquity reveals the proximity of the sentimental genre with another burgeoning subgenre, crime fiction, whose immense popularity spurred translations, adaptations, and original reimaginings whose exact contours have yet to be fully accounted for. Elliott Colla cites at least eight series of detective narratives that were published in the early decades of the twentieth century, including Nasīb al-Mashʿalānī's translations of Sherlock Holmes stories in *Al-Ḍiyāʾ* magazine and then *Majallat Sarkīs* (1904–1908), ʿAbd al-Qādir Hamza's translations of Maurice Leblanc's Arsène Lupin novels in *Musamarāt al-shaʿb* (1910), and Ḥāfiẓ Najīb's translations of the Johnson series (*Jūnsūn*, ca. 1920).[121] Ṭāniyūs ʿAbduh's translations of Ponson du Terrail's Rocambole novels (*Rūkāmbūl*) were so well read that several of his seventeen volumes had been printed three times by 1906.[122] Salīm Sarkīs remarks that the series captured readers' attention like nothing else. He writes of an audience so devoted that some members could not wait until the next installment arrived; he recounts an anecdote about a Cairo reader who telephoned a friend in Alexandria to learn how one *Rocambole* novel ended, rather than wait the single day that separated the two cities' delivery schedules.[123] These famous literary protagonists, whose names preceded and even eclipsed those of their translators and original authors on their title pages as in reader's imaginations, made up "an important if informal canon of great modern fictional heroes for three or four generations of Egyptian writers and readers," as Selim notes.[124]

As the popularity of the criminal trickster Rocambole attests, crime was not limited to the detective genre. It spanned subgenres and even genres, as Colla notes, informing autobiography, *maqāma*, and translations of fictionalized memoirs that explored the lives of criminals, prostitutes, and other marginalized urban actors.[125] To the roster of turn-of-the-century characters of famous detectives, thieves, and criminals, we must add wrongful imprisonment, virtuous courtesans, noble thieves, and villainous police. This expansive category can include Jean Valjean and Jean Vaubaron, the unjustly accused protagonists of melodramatic tearjerkers. Indeed, when seen from the perspective of the turn-of-the-century market and its critical apparatus, the boundary between crime novels and sentimental ones appears much more porous than previously understood. Readers faced with the titles and subtitles of works like *Al-Fatāh al-sijīna, aw Dhāt al-shaʿr al-dhahabī* (The imprisoned beauty; or, the golden-haired girl, ca. 1890–1900) or *Al-Būlīs al-sirrī aw al-Shayṭāna al-ẓarīfa* (The secret police; or, the charming devil-woman, 1900) might reasonably expect contents that simultaneously satisfied multiple narrative desires. Reading through the popular archive, politically motivated romances, crimes of passion and even maternal love, and a seemingly endless procession of wrongfully accused heroes and heroines blurred the boundary between romance and crime fiction. Take, for instance, a list of recent publications for sale at a Cairo bookshop around 1900 (figure 6.1). Out of the thirty-three new works for sale on this page, about a third are recognizably crime focused, even containing the word "crime" or "theft" in the title ("The murdered man's crime," "The child abductor," "The corpse thief," "The skill of the police"), and a bit less than a third are unmistakably romantic ("The power of love," "The lover's post," "The girl of beauty"). But then there are also several titles that could place the novels in either subgenre. "The martyr to love" and "Lovers' atrocities," for example, could contain stories of metaphorical violence (the violence of passion, for example) or actual violent crimes. Is the "Āh" of *Āh, yā ḥarāmī* (Oh, you thief) a sigh of admiration or an exclamation of agitated surprise? For a reader who has come to associate the novel genre itself with emotional excitement, either outcome might have been expected.

In fact, the pleasures that the crime genre promised appeared remarkably similar to the pleasures associated with the sentimental genre. In an early-1920s advertisement for the series of the Johnson (*Jūnsūn*) crime novels, its publisher ran a mock warning for readers that ironized the very complaints that critics lodged against the popular sentimental novel in previous decades (figure 6.2):

> Warning
>
> From Musṭafā Muḥammad, owner of the Commercial Bookshop, located at 1 Muḥammad ʿAlī Street in Cairo
>
> to
>
> The Readers of the Johnson Novels
>
> The bookstore warns all readers of the [forthcoming] *Johnson's Marriage*, translated by the writer Ḥāfiẓ Najīb, that we do not guarantee their sanity after they have ventured to read it and alert all to the fact that we will only sell this novel to those who have obtained the following assurances:
>
> First: a certificate from the director of a mental hospital confirming that there is ample space in the hospital to receive new patients;

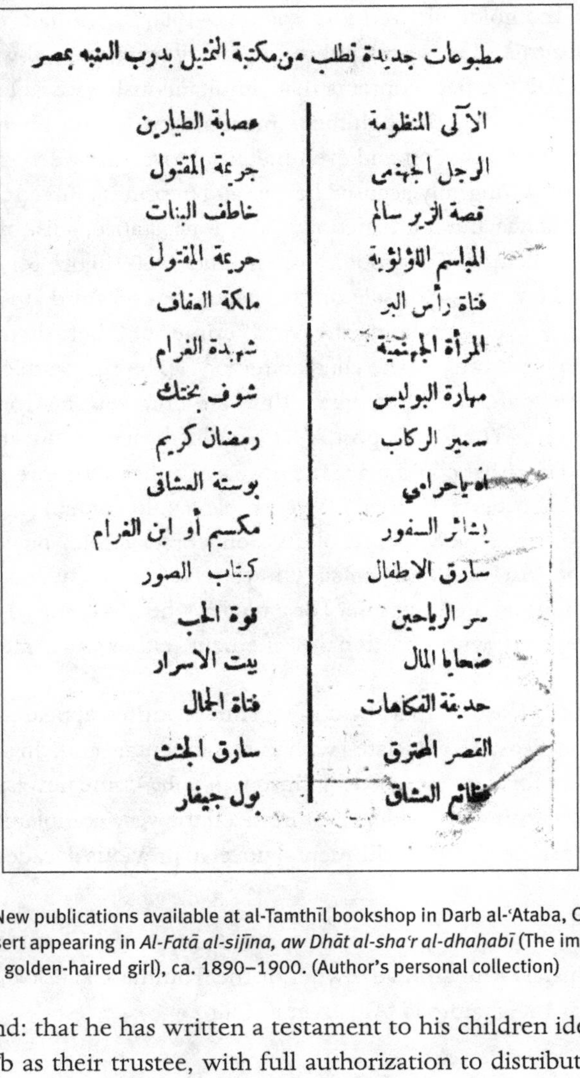

مطبوعات جديدة تطلب من مكتبة التمثيل بدرب العتبه بمصر

الآلى المنظومة	عصابة الطيارين
الرجل الجهنمى	جريمة المقتول
قصة الزير سالم	خاطف البنات
المباسم اللؤلؤية	جريمة المقتول
فتاة رأس البر	ملكة العفاف
المرأة الجهنمية	شهيدة الغرام
مهارة البوليس	شوف بختك
سمير الركاب	رمضان كريم
أه ياحرامي	بوستة العشاق
بشائر السفور	مكسيم أو ابن الغرام
سارق الاطفال	كتاب الصور
سر الرياحين	قوة الحب
ضحايا المال	بيت الاسرار
حديقة الفكاهات	فتاة الجمال
القصر المحترق	سارق الجثث
فظائع العشاق	بول جيفار

Figure 6.1. New publications available at al-Tamthīl bookshop in Darb al-ʿAtaba, Cairo, ca. 1900. Advertising insert appearing in *Al-Fatā al-sijīna, aw Dhāt al-shaʿr al-dhahabī* (The imprisoned beauty; or, the golden-haired girl), ca. 1890–1900. (Author's personal collection)

Second: that he has written a testament to his children identifying Mr. Najīb as their trustee, with full authorization to distribute the estate as he sees fit;

Third: that he has received a certification from the authorities that he displays [no] traces of madness in the present circumstances.

Fourth: that he has received a prescription from a specialist in mental illness permitting him to read *Johnson's Marriage* under his supervision.

[Signed,]
The owner of the Commercial Bookshop
Muṣṭafā Muḥammad[126]

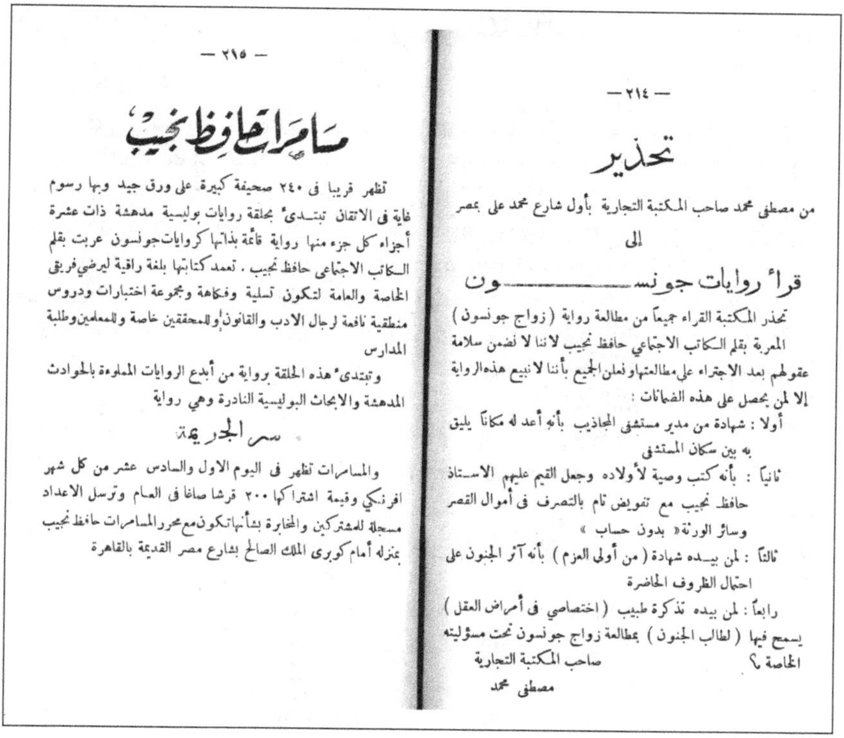

— ٢١٤ —

تحذير

من مصطفى محمد صاحب المكتبة التجارية بأول شارع محمد على بمصر

الى

قراء روايات جونســــــــون

تحذر المكتبة القراء جميعاً من مطالعة رواية (زواج جونسون) المعربة بقلم الكاتب الاجتماعي حافظ نجيب لاننا لا نضمن سلامة عقولهم بعد الاجتراء على مطالعتها ونعلن الجميع بأننا لا نبيع هذه الرواية إلا لمن يحصل على هذه الضمانات :

أولا : شهادة من مدير مستشفى المجاذيب بأنه أعد له مكاناً يليق به بين سكان المستشفى

ثانياً : بأنه كتب وصية لأولاده وجعل القيم عليهم الاستاذ حافظ نجيب مع تفويض تام بالتصرف فى أموال القصر وسائر الورثة « بدون حساب »

ثالثاً : لمن بيده شهادة (من أولى العزم) بأنه آثر الجنون على احتمال الظروف الحاضرة

رابعاً : لمن بيده تذكرة طبيب (اختصاصي فى أمراض العقل) يسمح فيها (لطالب الجنون) بمطالعة زواج جونسون تحت مسؤليته الخاصة ؟

صاحب المكتبة التجارية

مصطفى محمد

— ٢١٥ —

مسامرات حافظ نجيب

تظهر قريبا فى ٢٤٠ صحيفة كبيرة على ورق جيد وبها رسوم غاية فى الاتقان تبتدئ بحلقة روايات بوليسية مدهشة ذات عشرة أجزاء كل جزء منها رواية قائمة بذاتها كروايات جونسون عربت بقلم الكاتب الاجتماعى حافظ نجيب . تعمد كتابتها بلغة راقية ليرضي فريقى الخاصة والعامة لتكون تسلية وفكاهة ومجموعة اختبارات ودروس منطقية نافعة لرجال الادب والقانون ولمحققين خاصة وللمعلمين وطلبة المدارس

وتبتدئ هذه الحلقة برواية من أبدع الروايات المملوءة بالحوادث المدهشة والابحاث البوليسية النادرة وهي رواية

سر الجريمة

والمسامرات تظهر فى اليوم الاول والسادس عشر من كل شهر افرنكي وقيمة اشتراكها ٢٠٠ قرشا صاغا فى العام وترسل الاعداد مسجلة للمشتركين والمخابرة بشأنها تكون مع محرر المسامرات حافظ نجيب بمنزله أمام كوبرى الملك الصالح بشارع مصر القديمة بالقاهرة

FIGURE 6.2. "Warning" to readers of the Johnson crime series, appearing at the end of Ḥāfiẓ Najīb, *Jūnsūn: Ikhtifāʾ Banwā* (Johnson: The disappearance of Benoit), ca. 1920

The Johnson novels, which were themselves advertised like romantic novels often were, as "amusing, romantic, crime novels" (*būlisiyya gharāmiyya fukāhiyya*), recycled the very same warnings that conservative critics of the "amorous novel" voiced in their articles. Nervous conditions, illness, and even suicide, they had warned, were risks of novel reading. Here, Muṣṭafā Muḥammad turns that social panic into commercial currency. The commingling of these narrative pleasures, of the "agitation of emotions" that romances provoked and the frisson of fear and suspense that the crime novel promised, is what gave these novels a similar appeal in the popular market. In this case, translations performed for an affect-centered market reveal the similarity of these subgenres that were often believed to be distinct. Both, in fact, utilize the melodramatic mode, which Linda Williams has identified as a larger phenomenon than the "feminine, sentimental form." Indeed, as she writes, it should properly include "sensational pathos *and* action—the sufferings of innocent victims *and* the exploits of brave heroes or monstrous criminals." For her, "gothic horror . . . is the flip side of melodramatic pathos."[127]

But the history of reading is never wholly disconnected from the history of forms. To paraphrase Franco Moretti, we might observe that though the history of the book and literary history are indeed distant from each other, translation acts as a vital connecting bridge.[128] What have been understood as distinct and even opposed subgenres, the nonrational, unrealistic sentimental romance and the rational, hyperrealist detective novel, became in Arabic translation virtually the same form. Najīb (and the bookseller Muḥammad) translated crime fiction into the critical lexicon deployed against sentimental romance, to amusing ironic effect. Others translated crime novels that prominently featured romantic plots: *Rocambole* famously featured a courtesan with a heart of gold (another sentimental trope), and—as Selim points out—ʿAbd al-Qādir Ḥamza enhanced romantic elements in his translations of *Arsène Lupin*, even adding "expanded interior monologues and fragments of verse."[129] Missing fiancées, secret marriages, daughters with inappropriate suitors, and blackmailed wives fill the pages of the detective stories of *Al-Ḍiyāʾ* and *Majallat Sarkīs*; out of the twenty-four Holmes stories translated by al-Mashʿalānī, all but eight involve plots that would be equally appropriate in sentimental novels.

It is only logical, then, that the first appearance of a modern, scientific detective in Arabic would be found in a work that had all the outward appearances of a sentimental romance and that it would be pioneered—again—by Labība Hāshim. Four years before Sherlock Holmes's 1904 debut, Hāshim translated one of Émile Gaboriau's (1832–1873) Inspector Lecoq novels, *Le Dossier 113* (1867) and published it in *Al-Ḍiyāʾ* as "Fālantīn" (Valentine). It has gone undetected as crime fiction precisely because of the way that it resembles sentimental romantic novels, as Hāshim not only retitles it after a female character but also turns this over-four-hundred-page police novel into a ten-page narrative about a woman's ill-fated and scandalous youthful relationship. Inspector Lecoq makes an appearance in Hāshim's version but as an unnamed "chief inspector" who "is charged with investigating the truth" of a bank theft that perplexes its discoverers. While Gaboriau's version spends much of its time following the police in their pursuit of clues and witnesses to the theft, Hāshim brushes them aside to instead focus on the bank owner's wife, Valentine, whom Gaboriau introduces around page 200. She had previously and secretly married the love of her life, who she had thought died at sea, and had given birth to his son, whom she had sent to be raised in England. She turns out to be the culprit, having robbed her own current husband's bank in order to pay the debts of that son, who had returned to her, unbeknownst to anyone but herself and her former brother-in-law. In a central emotional scene, added by Hāshim, son and mother reunite in mutual recognition.

> "Yes, I am Raoul, son of Gaston de Clameran, and as for my mother . . ."
>
> Valentine screamed, "I am your mother!" and opened her arms. He threw himself upon her neck, in an affecting moment.[130]

Valentine's cry here recalls not just one melodramatic romance that preceded this novel but an entire mode of melodrama that turns on the recognition of (here, maternal) virtue. "The expressive means of melodrama," Brooks writes, "are all predicated on this subject: they correspond to the struggle toward the recognition of the sign of virtue and innocence."[131] It is Valentine's maternal virtue that leads her to steal the money, though the relationship that inspired it turns out to be an elaborate fraud: this man turns out to be an imposter, hired by the brother-in-law, who had in fact murdered her first husband.

In the French version, the romance plot is delegitimized by the detection plot, in which an identity attributed through sentimental ties and dramatic recognitions is eventually overturned by detailed police work. In this version, all identities and relationships are mediated through the police and therefore the state, who set those things right that sentiment had momentarily overturned. As Moretti has pointed out, this is detective fiction's "greatest obsession," which is "interested only in *perpetuating* the existing [legal, social, political] order, which is also a *legitimate* state of affairs."[132] Inspector Lecoq solves the crime, identifies the robber, delegitimizes Valentine's ties to her former husband and hidden son, and restores the reputation of the man accused of the crime.

In Hāshim's Arabic, however, that work of detection is itself entirely absent. Inspector Lecoq, whom Hāshim never names, follows no clues and interviews no suspects. He is mentioned at the beginning of the story as the officer in charge of the case and returns only in the last lines to explain the mystery to the befuddled husband. Then, yet again, Hāshim supplants detection with the romance plot. When the husband asks Lecoq how he can repay the detective, instead of Lecoq saying he wants the husband to clear the accused's name, Hāshim substitutes a more sentimental request: "Restore Prosper to his proper place and marry him to your daughter, Madeleine," he asks. His "proper place" is in a companionate marriage, which is the order that this detection perpetuates and legitimates and not Prosper's economic or social position. Then, in a final departure from Gaboriau's text, Hāshim ends the novel with a line that could have been taken from a romance: "The next day the newspapers announced the arrest of the Marquis as his brother's murderer, and he was sentenced to death after that. And Prosper and Madeleine married and lived together in happiness and innocence."[133] In this version, Hāshim enlists the police and the courts in enforcing a moral order that is dictated by the sentimental genre, subordinating them to the struggle toward the recognition of virtue. Crime fiction, in Hāshim's hands, is translated into a subgenre of the female-centered sentimental romance. If melodrama calls into question the smooth operation of reason and justice, here its integration into a crime novel brings about justice's narrative and legal resolution but on romance's terms. Hāshim's is a melodramatic state, one where the desire of young couples to be happy together is no longer outside the bounds of permissible social order but is legitimized by an agent of the law.

Al-Ḍiyā' was an important conduit for the ascendancy of crime fiction, the vast majority of which was translated from English. Along with another crime story translated by Hāshim, the magazine published twenty-three Sherlock Holmes works, as well as original crime stories by both Hāshim and Arthur Conan Doyle's translator Nasīb al-Mashʿalānī. After *Al-Ḍiyā'* ended its run in 1906, al-Mashʿalānī took his work to Salīm Sarkīs's *Majallat Sarkīs* (Sarkīs magazine, 1905–1926), where Sarkīs took enough interest in the endeavor to himself take over the project. He translated Doyle's *The Adventure of the Musgrave Ritual* as *Waṣiyat Mūsjrāf* in 1908 but also published a series of other stories "of that genre" that included both original creations and "translations" of real crime stories taken from European and American newspapers.[134] These included such titles as "Maryam Died," "The Ugly Deeds of New York's Wealthy," and "The Thirty-Two Wives of One Man." Like Hāshim's translation, Sarkīs's crime stories combined elements of genres and modes that contained what seemed like conflicting impulses but that worked together to produce a moral critique of social problems.

In "The Thief and the Rich American," for example, which was translated from the English from "the latest newspapers," Sarkīs transforms a crime report into a tear-soaked drama. Two London thieves try to rob the same American man and turn out to be husband and wife committing their first crimes unbeknownst to the other, in order to afford treatment for their sick daughter. Unlike detective fiction, the story is partially told from the pitiful thieves' point of view, and the reader sympathizes with their nerves, fear, and guilt. So, too, does their victim, in fact, who on hearing their story sheds two individual tears and gives them twice the money they need to treat their daughter. He explains, "Before I was rich I also had a daughter her age, and I found no one to help me. But I did not have your courage." The resolution to this crime story is not in the prosecution or arrest of the thief, nor does it involve rational decision-making in the service of "justice, . . . [that] impersonal thing," as Sherlock Holmes calls it.[135] Instead the resolution is so unexpected as to be unbelievable and is brought about not only by a sympathetic recognition of another's suffering but by the implausible coincidental sharing of the *exact same* suffering across time and continents. It leads not to *injustice* but to an alternative, extralegal form of justice.[136] Law and justice, time and again in sentimental crime stories as in criminal sentimental ones, are not perfectly coincidental but revise each other.

These sentimental crime narratives were, for Sarkīs, part of the zeitgeist. The Rocambole novel series was among the most popular in publication; over twenty-five Holmes stories had already appeared; and true crime stories filled the press. Sarkīs writes,

> Many among us are interested in criminals these days.
>
> They are surprised and fearful of the spread of corruption in our public morals.
>
> And suggest different solutions for purifying the social air of this rot. . . .
>
> But what is crime? Who is the criminal? Who is it that becomes a criminal?
>
> Have you ever wondered whether criminals appear among us because they have chosen to be so and want to spend their lives in misery? That they long to spend their days in prison or living in the shadows, fleeing the light of day and the police? Do you think they consented to a life of prison and shame?
>
> It is not logical that they have chosen this miserable life.[137]

It is not logical, the current social reality. And to contemplate its irrationality, Sarkīs offers none other than melodramatic sentimentality. He asks the reader to consider the misery of a woman whose poverty leads her to the impossible choices so common to melodrama and who turns to prostitution to feed her family. The prostitute is not someone who chose her profession, he explains, but a girl who is "cold and hungry," who "knows she has no place in this world," and who, if she finds a low-paying job, will "work for someone who has no respect for the health of her body and, if she arrives ten minutes late, will punish her with an entire day's wages."[138] To elicit tears for the prostitute, the thief, or the adulterer as a way to understand "public morals" and social structures is, to quote Berlant again, to identify "the place of painful feeling in the making of political worlds." In particular, as she argues, it is a way to construct "national sentimentality," the way by which a public uses affect to feel "being connected to strangers in a kind of nebulous *communitas*."[139] Feeling for the suffering of criminals, in this case, is to meditate on the margins of that community, on the mechanisms (social, economic, gendered) that create that marginality. The suffering of women, the poor, the ill, and the unjustly imprisoned, those stock figures of the turn-of-the-century translated novel, demand the contemplation of other societies, other forms of national community that might provide what Berlant calls "yet unlived better survival."[140] Tears, exaggerated emotions, coincidence, and unbelievable resolutions ask the reader to contemplate a community otherwise, whose social justice matches the narrative's emotional clarity.

These novels open a wedge between moral order and legal order in understanding the political community of the nation and do so via sensational, unrealistic, and melodramatic tropes. In this sense, they demonstrate what critics revising Brooks's account of melodrama have stressed. While for Brooks, the melodramatic imagination conjures a "universe bathed in the full, bright lighting of moral Manichaeism," scholars working in feminist and queer theoretical modes instead insist that its hyperbolic moral binaries often refuse moral clarity.[141] The interplay of moral opposites, coupled with the often impossible choices that protagonists are forced to make, points to a moral universe whose coordinates are difficult to locate and to a society that has a hard time "making good on goodness."[142] In melodrama's reliance on unlikely events and surprising coincidences for its moral resolution, it acts arbitrarily, "in its very structure calling into question the operation of law and justice."[143] The villain's perfidy and the damsel's virtue are revealed not by reason but by chance. More often, as Rey Chow explains in the case of Chinese popular "Butterfly literature" (a historical parallel to Badr's "entertainment novel"), the moral binaries present "a staging of conflicting, if not mutually exclusive, realities." "The visible 'crudities' of Butterfly literature," she writes, constitute "a space in which the parodic function of literature is not smoothed away but instead serves to reveal the contradictions of modern Chinese society in a disturbingly 'distasteful' manner."[144] If, as Brooks explains in his preface to the 1995 edition of *The Melodramatic Imagination*, melodrama is a product of modernity and its changing social codes, it often marks the locus of that change—the family, marriage models, national sentiment—as complex and inherently contradictory, whose resolution is often impossible.

So why was it not Dickens or Balzac that dominated the translation market in Arabic? This is a question often posed and only sometimes answered.[145] Why did the tear- and blood-soaked subgenres of crime fiction and sentimental romance become the image of the European novel that would be translated into Arabic popular culture? At the moment when national literary discourse was disciplining the novel into a social reform genre, these melodramatic novels opened up spaces of excessive popular emotion that were in fact directed at questioning the moral legitimacy of the state and forming multiple and alternate forms of national discourse. They were not apolitical but in fact utilized a political language that imagined politics otherwise, society otherwise, and the nation itself otherwise. Adding these translated popular novels to our understanding of national canon formation means locating the foreign within national discourse and locating both within discussions of rights, freedom, and justice that are posed as transnational. In doing so, the novel in translation contemplated justice itself in translation, as error laden and in need of revision.

Conclusion

Invader Fictions: National Literature after Translation

The final volume of Jurjī Zaydān's seminal *Tārīkh adāb al-lugha al-ʿarabiyya* (History of the literature and culture of the Arabic language, 1914), subtitled "The Latest *Nahḍa*," begins with a meditation on world relations: "The Arab World had changed during [this *nahḍa*] in a way unlike any other."[1] The verb he uses is *intaqala*; the Arab world, he writes, had *moved* or *shifted*. For Zaydān and others who wrote at the turn of the century, to say that the world had shifted was not overstatement. Writing in the wake of the British occupation and its reorganization of legal, educational, and social life, Zaydān's writings on the *nahḍa*—a topic of inquiry he may well have invented—belonged to a full-scale reevaluation of how Arab and Egyptian culture had absorbed European languages and literatures. If in 1858 Buṭrus al-Bustānī could conjure a history of literature as unchecked reciprocal circulation, a half century later Zaydān foregrounded movement channeled by colonial power. Collectively, he refers to translated literature, sciences, and arts as "al-ʿulūm al-dakhīla," the invading arts.[2] Zaydān, who with this work inaugurated national literary history in Arabic, inscribes the colonial relation into a literary modernity on the move.

Contemporaneous bibliographies, library card catalogues, and book reviews all appear to confirm Zaydān's characterization. In the years between the publication of the first volumes of his work in his journal, *Al-Hilāl* (1894–1895), and the publication of this final volume on the *nahḍa* period in 1914, translated and foreign-style novels had seemed to have taken over the literary market.[3] The number of journals serializing translated fiction likewise soared, competing with single-edition printing with detachable fascicles, by-subscription novel series, and stand-alone printings issued as annual supplements.[4] Some, like *Al-Rāwī* and *Musamarāt al-Sha'b*, were even principally devoted to fiction. Zaydān estimates in an 1897 article that "hundreds of thousands" of European novels existed, and he notes that they had already found many Arabic translators.[5] Foreign novels had indeed "invaded."

In the late 1910s and 1920s, novels, and especially translated ones, provided a special social and political danger that was being reimagined as a *national* one. Indeed, as Samah Selim has documented, the formation of the national canon, which took place in the first few decades of the twentieth century and in the context of anticolonialist nationalism, "was predicated on the suppression (through modern literary criticism) and management (through new quasi-official literary institutions) of this thriving contemporary field of popular fiction," in which claims of cultural danger "turned primarily on the trope of 'translation.'"[6] As she notes, literature and literacy were privileged subjects for nationalist writers and activists like Aḥmad Luṭfī al-Sayyid (1872–1963), just as the nation was a central organizing category for the modernists of the "New School" like Maḥmūd Taymūr (1894–1973). For both, "the new critical concept of 'national literature' was a pivotal element in the later development and canonization of the novel genre in Egypt."[7] By the 1920s, a retrospective reformation of the national canon rejected works that did *not* represent "Egyptian landscapes and Egyptian characters, urban and rural, and an overarching sense of national history." Such works were therefore cast out of the Arabic literary canon or, as Selim remarks, even blamed for colonialism.[8] Foreign literature was written out of the history of the Arabic novel at the same time that the countryside was being written *in*: it was then, as Elliott Colla has argued, that Muḥammad Ḥusayn Haykal's 1913 *Zaynab* became canonized as the first Arabic novel—as the first to depict the everyday life of the Egyptian peasantry.[9]

Yet though nationalist literary historians may have hoped to excise the translated origins of the novel from its now properly indigenized canon, Egyptian authors, translators, and critics still grappled with the changes that European literary influence brought to Arabic letters and the cross-pollination of novelistic traditions that occurred in the long *durée* of literary history.[10] They wrote literary history in translation and integrated their own works into that long arc of novelistic production considered in this book, narrating a history of the novel that emphasized bidirectional translation.[11] And in prefaces and in journalism, translators themselves theorized this history. In fact, the formation of national literary history coincided with the establishment of comparative literary studies in Arabic. Just three years after Zaydān inaugurated the modern study of Arabic literary history in *Al-Hilāl*, Najīb al-Ḥaddād, the translator of novels and theater pieces, published his "Muqābala bayn al-shi'r al-'arabī wa al-shi'r al-ifranjī" (Comparison between Arabic and European poetry) in *Al-Bayān*, establishing literary comparison as a subject of public interest and debate.[12] After summarizing an essay that Victor Hugo wrote on the history of French poetry, al-Ḥaddād declares Arabic not only superior to French poetry but inassimilable to Hugo's chronology of literary progress (French poetry at the apex of its progress, he explains, resembles Arabic poetry before Islam). Comparison yields an Arabic literature "unique unto itself" (*munfaradun fī nafsihi*) and particular to "the Arab countries in their specificity."[13] Five years later, Rūḥī al-Khālidī began a similarly titled series in *Al-Hilāl*, *Tārīkh 'ilm al-adab 'ind al-ifrānj wa al-'arab wa Victor Hugo* (History of the discipline of literature among the Westerners, the Arabs, and Victor Hugo), arguing for the Arab origins of European lyrical poetry via Islamic Spain and troubadour poets, who he argues would recite poems derived from Arabic sources.[14] As for so many of the translators whom *Stranger Fictions* studies, al-Khālidī's straight line from al-Ma'ārī to Victor Hugo complicates the line of influence (West to East) that scholars of world literature and the global novel trace and offers an alternative politics to its critique of Western hegemony. Al-Khālidī, who at the time of publication served as the consul general of the Ottoman Empire in Bordeaux, would have recognized the political provocation of positing the Arab conquest of Europe as the origin of European literary modernity. When he published his essays as a book in 1904, he addressed French readers as well as Arabic ones, explaining in a French-language preface that he wrote it in order to "participate in the centenary of the Great Poet that was being celebrated in the civilized world."[15] Such a statement would have been a sly commentary on what constitutes a geographically defined "civilized world" when Arabness—and especially Arab translation—is to be found in the heart of the French canon.[16] Arab authors of the *nahḍa*, as Verne's translators and others make clear, were concerned with the world of world literature, but that world-making is a comparative endeavor.

When we assess criticism of translated literature as *part* of the larger national conversation about the novel's purpose, the formation of the national literary canon comes to resemble a process of negotiating the foreignness that lies within it and not solely a process of casting the foreign out. In doing so, we ascribe historicity to the formation of national literary history itself, reformulating not just the position of Arabic in an imagined world literary canon but also the modern Arabic literary canon. The same year that al-Khālidī published his essays as a book, Sulaymān al-Bustānī, cousin of Buṭrus al-Bustānī, published a translation of Homer's *Iliad* with a lengthy introduction that included a history of European and Arab literary interaction, a comparison between Arabic and Greek poetic forms, and an extended comparison of what he called the *jāhiliyya* of the Arabs and the Greeks.[17] Yet comparison (*al-muqābala*), for al-Bustānī, was a technique that yielded above all a detailed analysis of Arab language and letters. The lengthiest section of the two-hundred-page introduction (over eighty pages) was devoted to a history of the "stages" (*ṭabaqāt*) of Arabic poetry, to which he even assimilated Greek literary history as *jāhaliyyat al-yūnān*.[18] Translating literary history did not always mean being seduced into colonial modes of evaluation; al-Bustānī assimilates Homer into Arabized historical categories like *al-Jāhiliyya*, rather than subsuming "the Arabic linguistic particular *within* the French linguistic universal."[19] *Al-Ilyādha* and its comparative method, the publication of which was celebrated by such nationalist leaders as Sa'd Zaghlūl (1857–1927) and 'Abd al-Khāliq Tharwat (1873–1928), was in the service of "elucidating the virtues of the Arabs in their use of language," al-Bustānī wrote.[20] Translation helped to shape a category of national literature that belonged in turn to a comparative process.

Reading the history of the novel in translation forces us to recast national literary histories, to read the nation in translation. To locate foreign literature within national literary history at the moment of its formation is only possible if one uncovers the impact that translations had on "original" writing, discourses and institutions of modernity, and reading practices. Understanding that history challenges us to read novels' depiction of even national environments or characters in the comparative critical context in which they were written and to see "national realism" as a mode that was canonized *through* comparative and translational methodologies and as perhaps the *culmination* of a history of translation. We might then understand what comparative work these novels—even novels nationalized through the canonization process—do. *Zaynab* became "the first Arabic novel" because it "endeavors to depict Egyptian life in a realistic way instead of adapting some Western theme."[21] The novel's national orientation, signaled by its subtitle—"Countryside viewpoints and morals"—promised symmetry between national character, national literature, and the land. But its title, the name of a female character, embeds the novel in a genealogy of foreign-inflected or foreign-produced sentimental fiction traced in previous pages. When one of its main characters, 'Azīza, takes to reading "novels" and "love stories" (*riwāyāt* and *aqāṣīṣ al-ḥubb*), it is a metonym for her larger isolation from the real world; it is not only in contrast to her cousin's socially useful reading to the peasants in the field but in connection with the abundance of translated romances on the print market.[22] A history of the novel that includes translated fiction is necessary in order to understand its particularly antinational dangers. The novel assumes this knowledge because it assumes that its readers, like ʿAzīza, *already* read literary history and the novel in translation.

I end with the Egyptian nation, but the history of the Arabic novel is not a nation-based one. It is a history of translation: of translators' role in forming and writing literary history, of translated concepts of modernity underpinning the novel's institutions, of practices of reading in translation that accustomed audiences to analyze comparatively and transnationally. And it is a history of mistranslation: of forms, concepts, and institutions that are transformed in the process of linguistic transfer. Translation—in its ability to put equivalence, translatability, and value at stake—produced not just intercommunication between languages but also failures of connectivity; it provided authors with the means not only for resolving difference but also for causing it to proliferate. In doing so, the translators of the long nineteenth century offer us a model for imagining transnational history not from the margins but from a translated center. It is a history that account not only for the genre's travels but for its transformations.

Notes

Introduction

1. Najīb Mīkhā'īl Gharghūr, *Al-Taʿisā' li-Fiktūr Hūjū, al-juz' al-awwul, Fāntīn* [*Les Misérables* by Victor Hugo, volume one, Fantine] (Alexandria: Printed at the behest of the Translator, 1888).

2. Mīkhā'īl Jūrj ʿAwrā, "Muqaddima fī ḥaqīqat tadwīn fann al-qiṣaṣ" [Introduction on the truth of the development of the art of novel-writing], in *Riwāyat al-Jinūn fī ḥubb Mānūn* (Alexandria: Maṭbaʿat al-Ahrām, 1886), 12. ʿAwrā explains in the first sentences that *qiṣaṣ* here refers to novels, or "what the Ifrānj [Franks, or Europeans] refer to . . . as '*rūmān*' [*romans*]" (3).

3. Jamāl al-Ghiṭānī, *Al-Majālis al-Maḥfūẓiyya* [The Mahfouz sessions] (Cairo: Dār Nahḍa, 2006), 130; Jurjī Zaydān, *Jurjī Zaydān, 1861–1914: Tarjama ḥayātihi, marāthī al-shuʿarā' wa al-kuttāb, ḥalflāt al-ta'bayn, aqwāl al-jarā'id wa al-majallāt fī al-rajul wa āthārihi* (Cairo: Maṭbaʿat al-Hilāl, 1915), 132–33; Ṣunʿallah Ibrāhīm, *Yawmiyāt al-Wāḥāt* [Memoirs of the oases] (Cairo: Dār al-Mustaqbal al-ʿArabī, 2004), 9. See also Ibrāhīm's short story "Arsène Lupin," *Tilka al-rā'iḥa wa qiṣaṣ ukhrā* (Cairo: Dar al-Shuhdī, 1980), cited in Elliott Colla, "Anxious Advocacy: The Novel, the Law, and Extrajudicial Appeals in Egypt," *Public Culture* 17, no. 3 (2005): 434.

4. Abdelfattah Kilito, *Thou Shalt Not Speak My Language*, trans. Waïl S. Hassan (Syracuse, NY: Syracuse University Press, 2008), 3.

5. ʿAwrā, "Introduction," 11–12.

6. Salīm dī Nawfal, preface to *Al-Mārkīz dī Fūntānj*, *Ḥadīqat al-akhbār* 50 (December 18, 1858): 4; Mikhā'īl al-Masabkī, introduction to *Kitāb mi'at ḥikāya* (Beirut: Maṭbaʿat al-Abā' al-Yasūʿīyīn, 1866), 2; Adīb Isḥāq, "Translator's Introduction," in *Al-Bārisiyya al-Ḥasnā'* (Beirut: Maṭbaʿat al-Qadīs Jāwrjīyūs, 1884), 5. Others emphasize the supralinguistic aspects of the genre, arguing that it exists in many cultures but is one "which the Franks perfected" or merely named. See, for example, Najīb Gharghūr, introduction to *Gharā'ib al-tadwīn* (Alexandria: Maṭbaʿat Jarīdat al-Mahrūsa, 1882), 7; and Nakhla Ṣāliḥ, preface to *Zawāj Jartrūda aw al-Kawkab al-munīr fī ḥubb ibnat al-amīr* (Cairo: M. Wādī al-Nīl, 1871), 2.

7. Khalīl Muṭrān, "Translator's Introduction," in *ʿUṭayl* [Othello], 6th ed. (Cairo: Dār al-Maʿārif, 1976), 7.

8. Muṭrān, 8.

9. As Margaret Litvin notes, Muṭrān's translations have been criticized for inaccuracies and awkward turns of phrase that were the result of his using intermediary

French translations; it is therefore crucial, as she insists, that we analyze Arabic translations in the larger intellectual and commercial networks in which they were created, rather than comparing them "one-to-one" with a stable original source text. Litvin, *Hamlet's Arab Journey: Shakespeare's Prince and Nasser's Ghost* (Princeton, NJ: Princeton University Press, 2011), 67, 8.

10. Masabkī, introduction to *Kitāb mi'at ḥikāya*, 5; Salīm Ṣaʿb, trans., *Riwāyat Amīr jazīrat Mūntū Krīstū ta'līf Mūsyū Iskandar Dīmās* [The novel of the prince of the island of Monte Cristo written by Alexandre Dumas], *Al-Shirāka al-Shahriyya* 4 (April 1866): 3.

11. Najīb Shaqra, trans., *Qiṣṣat Rūbart Bek* [The story of Robert Bey] (Beirut: al-Maṭbaʿa al-Adabiyya, 1885), 2–3. The translator lists the original title as *Christine*, a ten-page story that he expanded into a novel, but does not mention an author.

12. Khalīl al-Khūrī, *Wayy idhan lastu bi-ifranjī* [Alas, I am not a foreigner], 2nd ed. (Beirut: al-Maṭbaʿa al-Sūriyya, 1860), 30.

13. Quoted in ʿImād Sulḥ, *Aḥmad Fāris al-Shidyāq: Athāruhu wa ʿaṣruhu* (Beirut: Dar an-Nahār, 1980), 144.

14. See the essays in James L. Gelvin and Nile Green, eds., *Global Muslims in the Age of Steam and Print* (Berkeley: University of California Press, 2014).

15. See, for example, Benedict Anderson, *Imagined Communities: Reflections on the Origin and Spread of Nationalism*, rev. ed. (New York: Verso, 2006); Simone Müller, *Wiring the World: The Social and Cultural Creation of Global Telegraph Networks* (New York: Columbia University Press, 2016); and David S. Grewal, *Network Power: The Social Dynamics of Globalization* (New Haven, CT: Yale University Press, 2008).

16. On print interruptions, see especially On Barak, *On Time: Technology and Temporality in Modern Egypt* (Los Angeles: University of California Press, 2013); and Ami Ayalon, *The Arabic Print Revolution* (Cambridge: Cambridge University Press, 2016).

17. Jacques Derrida, "Des Tours de Babel," in *Psyche: Inventions of the Other, Volume One* (Stanford, CA: Stanford University Press, 2007), 199, 217.

18. See, for example, Susan Bassnett, *Comparative Literature: A Critical Introduction* (Oxford, UK: Blackwell, 1993), 138–61; Emily Apter, "A New Comparative Literature," in *The Translation Zone: A New Comparative Literature* (Princeton, NJ: Princeton University Press, 2006); and Steven Ungar, "Writing in Tongues: Thoughts on the Work of Translation," in *Comparative Literature in an Age of Globalization*, ed. Haun Saussy (Baltimore: Johns Hopkins University Press, 2006).

19. Harry Levin, "The Levin Report," in *Comparative Literature in the Age of Multiculturalism*, ed. Charles Bernheimer (Baltimore: Johns Hopkins University Press, 1994), 22; Thomas Greene, "The Greene Report," in Bernheimer, 31; Charles Bernheimer, "The Bernheimer Report," in Bernheimer, 44.

20. Gayatri Chakravorty Spivak, "The Politics of Translation," in *Outside in the Teaching Machine* (Abingdon, UK: Routledge, 1993), 202; Lawrence Venuti, *The Translator's Invisibility: A History of Translation* (Abingdon, UK: Routledge, 1995), 276.

21. Bassnett, *Comparative Literature*, 161.

22. Ungar, "Writing in Tongues," 129.

23. Lucas Klein, "Reading and Speaking for Translation: De-institutionalizing the Institutions of Literary Study," in *Futures of Comparative Literature: ACLA State of the Discipline Report*, ed. Ursula K. Heise (Abingdon, UK: Routledge, 2017), 217.

24. Gayatri Spivak, *Death of a Discipline* (New York: Columbia University Press, 2003), 18; Apter, *Translation Zone*, 10–11; Lawrence Venuti, *The Scandals of Translation: Towards an Ethics of Difference* (London: Routledge, 1998), 188–189.

25. Emily Apter, *Against World Literature: On the Politics of Untranslatability* (London: Verso, 2013), 2–3.

26. Venuti, *Translator's Invisibility*, 272.

27. Apter, *Translation Zone*, 251.

28. Ungar, "Writing in Tongues," 134.

29. Apter, for example, writes, "Saidian-Spitzerian philology portends the advent of a translational humanism that assumes the disciplinary challenges posed by Turkish and Arabic in their respective circumstances of institutional exile" (*Translation Zone*, 249).

30. As Shaden Tageldin recently remarks, Apter has helped make Arabic "an avatar of untranslatability in US comparative literary studies of late." Tageldin, "Untranslatability," in Heise, *Futures of Comparative Literature*, 216. Apter's *Translation Zone* offers yet another Arabic genealogy of the untranslatable in her chapter "'Untranslatable' Algeria" (94–108).

31. Franco Moretti, "Conjectures on World Literature," in *Distant Reading* (London: Verso, 2013), 46.

32. Immanuel Wallerstein, "The Rise and Future Demise of the World Capitalist System: Concepts for Comparative Analysis," *Comparative Studies in Society and History* 16, no. 4 (September 1974): 387.

33. Moretti uses the notion of "foreign debt" to characterize the relationship between the European novelistic core and its import-dependent non-European peripheries, while Pascale Casanova uses the metaphor of "literary capital" that "poor" national literatures can acquire through the translation of texts from "rich" ones. Moretti, "Conjectures," 46–47, 58; Casanova, *The World Republic of Letters*, trans. M. B. DeBevoise (Cambridge, MA: Harvard University Press, 2004), 256.

34. Casanova, *World Republic of Letters*, 134.

35. Moretti, "Conjectures," 54.

36. Elizabeth M. Holt, *Fictitious Capital: Silk, Cotton, and the Rise of the Arabic Novel* (New York: Fordham University Press, 2017).

37. Moretti, "Conjectures," 56.

38. Moretti, 57; Moretti, *Atlas of the European Novel, 1800–1900* (London: Verso, 1998), 187, 191. As Jahan Ramazani has pointed out, the gesture toward "compromise" is undercut by the verbs used in these essays: "*Engulfing, conquering, swallowing*—like Stevens' jar, the foreign form takes dominion over the local wilderness." Ramazani, "Form," in *A New Vocabulary for Global Modernism*, ed. Eric Hayot and Rebecca L. Walkowitz (New York: Columbia University Press, 2016), 116.

39. Khalīl Zayniyya al-Lubnānī, *Nājiyya: Riwāya gharāmiyya adabiyya* (Beirut: al-Maktaba al-ʿilmiyya, 1884), 3; Ṣaʿb, *Riwāyat Amīr jazīrat Mūntū Krīstū*, 3.

40. Zayniyya, *Nājiyya*, 3.

41. Michel de Certeau, *The Practice of Everyday Life*, trans. Steven Rendall (Berkeley: University of California Press, 1984), 34.

42. de Certeau, xiii.

43. de Certeau, xiii.

44. Bill Brown, "How to Do Things with Things (a Toy Story)," *Critical Inquiry* 24, no. 4 (Summer 1998): 954.

45. Al-Khūrī, *Wayy*, 30. The first usage of this quotation is by Salīm dī Nawfal in the prefatory remarks to his translation *Al-Mārkīz dī Fūntanj*, serialized in *Ḥadīqat al-akhbār* beginning in December 1858 (volume 50). Nawfal uses this quotation to excuse any deficiencies that the reader might find in his particular attempt at translation, while al-Khūrī uses it to describe the condition of translating as a whole.

46. Brown, "How to Do Things," 955.

47. Antoine Berman, *The Experience of the Foreign: Culture and Translation in Romantic Germany*, trans. S. Heyvaert (Albany: State University of New York Press, 1992), 155. Berman argues that such translation should not be considered "bad" but valued for its preservation of the alterity of the source text to the new literary context. Venuti concurs and refers to these translations as "foreignizing" ones, which he argues makes the translator visible. Venuti, *Translator's Invisibility*, 124.

48. Lital Levy, *Poetic Trespass: Writing between Hebrew and Arabic in Israel/Palestine* (Princeton, NJ: Princeton University Press, 2014).

49. See also Lawrence Venuti, "Hijacking Translation: How Comp Lit Continues to Suppress Translated Texts," *Boundary 2*, 43, no. 2 (2016): 179–204.

50. Matti Moosa, *Origins of Modern Arabic Fiction* (Boulder, CO: Three Continents Press, 1980), 107; 'Abd al-Muḥsin Ṭaha Badr, *Taṭawwur al-riwāya al-ʿarabiyya al-ḥadītha fī Miṣr, 1870–1938* [Development of the modern Arabic novel in Egypt, 1870–1938] (Cairo: Dār al-Maʿārif, 1963), 128; Anwar al-Jundī, *Taṭawwur al-tarjama fī al-adab al-ʿarabī al-muʿāṣir* [The development of translation in modern Arabic literature] (Cairo, n.d.), 14.

51. Badr, *Taṭawwur*, 129.

52. Badr, 130.

53. Samah Selim, "The People's Entertainments: Translation, Popular Fiction, and the Nahdah in Egypt," in *Other Renaissances: A New Approach to World Literature*, ed. Brenda Den Schildgen, Gang Zhou, and Sander L. Gilman (New York: Palgrave Macmillan, 2006), 38. I have benefitted greatly from this and Selim's other articles, as indicated throughout this book. Though I did not have the opportunity to learn from *Popular Fiction, Translation, and the Nahda in Egypt* (Cham, Switzerland: Palgrave Macmillan, 2019) before *Stranger Fictions* had been submitted for publication, I hope that our two books will be in conversation once both are available.

54. Sabry Hafez, *Genesis of Arabic Narrative Discourse: A Study in the Sociology of Modern Arabic Literature* (London: Saqi Books, 1993), 99.

55. The translator Ṭāniyūs 'Abduh himself is reported to have translated no fewer than seven hundred novels. See Anṭūn Bey al- Jumayyil's introduction to his anthology of 'Abduh's work, *Diwān Ṭāniyūs ʿAbduh* (Cairo, 1925). Cited in Moosa, *Origins of Modern Arabic Fiction*, 209n58. My own research has documented 319 titles that can be dated to earlier than 1913.

56. On the back cover of his translation, *Zawāj Jartrūda, aw al-Kawkab al-munīr fī ḥubb ibnat al-amīr*, Nakhla Ṣāliḥ is described as "ex-traducteur de la Direction Générale des Chemins de Fer Egyptiens," and 'Aṣṣāf is listed on the title page of his translation of *Le Tour du monde en quatre-vingt jours* as "Agent of the Egyptian Post."

57. "Salīm Bustrus," in Yūsuf Ilyān Sarkīs, *Muʿjam al-maṭbūʿāt al-ʿarabiyya* [Dictionary of Arabic printed books] (Cairo: Maṭbaʿat Sarkīs, 1928), 144.

58. Zayniyya, *Nājiyya*, 2.

59. Yūsuf al-Shalfūn, trans., *Riwāyat ḥifẓ al-widād*, *Al-Shirāka al-shahriyya fī Bayrūt* 1, no. 5 (April 1866): 2.

60. Iskandar Tuwaynī, trans., *Riwāyat yamīn al-armala* (Beirut, 1861), 2.

61. Al-Khūrī, *Wayy*, 2.

62. Al-Khūrī, 162.

63. Al-Khūrī, 163.

64. al-Khūrī, *Wayy idhan lastu bi-ifranjī*, 44.

65. Dilip Parameshwar Gaonkar and Elizabeth Povinelli, "Technologies of Public Forms: Circulation, Transfiguration, Recognition," *Public Culture* 15, no. 3 (Fall 2003): 387.

66. Gaonkar and Povinelli, 389.

67. Gaonkar and Povinelli, 395.

68. Gayatri Spivak, "Scattered Speculations on the Question of Value," *Diacritics* 15 (1985): 8–10.

69. Shaden M. Tageldin, *Disarming Words: Empire and the Seductions of Translation in Egypt* (Berkeley: University of California Press, 2011), 21.

70. William B. Warner, *Licensing Entertainment: The Elevation of Novel Reading in Britain, 1684–1750* (Los Angeles: University of California Press, 1998), 25.

71. James Beattie, "On Fable and Romance," in *Dissertations Moral and Critical*, vol. 2 (Dublin: Printed for Mess. Exshaw, Walker, Beatty, White, Byrne, Cash, and M'Kenzie, 1783), 234; Clara Reeve, *The Progress of Romance*, vol. 1 (Colchester, UK: Printed for the author, 1785), 112–22.

72. Georg Lukács, *The Theory of the Novel: A Historico-Philosophical Essay on the Forms of Great Epic Literature*, trans. Anna Bostock (Cambridge, MA: MIT Press, 1971), 41. Lukács argues that the novel arose as a response to a conception of the world in which it had become "infinitely large" and where "the distinctions between men have made an unbridgeable chasm." Placing the problem of foreignness at the center of the function of genre, he argues that the novel's function is to attempt to unify a world that cannot be unified. In other words, the problematic of the genre is the impossibility of translation.

73. Mikhail Bakhtin, *The Dialogic Imagination*, trans. Michael Holquist (Austin: University of Texas Press, 1981), 361. "Heteroglossia" has largely been interpreted to refer to the differing registers of a single language deployed in novelistic writing, but close examination of Bakhtin's writings on the novel and on language in general point to a more literal interpretation that implicates translation. If the novel is dialogic, it is only because it is "the artistic image of a language" that is dialogic itself—where meaning is elicited between (at least two) languages, or systems of signs, and where the meaning of any word "is shaped in dialogic interaction with an alien word" (266). For Bakhtin, that is, speaking is not a matter of selecting a word from a neutral and impersonal body of signs, for such a body does not exist; the word always already "exists in other people's mouths, in other people's contexts, serving other people's intentions: it is from there that one must take the word" (293–94). See also Mikhail Bakhtin, *Marxism and the Philosophy of Language*, trans. Ladislav Matejka and I. R. Titunik (New York: Seminar, 1973), 115.

74. For more on the intellectual recuperation of the novel for Egyptian national purposes, see Samah Selim, "The Narrative Craft: Realism and Fiction in the Arabic

Canon," *Edebiyat* 14, nos. 1–2 (2003): 109–28. Examples of this line of logic can be found in both the Anglophone and Arabophone academies: for Roger Allen, the novel is the benchmark for modernity itself, "*the* preferred modern fictional form"; for 'Abd al-Muḥsin Ṭaha Badr, the novel marks the transition out of a period of "decline" or "decadence." Allen, *The Arabic Novel: An Historical and Critical Introduction* (Syracuse, NY: Syracuse University Press, 1982), 3; Badr, *Taṭawwur*, 47. An important notable exception is in the work of Kamran Rastegar. Rastegar, *Literary Modernity between the Middle East and Europe: Textual Transactions in Arabic, English, and Persian Literatures* (New York: Routledge, 2007). More research remains to be conducted, however, in the field of early Arabic translations of poetry and drama, which also vied for dominance in the early *nahḍa*. For a notable exception to this, see Carol Bardenstein's analysis of the translations from French plays of Muḥammad 'Uthmān Jalāl (1829–1898): *Translation and Transformation in Modern Arabic Literature: The Indigenous Assertions of Muḥammad 'Uthmān Jalāl* (Wiesbaden: Otto Harrassowitz, 2005).

75. Yet even the multiple meanings of "national" in the instances of these figures needs to be teased out: Zaydān, a Syrian Christian émigré to Egypt, promoted forms of what is now recognized as pan-Arab nationalism, while Amīn explored gendered notions of national identity within Egypt. Riḍa, another Lebanese émigré, promoted the rejuvenation of the *umma* (often translated as "nation" but referring to the larger Muslim political community) at times through forms of Ottoman nationalism.

76. Sherene Seikaly, *Men of Capital: Scarcity and Economy in Mandate Palestine* (Stanford, CA: Stanford University Press, 2016), 16.

77. See, for example, Elizabeth Suzanne Kassab, *Contemporary Arab Thought: Cultural Critique in Comparative Perspective* (New York: Columbia University Press, 2010), 20–47.

78. Selim, "Narrative Craft," 110.

79. As Selim writes, "the canonicity of [*Zaynab*] lies in its being particularly situated at the confluence of two powerful and intersecting historical narratives; the narrative of Egyptian nationhood and the European narrative of the history of the novel." Selim, *The Novel and the Rural Imaginary in Egypt, 1880–1985* (London: Routledge, 2004), 103. For Elliott Colla, by contrast, the canonization of *Zaynab* occurs in a later nationalization phase, during Nasserist Egypt. Colla, "How *Zaynab* Became the First Arabic Novel," *History Compass* 7 (2009): 214–55.

80. As Aamir Mufti has argued in the case of South Asian literatures, "It is when a writing tradition has produced a literary history that its literary modernity, properly speaking, may be said to have begun," as its theorizers identify it as a distinct national literary territory operating on an allegedly universal plane of literariness. Mufti, *Forget English! Orientalisms and World Literatures* (Cambridge, MA: Harvard University Press, 2016), 141.

81. As Nadia Bou Ali writes, "the problematics of the Nahda are thereby themselves the problematics of the nation." Ali, "Collecting the Nation: Lexicography and National Pedagogy in *al-nahda al-'arabiyya*," in *Archives, Museums, and Collecting Practices in the Modern Arab World*, ed. Sonja Mejcher-Atassi and John Pedro Schwartz (London: Routledge, 2016), 33.

82. See Tageldin, *Disarming Words*.

83. After a fire that destroyed the Egyptian Citadel Records in 1820, no records of this or any of the other earliest student missions survive. The earliest records relate to

Niqūlā al-Masābikī, who studied printing in Milan between 1815 and 1820 and acted as the director of the Būlāq Press in Cairo. On these early educational missions, see Ibrahim Abu-Lughod, *The Arab Rediscovery of Europe* (Princeton, NJ: Princeton University Press, 1963); and Alain Silvera, "The First Egyptian Student Mission to France under Muhammad Ali," *Middle Eastern Studies* 16, no. 2 (May 1980): 1–22.

84. This process was far from voluntary. Delegates were required to produce a translation of a work of "scientific merit" as a condition of their European education. Mehmet Ali writes in an 1823 letter to a student named Jawāni, "Concerning the medical books, we hereby order their translation from Italian into Arabic. . . . He should be warned that if he is negligent in his work he will be punished." Quoted in Abu-Lughod, *Arab Rediscovery*, 38.

85. As Matti Moosa argues, al-Ṭahṭāwī's works "showed at least an initial departure from traditional and static literary models and opened a gate, however narrow, to future possibilities for the modernization of imaginative literature" (*Origins*, 6).

86. Ami Ayalon, *The Press in the Arab Middle East: A History* (Oxford: Oxford University Press, 1995), 30.

87. See Beth Baron, *The Women's Awakening in Egypt: Culture, Society, and the Press* (New Haven, CT: Yale University Press, 1997); Ziad Fahmy, *Ordinary Egyptians: Creating the Modern Nation through Popular Culture* (Stanford, CA: Stanford University Press, 2011); and Elaine Ursul Ettmüller, *The Construct of Egypt's National Self in James Sanua's Early Satire and Caricature* (Berlin: Klaus Schwarz Verlag, 2012).

88. Yūsuf al-Shalfūn, *Riwāyat ḥifẓ al-widād* (Beirut: al-Maṭbaʿa al-Amūmiyya, 1866), 2. It appears in the fifth (April) issue of his monthly subscription series *Al-Shirāka al-Shahriyya* (The monthly subscription).

89. Khalīl al-Khūrī, *Ḥadīqat al-Akhbār* (The garden of news) 153 (October 21, 1859): 4.

90. *Mawāqiʿ al-aflāk fī waqāʾi Tilīmāk* was serialized from August 15, 1861, to April 5, 1866, and February 5, 1867, to December 10, 1867, in *Ḥadīqat al-akhbār*. For a complete table of translations published in the periodical, see Basiliyus Bawardi, "First Steps in Writing Arabic Narrative Fiction: The Case of *Ḥadīqat al-akhbār*," *Die Welt des Islams* 48 (2008): 179.

91. Michael Allan, *In the Shadow of World Literature: Sites of Reading in Colonial Egypt* (Princeton, NJ: Princeton University Press, 2016).

92. Benedict Anderson, *Imagined Communities: Reflection on the Origin and Spread of Nationalism* (London: Verso Books, 1983), 25.

93. A full list of examples would be too large to include, but a sampling reveals the linguistic range of the phenomenon: Doris Sommer, *Foundational Fictions: The National Romances of Latin America* (Berkeley: University of California Press, 1993); Neil Larsen, *Determinations: Essays on Theory, Narrative, and Nation in the Americas* (London: Verso, 2001); Yasir Suleiman and Ibrahim Muhawi, eds., *Literature and Nation in the Middle East* (Edinburgh: Edinburgh University Press, 2006); and Patrick Parrinder, *Nation and Novel: The English Novel from Its Origins to the Present Day* (Oxford: Oxford University Press, 2006).

94. Ami Ayalon, "Private Publishing in the *Nahḍa*," *International Journal of Middle East Studies* 40, no. 4 (November 2008): 562.

95. On the Iranian and South Asian contexts, see Ronit Ricci, *Islam Translated: Literature, Conversion, and the Arabic Cosmopolis of South and Southeast Asia* (Chicago: University of Chicago Press, 2011); and Kamran Rastegar, *Literary Modernity between the*

Middle East and Europe: Textual Transactions in Nineteenth-Century Arabic, English, and Persian Literatures (London: Routledge, 2007).

96. See Philipp Bruckmayer, "Arabic and Bilingual Newspapers and Magazines in Latin America and the Caribbean," in *Islamic Manuscripts and Books: Historical Aspects of Printing and Publishing in Languages of the Middle East: Papers from the Symposium at the University of Leipzig, September 2008*, ed. Geoffrey Roper (Leiden: Brill, 2014), 245–69.

97. *Al-Naḥla*, for example, was published in Beirut from 1870 to 1877, when Ṣābūnjī moved to London. It reappeared in a bilingual edition in London in the same year and continued there until 1880 and then restarted briefly in 1884. L. Zolondek, "Sabunji in England 1876-91: his role in Arabic journalism," *Middle Eastern Studies* 14, no. 1: 105. In 1895, according to al-Ṭarrāzī, it reappeared in Cairo also under Ṣābūnjī's name. *Abū Naḍḍāra* was published in Cairo from 1877 to 1878, when Ṣannū' was exiled to France by Ismail I. It was published there under several titles until 1910. Fahmy, *Ordinary Egyptians: Creating the Modern Nation through Popular Culture* (Stanford, CA: Stanford University Press, 2011), 47–50.

98. Ayalon, "Private Publishing," 561.

99. The third year of *Al-Najāḥ* (Beirut, 1873), for example, lists twenty-three *amākin al-ishtirāk* (subscription locations), and the second year of *Ḥadīqat al-akhbār* lists ten, including in Paris and London. Ayalon also provides evidence of this phenomenon, most strikingly in his examples is *Al-Muqtaṭaf*, which began with twelve but after a year listed forty-five agents of international distribution (*Arabic Print Revolution*, 130).

100. For more on this, see Rebecca C. Johnson, "Importing the Novel: The Arabic Novel in and as Translation," *NOVEL: A Forum on Fiction* 48, no. 2 (2015): 243–60.

101. Examples of this are numerous. See, for example, an announcement in *Al-Jinān* about the delay of *Al-Jannah* due to the late arrival of a Viennese steamship. *Al-Jinān* 5, no. 4 (February 15, 1874): 119.

102. It was composed of material alliances as well: these early journals and newspapers were often either founded by emigrants or the product of binational investment (as was the case with the Franco-Egyptian ventures of *L'Echo des Pyramides*, founded in 1827, and *Al-Tanbīh*, founded in 1800) or featured foreign news translated from European newspapers and wire services, thanks to the use of the telegraph and the establishment of Reuters' first office outside Europe in Alexandria in 1865. Elisabeth Kendall, "Between Politics and Literature: Journals in Alexandria and Istanbul at the End of the Nineteenth Century," in *Modernity and Culture: From the Mediterranean to the Indian Ocean*, ed. Leila Tarazi Fawaz, Christopher Alan Bayly, and Robert Ilbert (New York: Columbia University Press, 2002), 350.

103. Examples of these links are too frequent to enumerate here, but one illustrative example is a positive review in the Jesuit-run *Al-Mashriq* (The Levant) of *Riwāyat Ḥasnā' Bayrūt* (The novel of the beauty of Beirut). Though *Al-Mashriq* might be seen as a publication that seeks to consolidate a Levantine Christian community, it did so by promoting an anonymous Egyptian novel (on the basis that it is a moral alternative to the books that inflame the passions of young women who read them). And yet it is an Egyptian novel that itself makes a cross-regional imaginative alliance, taking as its subject the contemporary society not of Cairo but of Beirut. "Review," *Al-Mashriq* 3 (February 1, 1899): 141–42.

104. Ilham Khuri-Makdisi, *The Eastern Mediterranean and the Making of Global Radicalism, 1860-1914* (Berkeley: University of California Press, 2010); Julia Clancy-Smith,

Mediterraneans: North Africa and Europe in an Age of Migration, 1800–1900 (Berkeley: University of California Press, 2011), 20.

105. Valeska Huber, *Channelling Mobilities: Migration and Globalization in the Suez Canal Region and Beyond, 1869-1914* (Cambridge: Cambridge University Press, 2013); Hala Auji, *Printing Arab Modernity: Book Culture and the American Press in Nineteenth-Century Beirut* (Leiden: Brill, 2016), 130.

106. James Gelvin and Nile Green, eds., *Global Muslims in the Age of Steam and Print* (Berkeley: University of California Press, 2014), 10.

107. Marwa Elshakry, *Reading Darwin in Arabic, 1860–1950* (Chicago: University of Chicago Press, 2013), 10.

108. Tarek El-Ariss, *Trials of Arab Modernity: Literary Affects and the New Political* (New York: Fordham University Press, 2013).

109. Laura Briggs, Gladys McCormick, and J. T. Way, "Transnationalism: A Category of Analysis," *American Quarterly* 60, no. 3 (September 2008): 628.

110. Briggs, McCormick, and Way, 627.

111. Jean-Jacques Lecercle, *The Violence of Language* (London : Routldege, 1990), 182. Cited in Lawrence Venuti, *The Scandals of Translation: Towards an Ethics of Difference* (London: Routledge, 1998), 10

112. Walter Benjamin, "Task of the Translator," in *Illuminations* (New York: Schocken Books, 1968), 78.

113. Lukács, *Theory of the Novel*, 39.

Part I. Reading in Translation

1. Examples include James T. Monroe, *The Art of Badī al-Zamān al-Hamadhānī as Picaresque Narrative* (Beirut: Center for Arab and Middle East Studies, 1983); and Jareer Abu-Haidar, "*Maqāmāt* Literature and the Picaresque Novel," *Journal of Arabic Literature* 5 (1974): 1–10.

2. Abdelfattah Kilito, *Thou Shalt Not Speak My Language*, trans. Waïl S. Hassan (Syracuse, NY: Syracuse University Press, 2008), 10. The original is ʿAbd al-Fattāḥ Kīlīṭū, *Lan tatakallama lughatī* (Beirut: Dār al-Ṭalīʿa li al-Ṭibāʿa wa al-Nashr, 2002).

3. Kilito, *Thou Shalt Not*, 18.

4. Kilito, 19.

5. Buṭrus al-Bustānī, "Khuṭba fī adāb al-ʿarab," in *Al-Jamʿiyya al-Sūriyya li al-ʿulūm wa al-funūn, 1847–1852* (Beirut: Dār al-Ḥamrāʾ, 1990), 117.

6. For an extended discussion of the "Khuṭba," see chapter 1 ("Unpacking the Native Subject") of Stephen Sheehi, *The Foundations of Modern Arab Identity Foundations of Modern Arab Identity* (Gainesville: University Press of Florida, 2004).

7. Buṭrus al-Bustānī, "*Nafīr Sūriyā* [Trumpet of Syria] (Beirut: Dār Fikr lil-Abḥāth wa al-Nashr, 1990), 50–51.

8. Al-Bustānī, "Khuṭba,"107.

9. Al-Bustānī, 115.

10. Sheehi, *Foundations of Modern Arab Identity*, 33.

11. Al-Bustānī, "Khuṭba," 35.

12. Al-Bustānī, 107; my emphasis.

13. Aḥmad Fāris al-Shidyāq, *Leg over Leg*, trans. Humphrey Davies, 4 vols., Library of Arabic Literature (New York: NYU Press, 2012–2014), 4:19 [4.1.9]. This was originally

published as *Al-Sāq ʿalā al-sāq fī mā huwa al-Fāryāq* [Leg over leg concerning that which is al-Fāryāq] (Paris: Benjamin Duprat, 1855). All references here refer first to the English page number of the four-volume bilingual edition of Davies's translation. To facilitate access to the Arabic text, I have also included the volume, chapter, and paragraph number. In the rare instances when I have differed from Davies's translation, I have indicated as much, but I defer to Davies, who has, as al-Shidyāq put it, "rendered his reputation white by covering pages in black." Al-Shidyāq, *Leg over Leg*, 1:37 [1.1.1].

14. Printed editions of dictionaries included at least six editions of al-Fīrūzābādī's dictionary, *Al-Qāmūs al-muḥīṭ* (The encompassing ocean; ca. 1450), four editions of Muḥammad Murtaḍā al-Zabīdī's comment on *Al-Qāmūs*, *Tāj al-ʿarūs min jawāhir al-Qāmūs* (The bride's crown inlaid with the jewels of the *Qāmūs*; ca. 1774), and a twenty-volume edition—edited by al-Shidyāq—of Ibn al-Manẓūr's thirteenth-century lexicon, *Lisān al-ʿarab* (The language of the Arabs; 1290). Saʿīd al-Shartūnī, *Aqrab al-mawārid fī al-fuṣuḥ al-ʿarabiyya wa al-shawārid* [The closest sources to the pure Arabic language and its anomalies], vol. 1 (Beirut: Maṭbaʿat Mursalī al-Yasūʿiyya, 1889), 12.

15. Al-Shartūnī, *Aqrab al-mawārid*, 12–13.

16. Buṭrus al-Bustānī, "Fātiḥat al-Kitāb," [preface to] *Muḥīṭ al-muḥīṭ* (Beirut: Maktabat Lubnān, 1977), i.

17. Aḥmad Fāris al-Shidyāq, *Al-Jāsūs ʿalā al-Qāmūs* (Istanbul: Maṭbaʿat al-Jawāʾib, 1882), 3.

18. Al-Shidyāq, 3; Ibrāhīm al-Yāzijī, "Al-Lugha wa al-ʿaṣr" [Language and the age], *Al-Bayān* [The bulletin] 1, no. 4 (June 1, 1897): 149.

19. On al-Shartūnī's refutation, see Abdulrazzak Patel, "Language Controversy and Reform in the *Nahḍa*: Saʿīd al-Sharūnī's Position as a Grammarian in *Sahm*," *Journal of Semitic Studies* 55, no. 2 (Autumn 2010): 509–38.

20. Al-Yāzijī's articles, which appeared in his journals *Al-Bayān* and *Al-Ḍiyāʾ*, al-Bustānī's *Al-Jinān*, and Yūsuf al-Shalfūn's *Al-Najāḥ* were the most ubiquitous and strident. They aimed not only to "point out [al-Shidyāq's] mistakes from the beginning to the end by publishing them one by one" but more broadly to defend the Arabic language from improper usage by adhering to the principles of the most conservative classical grammarians and lexicographers. Ibrāhīm al-Yāzijī, "Al-Radd ʿalā ṣāḥib *Al-Jawāʾib*" [A reply to the owner of *Al-Jawāʾib*], *Al-Najāḥ: Ṣaḥīfa siyāsiyya ʿilmiyya tijāriyya* [Success: A political, scientific, and commercial newspaper] 3, no. 6 (February 1, 1872): 88.

21. Al-Shidyāq, *Jāsūs*, 3.

22. Mikhāʾīl ʿAbd al-Sayyid, *Kitāb sulwān al-shajī fī al-radd ʿalā Ibrāhīm al-Yāzijī* [Book of solace for the distressed in the refutation of Ibrāhīm al-Yāzijī] (Istanbul: Maṭbaʿat al-Jawāʾib, 1872), 77. While *Kitāb sulwān* was published as the work of a friend of al-Shidyāq's who lived in Egypt, most scholars believe it to be the work of al-Shidyāq himself, as it conforms to both his linguistic views and his rhetorical style. It was also published by al-Shidyāq's press.

23. Al-Yāzijī, "Al-Lugha," 146.

24. Al-Bustānī, "Khuṭba," 108.

25. Al-Shartūnī, *Aqrab al-mawārid*, 8.

26. "In that age almost no foreign word entered their vocabulary (except in works of medicine, where they permitted themselves to translate [*naqal*] many words for

medical devices and disorders from foreign terms, similarly names of gems can only be translated [*yunqal*] by way of Arabization); . . . they used derivations in order to translate Persian and Greek terms into Arabic" (Al-Yāzijī, "Al-Lugha," 149).

27. Aḥmad Fāris al-Shidyāq. *Ghunyat al-ṭālib wa munyat al-rāghib* [The Enrichment of the Student and the Object of the Desirer] (Istanbul: Maṭba'at al-Jawā'ib, 1872), 3.

28. Al-Bustānī, "Khuṭba," 104.

29. "For there is a wide field for reform and the translation [*al-naql*] of what can be transmitted [*mā yumkinu naqalahu*] from those Bedouin expressions into modern subjects" (Al-Bustānī, 109).

30. Al-Bustānī, 115.

31. Al-Bustānī, 106.

32. Al-Shidyāq, *Ghunyat al-ṭālib*, 4. On these grammatical works, see Abdulrazzak Patel, *The Arab Nahḍah: The Making of the Intellectual and Humanist Movement* (Edinburgh: Edinburgh University Press, 2013), 108; and M. G. Carter, "Arabic Grammar," in *Religion, Learning, and Science in the 'Abbasid Period*, ed. M. J. L. Young et al. (Cambridge: Cambridge University Press, 1990), 134.

33. Aḥmad Fāris al-Shidyāq, *Kashf al-mukhabbā' 'an funūn Urūbā* [Uncovering the hidden arts of Europe] (Tunis: Maṭba'at al-Dawla al-Tūnisīyya, 1867), 125.

34. Al-Shidyāq, "Dhayl al-kitāb" [Appendix], in *Al-Sāq*, 1–24.

35. Seth Lerer, *Error and the Academic Self* (New York: Columbia University Press, 2002), 2.

36. Cited in Edward William Lane, *Arabic-English Lexicon*, vol. 1 (Beirut: Librarie du Liban, 1968), 761.

37. Lane, 761.

38. Zachary Sng, *The Rhetoric of Error from Locke to Kleist* (Stanford, CA: Stanford University Press, 2010), 4.

39. Sng, 4.

40. Timothy J. Reiss, *Against Autonomy: Global Dialectics of Cultural Exchange* (Stanford, CA: Stanford University Press, 2002), 67.

41. Al-Bustānī, *Khuṭba*, 111; Salīm al-Bustānī, "Rūḥ al-'aṣr," *al-Jinān* 1 (1870): 385–86.

1. *Crusoe*'s Babel, Missionaries' Mistakes

1. *Qiṣṣat Rūbinṣun Kurūzī* [The story of Robinson Crusoe] (Malta: Press of the Church Missionary Society, 1835), 122–123. Hereafter cited as *QRK* in the text.

2. Daniel Defoe, *Robinson Crusoe*, ed. Michael Shinagel, Norton Critical Edition (New York: Norton, 1993), 86. Hereafter cited as *RC* in the text.

3. These claims stem from the overwhelming prominence of Ian Watt's *The Rise of the Novel*, in which he argued that "*Robinson Crusoe* is certainly the first novel in the sense that it is the first fictional narrative in which an ordinary person's daily activities are the centre of continuous literary attention." Watt, *The Rise of the Novel: Studies in Defoe, Richardson, and Fielding*, 2nd American ed. (Berkeley: University of California Press, 2001), 74.

4. As Frank Donaghue writes, "Crusoe is never so solitary as he imagines himself." Donaghue, "Inevitable Politics: Rulership and Identity in Robinson Crusoe," *Studies in the Novel* 27, no. 1 (Spring 1995): 1. For examples of these arguments, see Peter

Hulme, *Colonial Encounters: Europe and the Native Caribbean, 1492–1797* (London: Methuen, 1986); John Richetti, *Defoe's Narratives, Situations, and Structures* (Oxford, UK: Clarendon, 1975), 21–62; and Carol Houlihan Flynn, "Consumptive Fictions: Cannibalism and Defoe," in *The Body in Swift and Defoe* (Cambridge: Cambridge University Press, 1990), 149–59.

5. Virginia Woolf, "*Robinson Crusoe*," in *The Second Common Reader*, ed. Andrew McNeillie (New York: Houghton Mifflin Harcourt, 2002), 58.

6. J. Weiss (Printer to Malta Press, 1829–1846) to Coates, December 18, 1844, C M/O 67/32, Church Missionary Society Archives, University of Birmingham, UK (hereafter cited as CMS Archives).

7. M. Peled, "Creative Translation: Towards the Study of Arabic Translations of Western Literature since the Nineteenth Century," *Journal of Arabic Literature* 10 (1979): 128–150; Samah Selim, "Pharaoh's Revenge: Translation, Literary History and Colonial Ambivalence," in *The Making of the Arab Intellectual: Empire, Public Sphere, and the Colonial Coordinates of Selfhood*, ed. Dyala Hamzah (Abingdon, UK: Routledge, 2013), 24.

8. Schlienz to Jowett, May 20, 1828, C M/O 65/4a, CMS Archives; Tarek El-Ariss, *Trials of Modernity: Literary Affects and the New Political* (New York: Fordham University Press, 2013).

9. Dagmar Glass, Geoffrey Roper, and Hrant Gabeyan, "Arabic Book and Newspaper Printing in the Arab World," in *Middle Eastern Languages and the Print Revolution: A Cross-Cultural Encounter*, ed. Eva Manebutt-Benz, Dagmar Glass, and Geoffrey Roper (Westhofen, Germany: WVA-Verlag Skulima, 2002), 192.

10. Print runs of the CMS Press in Malta often reached three thousand, while those of the Greek Catholic press in al-Shuwayr, Lebanon, fluctuated around eight hundred copies. Glass, Roper, and Gabeyan, 180.

11. A. L. Tibawi, *American Interests in Syria, 1800–1901: A Study of Educational, Literary, and Religious Work* (Oxford, UK: Clarendon, 1966), 54. While conversion between Christian sects and from Christianity to Islam and from Islam to Christianity (after 1844, when the ban on the execution of apostates was ordered) was a legally protected right in the Ottoman Empire, the distribution of "false books" was declared illegal in 1824 by imperial decree (*firman*) as a threat to public order. Furthermore, any contact with the missionaries was declared grounds for excommunication by the Maronite Patriarch. As a result, the Syrian mission was temporarily disbanded until diplomatic relationships between Great Britain and the United States were strengthened enough to offer the missionaries protection. It was not until 1850 that Protestantism was officially recognized as a protected religious minority, or *millet*. All non-Muslim subjects were declared equal to Muslim ones in 1856. See Ussama Samir Makdisi, *Artillery of Heaven: American Missionaries and the Failed Conversion of the Middle East* (Cornell: Cornell University Press, 2008), 96–99. Samir Khalaf, *Protestant Missionaries in the Levant: Ungodly Puritans, 1820–1860* (London: Routledge, 2012), 195–200.

12. Hala Auji, *Printing Arab Modernity: Book Culture and the American Press in Nineteenth-Century Beirut* (Leiden: Brill, 2016), 32. Missionaries began by teaching Italian, the lingua franca of commerce in the region, in order to communicate with potential converts but soon switched to their native English. Tibawi, *American Interests*, 33.

13. The role of secular education in the missionary schools was hotly debated by missionaries and their home administrations, with the latter arguing that education

"for the sake of it" was not the primary goal of their efforts and should be subordinated to the pulpit. The teaching of English was often the locus of this debate; while it was cited by the missionaries as useful for attracting pupils, the Prudential Committee saw English-language acquisition by native students as dangerous in its promotion of "Frank manners and customs" that would check "their sympathies with their people" and make them unfit for service. Tibawi, *American Interests*, 125, 134. As Samir Khalaf argues, the argument about whether to teach or preach, Christianize or civilize, was divisive among missionaries in the field as well, many of whom feared that they risked "denationalizing" their converts to become foreign in their sympathies (*Protestant Missionaries*, xvii).

14. ABCFM, *ABCFM Annual Report* (1834), 57, cited in Tibawi, *American Interests*, 63.

15. American Mission Press, *Illustrated Catalogue and Price List of Publications of the American Mission Press of the Presbyterian Board of Foreign Missions, Beirut, Syria, founded in Malta, 1822, and Beirut, 1834* (Beirut: American Mission Press, 1896), 100, 116–117.

16. Shmuel Moreh, *Modern Arabic Poetry: 1800–1970* (Leiden: Brill, 1976), 30.

17. Eugene Stock, *The History of the Church Missionary Society: Its Environment, Its Men, and Its Work*, vol.1 (London: Church Missionary Society, 1899), 224.

18. Church Missionary Society, "Foreign Intelligence Report: Mediterranean," *Missionary Register* 6 (December 1818): 292. As Jowett argued, the publication of schoolbooks, religious tracts, and society proceedings "would insensibly undermine false opinions, and diffuse sound principles and useful knowledge" as well as "apply the stimulus of example, and rouse by the force of Christian motives." William Jowett, *Christian Researches in the Mediterranean, 1815–1820, in Furtherance of the Objects of the Christian Missionary Society* (London: Church Missionary Society, 1822), 321, 326.

19. Church Missionary Society, *Church Missionary Atlas, Containing Maps of the Various Spheres of the Church Missionary Society, with Illustrative Letter-Press*, 2nd ed. (London: Church Missionary House, 1859), 7. The first edition was published in 1837.

20. Church Missionary Society, 10.

21. Samuel Gobat, *Samuel Gobat, Bishop of Jerusalem. His Life and Work. A Biographical Sketch Drawn Chiefly from His Own Journals* (London: James Nisbet, 1884), 190.

22. Vincente L. Rafael, *Contracting Colonialism: Translation and Christian Conversion in Tagalog Society under Early Spanish Rule* (Durham: Duke University Press, 1993), 28.

23. Letter dated July 5, 1854, series ABC: 2.1.1., vol. xx, ABCFM Archives, cited in Tibawi, *American Interests*, 134.

24. *Missionary Herald* 46 (1850): 362, cited in Tibawi, 125.

25. Tibawi, 123. Cornelius Van Alen Van Dyck wrote that he preferred "a Muslim to a Christian, as coming to the work with no preconceived ideas of what a passage ought to mean, and as being more extensively read in Arabic." Isaac H. Hall, "The Arabic Bible of Drs. Eli Smith and Cornelius V. A. Van Dyck," *Journal of the American Oriental Society* 11 (1882–1885): 280.

26. Lawrence Venuti, *The Scandals of Translation: Towards an Ethics of Difference* (London: Routledge, 1998), 5.

27. Venuti, 82.

28. Jacques Derrida, "Des Tours de Babel," in *A Derrida Reader: Between the Blinds*, ed. Peggy Kamuf (New York: Columbia University Press, 1991), 250.

29. See, for example, the Church Missionary Society's *Atlas*, in which the religious diversity of the world is enumerated in order to be "overthrown" (Buddhism

is characterized as "atheistic," Hinduism as "idolatrous," and Islam as "proud" and "fatalist"; 5).

30. Makdisi, *Artillery of Heaven*, 5.

31. Stock, *Church Missionary Society*, 223.

32. *Missionary Register* 7(February 1819): 70.

33. Church Missionary Society, *Atlas*, 7.

34. See Johann Strauss, "Who Read What in the Ottoman Empire (19th–20th Centuries)?," *Middle Eastern Literatures* 6, no. 1 (2010): 39–76.

35. The Ottoman language is Turkish in syntax but largely composed of Arabic (perhaps 40 percent of the total), Turkish, and Persian vocabularies (as well as loan words from central and western European languages). While Turkish was most often written in Arabic script, it was also written in the Armenian script among some Armenian communities and in the Greek alphabet among some Greek Christians. See Donald Quataert, *The Ottoman Empire, 1700–1922*, 2nd ed. (Cambridge: Cambridge University Press, 2005), 181.

36. "We almost daily read the Scriptures in Ancient Greek, Modern Greek, Ancient Armenian, Modern Armenian, Turkish Armenian (or Armeno-Turkish), Arabic, Italian, and English, and frequently hear them read in Syriac, Hebrew, and French. Seldom do we sit down to our meals without hearing conversation at the table in Armenian, Greek, Arabic, Turkish, Italian, and English, and prayer daily ascends from this house—I hope to heaven—in all these languages, excepting the Italian." Edward Dorr Griffin Prime, *Forty Years in the Turkish Empire, or, Memoirs of Rev. William Goodell, D.D., Late Missionary of the ABCFM at Constantinople*, 5th ed. (New York: Robert Carter and Brothers, 1878), 84.

37. Jowett, *Christian Researches*, 381.

38. John Kitto, who only began to learn Arabic after his arrival in Malta on July 30, 1827, was translating and "composing in Arabic" by November of the same year. John Kitto to Rev. Bickersteth, September 20, 1828, CMS/B/OMS/C M 14, CMS Archives.

39. The consequences were also dangerous to the native readers themselves, who braved social and political consequences for associating with the "Biblemen."

40. Auji, *Printing Arab Modernity*, 33.

41. Weiss to Coates, December 18, 1844. Two years earlier, Weiss had discontinued production when the "great influence of the Romish Priesthood over the Maltese printers" was suspected, preventing them from being "entrusted with Protestant Missionary Work." Weiss to Coates, February 24, 1842, C M/O 67/18, CMS Archives.

42. Henry Harris Jessup, *Fifty-Three Years in Syria*, vol. 2 (New York: Fleming H. Revell, 1910), 809. Historians of the Levantine missions have documented that the missions never succeeded in converting great numbers of Ottoman subjects in Syria and Lebanon. As Khalaf argues, though the missions became influential in "ungodly" matters—Puritan ethics of methodical work, virtues of honesty, sobriety, and moderate lifestyles, as well as models of education—their successes stopped short of actual conversion. Indeed, he posits that it was *because of* failed Christianization that the missionaries shifted their efforts "in the direction of 'civilizing' to better prepare students for secular and utilitarian employment opportunities" (*Protestant Missionaries*, xvii).

43. I[sa] Rassam to Secretary, March 22, 1834, CMS/B/OMS/CM 08/25, CMS Archives.

44. Stock, *Church Missionary Society*, 45; Jowett to Coates, September 23, 1825, C M/O 39/53, CMS Archives.

45. "Remarks on Ysa Petros's Arabic Translations," *Missionary Register* 16 (April 1828): 205–6. Petros's contract negotiations are recorded in the CMS Archives: Krusé to Schlienz, December 29, 1829, C M/O 73/40.

46. Jowett to Coates, September 23, 1825.

47. Krusé Gobat, Kugler, and Leider to Schlienz, September 30, 1829, C M/O 73/35, CMS Archives; Krusé to Brenner, July 2, 1830, C M/O 73/49, CMS Archives.

48. Eshediak to Rev. Temple, March 2, 1832, C M/O 73/61, CMS Archives.

49. Schlienz to Secretary, February 3, 1836, C M/O 65/44a, CMS Archives.

50. Jowett notes that even his first name (the Arabic rendering of "Jesus") provides an illustration of the danger of "mingling" for Christians living in Muslim countries, as they adopt names "not common among their brethren in other countries." "Rather," Jowett writes, "in the name Ysa they have adopted the orthography of the Koran" (*Christian Researches*, 220).

51. Kenneth Mills and Anthony Grafton, *Conversions: Old Worlds and New* (Rochester, NY: University of Rochester Press, 2003), x.

52. Gobat to Secretary, February 20, 1840, C M/O 28/37, CMS Archives.

53. Gobat, *Samuel Gobat, Bishop of Jerusalem*, 190–91.

54. Gobat to Dandeson Coates, Lay Secretary, July 12, 1841, C M/O 28/42, CMS Archives.

55. Venuti, *Scandals of Translation*, 15.

56. Paul Ricoeur, *On Translation* (London: Routledge, 2006), 6.

57. Gobat, *Samuel Gobat, Bishop of Jerusalem*, 190. In this passage, Gobat is again criticizing al-Shidyāq, this time for claiming that there were some words in the Bible with no Arabic equivalents. In this ideology of translation, all is translatable because no translation is necessary.

58. Schlienz to Jowett, May 20, 1828, C M/O 65/4a, CMS Archives.

59. Al-Shidyāq to Secretary, March 24, 1844, CMS/B/OMS/C M 08/51, CMS Archives. The poem, regrettably, is no longer attached to the letter.

60. Jurjī Zaydān, *Tārīkh adāb al-lugha al-ʿarabiyya*, vol. 16 of *Mu'alifāt Jurjī Zaydān al-kāmila* (Beirut: Dār al-Jīl, 1982), 222; originally published in 1911–1913 by Maṭbaʿa al-hilāl. It is unclear what role al-Shidyāq played at the CMS at the time that *Kurūzī* was published. After staying two years in Malta from 1826 to 1828, al-Shidyāq moved to Cairo and was employed by the Egyptian state and the CMS at one of its schools until his return to Malta, probably late in 1835, when Christopher Schlienz reports to the CMS secretariat that al-Shidyāq arrived by the *Alexandria* "packet," or steamship. Schlienz to Coates, December 9, 1835, C M/M 5/240, CMS Archives. Despite his physical removal from Malta, however, we cannot discount his continued involvement with the translation department. William Krusé reported from Cairo that al-Shidyāq had looked over and corrected the text of another translator, also residing in Cairo, Luigi Afsemani. In addition to al-Shidyāq, the CMS employed a "sheikh" to improve Afsemani's Arabic. Krusé to Schlienz, April 10, 1829, C M/O 73/30, CMS Archives.

61. Temple to Jowett, July 25, 1828, C M/O 39/121, CMS Archives (emphasis in the original).

62. ABCFM, *Missionary Herald* 23 (June 1827): 180.

63. ABCFM, *Annual Report of the ABCFM* 24–26 (September 1833): 42.

64. Müller to Schlienz, April 2, 1832, C M/O 65/20, CMS Archives; Krusé to Lay Secretary, January 25, 1835, C M/M 5/39, CMS Archives; Gobat to Secretary, February 20, 1840.

65. Müller to Schlienz, June 15, 1830, C M/O 73/47, CMS Archives. Müller was one of al-Shidyāq's great supporters in the mission, even defending him against charges of immorality.

66. Aḥmad Fāris al-Shidyāq, *Mumāḥakāt al-taʿwīl fī munāqiḍāt al-Injīl* (Amman: Dār Wāʾil lil-Nashr, 2003), 14. The manuscript, which was copied in 1900 from another 1865 copy, is dated February 20, 1851.

67. Al-Shidyāq, 21.

68. Al-Shidyāq, 14.

69. Aḥmad Fāris al-Shidyāq, *Leg over Leg*, trans. Humphrey Davies, 4 vols., Library of Arabic Literature (New York: NYU Press, 2012–2014), 1:17 [0.3.1]. As noted in the introduction, I have also included the volume, chapter, and paragraph number in brackets to facilitate access to the Arabic text. On the issue of the text's generic classification, see Luis ʿAwad, *Al-Muʿattirāt al-ajnabiyya fī al-adab al-ʿarabī al-ḥadīth* (Cairo, 1962), 28, and Shawqī Ḍayf, *Al-Matāmāt* (Cairo, 1964), both cited in Mattityahu Peled, "*Al-Sāq ʿalā al-Sāq*: A Generic Definition," *Arabica* 32, no. 1 (March 1985): 35; Raḍwā ʿĀshūr, *Al-Ḥadātha al-mumkina: Al-Shidyāq wa al-Sāq ʿalā al-sāq, al-riwāya al-ūlā fī al-adab al-ʿarabī al-ḥadīth* (Cairo: Dār al-Shurūq, 2009), 10; and Paul Starkey, "Voyages of Self-Definition: The Case of [Ahmad] Fāris al-Shidyāq," in *Sensibilities of the Islamic Mediterranean: Self-Expression in a Muslim Culture from Post-Classical Times to the Present Day*, ed. Robin Ostle (London; I. B. Tauris, 2008), 118–32.

70. Al-Shidyāq, *Leg over Leg*, 1:17 [0.3.1].

71. Al-Shidyāq, 1:17 [0.3.2].

72. Al-Shidyāq, 1:47 [1.1.7].

73. Lexically, the adverbial phrase *sāqan ʿala al-sāq* is also a figurative way of saying "one after another." Edward William Lane, *Arabic-English Lexicon*, vol. 4 (Beirut: Librairie du Liban, 1968), 1472.

74. Al-Shidyāq, *Leg over Leg*, 1:69 [1.2.7].

75. Quoted in ʿImād al-Ṣulḥ, *Aḥmad Fāris al-Shidyāq: Āthāruhu wa ʿaṣruhu* (Beirut, 1980), 144.

76. Walter Benjamin, "On Language and Such and the Language of Man," in *Reflections*, ed. Peter Demetz (New York: Harcourt Brace, 1978), 325, 331.

77. Derrida, "Des Tours de Babel," 250.

78. Joseph Wolff, *Narrative of a Mission to Bokhara, in the Years 1843–1845*, vol. 1 (London: John Parker, 1845), 90. Wolff traveled as a representative of the London Society for Promoting Christianity amongst the Jews. In the CMS papers, he is referred to both as an "independent missionary" and as a "traitor against [the] brethren." Krusé to Jowett, October 5, 1830, C M/O 73/50, CMS Archives.

79. J. Paul Hunter, *The Reluctant Pilgrim: Defoe's Emblematic Method and Quest for Form in Robinson Crusoe* (Baltimore: Johns Hopkins University Press, 1966), 46. As Hunter argues, Defoe might have used seventeenth-century accounts of Indian conversions as a source for Friday. Hunter, "Friday as Convert: Defoe and the Accounts of Indian Missionaries," *Review of English Studies* 14, no. 55 (August 1963): 243–48.

80. These particular examples appear in James Bickford, *James Bickford: An Autobiography of Christian Labour in the West Indies, Demerara, Victoria, New South Wales, and South Australia, 1838–1888* (London: Charles Kelly, 1890), 39; and John Campbell, *Travels in South Africa, Undertaken at the Request of the Missionary Society* (London: Black, Parry, 1815), 115. For more examples see Vanessa Smith, "Crusoe in the South Seas: Beachcombers, Missionaries and the Myth of the Castaway," in *Robinson Crusoe: Myths and Metamorphoses*, ed. Lieve Spaas and Brian Stimpson (London: Macmillan, 1996), 62–77.

81. Hulme, *Colonial Encounters*, 222.

82. Instead of simply finding Friday to have "a settled Affection" for Crusoe, as it appears in Defoe's version, the abridgement is expanded to a lengthy paragraph: "[Friday] found me not only his deliverer, but his preserver and comforter. . . . I was his physician, not only for his body, but his soul." Daniel Defoe, *The Life and Most Surprising Adventures of Robinson Crusoe, of York, Mariner* (Dublin: John Jones, 1819), 144. Andrew O'Malley argues that this is common among children's versions of *Crusoe* in the nineteenth century. See O'Malley, *Children's Literature, Popular Culture, and Robinson Crusoe* (Basingstoke, UK: Palgrave Macmillan, 2012), 48–75. After a survey of the abridgements listed in Robert W. Lovett's bibliography and a comparison of them to the translation, the likeliest candidate (the only one to end in the same way and at the same point in the original narrative) is a popular one printed in at least five editions before *Kurūzī*'s publication, beginning in 1819. The fourth edition of this abridgement was published by John Jones in 1826. Another edition from the same plates was published in New York in 1831 (John Lomax). Robert W. Lovett, *Robinson Crusoe: A Bibliographical Checklist of English Language Editions (1719–1979)* (New York: Greenwood, 1991), 70, 89.

83. The press was established in 1733 by al-Ṣā'igh's cousin ʿAbd Allah Zākhir (1680–1748), under al-Ṣā'igh's supervision. Abdulrazzak Patel, *The Arab Nahḍa: The Making of the Intellectual and Humanist Movement* (Edinburgh: Edinburgh University Press, 2013), 48.

84. Patel, 58. Al-Ṣā'igh, Zākhir, Farḥat Jarmānūs (1670–1732), Niʿmat Allah al-Ḥalabī (d. 1700), Buṭrus al-Tūlawī (d. 1746), and Mikirdīj al-Kasīḥ (d. 1666) formed this learned society. They are often considered the forefathers of the *nahḍa*.

85. Carston-Michael Walbiner counts fourteen manuscript copies of al-Ṣā'igh's *diwān* dating from 1766 to 1884 in the Monastery of al-Shīr (it was printed in 1859 and went through at least six editions at two presses by 1890). Walbiner, "Monastic Reading and Learning in Eighteenth-Century Bilād al-Šām: Some Evidence from the Monastery of al-Šuwayr (Mount Lebanon)," *Arabica* 51, no. 4 (October 2004): 472. Mārūn ʿAbbūd (1886–1962) recalls that during his days as a schoolboy, al-Ṣā'igh's poems were so well-known that they were referred to simply as "the priest's poetry" (*Dīwān al-khūrī*). Mārūn Abbūd, *Ruwwād al-nahḍa al-ḥadītha* (Beirut: Dār al-Thaqāfa, 1996), 40.

86. ʿAbbūd mentions that al-Ṣā'igh's poems were known to contain grammatical and metrical errors: "Ibrāhīm al-Yāzijī corrected many of his errors when he came across them." ʿAbbūd, *Ruwwād al-nahḍa*, 40.

87. Originating within the science of Ḥadīth authentication, the *isnād* extended to other genres including prose fiction (where the chain of transmission was often fictionalized) and documents the provenance of a narrative, citing not only the transmitters of a text but also the mode of transmission (recitation, extemporization, transcription). Poor transmitters, or unreliable methods of transmission, are grounds

for discrediting a story or account. See Abdelfattah Kilito, "The Paths of the Prophetic Hadith," in *The Author and His Doubles* (Syracuse, NY: Syracuse University Press, 2001), 34–44.

88. Daniel Beaumont, "Hard Boiled: Narrative Discourse in Early Muslim Traditions," *Studia Islamica* 83 (1996): 28.

89. Priya Joshi, *In Another Country: Colonialism, Culture, and the English Novel in India* (New York: Columbia University Press, 2002), 21.

90. Buṭrus al-Bustānī, *Muḥīṭ al-muḥīt* (Beirut, 1869), 655. Also cited in Reinhart Dozy, *Supplément aux dictionnaires arabes* (Beirut: Libraire du Liban, 1881), 459. Dozy suggests that *damnajāna* is a "grosse bouteille . . . contient environ vingt bouteilles ordinaires, et elle est revêtue d'osier ou de jonc" (large bottle . . . containing about twenty ordinary bottles, encased in wicker or rush). For *parkal*, see J. W. Redhouse, *A Lexicon, English and Turkish* (Constantinople: A. H. Boyajian, 1884), 154.

91. J. G. Hava, *Al-Farā'id al-durrīyah fī al-lughatayn al-ʿarabiyya wa al-ingilīzīyya* [Arabic-English dictionary for the use of students] (Beirut: Catholic Press, 1899), 201, 292.

92. On Barak, *On Time: Technology and Temporality in Modern Egypt* (Berkeley: University of California Press, 2013), 119.

93. The Gregorian and *hijrī* (the Islamic calendar, a lunar calendar that counts the years from the *hijra*, or the migration of the Prophet from Mecca to al-Madina) calendars were but two of several systems in use in North Africa and the Levant during the nineteenth century. On Barak has shown that four calendars were in use in nineteenth-century Egypt. He writes, "the Coptic solar year regulated agriculture and taxation, the 'Frankish' Gregorian calendar was used in banking and the Cotton Exchange, and the Hijrī calendar was used by the administration and the educated public. Finally, the '*rumi* months' probably referred to the Seleucid calendar or possibly the Julian calendar" (119).

In the Levant, as Avner Wishnitzer has shown, the Gregorian calendar was used only by a minority—the churches affiliated with Rome and by European communities in residence. The *hijrī* remained the dominant calendar in use, alongside a Byzantine one (based on the Julian calendar) used by Eastern Christian communities, as well as the Ottoman fiscal calendar, the *mālī* (a solar calendar that was roughly based on the Julian one but that counted the years from the *hijra*). By 1789, the *mālī* calendar was adopted by almost all departments of the Ottoman government, as Wishnitzer reports, and was made the standard official calendar of the state in 1839. See Wishnitzer, "The Transformation of Ottoman Temporal Culture during the Long Nineteenth Century" (PhD diss., Tel Aviv University, 2009).

94. The biblical passages appear to be original translations, though they most closely follow Fāris al-Shidyāq and Samuel Lee's 1857 translation of the Bible. Compare the translation of Psalms 78:19 that appears in *Kurūzī* (*hal yaqdiru allah an yahī'yā mā'ida fī al-barriya*) with that in Shidyāq and Lee (*wa qālū ayaqdiru allah an yahī'yā mā'ida fī al-barriya*); only two words have been altered. Other passages also appear as similar. *QRK*, 87. *Al-Kitāb al-muqaddasa*, trans. al-Shidyāq and Lee (London: William Watts, 1857), 805.

95. Makdisi, *Artillery of Heaven*, 5.

96. "The slave may only eat what is of his own labor." Al-Qurṭubī (Abū ʿAbd Allah Muḥammad b. Aḥmad b. Abī Bakr b. Faraj al-Anṣārī al-Khazrajī al-Andalusī) (d. 1272), *Al-Jāmiʿ li-aḥkām al-Qur'ān* (Cairo: Dār al-Ḥadīth, 1994).

97. *RC*, 72; Defoe, *Life and Most Surprising Adventures*, 56.

98. *The Holy Qur'an*, trans. Yusuf Ali (Ware, UK: Wordsworth Editions, 2000), 170.

99. Hulme, *Colonial Encounters*, 210.

100. This is what Naoki Sakai has called the "homolingual address," a mode of address that assumes "circulation within the interior of one language, within the putative homogeneity of one linguistic community." Sakai, *Translation and Subjectivity: On "Japan" and Cultural Nationalism* (Minneapolis: University of Minnesota Press, 1997), 1.

101. Walter Benjamin, "Task of the Translator," in *Illuminations* (New York: Schocken Books, 1968), 75.

102. As Ryan Dunch points out, missionary societies often expressed their transnational religious commitments in national terms, imagining a "modern international order of autonomous yet related nation-states" and figuring Christianity as both a religious and a national "awakening." Dunch, "Beyond Cultural Imperialism: Cultural Theory, Christian Missions, and Global Modernity," *History and Theory* 41 (October 2002): 320.

103. Christopher Hill argues that an understanding of reception that focuses on departures and arrivals obscures the "transformations of form that result from movement." Hill, "The Travels of Naturalism and the Challenges of a World Literary History," *Literature Compass* 6, no.6 (2009): 1199.

104. Edward Said, *Beginnings* (New York: Columbia University Press, 1985), 81, quoted in Franco Moretti, *Atlas of the European Novel, 1800–1900* (London: Verso, 1998), 187.

105. Indeed, generic travels are often figured as literal travels. Margaret Cohen's "Traveling Genres" and *The Novel of the Sea* are particularly complex and nuanced versions of this thesis, where a "traveling genre" has the ability to address "divergent publics or a public defined in its diversity, dispersion, and heterogeneity." Cohen, *The Novel and the Sea* (Princeton, NJ: Princeton University Press, 2010), 168. Nevertheless, maritime novels are still imagined to be transported to different "national contexts where [they] then take root." Cohen, "Traveling Genres," *New Literary History* 34, no. 3 (2003): 484. European sea fiction, for example, "returned back across the Atlantic to widespread practice by U.S. authors in the later 1830s and 1840s" who "defined the distinctiveness of the American tradition with an intense, if ambivalent relation to European writers, readers, and literary institutions." Cohen, *Novel and the Sea*, 135.

106. The most well-known examples of this idea are Watt's *Rise of the Novel* and *Myths of Modern Individualism* (Ian Watt, *Myths of Modern Individualism: Faust, Don Quixote, Don Juan, Robinson Crusoe* [Cambridge: Cambridge University Press, 1996]), though the importance of individualism to the novel as a form runs through diverse accounts of the English novel, including Nancy Armstrong's *Desire and Domestic Fiction: A Political History of the Novel* (Oxford: Oxford University Press, 1987) and her more recent *How Novels Think: The Limits of British Individualism, 1719–1900* (New York: Columbia University Press, 2005); and Michael McKeon, *The Secret History of Domesticity: Public, Private, and the Division of Knowledge* (Baltimore: Johns Hopkins University Press, 2005).

107. Richetti, *Defoe's Narratives, Situations and Structures*, 35.

108. Hulme, *Colonial Encounters*, 189.

109. Woolf, "*Robinson Crusoe*," 52.

110. Hulme, *Colonial Encounters*, 198.

111. For Christopher Flynn, to see Crusoe only as an individual in direct encounter with his environment is to deny his status as an agent of British commerce, a

representative of the imperial commercial vanguard in the Caribbean. For Robert Markley, meanwhile, it is to discount the East Indian, South Seas, and East Asian "networks of communication and credit . . . and Crusoe's implication in these networks." For Lydia H. Liu, it is to obscure the fact that Crusoe participates in global network of metonymic exchange with China that predated and preconditioned European colonialism. Flynn, "Nationalism, Commerce, and Imperial Anxiety in Defoe's Later Works," *Rocky Mountain Review of Language and Literature* 54, no. 2 (2000): 12–13; Markley, *The Far East and the English Imagination, 1600–1730* (Cambridge: Cambridge University Press, 2006), 179, 183; Liu, "Robinson Crusoe's Earthenware Pot," *Critical Inquiry* 25, no. 4 (Summer 1999): 730.

112. Liu, "Earthenware Pot," 732, 747 (emphasis in the original).

113. Liu, 747.

114. While Woolf and Liu both note the singularity of the vessel that Crusoe makes, Crusoe in fact succeeds in making a total of five pots: "three very good, I will not say handsome Pipkins; and two other Earthen Pots" (*RC*, 88). It is not clear, however, that all of them were suitable for use on the fire—as Crusoe continues to refer to his having made "an Earthen Pot that would bear the Fire" (*RC*, 89).

115. A *ṭājin* (pl. *ṭawājin*), for example, is a shallow earthenware dish often used for stewing meats (or tajines), while a *dawraq* (pl. *dawāriq*) refers to a round pitcher with a long, slender neck used for serving beverages (in modern Arabic, it is also used to refer to the glass flasks, such as the Erlenmeyer flask used in laboratories).

116. Gobat to Coates, July 12, 1841.

117. Defoe, *Life and Most Surprising Adventures*, 71.

118. Watt, *Rise of the Novel*, 12, 29.

119. Lynn Festa, "Crusoe's Island of Misfit Things," *Eighteenth Century* 52, nos. 3–4 (Fall–Winter 2011): 453 (emphasis in the original).

120. It is significant that Crusoe's naming involves giving the thing a name that belongs to something else; the Latin *translation* and Greek *metaphora* meant both translation and metaphor, pointing to the indistinguishability of inter- and intralingual translation.

121. Benjamin, "Task of the Translator," 76, 78.

122. See David Fausett, *The Strange and Surprizing Sources of Robinson Crusoe* (Amsterdam: Rodopi, 1994). As Srinivas Aravamudan notes, the first serializations of both *Robinson Crusoe* and *The Voyages of Sindbad the Sailor* were concurrent. Aravamudan, "In the Wake of the Novel: Oriental Tale as National Allegory," *Novel: A Forum on Fiction* 33, no. 1 (Autumn 1999): 11.

123. Daniel Defoe, *A Continuation of Letters Written by a Turkish Spy at Paris* (London: W. Taylor, 1718), iv.

124. Daniel Defoe, *The Conduct of Christians Made the Sport of Infidels, in a Letter from a Turkish Merchant at Amsterdam to the Grand Mufti at Constantinople* (London: S. Baker, 1717), 5.

125. Defoe, 7–8.

126. Defoe, as Mary Helen McMurran argues, integrates translation into *Crusoe*'s intercultural scenarios: he speaks Portuguese, Spanish, and even Friday's native language to a Spanish sailor, who replies in Latin, portraying the "reality of Atlantic multilinguality." Yet it is a multilinguality that is rife with errors, miscommunications, and intermediary transmitters; Crusoe speaks only as much Spanish as he could

"make up" and uses Friday as his "interpreter." McMurran, *The Spread of Novels: Translation and Prose Fiction in the Eighteenth Century* (Princeton, NJ: Princeton University Press, 2010), 139.

127. Mīkhā'īl Jūrj 'Awrā, "Muqaddima fī ḥaqīqat tadwīn fann al-qiṣaṣ" [Introduction on the truth of the development of the art of novel-writing], *Riwāyat al-Jinūn fī ḥubb Mānūn* (Alexandria: Maṭba'at al-Ahrām, 1886), 12.

128. Clara Reeve, *The Progress of Romance through Times, Countries and Manners* (London, 1785), ix.

129. Srinivas Aravamudan, *Enlightenment Orientalism: Resisting the Rise of the Novel* (Chicago: University of Chicago Press, 2012), 74.

130. Georg Lukács, *The Theory of the Novel: A Historico-Philosophical Essay on the Forms of Great Epic Literature*, trans. Anna Bostock (Cambridge, MA: MIT Press, 1971), 39.

131. Mikhail Bakhtin, *The Dialogic Imagination: Four Essays*, trans. Caryl Emerson and Michael Holquist (Austin: University of Texas Pres, 1981), 49, 276.

132. Bakhtin, 277–78.

133. Bakhtin, 278.

134. Derrida, "Des Tours de Babel," 244.

135. Lukács, *Theory of the Novel*, 84.

2. Stranger Publics

1. *Al-Sāq* did not see wide circulation in al-Shidyāq's lifetime. Apart from excerpts published in the Tunisian newspaper *Al-Rā'id al-Tunīsī* and an early twentieth-century reprinting by the Cairo publishing house al-Maktaba al-Tijāriyya, it was only republished in 1966. Raḍwā 'Āshūr describes finding a copy of this rare Cairo edition in the 'Ayn Shams University library, only for it to have vanished on her next visit. 'Āshūr, *Al-Ḥadātha al-Mumkina: Al-Shidyāq wa al-Sāq 'alā al-sāq, al-riwāya al-ūlā fī al-adab al-'arabī al-ḥadīth* (Cairo: Dār al-Shurūq, 2009), 15.

2. Of the 243 works published by the Būlāq Press in Egypt, for example, J. Heyworth-Dunne classifies only two as Arabic poetry and two (*Kalīla wa Dimna* and *Alf Layla wa layla*) as Arabic "belles-lettres." Heyworth-Dunne, "Printing and Translations under Muḥammad 'Alī of Egypt: The Foundation of Modern Arabic," *Journal of the Royal Asiatic Society of Great Britain and Ireland* 3 (July 1940): 334. The vast majority of literary works published by the press were in Turkish, either for export to Turkey or, as Richard N. Verdery suggests, for the officer class of Muḥammad 'Alī's army. Verdery, "The Publications of the Būlāq Press under Muḥammad 'Alī of Egypt," *Journal of the American Oriental Society* 91, no. 1 (January–March 1971): 131–32.

3. See Buṭrus al-Bustānī, "Khuṭba fī adāb al-'arab," in *Al-Jam'iyya al-Sūriyya li al-'ulūm wa al-funūn, 1847–1852* (Beirut: Dār al-Ḥamrā', 1990), 12. For an overview of these societies see Abdulrazzak Patel, *The Arab Nahḍa: The Making of the Intellectual and Humanist Movement* (Edinburgh: Edinburgh University Press, 2013), 216–21.

4. See al-Bustānī, "Khuṭba," 123–27.

5. See Yusuf Q. Khūrī, preface to *A'māl al-jam'īyya al-'ilmiyya al-sūriyya*, 2. The "Khuṭba," at least, was advertised for sale in *Ḥadīqat al-akhbār* as a tract "that everyone is recommended to read." It was for sale at the American Press and at the bookstore of al-Khuwāja Liyās Fuwāz in Beirut. *Ḥadīqat al-akhbār* 100 (December 1/19, 1859): 4.

6. Al-Bustānī, "Khuṭba," 115.

7. As Jeff Sacks notes, the appeal to promote print "violently reorganizes an understanding of language in Arabic," subordinating an older "Arabic-Islamic, juridical-logocentric one." The disciplining of the public went hand in hand with the redisciplining of the Ottoman legal and economic systems. Sacks, *Iterations of Loss: Mutilation and Aesthetic Form, from al-Shidyaq to Darwish* (New York: Fordham University Press, 2015), 81.

8. Al-Bustānī, "Khuṭba," 115.

9. The speech was originally given in 1868 and published in 1869. Buṭrus al-Bustānī, *Al-Khiṭāb fī al-hay'a al-ijtimā'īyya wa al-muqābala bayn al-'awā'id al-'arabiyya wa al-ifranjiyya* (Beirut: Maṭba'at al-Ma'ārif, 1869), 11.

10. The Egyptian Khedive Ismā'īl has been credited for liberalizing the press in Egypt, but Ami Ayalon explains how Ismā'īl wavered between "a desire to encourage cultural activity and the political implications of such activity," closing the first private periodicals after only a few issues. The first to successfully navigate the political climate and remain in publication was *Al-Ahrām*, founded in 1876 and now the state newspaper of Egypt. Ayalon, *The Press in the Arab Middle East: A History* (New York: Oxford University Press, 1995), 43.

11. No comprehensive study of the semantic emergence of the term "public" has yet been undertaken, but corollary terms have been examined. Notably, Dyala Hamza has excavated an extensive genealogy of the term "public interest" (*al-maṣlaḥa al-'āmm*), Anne-Laure Dupont has written on the emergence of the *kātib 'āmm* (public writer), and Ami Ayalon has written on the emergence of the term *jumhūr*. Hamza, "From *'ilm* to *Ṣiḥāfa* or the politics of the Public Interest (*maṣlaḥa*): Muḥammad Rashīd Riḍa and His Journal *al-Manār* (1898–1935)," in *The Making of the Arab Intellectual: Empire, Public Sphere, and the Colonial Coordinates of Selfhood*, ed. Hamza (London: Routledge, 2013), 90–127; Dupont, "What Is a *Kātib 'Āmm*? The Status of Men of Letters and the Conception of Language According to Jurjī Zaydān," *Middle Eastern Literatures* 13, no. 2 (August 2010): 171–81; Ayalon, *Language and Change in the Arab Middle East: The Evolution of Modern Arabic Political Discourse* (New York: Oxford University Press, 1987), 43–53.

12. The nineteenth-century Egyptian chronicler Mikhā'īl Sharubim refers to literature and illiterate members of *al-'āmma* when describing newspaper consumption in the streets of Cairo: "those who were literate among the common people [*al-'āmma*] relied on those who could read." Ziad Fahmy, *Ordinary Egyptians: Creating the Modern Nation through Popular Culture* (Stanford, CA: Stanford University Press, 2011), 53. Both Fahmy and Hoda A. Youssef argue for an expanded understanding of periodical audiences, based on Egyptian periodicals' incorporation of dialect (*al-'ammiyya*, the language of the common people). See especially Fahmy, 1–19. As Youssef writes, "the 'modern' Arabic of the newspapers and journals sought to reach a wider audience, not only the minority who were actually literate." Youssef, *Composing Egypt: Reading, Writing, and the Emergence of a Modern Nation, 1870–1930* (Stanford, CA: Stanford University Press, 2016), 128.

13. Khalīl al-Khūrī, "Al-Muṭāli'a" [Reading], *Ḥadīqat al-akhbār* 250 (January 18/29, 1863).

14. Buṭrus al-Bustānī, "Al-Sharq," *Al-Jinān* 1, no. 1 (January 1870): 17.

15. Fransīs al-Marrāsh, "Al-Jarā'id" [Newspapers], *Al-Jinān* 2, no. 5 (March 1871): 157–58.

16. Al-Bustānī, "Khuṭba," 115.

17. *Ḥadīqat al-akhbār* criticized a new journal published in Bayt al-Dīn, Lebanon, for printing content that was "self-interested," rather than "in the spirit of general periodicals." *Ḥadīqat al-akhbār* 10, no. 455 (April, 11/23 1867). For other examples, see *Ḥadīqat al-akhbār* 98 (November 5/17, 1859), 1; and *Ḥadīqat al-akhbār* 104 (December 17/29, 1859).

18. Youssef, *Composing Egypt*, 39–42; Elizabeth M. Holt, "Narrative and the Reading Public in 1870s Beirut," *Journal of Arabic Literature* 40 (2009): 37–70.

19. Jürgen Habermas, *The Structural Transformation of the Public Sphere*, trans. Thomas Burger (Cambridge, UK: Polity, 1989), 43; Holt, "Narrative and the Reading Public," 43.

20. Holt, "Narrative and the Reading Public," 49, 39.

21. Habermas, *Structural Transformation*, 37.

22. Youssef, *Composing Egypt*, 7–8.

23. See Fahmy, *Ordinary Egyptians*, 37.

24. "Opening," *Al-Zahra* 1, no. 1 (January 7, 1870): 3.

25. Al-Marrāsh, "Al-Jarā'id," 158.

26. See, for example, *Al-Jinān* 1, no. 20 (October 1870): 619; 2, no. 24 (December 15, 1871): 869; *Al-Bashīr* 74 (January 27, 1872); *Ḥadīqat al-akhbār* 89 (August 3/15, 1859); 184 (October 12/24, 1861); 193 (December 14/26, 1861); 391 (February 20/1, 1866). An advertisement for the book-subscription scheme *Al-'Umda al-adabiyya* also reveals subscription problems, as it asks current subscribers to pay their second installment. *Ḥadīqat al-akhbār* 126 (May 19/31, 1860).

27. Ayalon, *Language and Change*, 208–11.

28. *Al-Bashīr* 437 (January 24, 1879); 474 (October 10, 1879); 475 (October 17, 1879).

29. See *Al-Jawā'ib* (April 21, 1868), 1; and *Al-Jinān* 1, no. 17 (August 1870): 515–16.

30. "Tanbīh" [Announcement], *Al-Bashīr* 475 (October 17, 1879).

31. "Muqaddima" [Introduction], *Al-Muqtaṭaf* 1 (June 1876): 2.

32. Stephen Sheehi, "Toward a Critical Theory of *al-Nahḍah*: Epistemology, Ideology, and Capital," *Journal of Arabic Literature* 43 (2012): 271.

33. Sheehi, 291.

34. Marrāsh, "Al-Jarā'id," 159.

35. Al-Khūrī, "Al-Muṭāli'a," *Ḥadīqat al-akhbār* 250 (January 18/29, 1863), 3.

36. As Ayalon points out, the cost of a single issue of *Lisān al-ḥāl* in 1878 was 1 *qirsh*, which in 1870s Beirut could provide enough food for one adult for one day; it was the equivalent of one pound of rice, one and a half pounds of flour, or two pounds of broad beans. In Ayalon's assessment, those who could afford to regularly purchase a periodical would have to have had incomes significantly above the requirement for basic survival: "skilled workers, successful merchants, state functionaries, and a small but growing group of modern professionals, including journalists, along with the tiny wealthy class." While this amounted to a tiny fraction of the entire community, Ayalon notes that this meant tens or hundreds of thousands (depending on the country) of potential readers in the nineteenth century. Ayalon, *Language and Change*, 193–94.

37. Ayalon, 155, 157; Fahmy, *Ordinary Egyptians*, 33; On Barak, *On Time, Technology, and Temporality in Modern Egypt* (Berkeley: University of California Press, 2013), 130.

38. Mikhā'īl Sharubīm, *Al-Kāfī fī tarīkh Miṣr* [The complete history of Egypt] 5, no. I.ii (Cairo: Maṭba'at Dār al-Kutub wa al-Wathā'iq al-Qawmiyya bi al-Qāhira, 2003),

660, cited in Fahmy, *Ordinary Egyptians*, 35; *Al-Hilāl*, October 1897, 131, cited in Ayalon, *Language and Change*, 157.

39. Fahmy, *Ordinary Egyptians*, 36.

40. "*Jinān* sanna 1872" [*Al-Jinān*, year 1872], *Al-Jinān* 2, no. 24 (December 15, 1871): 830.

41. Khalīl al-Khūrī, "Mudīr jurnāl wa al-mushtarikīn bihi" [A journal editor and his subscribers], *Ḥadīqat al-akhbār* 173 (August 27/8, 1861), 2.

42. Nancy Fraser, "Rethinking the Public Sphere: A Contribution to the Critique of Actually Existing Democracy," *Social Text* 25/26 (1990): 116.

43. Michael Warner, *Publics and Counterpublics* (Brooklyn, NY: Zone Books, 2002), 55.

44. Because print promises to address anybody, Warner argues, it "commits itself in principle to the possible participation of any stranger" (55).

45. Khalīl al-Khūrī, "Request for Forgiveness," *Ḥadīqat al-akhbār* 31 (August 26/7, 1858): 2.

46. Al-Khūrī, 2.

47. "Al-Jarā'id wa wājibātuhā wa adābuhā," *Al-Hilāl* 4, no. 1 (September 1, 1895): 16.

48. "Al-Jarā'id wa wājibātuhā wa adābuhā," 17.

49. Ibrāhīm al-Yāzijī, *Lughat al-jarā'id* (Cairo: Maṭbaʿat Maṭar, n.d.), 2.

50. Ayalon lists many examples of this in *Language and Change in the Arab Middle East*. See, for example, pages 104 and 108.

51. "Al-Jinān," *Al-Jinān* 1, no. 1 (January 1870): i.

52. Al-Marrāsh, "Al-Jarā'id," 157–58

53. Yaʿqūb Ṣarrūf and Fāris Nimr, "Muqaddima," *Al-Muqtaṭaf* 1, no. 1 (1876): 1–2.

54. As he writes, periodicals like *Al-Muqtaṭaf* avoided "eloquently arranged sentences, subtly chosen words, [and] brilliantly figured expressions." Salāma Mūsā, *The Education of Salāma Mūsā*, trans. L. O. Schuman (Leiden: Brill, 1961), 38.

55. Salāma Mūsā, *Al-Ṣiḥāfa, ḥirfa wa risāla* (Cairo: Salāma Mūsā li al-Nashr wa al-tawzīʿ, 1963).

56. Mūsā, 46–47.

57. Al-Khūrī, "Mudīr jurnāl wa al-mushtarikīn bihi," 2.

58. Al-Marrāsh, "Al-Jarā'id," 159.

59. Scientific terms like "horizon" and "friction," places names like "Hungary" or "Albania," foreign terms like "geology" or "zoology," and obscure synonyms like *suhd* for "insomnia" ("with a *ḍamma* meaning *al-araq*, or the absence of sleep") were all glossed either inside parentheses or in the text itself. "Al-Shafaq al-quṭbī" [Polar lights], *Al-Jinān* 1, no. 22 (November 1870): 690; Salīm al-Bustānī, "Khaṣā'iṣ al-Mawād" [Material properties], *Al-Jinān* 9, no. 12 (June 15, 1878): 393; Bishāra Zilzal, "Al-Tārīkh al-Ṭabīʿī" [Natural history], *Al-Muqtaṭaf* 1, no. 5 (1876): 101; "Aḥwāl al-Ṣirb qadīman wa ḥadīthan qabl istiqlālihā" [The condition of the Serbians before independence], *Al-Jawā'ib*, cited in Salīm al-Shidyāq, *Kanz al-raghā'ib fī muntakhabāt al-Jawā'ib* [Treasures from *Al-Jawā'ib* magazine], vol. 6 (Istanbul: Maṭbaʿat al-Jawā'ib, 1871–1881), 369. See also a poem written by al-Shidyāq in *Al-Jawā'ib* and reprinted in *Kanz* 3 (1880): 115.

60. Khalīl al-Khūrī, "On Periodical Writing" [Fī qirā'at al-jarā'id] *Ḥadīqat al-akhbār* 51 (December 10/22, 1858): 2.

61. See Sasson Somekh, *Genre and Language in Modern Arabic Literature* (Wiesbaden: Otto Harrassowitz, 1991), 11–17; and Jaroslav Stetkevych, *The Modern Arabic Literary*

Language: Lexical and Stylistic Developments, 2nd ed. (Washington, DC: Georgetown University Press, 2006), 15–18; as well as Joshua Blau, *The Renaissance of Modern Hebrew and Modern Standard Arabic: Parallels and Differences in the Revival of Two Semitic Languages* (Berkeley: University of California Press, 1981).

62. *Al-Jawāʾib* 43 (March 28, 1862): 1.

63. While a system of transliteration for Ottoman Turkish telegrams was devised relatively early in the telegraph's history in 1856, French continued to be the dominant language for both transmissions and the daily operations of telegraph offices in the Ottoman Empire. Roderic H. Davison, "The Advent of the Electric Telegraph in the Ottoman Empire," in *Essays in Ottoman and Turkish History 1774–1923: The Impact of the West* (Austin: University of Texas Press, 1990), 151–53; Yakup Bektas, "The Sultan's Messenger: Cultural Constructions of Ottoman Telegraphy, 1847–1880," *Technology and Culture* 41, no. 4 (2000): 687.

64. Esperança Bielsa and Susan Bassnet, *Translation in Global News* (New York: Routledge, 2009), 56.

65. Barak, *On Time*, 127; Bektas, "Sultan's Messenger," 688.

66. *Ḥadīqat al-akhbār* 180 (September 14/26, 1861): 1. An article announcing the completion of the Beirut-Damascus cable appeared in *Ḥadīqat al-akhbār* on November 17/29, 1860, and an article announcing that the line was operational appeared six months later, on July 22/4, 1861.

67. Al-Bustānī, "Al-Sharq," 1.

68. In Pettegree's chapter "The First Newspapers," almost all of his earliest examples mention a reliance on translation. Andrew Pettegree, *The Invention of the News: How the World Came to Know about Itself* (New Haven, CT: Yale University Press, 2014), 75, 195.

69. *Al-Najāḥ* 2, no. 32 (March 8, 1871): 503; *Al-Najāḥ* 2, no. 37 (May 22, 1871): 556.

70. *Al-Jinān* 4, no. 11 (June 1, 1873): 442. Though Ayalon lists this journal as weekly, following Tarrazi III (*Language and Change*, 48–50), al-Ḥamawī in this article advertises it as daily.

71. *Al-Najāḥ* 3, no. 1 (January 6, 1872): 1.

72. See Itamar Even-Zohar, "Polysystem Theory," *Poetics Today* 1, nos. 1–2 (Autumn 1979): 287–310; and Pascale Casanova, *The World Republic of Letters* (Cambridge, MA: Harvard University Press, 2004).

73. Khalīl al-Khūrī, "Al-ʿAsr al-Jadīd," *Ḥadīqat al-akhbār* 1 (January 1, 1858): 1.

74. "Translation Lexicon" [Muʿjam al-muʿarrabāt], *Al-Muqtaṭaf* 8, no. 2 (November 1883): 108.

75. For examples of readers' translation questions, see "Questions and Answers," *Al-Muqtaṭaf* 3, no. 9 (February 1789): 254; 4, no. 12 (May 1880): 333, and 6, no. 11 (April 1882): 300. For examples of lexicons for translation being advertised, see 6, no. 2 (July 1881): 56; 6, no. 3 (August 1881): 79; 6, no. 5 (October 1881): 136; and 6, no. 12 (May 1882): 328. *Al-Muqtaṭaf* considered the translation of scientific terms to be part of its essential mission and began serializing an alphabetical "Glossary of Translated Terms" (Muʿjam al-muʿarabāt) in 1883. As Marwa Elshakry explains, *Al-Muqtaṭaf*'s editors used the journal "to create a systematic and extensive vocabulary for the new sciences": the glossaries of translated terms were central to their publishing mission. Elshakry, *Reading Darwin in Arabic, 1860–1950* (Chicago: University of Chicago Press, 2013), 712.

76. *Al-Jinān* 2, no. 4 (February 5, 1871): 132.

77. Al-Yāzijī enumerates many examples of these in *Lughat al-jarā'id*.

78. ʿAbd al-Qādir afandī al-Mu'ayid, "Fī al-tarjama" [On translation], *Al-Jinān* 1, no. 23 (December 1870): 728–29.

79. Ayalon, *Press in the Arab Middle East*, 24.

80. Jūzīf Iliyās, *Taṭawwur al-ṣiḥāfa al-Sūriyya fī mi'at ʿām*, vol. 1, *1865–1965* (Beirut: Dār al-Niḍāl li al-Ṭibāʿa wa al-Nashr wa al-Tawzīʿ, 1982), 163, 196–97, 114. Even European-language journals appearing in the Ottoman Empire were often printed in multiple languages: in Alexandria, *Il Popolo*, *L'Argus*, and *La Revista* were all published in French and Italian, and *Le Bavard égyptien* was published in eight languages. Grilles Kraemer, *La Presse francophone en mediterranée* (Paris: Maisonneuve et Larose, 2001), 114–17. Kraemer lists eight multilingual periodicals published in Egypt between the years of 1851 and 1897, to which Jean-Jacques Luthi adds four more. Luthi, *Lire la presse d'expression française en Egypte: 1798–2008* (Paris: L'Harmattan, 2010), 18.

81. I counted 907 periodicals published before 1913 in either Hasan Duman's index or the *Jarā'id* chronology compiled by the Leibniz-Zentrum Moderner Orient in Berlin (https://www.zmo.de/jaraid/index.html). Of them, nearly 200 were multilingual. Duman, *İstanbul kütüphaneleri Arap harfli süreli yayınlar toplu kataloğu, 1828–1928* [Union catalogue of the periodicals in Arabic script in the libraries of Istanbul, 1828–1928] (İstanbul: İslâm Tarih, Sanat, ve Kültür Araştırma Merkezi, 1986).

82. Nancy Fraser, *Transnationalizing the Public Sphere* (Cambridge, UK: Polity Press), 10.

83. In both *Inclusion of the Other* and *The Postnational Constellation*, Habermas explores the possibility of a "European-wide political public sphere embedded in a shared political culture." Jürgen Habermas, *Inclusion of the Other: Studies in Political Theory*, edited by Ciaran Cronin and Pablo De Greill (Cambridge, UK: Polity Press, 1999), 153. Jürgen Habermas, *The Postnational Constellation: Political Essays* (Cambridge: The MIT Press, 2001).

84. Habermas, *Structural Transformation*, 34.

85. This is despite the body of scholarship that has posited the formative role of translation and other forms of multilingual circulation in the rise of these cultural institutions and their literary corollaries. See, for example, Mary Helen McMurran, *The Spread of Novels: Translation and Prose Fiction in the Eighteenth Century* (Princeton, NJ: Princeton University Press, 2010).

86. Benedict Anderson, *Imagined Communities: Reflections on the Origin and Spread of Nationalism* (London: Verso, 1983), 44.

87. Timothy Brennan, "The National Longing for Form," in *Nation and Narration*, ed. Homi Bhabha (New York: Routledge, 1990), 49.

88. Anderson, *Imagined Communities*, 43.

89. Anderson, 62–63.

90. See, for example, Raúl Coronado, *A World Not to Come: A History of Latino Writing and Print Culture* (Cambridge, MA: Harvard University Press, 2013). Though the book explores, through Tejano print culture, the "space of overlap between Spanish America and the United States," it does so without examining the bilingual or multilingual publications or indeed Anglophone ones (17). As Kristen Silva Gruesz, whose work has focused on the "vibrant polyglot print cultures in New Orleans" and the "Gulf Stream" more generally, argues, though scholars have called for multilingual studies

of American literature, linguistic nativism and responses to it has inhibited cross-linguistic study, with scholars largely producing comparisons of linguistically discrete literary cultures. Gruesz, *Ambassadors of Culture: The Transamerican Origins of Latino Writing* (Princeton, NJ: Princeton University Press, 2002), 111; Gruesz, "Alien Speech, Incorporated: On the Cultural History of Spanish in the US," *American Literary History* 25, no. 1 (Spring 2013): 9. Though Anderson's assertion that "then and now the bulk of mankind is and was monoglot" was not applicable to eighteenth- and nineteenth-century South Asia, as Lisa Mitchell argues, print helped to construct audiences that defined themselves in relation to the language of publication. Mitchell, *Language, Emotion, and Politics in South India: The Making of a Mother-Tongue* (Bloomington: Indiana University Press, 2009), 73.

91. Benedict Anderson, *The Spectre of Comparisons: Nationalism, Southeast Asia, and the World* (London: Verso, 1998), 33.

92. "Issue 41 of *Barjīs Barīs*," *Ḥadīqat akhbār* 146 (January 19/31, 1861): 1. See also an unfavorable review of *Jabal Lubnān*, a new official journal published bilingually in Mount Lebanon. Among its flaws are its small size, its unattractive type, and the fact that "it is clear from its spirit of expression that [its Arabic section] is translated from the French." "Jabal Lubnān," *Ḥadīqat al-akhbār* 455 (April 11/23, 1867): 3.

93. These articles are published in issues 54 through 62 (September 9, 1871–November 4, 1871), then reprised in issues 70, 75, 141, and 144.

94. "On the Distortions Found in a Copy of the Protestant Bible Published in Beirut," *Al-Bashīr* 54 (September 9, 1871): 487.

95. Stetkeyvich, *Modern Arabic Literary Language*, 14; Ayalon, *Language and Change*, 7.

96. Ayalon, *Language and Change*, 34–39.

97. See *Annales de l'assemblée nationale, compte-rendu in extensor des séances*, vol. 1, February 12–March 11, 1871 (Paris: Imprimerie et librairie du journal officiel, 1871), 106–9.

98. Marshall McLuhan, *Counterblast* (New York: Harcourt and Brace, 1969), 112–13.

99. McLuhan, in fact, has done just that: "All media are active metaphors in their power to translate experience into new forms," as he writes. McLuhan, "Media as Translators," in *Understanding Media: Extensions of Man* (Cambridge, MA: MIT Press, 1964), 57.

100. Martin Heidegger, *Unterwegs zur Sprache*, vol. 12 of *Gesamtausgabe* (Frankfurt: Klostermann, 1985), 149, cited in Antoine Berman, *The Experience of the Foreign: Culture and Translation in Romantic Germany* (Albany: SUNY Press, 1992), vii.

101. Ashraf Eissa, "Majallat al-Jinān: Arabic Narrative Discourse in the Making," *Quaderni di Studi Arabi* 18 (2000): 41–49.

102. Michael Mckeon, *Secret History of Domesticity: Public, Private, and the Division of Knowledge* (Baltimore: Johns Hopkins University Press, 2005), 75.

3. Errant Readers

1. Ḥamdī Sakkūt, *Al-Riwāya al-ʿarabiyya: Bibliyūjrāfiyā wa madkhal naqadī, 1865–1995* [The Arabic novel: Bibliography and critical introduction, 1865–1995], vol. 5 (Cairo: American University in Cairo Press, 2000), 2845–47. Matti Moosa, *Origins of Arabic Fiction* (Washington, DC: Three Continents Press, 1997), 157. Basilius Bawardi and Fruma Zachs, "Between Adab al-Rihlat and 'Geo-Literature': The Constructive

Narrative Fiction of Salim al-Bustani," *Middle Eastern Literature* 10, no. 3 (2007): 203–17; Sharon Halevi and Fruma Zachs, "The Early Arabic Novel as Social Compass," *Studies in the Novel* 39, no. 4 (2007): 416–30. These novels are *Al-Huyām fī jinān al-Shām* (1870), *Zanūbya* (1871), *Budūr* (1872), *Asmā'* (1873), *Al-Huyām fī futūḥ al-Shām* (1874), *Bint al-'aṣr* (1875), *Fātina* (1877), *Salmā* (1878–1879), and *Samiyā* (1882).

2. Al-Bustānī, "Al-Jinān," *Al-Jinān* 1, no. 1 (January 1870): n.p.; "Advertisement," *Al-Jinān* 1, no. 20 (October 1870): 619; "Gil Blas's Introduction to the Reader," *Al-Jinān* 15, no. 5 (March 1, 1884): 153. *Al-Jinān*, as the editors explain in its inaugural issue, is the plural of *janna*, or "garden." Alain-René Lesage fortuitously uses the phrase "tirer les fruits" (reap the fruits) in the French introduction, which Mudawwar amplifies and ties to *Al-Jinān*.

3. *Riwāyat al-Markīz dī Fūntānj* [Novel of the Marquis de Fontanges], trans. Salīm dī Nawfal, *Ḥadīqat al-akhbār* 50 (December 6/18, 1858): 3. The translation, which was serialized from December 18, 1858, to February 14, 1859, took as its source text Léocadie Aimée Doze Beauvoir's *Confidences et causeries de Mlle Mars*, which was published under the pseudonym of Mademoiselle Mars in 1852 (Brussels: Kiessling). Nawfal probably obtained a copy of its 1855 Paris republishing (Librairie Nouvelle).

4. "Advertisement," *Al-Bashīr* 145 (June 7, 1873). *Wardat al-Maghrib*, originally *Rosa von Tannenburg* and translated by Jirjis Zuwayn, was serialized from February 3, 1872, to August 24, 1872 (issues 75–104); this advertisement was for its publication as a single-volume edition. Though it was written in German by Christoph von Schmid, *The Catalogue of Arabic Books in the British Museum* lists it as having been translated from the French version—a more likely scenario considering the prevalence of French-language learning in *nahḍa*-era schools. British Museum, Department of Oriental Printed Books and Manuscripts, A. S. (Alexander Strathern) Fulton, and W.W. Elliott, eds., *Catalogue of Arabic Books In the British Museum* (London: British Museum, 1967), 589. On the orientation of *Al-Bashīr* and other Jesuit publications in Beirut, see Rafael Herzstein, "The Oriental Library and the Catholic Press at Saint-Joseph University in Beirut," *Journal of Jesuit Studies* 2, no. 2 (2015): 248–64.

5. "Advertisement," *Al-Bashīr* 145 (June 7, 1873).

6. Lūwīs Shaykhū [?], introduction to *Wardat al-Maghrib* (Beirut: Maṭba'a al-Abā' al-Yasū'īyīn, 1873), ii, i.

7. *Riwāyat al-Markīz dī Fūntānj*, *Ḥadīqat al-akhbār* 50 (December 6/18, 1858): 4. The author attributes the quotation to Voltaire.

8. Jürgen Habermas, *The Structural Transformation of the Public Sphere*, trans. Thomas Burger (Cambridge, UK: Polity, 1989), 51.

9. Benedict Anderson, *Imagined Communities: Reflections on the Origin and Spread of Nationalism* (London: Verso, 1983), 30.

10. Anderson, 30, 35-36.

11. Clifford Siskin, *The Work of Writing: Literature and Social Change in Britain, 1700–1830* (Baltimore: Johns Hopkins University Press, 1998), 180.

12. Siskin, 187. As he argues, the domestication of the novel did not resolve but regulated difference by portraying what William Godwin called "things as they are," and Jane Austen called "bits" of the "ordinary" (186).

13. Michael Warner, *Publics and Counterpublics* (New York: Zone Books, 2002), 115.

14. Warner, 115.

15. Salīm al-Bustānī, *Asmā'*, *Al-Jinān* 4, no. 1 (January 1, 1873): 31.

16. Al-Bustānī, 31–32.

17. Salīm al-Bustānī, *Asmā'*, *Al-Jinān* 4, no. 23 (December 1, 1873): 826–27. This is an argument he elaborates from a similar aside in his first serialized novel, *Al-Huyām fī jinān al-Shām*. See *Al-Jinān* 1, no. 22 (November 1870): 702.

18. Al-Bustānī, *Asmā'*, *Al-Jinān* 4, no. 23 (December 1, 1873): 826–27.

19. Al-Bustānī, *Al-Jinān* 4, no. 1 (January 1, 1873): 31.

20. It is a problem with which al-Bustānī had some practical experience, as readers objected to his "indecent" portrayal of a romantic reunion in *Huyām* in which the protagonist recognizes Warda by the mole on her breast. *Wardat al-Huyām* [Warda of al-Huyām], *Al-Jinān* 1, no. 24 (December 1870): 752.

21. Al-Bustānī, *Asmā'*, *Al-Jinān* 4, no. 3 (February 1, 1873): 102.

22. Salīm al-Bustānī, *Bint al-'aṣr*, *Al-Jinān* 6, no. 1 (January 1, 1875): 31.

23. Al-Bustānī, *Asmā'*, *Al-Jinān* 4, no. 4 (February 15, 1873): 138.

24. Al-Bustānī, *Asmā'*, *Al-Jinān* 4, no. 7 (May 15, 1873): 212–14; no. 9 (May 1, 1873): 318–19; no. 20 (October 15, 1873): 717–19.

25. Al-Bustānī, *Bint al-'aṣr* 6, no. 2 (January 15, 1875): 71.

26. Michael Allen, "How *Adab* Became Literary: Formalism, Orientalism, and the Institutions of World Literature," *Journal of Arabic Literature* 43 (2012): 172–96.

27. Hilary Kirkpatrick, "Selection and Presentation as Distinctive Characteristics of Mediaeval Arabic Courtly Prose Literature," in *Courtly Literature: Culture and Context; Selected Papers from the 5th Triennial Congress of the International Courtly Literature Society*, ed. Keith Busby and Erik Kooper (Amsterdam: John Benjamins, 1990), 339.

28. This comes from Rina Drory's influential article "Three Attempts to Legitimize Fiction in Classical Arabic Literature," *Jerusalem Studies in Arabic and Islam* 18 (1994): 146–64.

29. Muhsin Mahdi, preface to *The Arabian Nights*, trans. Husain Haddawy (New York: Norton, 1990), 3.

30. Al-Bustānī, *Asmā'*, *al-Jinān* 4, no. 23 (December 1, 1873): 827.

31. Al-Bustānī, *Asmā'*, *al-Jinān* 4, no. 11 (June 1, 1873): 390; no. 1 (January 1, 1873): 31; no. 10 (May 15, 1873): 358.

32. See Elizabeth M. Holt, "Narrative and the Reading Public in 1870s Beirut," *Journal of Arabic Literature* 40 (2009): 37–70.

33. *Al-Jinān* 1, no. 4 (February 1870): 109. And even al-Bustānī's first original novel, serialized concurrently with "Idwār wa Sīlfā," *Al-Huyām fī jinān al-shām*, separated and united its lovers several times over, promising the reader "strange events and anecdotes" (*gharā'ib al-ḥawādith wa al-akhbār*). Salīm al-Bustānī, *Al-Huyām fī jinān al-shām* [Love in a Levantine garden], *Al-Jinān* 1, no. 1 (January 1870): 23.

34. Though best known as Comtesse Dash, she also used or was known by eleven other names, including pen names under which she published articles in *Le Figaro*, *La Gazette des Femmes*, *La Mode nouvelle*, *Le Constitutionnel*, and two of Alexandre Dumas's (*père*) journals, *Le Mousquetaire* and *Le Dartagnan*. Claude Schopp, "Sous le manteaux d'Alexandre Dumas, ou les douze noms de la Comtesse Dash," in *Les Romancières sentimentales: Nouvelles approches, nouvelles perspectives*, ed. Àngels Santa and M. Carme Figuerola (Lleida, Spain: Edicions de la Universitat de Lleida, 2014), 91–116.

35. This phrase can be found in Madām Kārlūs Rīyu, *Mādamyāzīl Mālābyār*, trans. from the French by Salīm Bustrus (Beirut: al-Maṭba'a al-Sūriyya, 1860), 16. Page numbers for this text are taken from this single printing, but the translation was originally

serialized in *Ḥadīqat al-akhbār* from May 1860 to July 1861. The same plates were used in serialized and single-edition printings, probably in order to coordinate release with the last date of serialization. *Mālābyār*, for example, is advertised for sale beginning one month after its serialization concludes. *Ḥadīqat al-akhbār* 172 (August 1, 1861): 4.

36. See, for example, Salīm dī Nawfal, trans., *Riwāyat al-Jirjisayn* [The two Georges] *Ḥadīqat al-akhbār* 66 (April 28/9, 1859): 4; Salīm dī Nawfal, *Al-Markīz dī Fūntānj*, *Ḥadīqat al-akhbār* 50 (December 18/6, 1858): 1; and *Faṣl fī Bādīn* [A season in Baden-Baden], *Ḥadīqat al-akhbār* 88 (August 27/7, 1859): 4.

37. Margaret Cohen, *The Sentimental Education of the Novel* (Princeton, NJ: Princeton University Press, 1999), 30.

38. Cohen, 79, 84.

39. Cohen, 84.

40. Al-Bustānī, *Asmā', al-Jinān* 4, no. 10 (May 15, 1873): 358.

41. *Ḥadīqat al-akhbār* 24 (June 19/7, 1858): 2.

42. *Ḥadīqat al-akhbār* 50 (December 18/6, 1858): 3–4.

43. Nawfal, *Al-Jarjasīn*, *Ḥadīqat al-akhbār* 61 (March 20, 1859): 3.

44. *Faṣl fī Bādīn*, *Ḥadīqat al-akhbār* 81 (July 9, 1859): 3; and *Riwāyat Būlīna Mūlyān* [Novel of Pauline Meulien], *Ḥadīqat al-akhbār* 98 (November 5/17, 1859): 4.

45. Rifā'a Rāfi' al-Ṭahṭāwī, "Translator's Introduction," *Ḥadīqat al-akhbār* 174 (August 15, 1861): 4.

46. Iskandar Tuwaynī, trans., *Yamīn al-armala* [The widow's oath] (Beirut: al-Maṭba'a al-Waṭaniyya, 1861), 66. This refers to the single-volume edition.

47. Iskandar Tuwaynī, trans., *Riwāyat yamīn al-armala* [The widow's oath], *Ḥadīqat al-akhbār* 176 (August 17/29, 1861), 3. The affinity of this work with the Sindbad cycle is made even more evident by perusing the further contents of the collection: alongside "Le Serment de la veuve" [The widow's oath], Tuwaynī would have found advertisements for novels entitled *Le Cabinet noir* and *L'Homme de minuit*, the latter of which offers "un frisson de terreur" (a thrill of terror) for its readers. Gonzalès, *Une Princesse Russe*, vol. 1 (Paris: L. de Potter, 1857): n.p.

48. Anthony Ashley Cooper, third Earl of Shaftesbury, *Characteristics of Men, Manners, Opinions, and Time*, ed. Lawrence E. Klein (Cambridge: Cambridge University Press, 1999), 155–56. And a century later, Balzac would list among the modern novel's literary ailments its being "filled with Spain, the Orient, torture, and pirates." Honoré de Balzac, *La Peau de Chagrin* (Paris: Pléiade, 1979), volume 10, 54.

49. 'Abd al-Muhsin Ṭaha Badr, *Taṭawwur al-riwāya al-'arabiyya al-ḥadītha fī Miṣr* [Development of the modern Arabic novel in Egypt] (Cairo: Dār al-Ma'ārif, 1992), 121.

50. Jurjī Zaydān, *Tārīkh adāb al-lugha al-'arabiyya*, vol. 4 (Cairo: Maṭba'at al-Hilāl, 1914), 230. Badr elaborates, explaining that these men read "to fill their need for entertainment and forget the concerns of their reality" (*Taṭawwur*, 121).

51. Zaydān, *Tārīkh adāb al-lugha al-'arabiyya*, vol. 4, 230.

52. See David Pinault, *Story-Telling Techniques in the Arabian Nights* (Leiden: Brill, 1992), 106–7. See also Peter Molan, "The Arabian Nights: The Oral Connection," *Edebiyāt* 2, nos. 1–2 (1988): 191–99.

53. *Faṣl fī Bādīn*, *Ḥadīqat al-akhbār* 81 (July 21/9, 1859): 3.

54. *Faṣl fī Bādīn*, *Ḥadīqat al-akhbār* 81 (July 21/9, 1859): 3.

55. *Faṣl fī Bādīn*, *Ḥadīqat al-akhbār* 81 (July 21/9, 1859): 4.

56. La Comtesse Dash [Gabrielle Anne Cisterne de Courtiras Vicomtesse de Saint-Mars], *Les Bals masqués* (Paris: Michel Lévy Frères, 1857), 95. *Faṣl fī Bādīn, Ḥadīqat al-akhbār,* 87 (23/3 September, 1859), 3.

57. See Tzvetan Todorov, "Narrative Men," in *The Poetics of Prose* (Oxford, UK: Blackwell, 1977), 66–79.

58. *Faṣl fī Bādīn, Ḥadīqat al-akhbār*, 81 (July 21/9, 1859): 3.

59. *Faṣl fī Bādīn*, 3.

60. *Faṣl fī Bādīn, Ḥadīqat al-akhbār* 95 (October 15/27, 1859): 3–4. The translator softens the original's critique of women, translating *stupides* as *tandhahilu*, or "baffled." La Comtesse Dash, *Les Bals masqués*, 185.

61. *Al-Jirjisayn, Ḥadīqat al-akhbār* 66 (April 28/9, 1859): 4.

62. *Al-Jirjisayn, Ḥadīqat al-akhbār* 62 (March 11/26, 1859): 2.

63. *Al-Jirjisayn, Ḥadīqat al-akhbar* 69 (May 18/1, 1859): 4; 74 (July 4/23, 1859): 3.

64. *Al-Jirjisayn, Ḥadīqat al-akhbār* 63 (March 4/16, 1859): 3.

65. As Stephen Sheehi writes, taste was "the aesthetic of *al-nahdah*, integral to the process of *embourgeoisement*." Sheehi, *The Arab Imago: A Social History of Portrait Photography, 1860–1910* (Princeton, NJ: Princeton University Press, 2016), 122.

66. "Fī al-Tamaddun," *Ḥadīqat al-akhbār* 28 (July 5/17, 1858): 2.

67. Similar to the tension I find between "proper" reading and actual reading habits, Abou-Hodeib describes a tension between the "aesthetics of moderation and authenticity propagated by the intellectual literature" and actual consumption habits. Toufoul Abou-Hodeib, "Taste and Class in Late Ottoman Beirut," *International Journal of Middle East Studies* 43, no. 3 (2011): 477, 487.

68. *Būlīna Mūlyān, Ḥadīqat al-akhbār* 101 (December 26/8, 1859): 4.

69. These are the three major private publishers active in the nineteenth century, according to Ami Ayalon; between them they accounted for much of the century's literary output. Of the thirty titles Ayalon mentions as the press's publications in the first six years, at least five are translations, but there are most certainly more. Camille Bodin, *Le Monstre, Riwāyat al-ʿajāʾib wa al-gharāʾib* (1865), Salīm al-Ḥalyānī, *Riwāyat maʿdan al-Ddhahab* (1868), Salīm Ṣaʿb, *Riwāyat Būl wa Firjīnī* (before 1865), *Būlīna Mulyān* (1865), Salīm Ṣaʿb, *Amīr jazīrat Mūntū Krīstū* (1866). Ayalon, "Private Publishing in the Nahḍa," *International Journal of Middle East Studies* 40, no. 4 (November 2008): 565.

70. *Amīr jazīrat Mūntū Krīstū*, trans. Salīm Ṣaʿb under the supervision and Arabization of Yūsuf al-Shalfūn, *Al-Shirāka al-shahriyya fī Bayrūt* 4 (March 1866): 2.

71. See Ayalon, "Private Publishing in the Nahḍa," 565–66.

72. Salīm Ṣaʿb, trans., *Riwāyat al-ʿajāʾib wa al-gharāʾib* [Novel of the wondrous and the strange] (Beirut: al-Maṭbaʿa al-ʿUmūmiyya, 1865), 2. The author of this text is identified only as "Mūsyū Kāmīl."

73. Ḥunayn Khūrī, trans., *Kitāb raʾs ṣakhrat al-shayṭān* [The Devil's Peak] (Beirut: Dār al-Maʿārif, 1874), 2.

74. Salīm Afandī Abī Ḥamad al-Ḥalyānī, trans., *Riwāyat maʿdan al-dhahab* [The Gold Mine] (Beirut: al-Maṭbaʿa al-ʿAmūmiyya, 1868), 2. The title page acknowledges Elia Berthet, the "famous historian" as its author.

75. Advertisement, *Ḥadīqat al-akhbār* 353 (January 7/19, 1865): 4.

76. Anthony Glinoer cites *Le Monstre* as a paradigmatic example of *les romans frénétiques classiques*—popular gothic novels inspired by Anne Radcliffe that "headed the

list of novelistic sub-genres in the circulating libraries under the Restoration." Glinoer, *La Littérature frénétique* (Paris: Presses Universitaires de France, 2009), 182.

77. He reuses the line from the preface to *Monte Cristo* here, writing "after seeing the largest part of the young, intelligent audience of our country preferring to read novels, especially French ones." Yūsuf al-Shalfūn, *Riwāyat ḥifẓ al-widād*, *Al-Shirāka al-shahriyya fī Bayrūt* 5 (April 1866): 2.

78. Badr, *Taṭawwur*, 141. Badr cites as an example Muṣṭafā Ibrāhīm, a post office employee whose *Shuhadā' al-Abā'* appeared in the Egyptian serial *Musāmarāt al-sha'b* (The people's entertainment).

79. Samah Selim, "Narrative Craft: Realism and Fiction in the Arabic Canon," *Edebiyat* 14, nos. 1–2 (2004): 110.

80. Selim, 112.

81. Al-Shalfūn, *Ḥifẓ al-widād*, 5.

82. Al-Shalfūn, 6.

83. Khalīl al-Khūrī, *Wayy idhan lastu bi ifranjī* [Alas, I am not a foreigner], 2nd ed. (Beirut: al-Maṭba'a al-Sūriyya, 1860), 94.

84. Al-Khūrī, 87.

85. Khalīl al-Khūrī, "On Periodical Writing" [Fī qirā'at al-jarā'id] *Ḥadīqat al-akhbār* 51 (December 10/22, 1858): 2.

86. Al-Bustānī, *Asmā'*, *al-Jinān* 4, no. 7 (April 1, 1873): 250.

Part II. The Transnational Imagination

1. Simone M. Müller, *Wiring the World: The Social and Cultural Creation of Global Telegraph Networks* (New York: Columbia University Press, 2016).

2. Juan Ricardo Cole, *Colonialism and Revolution in the Middle East: Social and Cultural Origins of Egypt's 'Urabi Movement* (Cairo: American University in Cairo Press), 112, cited in Dwayne R. Winseck and Robert M. Pike, *Communication and Empire: Media, Markets, and Globalization, 1860–1930* (Durham, NC: Duke University Press, 2007), 98.

3. Travelers in the 1880s could board steamers between Marseille and Istanbul, for example, for a fraction of what it cost in the 1840s, arriving in six days instead of fifteen. Londoners could book package tours of the Holy Land that made the trip around the Mediterranean by railway and steamer in merely twenty days. Thomas Cook & Son, *Programmes and Itineraries of Cook's Arrangements for Palestine Tours* (London, 1880), 29. As James Gelvin and Nile Green point out, by the 1880s, with technology that allowed larger steamships to run on smaller amounts of coal, more people were traveling at lower rates. "Cheap tickets on such vessels enabled migration and pilgrimage, trade and tourism, in ways that were out of reach a generation before." Gelvin and Green, introduction to *Global Muslims in the Age of Steam and Print*, ed. Gelvin and Green (Berkeley: University of California Press, 2014), 6.

4. Fāris al-Shidyāq, *Leg over Leg*, vol. 1, trans. Humphre Davies (Library of Arabic Literature) (New York: NYU Press, 2013), 153.

5. Buṭrus al-Bustānī, *Nafīr Sūriyā* [Trumpet of Syria] (Beirut: Dār Fikr lil-Abḥāth wa al-Nashr, 1990), 50–51.

6. Khalīl al-Khūrī, *Ḥadīqat al-akhbār* 186 (October 7, 1861): 1.

7. Talexy quoted in Müller, *Wiring the World*, 1; Rudyard Kipling, "McAndrew's Hymn," in *Selected Poems* (New York: Penguin Classics, 2006), 66; Lord Tennyson,

"Locksley Hall," in *The Major Works* (Oxford: Oxford University Press, 2000), 101. Not all depictions of transportation technology were positive: Wordsworth, famously, denounced the railroad that was to run through his beloved Lake District as "a rash assault" on beauty. William Wordsworth, *Kendal and Windermere Railway*, in W.J.B. Owen and J.W. Smyser, eds., *The Prose Works of William Wordsworth*, volume 3 (Oxford: Clarendon Press, 1974), 331.

8. Müller, *Wiring the World*, 83–84.

9. Rifā'a Rāfi' al-Ṭahṭāwī, *Manāhij al-albāb al-Miṣriyya fī mabāhij al-ādāb al-'aṣriyya*, 2nd ed. (Cairo: Maṭba'at Sharikat al-Raghā'ib, 1912), 124.

10. Abd al-Muḥsin Ṭaha Badr, *Taṭawwur al-riwāya al-'arabiyya al-ḥadītha fī Miṣr, 1870–1938* [Development of the modern Arabic novel in Egypt, 1870–1938] (Cairo: Dār al-Ma'ārif, 1963), 124.

11. Advertisement for *Al-Markīza Blānsh* [The white marquise, original author unknown], *Al-Hilāl* 7, no. 4 (November 1, 1898): 124. The latter quote appears in an advertisement for *Al-Burj al-hā'il* [The man in the iron mask] in *Al-Hilāl* 7, no. 8 (February 1, 1899): 253.

12. Japanese translations of *Le Tour du monde* appeared in two volumes in 1878 and 1880. Judy Wakabayashi, "Foreign Bones, Japanese Flesh: Translations and the Emergence of Modern Children's Literature in Japan," *Japanese Language and Literature* 42, no. 1 (April 2008): 235. Dumas, as Priya Joshi estimates, appeared in at least 80 percent of the English-language Indian libraries she surveyed, and both Dumas and Verne were multiply translated into Indian languages between 1850 and 1900. Joshi, *In Another Country: Colonialism, Culture, and the English Novel in India* (New York: Columbia University Press, 2002), 66, 133.

13. Franco Moretti, *Atlas of the European Novel, 1800–1900* (London: Verso, 1998), table 87 ("Diffusion of French and British Novels in Nineteenth-Century Europe"), 182.

14. The UNESCO index aggregates date from over 150 countries and includes works published from 1979 to 2015. Dumas is the thirteenth-most-translated author according to the index.

15. These translations were of *Le Tour du monde en quatre-vingt jours* (1885), *Voyage au centre de la terre* (1885, 1889), and *Voyage au pole nord* (1894). Arthur B. Evans, "Jules Verne's English Translations," *Science Fiction Studies* 32, no. 1 (March 2005): 80–104.

16. Mariano Siskind, *Cosmopolitan Desires: Global Modernity and World Literature in Latin America* (Evanston, IL: Northwestern University Press, 2014), 26.

17. In Kipling's "McAndrew's Hymn," the steam engine brings "Interdependence absolute" via a jolly "Law, Order, Duty an' Restraint, Obedience, Discipline!" Rudyard Kipling, "McAndrew's Hymn," *Scribner's Magazine* 16, no. 6 (December 1894): 674.

18. Jules Verne, *Le Tour du monde en quatre-vingts jours* (Paris: Gallimard, 2009), 99.

19. Both Samera Esmeir and Valeska Huber outline the forced immobilities (in the form of imprisonment) that Egyptian infrastructure projects required. See Esmeir, "On the Coloniality of Modern Law," *Critical Analysis of Law* 2, no. 1 (2015): 23; and Huber, *Channeling Mobilities: Migration and Globalisation in the Suez Canal Region and Beyond, 1869–1914* (Cambridge: Cambridge University Press, 2013), 28–29.

20. Winseck and Pike, *Communication and Empire*, 100.

21. Bernhard Siegert, *Relays: Literature as an Epoch of the Postal System*, trans. Kevin Repp (Stanford, CA: Stanford University Press, 1999), 2.

22. Zachary Lockman, "'Worker' and 'Working Class' in Pre-1914 Egypt: A Rereading," in *Workers and Working Classes in the Middle East: Struggles, Histories, Historiographies*, ed. Lockman (Albany: SUNY Press, 1994), 82.

23. If, as Wen-Chin Ouyang posits, we might locate the politics of modernity and modernization in the chronotope of the "journey to the West," what does it mean that the West is never reached and remains always virtual? Ouyang, "Fictive Mode, 'Journey to the West,' and Transformation of Space: 'Ali Mubarak's Discourses of Modernization," *Comparative Critical Studies* 4, no. 3 (October 2007): 331–58.

24. See Roger Allen, introduction to *What 'Isā ibn Hishām Told Us*, by Muḥammad al-Muwayliḥī, vol. 1 (New York: NYU Press, 2015), xvii.

25. Al-Muwayliḥī, *What 'Isa ibn Hisham Told Us*, 235.

4. Fictions of Connectivity

1. Alexandre Dumas, *Le Comte de Monte-Cristo*, 2 vols. (Paris: Éditions Gallimard, 1981), 1:3.

2. See for example Dumas, 1:383, 393, 680.

3. Jennifer Yee tracks the use of "populuxe" (cheap copies of luxury items) products in late eighteenth-century French realist novels, where they were linked to duplicity, fraud, and colonial financial scams. Yee, *The Colonial Comedy: Imperialism in the French Realist Novel* (Cambridge: Cambridge University Press, 2016), 86.

4. Walter Benjamin, *The Arcades Project*, trans. Howard Eiland and Kevin McLaughlin (Cambridge, MA: Harvard University Press, 1999), 55, cited in Susan Hiner, "Lust for *Luxe*: 'Cashmere Fever' in Nineteenth-Century France," *Journal for Early Modern Cultural Studies* 5, no. 1 (Spring–Summer 2005): 76.

5. Dumas, *Cristo*, 1:346.

6. Frank Ames, *The Kashmir Shawl and Its Indo-French Influence* (Woodbridge, England: Antique Collector's Club, 1997), 134. Cited in Susan Hiner, *Accessories to Modernity: Fashion and the Feminine in Nineteenth-Century France* (Philadelphia: University of Pennsylvania Press, 2010), 83-84. As Hiner demonstrates, cashmere shawls became essential fashion accessories and often the centerpiece of the *corbeille de marriage* in the first half of the nineteenth century.

7. Catherine Hall and Sonya O. Rose, introduction to *At Home with Empire: Metropolitan Culture and the Imperial World*, ed. Hall and Rose (Cambridge: Cambridge University Press, 2006), 3.

8. Indeed, the first original Arabic novel, Khalīl al-Khūrī's *Wayy . . . Idhan lastu bi-ifranjī* [Alas, I am not a foreigner] (1858), opens with the image of the Beirut harbor filled with steamships packed with undyed cloth and yarn destined for "the mouths of Manchester or Liverpool factories." Al-Khūrī, *Wayy . . . Idhan lastu bi-ifranjī*, 2nd ed. (Beirut: al-Maṭbaʿa al-Sūriyya, 1860), 4–5.

9. Elizabeth M. Holt, *Fictitious Capital: Silk, Cotton, and the Rise of the Arabic Novel* (New York: Fordham University Press, 2017), 15.

10. Holt, 64–65.

11. Elizabeth Holt, *Fictitious Capital: Silk, Cotton, and the Rise of the Arabic Novel* (New York: Fordham University Press, 2017), 137.

12. Lydia Liu, *Tokens of Exchange: The Problem of Translation in Global Circulations* (Durham, NC: Duke University Press, 1999), 13.

13. Gayatri Spivak, "The Practical Politics of the Open End," in *The Post-Colonial Critic*, ed. Sarah Harasym (New York: Routledge, 1990), 96.

14. Gayatri Spivak, "Scattered Speculations on the Question of Value," *Diacritics* 15, no. 4 (Winter 1985): 81.

15. Karl Marx, *A Contribution to the Critique of Political Economy*, trans. S.W. Ryazanskaya (New York: International Publishers, 1970), 108. Cited in Spivak, "Scattered Speculations," 81.

16. See Sevket Pamuk, *A Monetary History of the Ottoman Empire* (Cambridge: Cambridge University Press, 2000), 194–97, 206–13.

17. Spivak, "Scattered Speculations," 81.

18. As Roger Owen puts it, while in the eighteenth century "over half of the seaborne trade was controlled by the French merchants of Marseilles . . . this pattern was changed out of all recognition by the Napoleonic wars and the first stages of the Industrial Revolution in Britain." Owen, *The Middle East in the World Economy, 1800–1914* (London: I. B. Taurus, 1981), 85.

19. Dumas, *Cristo*, 1:53. French readers were attuned to references to imperial decline. In the decades after Waterloo, songs, poems, and broadsheets lamented France's military defeat, and by the 1840s, public discussions of France's global status had turned to ruminations on its weakness relative to the other imperial powers, as well to nostalgic images of former glory. Barbara Ann Day-Hickman, *Napoleonic Art: Nationalism and the Spirit of Rebellion in France (1815–1848)*, 21–35. See also Wolfgang Schivelbusch, *The Culture of Defeat: On National Trauma, Mourning, and Recovery* (New York: Picador, 2001).

20. As the reader will recall, Saʿb also translated Camille Bodin's *Le Monstre* (*Riwāyat al-ʿajāʾib wa al-gharāʾib*) for al-Shalfūn's ʿAmūmiyya Press one year earlier (1865).

21. Yūsuf al-Shalfūn, "Notice," *Al-Shirāka al-shahriyya fī Bayrūt* 1, no. 5 (May 1866): 3; al-Shalfūn, "Notice," *Al-Najāḥ* 1, no. 3 (January 16, 1871): 45. Al-Shalfūn notes that he will still maintain an editorial and supervisory role in the translation, "Arabizing and improving the grammar" of Misk's translation. At least one other translator may have been involved: when Luwīs Ṣābūnjī, co-owner of *Al-Najāḥ*, announced his resignation, he also announced that he would end his involvement in the translation of *Monte Cristo*. Ṣābūnjī, "Announcement," *Al-Zahra* 1, no. 43 (1870): 314.

22. As Wādī al-Nīl often published single-volume editions of texts that had previously appeared as serialized in its journal of the same name, it is possible that Shadīd's translation was published serially before 1871. Though I have been unable to locate Shadīd in any biographical dictionary, he is listed as one of the founding members of the Syrian Scientific Society in its 1859 circular. In his translator's note, he indicates that as of the date of the translation's completion, August 8, 1869, he is living in Alexandria. Bishāra Shadīd, trans., *Qiṣṣat al-Kūnt dū Muntū Krīstū* (Cairo: M. Wādī al-Nīl, 1871), 231.

23. Owen, *Middle East in the World Economy*, 249.

24. Owen, 165.

25. Though "men of capital" refers to a term used by mandate-era Palestinian entrepreneurs to describe themselves, Sherene Seikaly notes that its definition—men who "preached to their elite brethren about the proper spending and saving patterns that would ensure Palestinian progress"—has its roots in *nahḍa* economic thinking and may be used fruitfully here. Seikaly, *Men of Capital: Scarcity and Economy in Mandate Palestine* (Stanford, CA: Stanford University Press, 2016), 1.

26. As Owen notes, Beirut beginning in the 1840s saw a great increase in the construction of European-style accommodations, with 365 such dwellings built in a single year (*Middle East in the World Economy*, 98).

27. Jens Hanssen, *Fin-de-Siècle Beirut: The Making of an Ottoman Capital* (Oxford: Oxford University Press, 2005), 13.

28. Toufoul Abou-Hodeib, "The Material Life of the Ottoman Middle Class," *History Compass* 10, no. 8 (2012): 585.

29. Yūsuf al-Shalfūn, "Muqaddima," in *Riwāyat Amīr jazīrat Mūntū Krīstu*, trans. Salīm Ṣaʿb and ed. Yūsuf al-Shalfūn, *Al-Shirāka al-shahriyya fī Bayrūt* 1, no. 4 (April 1866): 2.

30. Al-Shalfūn, 3.

31. Liu, *Tokens of Exchange*, 21.

32. Liu, 21.

33. Yūsuf al-Shalfūn, "Muqaddima," *Al-Najāḥ* 2, no. 1 (January 1, 1871): 2.

34. Al-Shalfūn, "Muqaddima" (*Al-Shirāka*), 2.

35. Yūsuf al-Shalfūn, "Muqaddima" [Introduction], *Ḥifẓ al-widād, al-Shirāka al-shahriyya fī Bayrūt* 1, no. 5 (May 1866): 14.

36. Yūsuf al-Shalfūn, "Notice," *Al-Shirāka al-shahriyya fī Bayrūt* 1, no. 5 (May 1866): 3; al-Shalfūn, "Notice," *Al-Najāḥ* 1, no. 3 (January 16, 1871): 45.

37. Lūwīs Ṣābūnjī, "Notice," *Al-Zahra* 1, no. 43 (1870): 314. The notice also appeared in the Catholic weekly *Al-Bashīr*. "Notice from Luwīs Ṣābūnjī," *Al-Bashīr* 51 (August 19, 1871), cited in and translated by Elizabeth Holt, "Narrative and the Reading Public in 1870's Beirut," *Journal of Arabic Literature* 40, no. 1 (2009): 63.

38. Ṣābūnjī was forced out of his partnership after he published an attack on *Al-Jinān* and the al-Bustānī family in *Al-Naḥla* in 1871. The al-Bustānī family pressured the *vali* to suspend *Al-Naḥla*, making it one of only three known cases of censorship in Beirut before 1876. While *Al-Naḥla* closed that year, *Al-Najāḥ*, which was co-owned by al-Shalfūn, was allowed to continue only on the condition that Ṣābūnjī turn it over to al-Shalfūn as sole proprietor. Donald J. Cioeta, "Ottoman Censorship in Lebanon and Syria, 1876–1908," *International Journal of Middle East Studies* 10, no. 2 (May 1979): 170.

39. Compare Saʿb and al-Shalfūn, *Amīr jazīrat Mūntū Krīstu* (*Al-Shirāka*), 30, to Yūsuf al-Shalfūn, trans., *Amīr jazīrat Mūntū Krīstu*, *Al-Najāḥ* 2, no. 7 (February 6, 1871): 80.

40. Franco Moretti, "Conjectures on World Literature," in *Distant Reading* (London: Verso, 2013), 58.

41. It is difficult to say when *Cristo* ceased to be serialized. In the American University of Beirut's collection (the longest extant holding), which is not complete, it was still running at the end of 1873 but had already stopped by the beginning of 1875.

42. Dumas, *Cristo*, 1:20–21; Ṣaʿb and al-Shalfūn, *Amīr jazīrat Mūntū Krīstu* (*Al-Shirāka*), 35.

43. Dumas, *Cristo*, 1:21; Ṣaʿb and al-Shalfūn, *Amīr jazīrat Mūntū Krīstu* (*Al-Shirāka*), 35.

44. Al-Shalfūn, *Amīr jazīrat Mūntū Krīstu*, *Al-Najāḥ* 2, no. 63 (September 21, 1871): 1016.

45. Dumas, *Cristo*, 1:169.

46. David F. Bell calls this method "algorithmic." Bell, *Real Time: Accelerating Narrative from Balzac to Zola* (Urbana: University of Illinois Press, 2004), 128.

47. Lisa Parks, "Kinetic Screens: Epistemologies of Movement at the Interface," in *MediaSpace: Place, Scale, and Culture*, ed. Nick Couldry and Anna McCarthy (London: Routledge, 2004), 47.

48. Dumas, *Cristo*, 1:232.

49. Karla Malette, *European Modernity and the Arab Mediterranean: Toward a New Philology and a Counter-Orientalism* (Philadelphia: University of Pennsylvania Press, 2010), 104.

50. Dumas, *Cristo*, 1:232.

51. He uses the phrase *buwāṭin ẓuwāhir wa ẓuwāhir buwāṭin*, which makes reference to modes of Qur'anic interpretation and can also be translated "from [inner] meaning to [outer] word and from word to meaning." Nakhla Qalfāṭ, trans., *Qiṣṣat al-Kūnt dī Mūntū Krīstū* (Beirut: Maṭba'at al-Ma'ārif, 1883), 2.

52. Qalfāṭ, 2. It is not clear from either the preface or the title page whether Qalfāṭ claimed to have translated the work from the French or merely "corrected" Shadīd's translation (which is clearly what he did, as it follows Shadīd's additions and omissions to the source text). The full title is *Qiṣṣat al-Kūnt dī Mūntū Krīstū mutarjama 'an al-lugha al-faransiyya, Subikat fī qālib 'arabī wa ḍubiṭat bi-qalam Nakhlā afandī Qalfāṭ* [The story of the Count of Monte Cristo translated from the Arabic, poured into an Arabic mold and corrected by Nakhlā Qalfāṭ].

53. Shadīd, *Qiṣṣat al-Kūnt dū Muntū Krīstū*, 5; Qalfāṭ, *Qiṣṣat al-Kūnt dī Muntū Krīstū*, 3.

54. Shadīd, *Qiṣṣat al-Kūnt dū Muntū Krīstū*, 5.

55. This was Louis Calligaris, *Sīrat Nabulyūn al-awwal* (Paris, 1856). A revised edition was published in Beirut in 1868. Ami Ayalon notes that the revision "included many illuminating changes in language." Ayalon, *Language and Change in the Arab Middle East: The Evolution of Modern Political Discourse* (New York: Oxford University Press, 1987), 169.

56. Shaden Tageldin, *Disarming Words: Empire and the Seductions of Translation in Egypt* (Stanford, CA: Stanford University Press, 2011), 126.

57. Liu, *Tokens of Exchange*, 21.

58. Shadīd, *Qiṣṣat al-Kūnt dū Muntū Krīstū*, 3; Qalfāṭ, *Qiṣṣat al-Kūnt dī Muntū Krīstū*, 3.

59. Samera Esmeir, *Juridical Humanity: A Colonial History* (Stanford, CA: Stanford University Press, 2012), 154–55.

60. Khaled Fahmy, *All the Pasha's Men: Mehmed Ali, His Army, and the Making of Modern Egypt* (Cairo: American University Press, 1997), 137.

61. Khaled Fahmy, "The Era of Muhammad 'Ali Pasha, 1805–1848," in *The Cambridge History of Egypt*, vol. 2, *Modern Egypt, from 1518 to the End of the Twentieth Century*, ed. M. W. Daly, (Cambridge: Cambridge University Press, 1998), 162.

62. Valeska Huber, *Channeling Mobilities: Migration and Globalisation in the Suez Canal Region* (Cambridge: Cambridge University Press, 2013), 1. As Huber notes, *corvée* was discontinued in the canal zone in 1864. It did, however, continue in other public-works projects into the 1890s. As Esmeir argues, under the British "*corvée* labor was not abolished . . . [but] regulated" (*Juridical Humanity*, 90).

63. Owen, *Middle East in the World Economy*, 157.

64. Buṭrus al-Bustānī, "*Nafīr Sūriyā* [Trumpet of Syria] (Beirut: Dār Fikr li al-Abḥāth wa al-Nashr, 1990), 51.

65. Shadīd is listed in none of the major biographical indexes, and I have not been able to locate any reference to any other publications.

66. As Hala Halim has argued, the image of cosmopolitanism in Alexandria has been de-Arabized and understood in relationship to a Europeanized image of Hellenic civilization, in which intercultural and interlinguistic relationships are imagined as

fluid. Halim, *Alexandrian Cosmopolitanism: An Archive* (New York: Fordham University Press, 2013), 18.

67. One of the offending titles, Abd al-Rahman Kawakibi's *Umm al-qurā*, was itself the product of illicit circulations. A critique of the Ottoman caliphate narrated as an imaginary future conference, it was composed in Aleppo but published in Egypt, where Khedive Abbas Hilmi II looked favorably on his advocacy of an independent "Arab caliphate." Copies of it and Kawakibi's later *The Nature of Tyranny and the Injuries of Enslavement* were quickly put on the proscribed list of books but circulated outside Egypt nonetheless. See Itzchak Weismann, *Abd al-Rahman al-Kawakibi: Islamic Reform and Arab Revival* (London: Oneworld Books, 2015), 126.

68. Bell, *Real Time*, 104.

69. Dumas, *Cristo*, 2:1056.

70. As Adam Barrows argues, the global standardization of time "remov[ed] many of the formerly existent barriers to empire" and allowed "the authoritarian management of bodies, communities, and nations" that attended it. Barrows, *The Cosmic Time of Empire: Modern Britain and World Literature* (Berkeley: University of California Press, 2011), 8, 2.

71. Bell, *Real Time*, 130.

72. Compare al-Shalfūn, *Amīr jazīrat Mūntū Krīstu*, *Al-Najāḥ* 3, no. 1 (January 6, 1872): 16; Shadīd, *Qiṣṣat al-Kūnt dū Muntū Krīstū*, 54; Qalfāṭ, *Qiṣṣat al-Kūnt dī Muntū Krīstū*, 34.

73. See, for example, Shadīd, *Qiṣṣat al-Kūnt dū Muntū Krīstū*, 197; and Qalfāṭ *Qiṣṣat al-Kūnt dī Muntū Krīstū*, 130.

74. Qalfāṭ, *Qiṣṣat al-Kūnt dī Muntū Krīstū*, 78.

75. Qalfāṭ, 40.

76. The *Al-Najāḥ* version preserves the mystery of the French source, describing him as "a man with black beard covering half of his face." Al-Shalfūn, *Amīr jazīrat Mūntū Krīstu*, *Al-Najāḥ* 3, no. 9 (April 2, 1872): 143.

77. Shadīd, *Qiṣṣat al-Kūnt dū Muntū Krīstū*, 76.

78. Qalfāṭ, *Qiṣṣat al-Kūnt dī Muntū Krīstū*, 48.

79. Bell, *Real Time*, 15.

80. The *Al-Najāḥ* version preserves the exoticism of the text by transliterating this name, *Sinbār līmārīn* ("Sindbad le marin"), rather than rendering it in its more recognizable form, *Sindbād al-bahrī*. Al-Shalfūn, *Amīr jazīrat Mūntū Krīstu*, *Al-Najāḥ* 2, no. 12 (February 23, 1817): 191.

81. Shadīd, *Qiṣṣat al-Kūnt dū Muntū Krīstū*, 108.

82. Tzvetan Todorov, "Narrative-Men," in *The Poetics of Prose* (New York: Cornell University Press, 1977), 71. "The appearance of a new character involves the interruption of the preceding story, so that a new story, the one which explains the 'now I am here' of the new character, may be told to us."

83. Shadīd, *Qiṣṣat al-Kūnt dū Muntū Krīstū*, 80. Qalfāṭ, *Qiṣṣat al-Kūnt dī Muntū Krīstū*, 50.

84. Todorov, "Narrative-Men," 78.

85. Shadīd, *Qiṣṣat al-Kūnt dū Muntū Krīstū*, 122; Qalfāṭ, *Qiṣṣat al-Kūnt dī Muntū Krīstū*, 84.

86. Shadīd, *Qiṣṣat al-Kūnt dū Muntū Krīstū*, 111, Qalfāṭ *Qiṣṣat al-Kūnt dī Muntū Krīstū*, 76.

87. Shadīd, *Qiṣṣat al-Kūnt dū Muntū Krīstū*, 78; Qalfāṭ, *Qiṣṣat al-Kūnt dī Muntū Krīstū*, 49. In *Al-Najāḥ*, by contrast, the furnishings are all described as "ʿarabiyya," or Arab, without specific origins. Al-Shalfūn, *Amīr jazīrat Mūntū Krīstu*, *Al-Najāḥ* 2, no. 12 (April 23, 1872): 192.

88. Shadīd, *Qiṣṣat al-Kūnt dū Muntū Krīstū*, 90.

89. Margaret Cohen, *The Novel and the Sea* (Princeton, NJ: Princeton University Press, 2010), 150.

90. Julia A. Clancy-Smith, *Mediterraneans: North Africa and Europe in an Age of Migration, c. 1800-1900* (Berkeley: University of California Press, 2011), 243.

91. Palmira Brummett, "Visions of the Mediterranean: A Classification," *Journal of Medieval and Early Modern Studies* 37, no. 1 (2007): 10. Brummett and Clancy-Smith represent just two examples of a recent historiographical turn away from "Mediterranean studies" that—beginning with Fernand Braudel—posits the sea as an integral unit of analysis. For examples of that perspective, see Braudel, *The Mediterranean and the Mediterranean World in the Age of Philip II*, 2 vols., trans. Siân Reynolds (Berkeley: University of California Press, 1995); and Peregrine Horden and Nicholas Purcell, *The Corrupting Sea: A Study of Mediterranean History* (Oxford, UK: Blackwell, 2000).

92. Dumas, *Cristo*, 1:616.

93. Shadīd, *Qiṣṣat al-Kūnt dū Muntū Krīstū*, 102. There are slight variations between these two texts: Qalfāṭ omits any reference to language and characterizes Haydée as a "[servant] girl" he has (*Qiṣṣat al-Kūnt dī Muntū Krīstū*, 68).

94. Qalfāṭ, *Qiṣṣat al-Kūnt dī Muntū Krīstū*, 68.

95. Pheng Cheah, *What Is a World? On Postcolonial Literature as World Literature* (Durham, NC: Duke University Press, 2016), 3.

96. Eric Hayot, *On Literary Worlds* (Oxford: Oxford University Press, 2012), 25.

5. The Novel in the Age of the Comparative World Picture

1. "ʿAdad jarāʾid al-ʿālam," *Al-Muqtaṭaf* 4, no. 3 (August 1, 1879): 88; "Jarāʾid al-ʿālam," *Al-Nashra al-usbūʿiyya* 44 (November 2, 1885): 247; "Sakak ḥadīd fī al-ʿālam," *Al-Bashīr* 151 (July 19, 1873); "Railroads," *Al-Jinān* 1, no. 3 (April 4, 1870): 302.

2. *Al-Zahra* 1, no. 39 (September 24, 1870): 280; "On the Division of the World," *Al-Zahra* 1, no. 42 (October 1870): 43.

3. *Al-Bashīr* 74 (January 27, 1872): 3. *Trade Gazette* probably refers to the *Monthly Trade Gazette*, published from 1855 to 1872 in New York, a publication designed to circulate among booksellers. Frank Luther Mott, *A History of American Magazines, 1850–1865* (Cambridge, MA: Harvard University Press, 1966), 159.

4. Yūsuf Sarkīs, trans., *Al-Riḥla al-jawwiyya fī al-markaba al-huwāʾiyya al-maʿrūfa bi al-bālūn*, serialized in *Al-Bashīr* 212–72 (September 18, 1874–November 12, 1875).

5. These were Jirjis Zuwayn, trans., *Wardat al-Maghrib* [Warda/Rose of the West], which ran from February to August 1872; *Sūsana al-Maghrib* [Susanna of the West], which ran from August to October 1872; and *Farīdat al-Maghrib* [Farida of the West], which ran from October 1872 to August 1873. All were translated by Jirjis Zuwayn "from the French" and later appeared in single-volume printings published by *Al-Bashīr*'s sister press, the Jesuit Press (Beirut). I have only been able to identify one of the source texts for these translations: *Wardat al-Maghrib* appears to

be a translation of a French translation of Christoph von Schmid's *Rosa von Tannenburg* (ca. 1830).

6. "Baḥthun fī al-jughrāfiyya wa al-khāriṭāt," *Al-Bashīr* 242 (April 16, 1875): 3; "Irsālīyyat Inklatarā ilā al-jazīra Karghwālān Lānd," *Al-Bashīr* 256 (July 23, 1875): 3; "Ifādāt fī al-irsālīyya al-inkalīziyya al-ʿilmiyya ilā al-aqṭār al-sharqiyya," *Al-Bashīr* 259–61 (August 13–27, 1875). Elizabeth Holt notes that articles about balloon travel and construction appeared regularly in *Al-Bashīr* and *Al-Najāḥ* in 1870 and 1871. For that information as well as a beautiful reading of the silk threads that precariously suspend the travelers and the Lebanese economy of the time, see Holt, "Narrative and the Reading Public in 1870s Beirut," *Journal of Arabic Literature* 40 (2009): 68–69.

7. Martin Heidegger, "The Age of the World Picture," in *The Question Concerning Technology and Other Essays*, trans. William Lovitt (New York: Harper and Row, 1977), 134, 129.

8. Tanya Agathacleous, *Urban Realism and the Cosmopolitan Imagination in the Nineteenth Century: Visible City, Invisible World* (Cambridge: Cambridge University Press, 2011), xvi.

9. Sanjay Krishnan, *Reading the Global: Troubling Perspective s on Britain's Empire in Asia* (New York: Columbia University Pres, 2007), 2.

10. Krishnan, 2.

11. Heidegger, "Age of the World Picture," 134.

12. Jules Verne, "Souvenirs d'enfance et de jeunesse," in *Jules Verne*, ed. Pierre-Andrew Touttain, *L'Herne* 25 (October 14, 1974): 57–62, quoted and translated in Rosalind Williams, *The Triumph of Human Empire: Verne, Morris, and Stevenson at the End of the World* (Chicago: University of Chicago Press, 2013), 2; "Avertissement de l'éditeur," in *Voyages et aventures du Capitaine Hatteras* (Paris: Hetzel, 1866), 1–2.

13. Timothy Unwin, *Jules Verne: Journeys in Writing* (Liverpool, UK: Liverpool University Press, 2005), 26; Edmund Smyth, "Verne, SF, and Modernity," in *Jules Verne: Narratives of Modernity* (Liverpool, UK: Liverpool University Press, 2000), 3. Smyth cites a genealogy of this mode of analysis, beginning with Michel Butor's incorporation of Verne into his *Essais sur les modernes* in 1966, which is itself a reprint of a 1949 article ("Verne, SF, and Modernity," 2–6).

14. Heidegger, "Age of the World Picture," 132.

15. As Mariano Siskind argues, the novelization of the global was actualized by novels that joined scientific methods of mapping and measuring with colonialist symbolic relations to present the world as "an imaginary of global availability"; indeed, he goes as far as to write that combining this new sense of the world's measurability with the adventure genre helped Verne and other novelists to produce the "discursive conditions of globalization" as a whole. Siskind, *Cosmopolitan Desires: Global Modernity and World Literature in Latin America* (Evanston, IL: Northwestern University Press, 2014), 43.

16. Sarkīs also translated one of Verne's nonfictional source texts, *Les Naufragés au Spitzberg* (The shipwrecks at Spitsbergen), written by Louis Friedel (1839), as *Al-ʿĀṣ wa shajʿān* (Beirut: Press of the Jesuit Fathers, 1874). Verne's novel about a shipwreck in Spitsbergen, *Les Voyages et aventures du capitaine Hatteras* (1864–1866), probably used Friedel's work as a source. The British Library lists the source as Johann Andreas Christoph, *Winter auf Spitzbergen*, but upon comparing the Arabic to Christoph's and Friedel's texts, it is clear that it is a translation of the latter. Verne's death notice in *Al-Mashriq*

incorrectly attributes *Al- āṣ wa shajʿān* to Verne. "Jules Verne," *Al-Mashriq* 2, no. 9 (May 1, 1905): 435.

17. *Al-Hilāl* 5, no. 10 (January 15, 1897): 2. On the *Al-Hilāl* bookshop, see Ami Ayalon, *The Arabic Print Revolution: Cultural Production and Mass Readership* (Cambridge: Cambridge University Press, 2016), 112.

18. Verne referred in an interview to a Thomas Cook advertisement as his source, but the same year (October 3, 1869) the periodical *Le Tour du monde* published a piece entitled "Around the World in Eighty Days," which gave the exact itinerary of Verne's novel. This itinerary was reprinted in at least three different French periodicals in 1869 and 1870 and was probably reprinted in the wake of the success of *Around the World in Eighty Days* in 1872. William Butcher, "Appendix A. Principal Sources," in *Around the World in Eighty Days*, ed. Butcher (Oxford: Oxford World's Classics, 1995), 204.

19. Jules Verne, *Le Tour du monde en quatre-vingts jours*, ed. William Butcher (Paris: Gallimard, 2009), 49.

20. Roger Luckhurst, "Laboratories for Global Space-Time: Science-Fictionality and the World's Fairs, 1851–1939," *Science Fiction* Studies 39, no. 3 (November 2012): 392. Jules Verne himself joined Bly for one leg of her journey, which she completed in only seventy-two days.

21. A description of the journey around the world undertaken by General J. C. Smith was offered to readers of *Al-Muqtaṭaf* in "Al-Ṣiyāḥa ḥawl al-arḍ," February 1896, 139.

22. According to a WorldCat search, these languages are Arabic, Hebrew, Ottoman Turkish, Persian, and Armenian.

23. The first translation is the American version of *Cinq semaines en ballon*, *Five Weeks in a Balloon*, trans. William Lackland (New York: Appleton, 1869). An illustrative example of translation work begun simultaneously with serialization is the translation of *Le Village aérien*, published in French in 1901 and appearing in Hungarian, Turkish, and German in 1902.

24. Roland Barthes, "The *Nautilus* and the Drunken Boat," in *Mythologies*, trans. Annette Lavers (New York: Farrar, Straus and Giroux, 1972), 65.

25. In 1875, one year after Sarkīs began the serialization of *Al-Riḥla*, the seminary moved to Beirut and became known as the Jesuit College. It is today known as l'Université Saint-Joseph (USJ).

26. Yūsuf Ilyān Sarkīs, *Muʿjam al-maṭbūʿāt al-ʿarabīyya wa al-muʿarraba* [A bibliography of Arabic and translated publications], 1022–23.

27. Sarkīs, ii. Michael W. Albin, "Sarkīs, Yūsuf Ilyān," in *Encyclopedia of Library and Information Science* 39, supp. 4 (New York: Marcel Dekker, 1985), 395.

28. Sarkīs, *Muʿjam*, ii.

29. Verne, *Cinq semaines*, 9.

30. Verne, 238–39; Sarkīs, *Al-Riḥla*, 205–6.

31. Sarkīs, *Al-Riḥla*, 3.

32. Sarkīs, 105, 205. "A Byzantine scholar added the numerals [that correspond to the letters] of the Ancient Greek name 'Nilus' and found that their sum was 365, exactly the same number as the days in the year" (105).

33. Verne, *Cinq semaines*, 83; Sarkīs, *Al-Riḥla*, 54.

34. Verne, *Cinq semaines*, 288, 293; Sarkīs, *Al-Riḥla*, 256, 260.

35. Heidegger, "Age of the World Picture," 148.

36. Eric Hayot, *On Literary Worlds* (Oxford: Oxford University Press, 2012), 106.

37. Tim Mitchell, *Colonising Egypt* (Berkeley: University of California Press, 1988).

38. On globes and atlases, see Sumathi Ramaswamy, *Terrestrial Lessons: The Conquest of the World as a Globe* (Chicago: University of Chicago Press, 2017).

39. David Harvey, *Spaces of Capital: Towards a Critical Geography* (New York: Routledge, 2001), 225–26.

40. David Harvey, "The Cartographic Imagination: Balzac in Paris," in *Cosmopolitan Geographies: New Locations in Literature and Culture*, ed. Vinay Dharwadker (New York: Routledge, 2001), 64.

41. Mary Louise Pratt, *Imperial Eyes: Travel Writing and Transculturation*, 2nd Ed. (London: Routledge, 2007), 15.

42. A. Le Braz, in Charles Lemire, *Jules Verne* (Paris: Berger-Levrault, 1908), 110, quoted and translated in Williams, *Triumph of Human Empire*, 1. Williams argues that Verne's fictions, along with those of William Morris and Robert Louis Stevenson, dealt with "the rise of human empire": the understanding of the world as finite, as "more tightly wired by systems of communication and transportation" (15).

43. Pratt, *Imperial Eyes*, 101, 202.

44. See Verne, *Cinq semaines*, 75, 163, 97, 112, 202, 242.

45. Verne, 10; Sarkīs, *Al-Riḥla*, 3.

46. Wael Abu-ʿUksa, *Freedom in the Arab World: Concepts and Ideologies in Arabic Thought in the Nineteenth Century* (Cambridge: Cambridge University Press, 2016), 52.

47. Verne, *Cinq semaines*, 105.

48. Verne, 105.

49. Sarkīs, *Al-Riḥla*, 71

50. Sarkīs, 72.

51. The Arabic uses the term *barābara*, literally "barbarians," as a translation for "savage tribes." Sarkīs, 47, 77, 128, 209.

52. Sarkīs, 46.

53. Verne, *Cinq semaines*, 318–19; Sarkīs, *Al-Riḥla*, 285.

54. Sarkīs, *Al-Riḥla*, 81; Verne, *Cinq semaines*, 116. Compare this passage to another found on page 59 of the Arabic text, where Ferguson compares the sizes of mountain ranges in Africa, Europe, and Asia. There, "Europe" is rendered as *ūrubā* and "Asia" as *Asiyā*. The substitution of *Mashriq* for *Asiyā* and *Maghrib* for *Ūrubā* is deliberate and significant. Sarkīs, *Al-Riḥla*, 59.

55. Sarkīs, *Al-Riḥla*, 81–82; Verne, *Cinq semaines*, 116–17.

56. Sarkīs, *Al-Riḥla*, 43. No such footnote exists in the French source text.

57. Sarkīs, 113.

58. As Adrian S. Wisnicki argues, the "blank space" that constituted the center of maps of the African continent during this period was actually the result of "too much information [being] in circulation." As he shows, Speke, Burton, and others relied on many "native" sources of information, which they sought to efface. Wisnicki, "Charting the Frontier: Indigenous Geography, Arab-Nyamwezi Caravans, and the East African Expedition of 1856–59," *Victorian Studies* 51, no. 1 (Autumn 2008): 114.

59. Jules Verne, *Five Weeks in a Balloon; or, Journeys and Discoveries in Africa by Three Englishmen*, trans. William Lackland (New York: Hurst, 1869), 155; Verne, *Five Weeks in a Balloon: A Journey of Discovery by Three Englishmen in Africa*, trans. Frederick Paul Walter (Middleton, CT: Wesleyan University Press, 2015), 127.

60. Heidegger, "Age of the World Picture," 130.

61. "On the Division of the World According to European Geographers," *Al-Zahra* 1, no. 42 (October 1870): xx.

62. See, for example, Dīmitrī Khalāṭ, "Kilām 'an jughrāfiyā al-'arab" [Remarks on Arab geography], *Al-Muqtaṭaf* 13, no. 3 (December 1, 1888): 150.

63. Sarkīs, *Al-Riḥla*, 14, 31.

64. Sarkīs, 51, 272, 310.

65. Sarkīs, 310.

66. Heidegger, "Age of the World Picture," 134.

67. Heidegger, 134.

68. Kenneth Silverman, *Lightning Man: The Accursed Life of Samuel F. B. Morse* (New York: Knopf, 2003), 240–24, quoted in James L. Gelvin and Nile Green, introduction to *Global Muslims in the Age of Steam and Print*, ed. Gelvin and Green (Berkeley: University of California Press, 2014), 3. James W. Carey describes a "general uniformity of reaction" to the telegraph that similarly anticipated "the Universal Brotherhood of Universal Man." Carey, *Communication as Culture: Essays on Media and Society* (London: Routledge, 1989), 207–8.

69. Rifā'a Rāfi' al-Ṭahṭāwī, *Manāhij al-albāb al-Miṣriyya fī mabāhij al-ādāb al-'aṣriyya*, 2nd ed. (Cairo: Maṭba'at Sharikat al-Raghā'ib, 1912), 124.

70. Amīn afandī Shumayyal, "Kanz al-munā" [The treasure of destiny], *Al-Muqtaṭaf* 10, no. 2 (November 1885): 100.

71. "*Al-Najāḥ al-akīd mawqūf 'alā 'aqdar wa urīd*,'" Certain Success Relies on Ability and Desire," *Al-Muqtaṭaf* 10, no. 9 (June 1886): 542. The subject matter would not have been foreign to Shumayyal, who before entering the legal profession was engaged in the international cotton trade and in fact rented steamships for the purpose of exporting cotton to Liverpool. Yūsuf 'Aṣṣāf, *Dalīl Miṣr* (Cairo: al-Maṭba'a al-'Amūmiyya, 1890), 343.

72. Holt, "Narrative and the Reading Public," 12.

73. See, for example, the local news section of *Al-Bashīr* for September 17, 1875, where news of the disease's spread is accompanied by a chart detailing the death toll in Beirut, Aleppo, and elsewhere (4). The August–September issue of *Al-Jinān* was delayed that same year due to cholera and appeared in October after the progress of the disease had been halted. "Notice," *Al-Jinān* 6, nos. 16–18 (August 15–September 15, 1875): 1.

74. Eric Tagliacozzo, "Hajj in the Time of Cholera: Pilgrim Ships and Contagion from Southeast Asia to the Red Sea," in Gelvin and Green, *Global Muslims in the Age of Steam and Print*, 104.

75. On international public health initiatives, see LaVerne Kuhnke, *Lives at Risk: Public Health in Nineteenth-Century Egypt* (Berkeley: University of California Press, 1990), 92–110. Many of the public-health policies used in Egypt in the nineteenth century, including those decreed by Mehmet Ali, like autopsy, mandatory public bathing, and a penalty of execution for heads of households who did not report a death, were particularly ill received by the Egyptian people. Myron Echenberg, *Plague Ports: The Global Urban Impact of the Bubonic Plague, 1894–1901* (New York: NYU Press, 2007), 97–98.

76. Akram Fouad Khater estimates the population drain of Mount Lebanon as a third by the time of the First World War. Khater, *Inventing Home: Emigration, Gender,*

and the Middle Class in Lebanon, 1870–1920 (Berkeley: University of California Press, 2001), 8.

77. Yūsuf ʿAṣṣāf, *Dalīl Miṣr* (Cairo: al-Maṭbaʿa al-ʿAmūmiyya, 1890), 322.

78. Samera Esmeir, *Juridical Humanity: A Colonial History* (Stanford, CA: Stanford University Press, 2012), 21.

79. Al-ʿAṭf, or Atfé in British colonial documents, is a town situated where the Mahmudiyya canal connects to the Nile and its small postal steamboats. It acted as a mail hub for parcels moving to and from Alexandria.

80. Yūsuf ʿAṣṣāf, trans., *Riwāyat al-Ṭawwāf ḥawl al-arḍ fī thamānīn yawman* (Alexandria: Maṭbaʿat al-Maḥrūsa, 1885), 1.

81. Darko Suvin, *Metamorphoses of Science Fiction: On the Poetics and History of a Literary Genre*, ed. Gerry Canavan, Ralahine Utopian Studies 18 (Oxford, UK: Peter Lang, 2016), 150. Cited in Williams, *Triumph of Human Empire*, 107.

82. Verne, *Tour du monde*, 50.

83. Jules Verne, *Voyage au centre de la terre* (Paris: Gallimard, 2014), 102.

84. Verne, 102.

85. ʿAṣṣāf, *Al-Ṭawwāf*, 21.

86. Verne, *Tour du monde*, 170.

87. ʿAṣṣāf, *Al-Ṭawwāf*, 120; Verne, *Tour du monde*, 174.

88. Iskandar Anṭūn ʿAmmūn, *Al-Riḥla al-ʿilmiyya fī qalb al-kura al-arḍiyya* (Alexandria: Maṭbaʿat jarīda tal-Maḥrūsa, 1885), 206.

89. Verne, *Tour du monde*, 52; ʿAṣṣāf, *Al-Ṭawwāf*, 44.

90. "Announcement," *Ḥadīqat al-akhbār* 403 (April 5 / 17, 1866): 1. *Ḥadīqat al-akhbār* is full of stories of circulation breakdown: steamers that do not arrive (such as in issues 113, 150, 241); cargo that is lost (121); pirates that commandeer ships (241).

91. *Al-Jinān* 4, no. 5 (March 1, 1873): 152.

92. "Amā returned with *The Times*, which she opened next to the lamp. She read the correspondence from the Reuter's telegram company: We have received reports of the wreck of the ship named the Sultana on its way from Calcutta to Galle, as it was carrying the post of the 15th of October." Salīm al-Bustānī, trans., *Summ al-afaʿi* [The poison of the asps], *Al-Jinān* 7, no. 5 (February 1876): 356. Originally published in English as Florence Marryat (Mrs. Ross Church), "The Poison of Asps," *Appletons'* 4, nos. 81–90 (October 14–December 17, 1870).

93. Yakup Bektas, "The Sultan's Messenger: Cultural Constructions of Ottoman Telegraphy, 1847–1880," *Technology and Culture* 41, no. 4 (2000): 692–93.

94. Britain, *Memorial Calcutta and Bombay Telegraph Communications. Memorial to Governor General from Commercial Communities of Calcutta and Bombay on Telegraph Communications*, British Parliamentary Papers, 1867–68 (269), 15, cited in Dwayne R. Winseck and Robert M. Pike, *Communication and Empire: Media, Markets, and Globalization, 1860–1930* (Durham, NC: Duke University Press, 2007), 36n43.

95. See, for example, an apology in *Al-Muqtaṭaf* to its Syrian readers for a delay in delivery caused by an embargo of Egyptian publications. *Al-Muqtaṭaf* 9, no. 8 (May 1885): 449.

96. *Ḥadīqat al-akhbār* 432 (November 1 / 13, 1866), 2. A similar complaint about *Lubnān*, an official journal printed in Bayt al-Dīn, Lebanon, was leveled by the same newspaper. According to *Ḥadīqat al-akhbār*, *Lubnān* used an "unattractive type" and

stilted Arabic, probably translated from French. *Ḥadīqat al-akhbār* 455 (April 11 / 23, 1867), 2.

97. Benedict Anderson, *The Spectre of Comparisons: Nationalism, Southeast Asia, and the World* (London: Verso, 1998), 34.

98. Verne, *Tour du monde*, 21.

99. ʿAṣṣāf, *Al-Ṭawwāf*, 19.

100. Nakhla Qalfāṭ, trans., *Qiṣṣat al-Kūnt dī Mūntū Krīstū* (Beirut: Maṭbaʿat al-Maʿārif, 1883), 98; Bishāra Shadīd, trans., *Qiṣṣat al-Kūnt dū Muntū Krīstū* (Cairo: M. Wādī al-Nīl, 1871), 144.

101. On Barak, *On Time: Technology and Temporality in Modern Egypt* (Berkeley: University of California Press, 2013), 3, 8.

102. Verne, *Cinq semaines*, 345; Sarkīs, *Al-Riḥla*, 311 (my emphasis).

103. Martin Heidegger, "The Origin of the Work of Art," trans. Julian Young and Kenneth Haynes in, *Off the Beaten Track* (Cambridge: Cambridge University Press, 2002), 22, 21.

104. Pheng Cheah, *What Is a World? On Postcolonial Literature as World Literature* (Durham, NC: Duke University Press, 2016), 5.

105. Heidegger, "Origin," 32.

106. Sam Weber, *Mass Mediauras: Form, Technics, Media* (Stanford, CA: Stanford University Press, 1996), 73.

107. Heidegger, "Origin," 36.

108. ʿAṣṣāf, *Al-Ṭawwāf*, 50.

109. ʿAṣṣāf, 122.

110. Cheah, *What Is a World?*, 13.

111. Unwin, *Jules Verne: Journeys in Writing*, 29.

112. Barak, *On Time*, 79.

113. Donald Read, *The Power of News: The History of Reuters* (Oxford: Oxford University Press, 1992), 57.

114. Roderic H. Davison, *Essays in Ottoman and Turkish History, 1774–1923: The Impact of the West* (Austin: University of Texas Press, 1990), 151. As Davison notes, Ottoman telegraph agencies were staffed by recruiting from translation bureaus (152–53).

115. Esperança Bielsa and Susan Bassnet, *Translation in Global News* (New York: Routledge, 2009), 39.

116. Bielsa and Bassnett, 56.

117. Buṭrus al-Bustānī, "Al-Jinān," *Al-Jinān* 1, no. 17 (August 1870): 515.

118. Verne, *Voyage au centre de la terre*, 59.

119. ʿAmmūn, *Al-Kura al-arḍiyya*, 23.

120. ʿAmmūn, 14.

6. The Melodramatic State

1. Amīdī Lūryūl, "Fī al-riwāyāt al-khayāliyya" [On imaginative novels], *Al-Mashriq* 14 (July 15, 1898): 655.

2. "Ḍarar al-riwāyāt wa al-ashʾār al-ḥubiyya" [The ill effects of novels and romantic feelings], *Al-Muqtaṭaf* 7, no. 3 (August 1882): 174–75.

3. Jurjī Zaydān, "Kuttāb al-ʿarabiyya wa qurrāʾuhā" [Writers of Arabic and its readers], *Al-Hilāl* 5, no.12 (February 15, 1897): 457. He lists one in particular, *Al-Intiqām al-ʿādal* [The just revenge], that would embarrass a young reader. The second half of Zaydān's essay has been translated by Hilary Kilpatrick and appears in Thomas Philipp, *Jurji Zaidan and the Foundations of Arab Nationalism* (Bethesda, MD: Zaidan Foundation and Syracuse University Press, 2010), 199–225.

4. Lūriyūl "Fī al-Riwāyāt al-khayāliyya," 657. Zaydān, "Kuttāb al-ʿarabiyya," 457.

5. "Introduction to *Riwāyat Amīna* [Amina]," *Al-Muqtaṭaf* 26, no. 2 (February 1901): 145.

6. As Samah Selim argues, "when [early twentieth-century] Arab critics use the term 'reality' to talk about Arabic fiction, they mean 'national reality.'" Selim, "The Narrative Craft: Realism and Fiction in the Arabic Canon," *Edebiyet: Journal of Middle Eastern Literatures* 14, nos. 1–2 (2003): 110.

7. Sainte-Beuve, "De la littérature industrielle," in *La Querelle du roman-feuilleton: Littérature, presse, et politique, un débat précurseur (1836–1848)*, ed. Lise Dumasy (Grenoble: Université Stendhal, 1999), 25–43. The essay originally appeared in *Revue des Deux-Mondes*, September 1, 1839.

8. Saite-Beuve, 29.

9. Shaden Tageldin, *Disarming Words: Empire and the Seductions of Translation in Egypt* (Berkeley: University of California Press, 2011), 158. *The Woman in White* was translated as *Riwāyat Dhāt al-thawb al-abyaḍ li wāḍiʿihā al-kātib al-qiṣaṣī al-inkilīzī al-shahīr Kūlins*, 4 vols., *Musāmarāt al-shaʿb* 6, nos. 114–17 [1909?], cited in Tageldin, 315.

10. Lūryūl, "Fī al-riwāyāt al-khayāliyya," 655.

11. Quoted in Samah Selim, "The People's Entertainments: Translation, Popular Fiction, and the Nahdah in Egypt," in *Other Renaissances: A New Approach to World Literature*, ed. Brenda Den Schildgen, Gang Zhou, and Sander L. Gilman (New York: Palgrave Macmillan, 2006), 47.

12. Lūryūl, "Fī al-riwāyāt al-khayāliyya," 657.

13. Selim, "People's Entertainments," 48.

14. Schools for girls had been in operation since at least the 1840s in major metropolitan centers, but during the 1890s, as Beth Baron explains, support for educating girls and women went from a minority opinion to a majority one, with increasing state interest in the project of girls' education. Baron, *The Women's Awakening in Egypt: Culture, Society, and the Press* (New Haven, CT: Yale University Press, 1994), 125.

15. "Ḍarar al-riwāyāt wa al-ashʿār al-ḥubiyya," 174–75. On the class-related aspects of this debate, see Selim, "People's Entertainments," 47.

16. "Al-Riwāyāt wa al-akhlāq" [Novels and morals], *Al-Jawāʾib al-miṣriyya* 8 (September 19, 1907): 3.

17. "Al-Fatā" [The young woman], *Al-Muqtaṭaf* 31, no. 4 (April 1906): 338.

18. Quoted in Selim, "People's Entertainments," 47; Zaydān, "Kuttāb al-ʿarabiyya," 457.

19. Salīm al-Khūrī, "Al-Riwāyāt wa l-riwāʾiyūn" [Novels and novelists], *Al-Ḍiyāʾ* 15 (April 15, 1899): 460.

20. Zaydān, "Kuttāb al-ʿarabiyya," 456–57.

21. Mikhāʾīl Jahshān, *Riwāyat Janafyāf* (Beirut: al-Maṭbaʿa al-Waṭaniyya, 1866); Lūryūl, "Fī al-riwāyāt al-khayāliyya," 656; Zaydān, "Kuttāb al-ʿarabiyya," 457.

22. Jurjī Zaydān, *Jurjī Zaydān, 1861–1914: Tarjama ḥayātihi, marāthī al-shu'arā' wa al-kuttāb, ḥalflāt al-ta'bayn, aqwāl al-jarā'id wa al-majallāt fī al-rajul wa āthārihi* [Jurji Zaydan, 1861-1914: His Biography, elegies by poets and authors, his memorial service, and commentary on the man and his legacy that appeared in the newspapers and magazines] (Cairo: Maṭba'at al-Hilāl, 1915), 132–33. At least two of Scott's novels, *The Talisman* and *Ivanhoe*, had appeared before Zaydān's first novel was published. Kamran Rastegar, "Literary Modernity between Arabic and Persian Prose: Jurji Zaydān's *Riwayat* in Persian Translation," *Comparative Critical Studies* 4, no. 3 (2007): 375.

23. Faraḥ Anṭūn, "Preface to *The New Jerusalem*," trans. Ghenwa Hayek, in *The Arab Renaissance: A Bilingual Anthology of the Nahda*, ed. Tarek El-Ariss (New York: MLA, 2018), 199.

24. Khalīl Baydas, "Stages of the Mind: Introduction to the First Edition," trans. Spencer Scoville in El-Ariss, *Arab Renaissance*, 208.

25. Baydas, 210.

26. Niqūlā Rizqallah, "Fann al-Riwāyāt wa ta'rībuhā" [The Art of novels and their translation], *Al-Amāl* 17 (March 9, 1899): 4.

27. "Opening," *Al-Kināna* [The quiver] 1, no. 1 (April 1, 1895): 2–3. The novels *Al-Kināna* published included *Asrār al-ẓalām* (The secrets of darkness) and *Bint al-ḥān* (Tavern girl).

28. *Mawsū'āt* 2, no. 1 (November 1899): 2. *Al-Rāwī* framed its incorporation of translated fiction in similar terms. "Introduction," *Al-Rāwī* 1, no.1 (January 15, 1893): 1.

29. Samah Selim, *The Novel and the Rural Imaginary* (New York: Routledge Curzon, 2004), 13.

30. Matti Moosa, *Origins of Modern Arabic Fiction*, 2nd ed. (Boulder, CO: Lynne Rienner, 1997), 101.

31. Peter Brooks, *The Melodramatic Imagination: Balzac, Henry James, Melodrama, and the Mode of Excess* (New Haven, CT: Yale University Press, 1976), ix.

32. Beth Baron, *Egypt as a Woman: Nationalism, Gender, and Politics* (Berkeley: University of California Press, 2005), 80.

33. Salīm Ṣa'b, trans., *Riwāyat al-'Ajā'ib wa al-gharā'ib* (Beirut: al-Maṭba'a al-'Amūmiyya, 1865), 32. Bodin's original was published in Paris in 1824 under the pseudonym Jenny Bastide, but as Ṣa'b refers to the author as "al-mu'allim Kāmīl" (the learned [male] Camille), he was probably using the 1864 edition that was published under the name Bodin.

34. Ṣa'b, 2.

35. Margaret Cohen, *The Sentimental Education of the Novel* (Princeton, NJ: Princeton University Press, 1999), 142.

36. Melodrama still underwrites many forms of Arab popular culture until today. See, for example, Lila Abu-Lughod, "Modern Subjects: Egyptian Melodrama and Postcolonial Difference," in *Questions of Modernity*, ed. Timothy Mitchell (Minneapolis: University of Minnesota Press, 2000), 87–114; Abu-Lughod, "Egyptian Melodrama—Technology of the Modern Subject?," in *Media Worlds: Anthropology on New Terrain*, ed. Faye D. Ginsburg, Lila Abu-Lughod, and Brian Larkin (Berkeley: University of California Press, 2002), 115–33.

37. Brooks, *Melodramatic Imagination*, 40.

38. Brooks, 41.

39. ʿAbd al-Muḥsin Ṭaha Badr, *Taṭawwur al-riwāya al-ʿarabiyya al-ḥadītha fī Miṣr, 1870–1938* [Development of the modern Arabic novel in Egypt, 1870–1938] (Cairo: Dār al-Maʿārif, 1963), 134. Contemporary critics often omit these novels from their histories or describe them as simply "market driven" and devoid of social or literary import. See, for example, Sālam al-Maʿūsh, *Ṣūrat al-gharb fī al-riwāya al-ʿarabiyya* [Image of the west in the Arabic novel] (Beirut: Mu'asasat al-Riḥāb al-ḥadītha, 1998), 137, 166; Muḥammad ʿAbd al-Tuwāb, *Buwākir al-riwāya: Dirāsa fī tashkīl al-riwāya al-ʿarabiyya* [Earliest novels: a study in the formation of the Arabic novel] (Cairo: al-Hay'a al-Miṣriyya al-ʿĀmma li al-Kitāb, 2007), 169–72.

40. Baron, *Women's Awakening*, 4–5.

41. Ṣaʿb, *Al-ʿAjā'ib wa al-gharā'ib*, 2.

42. "Advertisement," *Ḥadīqat al-akhbār* 353 (January 7/19, 1865): 4.

43. Marilyn Booth calls it a "hot-button issue" of the *nahḍa*. Booth, "Women and the Emergence of the Arabic Novel," in *The Oxford Handbook of Arab Novelistic Traditions*, ed. Waïl S. Hassan (Oxford: Oxford University Press, 2017), 141.

44. See for example the titles of the following novels: Aḥmad Sayyid, Al-Wālida al-ẓālima [The oppressive mother], 1903, Shākir Shuqayr, *Qiṣṣat al-Yatīm al-maẓlūm* [Story of the oppressed orphan], 1886; Fransīs Mīkha'īl, *al-Ab al-ẓālim* [The oppressive father], 1901.

45. Najīb Gharghūr, *Gharā'ib al-tadwīn* (Alexandria: Maṭbaʿat Jarīdat al-Mahrūsa, 1882), 25, 29, 61.

46. ʿAzīz Fahmī, *Riwāyat ghādat Fanīs* [The Maiden of Venice] (Cairo: Maṭbaʿat al-Waṭan, 1903).

47. Labība Hāshim, *Al-Ghāda al-Ingiliziyya* [The English maiden] (Cairo: Mu'assasat Hindāwī il al-taʿlīm wa al-thiqāfa, 2012), 25. The translation was originally published in 1895.

48. Labība Hāshim, *Kitāb fī tarbiyya* [Book on education] (Cairo: Maṭbaʿat al-Maʿārif, 1911), 97. Hoda A. Yousef gives examples of this same argument elsewhere in Hāshim's nonfiction writing. Yousef, *Composing Egypt: Reading, Writing, and the Emergence of a Modern Nation, 1870–1930* (Stanford, CA: Stanford University Press, 2016), 20.

49. Kenneth Cuno, *Modernizing Marriage: Family, Ideology, and Law in Nineteenth- and Early Twentieth-Century Egypt* (Syracuse, NY: Syracuse University Press, 2015), 114.

50. Quoted in Marilyn Booth, *Classes of Ladies, of Cloistered Spaces: Writing Feminist History through Biography in Fin-de-Siècle Egypt* (Edinburgh: Edinburgh University Press, 2015), 258.

51. Hanan Kholoussy, *For Better or for Worse: The Marriage Crisis That Made Modern Egypt* (Cairo: American University in Cairo Press, 2010), 3.

52. Hugh Conway was the pseudonym of Frederick John Fargus.

53. Paul Raphael Rooney, *Railway Reading and Late-Victorian Literary Series* (London: Routledge, 2018), 126.

54. José Martí, *Misterio* (New York: Appleton, 1886).

55. Margaret Oliphant, "Three Young Novelists," *Blackwood's Edinburgh Magazine*, September 1884, 296–316, quoted in Rooney, *Railway Reading*, 126.

56. Hāshim, *Al-Ghāda al-Ingiliziyya*, 62.

57. Hāshim, 88.

58. Hāshim, 85.

59. Hāshim, 87.

60. Wael Abu-ʿUksa, *Freedom in the Arab World: Concepts and Ideologies in Arabic Thought in the Nineteenth Century* (Cambridge: Cambridge University Press, 2016), 37.

61. Lauren Berlant, "The Subject of True Feeling: Pain, Privacy, and Politics," in *Left Legalism / Left Critique*, ed. Wendy Brown and Janet Halley (Durham, NC: Duke University Press, 2002), 107.

62. Marilyn Booth, *May Her Likes Be Multiplied: Biography and Gender Politics in Egypt* (Berkeley: University of California Press, 2001), 151.

63. Baron, *Women's Awakening*, 165.

64. Booth, *May Her Likes Be Multiplied*, 46, 334n34.

65. Note: Berlant, "Subject of True Feeling," 127.

66. Samera Esmeir, *Juridical Humanity: A Colonial History* (Stanford, CA: Stanford University Press, 2012).

67. Qāsim Amīn, *The Liberation of Women and the New Woman: Two Documents in the History of Egyptian Feminism*, trans. Samiha Sidhom Peterson (Cairo: AUC Press, 1992), 7–8, 72.

68. Esmeir, *Juridical Humanity*, 80; Amīn, *Liberation of Women*, 59–60.

69. Booth, "Women and the Emergence of the Arabic Novel," 145.

70. Amīn, *Liberation of Women*, 334, also quoted in Hoda Elsadda, *Gender, Nation, and the Arabic Novel: Egypt, 1892–2008* (Edinburgh: Edinburgh University Press, 2012), 24–25.

71. It stages, as Tarek El-Ariss has put it, through experiences or events (*aḥdāth*), a political engagement with modernity (*ḥadātha*). El-Ariss, *Trials of Arab Modernity: Literary Affects and the New Political* (New York: Fordham University Press, 2013), 172.

72. Aḥmad Ḥassan al-Zayyāt, *Tārīkh al-adab al-ʿarabī lil-madāris al-thāniwiyya wa al-ʿulyā* [History of the Arabic novel for secondary schools and higher education] (Cairo: Dār al-Nahḍa), 462. Shaden Tageldin rightly describes his overall argument, which posits Arabic literature as a backwater awaiting Western rejuvenation, as self-Orientalization that is "absolute." Tageldin, "Proxidistant Reading: Toward a Critical Pedagogy of the *Nahḍah* in U.S. Comparative Literary Study," *Journal of Arabic Literature* 43 (2012): 240.

73. Elsadda, *Gender, Nation, and the Arabic Novel*, 108n41.

74. Ḥanā Ṣāwah, *Ḍaḥiyat al-gharām* (Cairo: Maṭbaʿat al-Nīl, 1905), 4. This is a translation of Louis Latourette, *Une Courtisane sous la revolution*.

75. Adīb Isḥāq, trans., *Al-Bārisiyya al-ḥasnāʾ* (Beirut: Maṭbaʿat al-Qadīs Jāwrjiyās, 1884), 46. There is no use of "independence" in the French source text, for example. The phrase *ṣāḥibat al-ḥaqq*, "she who is in the right," occurs repeatedly in the text.

76. Isḥāq, 10.

77. La Comtesse Dash (Gabrielle Anne Cisterne de Courtiras, Vicomtesse de Saint-Mars), *La Belle Parisienne: Nouvelle Édition* (Paris: Michel Lévy Frères, 1869), 3.

78. Booth, "Women and the Emergence of the Arabic Novel," 136.

79. Niqūlā Ilyās, trans., *Riwāyat al-qulūb al-kasīra* [Novel of the shattered hearts], serialized in *Al-Thurayyā* (July 15, 1896–September 15, 1897): 122.

80. Labība Hāshim, *Al-Ghāda al-Ingiliziyya* (The English maiden, 1895), page 7.

81. Isḥāq, *Al-Bārisiyya al-ḥasnāʾ*, 118.

82. Ḥanā Asʿad Fahmī, trans., *Qarīnat al-sūʾ, aw al-fatāh al-bāghiyya* (Cairo, M. al-Taqaddum, 1904), 49. The title page lists it as a translation of a novel by Émile Richebourg. Fahmī, a lawyer and graduate of Paris Law School, is best known for his

philosophical works, both translated and original, but he was also a prolific translator of French sentimental novels. According to my research, he published at least seven novels, including two by Émile Richebourg, between 1903 and 1905 alone.

83. Najīb Jirjis ʻAbd Allah, trans. *Ḥasnāʼ Niyū Yurk* [The belle of New York] (New York: Al-Hoda, 1905). This is a translation of Laura Jean Libbey's paradigmatic "working girl dime novel," *Leonie Locke: or The Romance of a Beautiful New York Working-Girl*, 1884. Nan Enstad, *Ladies of Labor, Girls of Adventure: Working Women, Popular Culture, and Labor Politics at the Turn of the Twentieth Century* (New York: Columbia University Press, 1999), 42.

84. Quoted in Margot Badran, *Feminists, Islam, and Nation: Gender and the Making of Modern Egypt* (Princeton, NJ: Princeton University Press, 2001), 17.

85. Baron lists a number of plays and polemical works with the same argument, including notably by Yaʻqūb Ṣannūʻ (founder of *Al-Muqtaṭaf*) and Niqūlā Ḥaddād, who was the translator of at least three novels at the turn of the century. Ḥaddād's polemic arguing for companionate marriage, *Al-Ḥubb wa al-zawāj*, was published 1901. Beth Baron, "The Making and Breaking of Marital Bonds in Modern Egypt," in *Women in Middle Eastern History: Shifting Boundaries in Sex and Gender*, ed. Nikki R. Keddie and Beth Baron (New Haven, CT: Yale University Press, 1991), 278.

86. It is only when "women are freed from tyrannies in their everyday family lives," as Badran summarizes the argument of Fahmī's play, that "the family will be strengthened and, in turn, the nation" (*Feminists, Islam, and Nation*, 18).

87. Amīn, *Liberation of Women*, 6, 80.

88. These are novels in which the protagonist (often a woman) is "caught between two moral imperatives," collective welfare (manners, society, the public good) and "individual freedom" (choice, sentiment, erotic love) (Cohen, *Sentimental Education*, 34).

89. In Ḥamdī Sakkūt's bibliography of original novels, he lists fifteen *Ghāda* (maidens) novels published between 1889 and 1911. Among these were also local maiden novels, including Jurjī Zaydān's *Ghādat Karbalāʼ* (1901) and ʻAfīfa Karam's *Ghādat ʻAmshīt* (1910), which was described in *Al-Ḥasnāʼ* as "a social novel . . . that examines the harms of forced marriage for girls and the absence of [romantic] feeling between spouses." "Maṭbūʻāt ḥadītha" [Recent publications], *Al-Ḥasnāʼ* 2 (1910–1911): 78.

90. Aḥmad Saʻīd al-Baghdādī, *Ghādat Jabal Anāṣyā* (1897), for example.

91. "Al-Taqrīẓ wa al-intiqād," *Al-Jāmiʻa* 4, no. 4 (June 1903): 258.

92. ʻAbd al-Raḥmān al-Jabartī, *Napoleon in Egypt: Al-Jabartī's Chronicle of the French Occupation, 1798*, trans. Shmuel Moreh (Princeton, NJ: Markus Wiener, 2010), 24.

93. Al-Jabartī, 31.

94. Al-Jabartī, 28.

95. Abu-ʻUksa, *Freedom in the Arab World*, 27.

96. Abu-ʻUksa, 156.

97. Abu-ʻUksa, 158.

98. These included "mixing of sexes in al-Azbakiyya park, the involvement of women in public life, taking off the *ḥijāb* and dressing in French style, and Egyptian women imitating their French counterparts by seeking pleasures such as public drinking, dancing, and laughing." Abu-ʻUksa, 33.

99. "Al-Marʼa bayn al-tabadhdhul wa al-ḥijāb" [Woman between vulgarity and the hijab], *Al-Hilāl* 19, no. 2 (November 1, 1910): 106–7.

100. "Al-Mar'a" [Woman], *Al-Ḍiyā'* 4, no. 9 (January 15, 1902), 269–70.
101. Amīn, *Liberation of Women*, 130.
102. Amīn, 130. He repeats this idea on page 145 (emphasis added).
103. "Āfāt al-zawāj" [Ills of marriage], *Fatāt al-sharq* 1, no. 5 (February 15, 1907): 166.
104. Fāṭima Rashīd, "Baḥth ijtimā'ī," *Tarqiyat al-Mar'a* 1, no. 4 (1908): 58–61, quoted in Booth, *May Her Likes Be Multiplied*, 47.
105. Malak Ḥifnī Nāṣif (Bāḥithat al-Bādiya, pseud.), "Ḥurriyat al-mar'a fī al-islām" [Women's freedom in Islam], *Al-Manār* 4, no. 14 (April 29, 1911): 308.
106. Hoda Yousef defines three separate discourses in Nāṣif's writing and reminds us not to collapse "European" into "colonial" when understanding her employment of Western legal and political terminology. Yousef, "Malak Hifni Nasif: Negotiations of a Feminist Agenda between the European and the Colonial," *Journal of Middle East Women's Studies* 7, no. 1 (Winter 2011): 76.
107. Nāṣif, "Ḥuriyyat al-Mar'a," 310.
108. Naoki Sakai, *Translation and Subjectivity: On "Japan" and Cultural Nationalism* (Minneapolis: University of Minnesota Press, 1997), 85 (emphasis in the original).
109. Tageldin, *Disarming Words*, 200.
110. Tageldin, 222.
111. Badran, *Feminists, Islam, and Nation*, 17–18.
112. Quoted in Booth, *May Her Likes Be Multiplied*, 23.
113. Fāṭima 'Aliya, *Nisā' al-Islām* [Women of Islam], trans. Ibrāhīm Fāris? (Cairo: Maṭba'at 'Ayn Shams, 189?), 11.
114. 'Aliya, 174.
115. 'Aliya, 34.
116. "Al-Mar'a al-fāḍila" [The favored woman], *Al-Ḥasnā'* 1, no. 9 (February 20, 1910): 269.
117. Hāshim, *Al-Ghāda al-Ingiliziyya*, 7.
118. Booth, *May Her Likes Be Multiplied*, xx.
119. El-Ariss, *Trials of Arab Modernity*, 7, 5.
120. Charles Hirschkind calls these "visceral modes of appraisal." Hirschkind, *The Ethical Soundscape: Cassette Sermons and Islamic Counterpublics* (Cambridge, MA: Harvard University Press, 2002), 18, quoted in El-Ariss, *Trials of Arab Modernity*, 6. "Trials of modernity" is the apt name that El-Ariss gives to this affective, somatic critical process, as it produces modes of experimentation through and with the body. There are yet still other resonances to be tapped from this phrase, however; in this section, I show how these particular romantic "trials" also have legal implications.
121. Elliott Colla, "Anxious Advocacy: The Novel, the Law, and Extrajudicial Appeals in Egypt," *Public Culture* 17, no. 3 (2005): 417-443.
122. Salīm Sarkīs, "Ja'bat al-muḥarir" [Word from the editor], *Majallat Sarkīs* 2, no. 10 (September 15, 1906): 307.
123. Salīm Sarkīs, "Ja'bat al-muḥarir" [Word from the editor], *Majallat Sarkīs* 2, nos. 5–6 (July 15, 1906): 175.
124. Samah Selim, "Fiction and Colonial Identities: Arsène Lupin in Arabic," *Middle Eastern Studies* 13, no. 2 (2010): 191.
125. Elliott Colla, "Anxious Advocacy: The Novel, the Law, and Extrajudicial Appeals in Egypt," *Public Culture* 17, no. 3 (2005): 428.

126. Ḥāfiẓ Najīb, *Jūnsūn: Ikhtifāʾ Banwā* [Johnson: The disappearance of Benoit] (Cairo: Maṭbaʿat al-Saʿāda, 1921?), 214. An advertisement on the interior title page indicates that two new issues will be available in January 1922, and so the latest this could be dated is December 1921. Though this same title indicates that nine titles in the series had already been published by that time, making it a significant series, I have found no trace of a corresponding "Johnson" series in French or English in any major bibliography. A WorldCat search turned up a single possible source, but neither is it in French, as *Jūnsūn* indicates, nor is it a series: Harry Hancock, *Detective Johnson of New Orleans. A Tale of Love and Crime* (New York: Ogilvie, 1891).

127. Linda Williams, *Playing the Race Card: Melodramas of Black and White from Uncle Tom to O. J. Simpson* (Princeton, NJ: Princeton University Press, 2001), 19–20.

128. Franco Moretti, *Atlas of the European Novel, 1800–1900* (London: Verso, 1998), 143. For Moretti, geography is that bridge.

129. Selim, "Fiction and Colonial Identities," 208n58.

130. Labība Hāshim, "Fālantīn," *Al-Ḍiyāʾ* 3, no. 7 (December 15, 1900): 218.

131. Brooks, *Melodramatic Imagination*, 28.

132. Franco Moretti, "Clues," in *Signs Taken for Wonders: On the Sociology of Literary Forms* (London: Verso, 1983), 140 (emphasis in the original).

133. Hāshim, "Fālantīn," 224.

134. Sarkīs describes his own interests in crime fiction as long-standing ones. He recounts a meeting he had with Arthur Conan Doyle in Giza when Doyle visited Egypt in 1897. He asked Doyle permission that day to translate his stories, and Doyle granted it. Salīm Sarkīs, "Ḥikāyāt Shirlūk Hūlmz," *Majallat Sarkīs* 4, no. 1 (May 1, 1908): 12.

135. Arthur Conan Doyle, "Adventure of the Copper Beeches," quoted in Moretti, "Clues," 142.

136. Sarkīs is keen to add that the man is from California, an outlaw state "where they are not afraid of the laws of the government" and "arrest wrongdoers . . . themselves"). Salīm Sarkīs, "Al-Sāriq wa al-ghaniyy al-amīrikī" [The Thief and the wealthy American], *Majallat Sarkīs* 4, nos. 3–4 (June 1, 1908): 76.

137. Salīm Sarkīs, "*Farīq al-mujrimīn (Hal khaṭara laka mithl hadhā min qablin?*" [The Band of Criminals (Have You Ever Thought of Something Like This Before?)], *Majallat Sarkīs* 3, nos. 21–22 (March 15, 1908): 641.

138. Sarkīs, "*Farīq al-mujrimīn*," 643.

139. Lauren Berlant, *The Female Complaint: The Unfinished Business of Sentimentality in American Culture* (Durham, NC: Duke University Press, 2008), xi.

140. Berlant, 271.

141. Brooks, *Melodramatic Imagination*, 43.

142. Jonathan Goldberg, *Melodrama: An Aesthetics of Impossibility* (Durham, NC: Duke University Press, 2016), x.

143. Judith Walkowitz, *City of Dreadful Delight: Narratives of Sexual Danger in Late-Victorian London* (Chicago: University of Chicago Press, 1992), 86.

144. Rey Chow, *Woman and Chinese Modernity: The Politics of Reading between West and East*, Theory and History of Literature 75 (Minnesota: University of Minnesota Press, 1991), 55.

145. Selim, "People's Entertainments," 192.

Conclusion

1. Jurjī Zaydān, *Tārīkh adāb al-lugha al-ʿarabiyya*, vol. 4 (Cairo: Maṭbaʿat al-Hilāl, 1914), 9.

2. Zaydān, *Tārīkh adāb al-lugha al-ʿarabiyya*, 4:9. The figure of *al-dakhīl*, as Zachary Lockman explains, was one in currency in Egyptian nationalist discourse at the turn of the twentieth century; Muṣṭafā Kāmil, the publisher, lawyer, and activist sometimes known as the "father of Egyptian nationalism," frequently referred to *al-dukhalāʾ* (plural) in his speeches and writings, as did others. As Lockman and Ami Ayalon have noted, this was, by the mid-1890s, a term used to describe Syrian-Lebanese (Christian) immigrants to Egypt, who often supported British colonial efforts. Zaydān's use here reorients that term back toward Europe, creating a unified Arabo-Syrio-Egyptian response to colonial "invaders." Lockman, "The Egyptian Nationalist Movement and the Syrians in Egypt," *Immigrants and Minorities: Historical Studies in Ethnicity, Migration, and Diaspora* 3, no. 3 (1984): 243.

3. ʿĀʾida Ibrāhīm Nuṣayr (1990) lists twenty-eight translated and original novels published between 1891 and 1895 and twenty-four novels (also original and translated) between 1880 and 1890. ʿĀʾida Ibrāhīm Nuṣayr, *Al-Kutub al-ʿarabiyya alatī nushirat fī Miṣr fī al-qarn al-tāsiʿ ʿashr* [Arabic books published in Egypt in the nineteenth century] (Cairo: American University in Cairo Press, 1990).

4. Zaydān himself pioneered these techniques in *Al-Hilāl*. Elizabeth M. Holt, *Fictitious Capital: Silk, Cotton, and the Rise of the Arabic Novel* (New York: Fordham University Press, 2017), 108.

5. Jurjī Zaydān, "Kuttāb al-ʿarabiyya wa qurrāʾuhā" [Writers of Arabic and its readers], *Al-Hilāl* 5, no. 12 (February 15, 1897): 456. The second half of Zaydān's essay has been translated by Hilary Kilpatrick and appears in Thomas Philipp, *Jurji Zaidan and the Foundations of Arab Nationalism* (Syracuse, NY: Syracuse University Press, 2010), 199–215.

6. Samah Selim, "The People's Entertainments: Translation, Popular Fiction, and the Nahdah in Egypt," in *Other Renaissances: A New Approach to World Literature*, ed. Brenda Den Schildgen, Gang Zhou, and Sander L. Gilman (New York: Palgrave Macmillan, 2006), 39.

7. Samah Selim, *The Novel and the Rural Imaginary* (New York: Routledge Curzon, 2004), 75–77.

8. Selim, 62.

9. Elliott Colla, "How *Zaynab* Became the First Arabic Novel," *History Compass* 7, no. 1 (2009): 217.

10. Aamir Mufti, *Forget English! Orientalisms and World Literatures* (Cambridge, MA: Harvard University Press, 2016), 143.

11. Yet even Zaydān, that pioneer of national literary history, who characterized the novel as one of the "invading arts," still argued that the Arabs had possessed the form "earlier." Jurjī Zaydān, *Tārīkh adāb al-lugha al-ʿarabiyya*, vol. 4 (Cairo: Maṭbaʿat al-Hilāl, 1914), 230.

12. Najīb al-Ḥaddād, "Muqābala bayn al-shiʿr al-ʿarabī wa al-shiʿr al-ifranjī," *Al-Bayān* 1, no. 7 (September 1, 1897) and 1, no. 9 (October 1, 1897). As Geert Jan van Gelder notes, it was reproduced in al-Manfalūṭī's *Al-Mikhtārāt* in 1937. Van Gelder,

"Najīb al-Ḥaddād's Essay on the Comparison of Arabic and European Poetry," in *Tradition and Modernity in Arabic Language and Literature*, ed. J. R. Smart (Richmond, UK: Curzon, 1996), 144.

13. Al-Ḥaddād, "Muqābala," 9: 335.

14. Rūḥī al-Khālidī, *Tārīkh 'ilm al-adab 'ind al-ifrānj wa al-'arab wa Victor Hugo*, 4th ed. (Damascus: Al-Hilāl, 1984), 126. This printing is based on the second 1912 edition.

15. Al-Khālidī, 6. On this preface see also H. Al-Khateeb, "Rūḥī al-Khālidī: A Pioneer of Comparative Literature in Arabic," *Journal of Arabic Literature* 18 (1987): 83.

16. Khālidī, *Tārīkh*, 128–30.

17. Sulaymān al-Bustānī, *Ilyādhat Hūmīrūs* (Cairo: Maṭba'at al-Hilāl, 1904), 6.

18. As Bo Holmberg argues, "contact with European ideas and modes of expression became an impetus to dig deep into the soil of the indigenous Arab tradition." Holmberg, "Transculturating the Epic: The Arab Awakening and the Translation of the *Iliad*," in *Literary History: Towards a Global Perspective*, vol. 3, ed. Gunilla Lindberg-Wada (Berlin: Walter de Gruyter, 2006), 165.

19. Shaden Tageldin, "One Comparative Literature? 'Birth' of a Discipline in French-Egyptian Translation, 1810–1834," *Comparative Literature Studies* 47, no. 4 (2010): 437.

20. al-Bustānī, *Ilyādhat Hūmīrūs*, 6. For an account of this celebration, including its attendees and the speeches given, see "Al-Iḥtifāl bi-mutarjim al-Ilyādha" [Celebration of the translator of *The Iliad*], *Al-Muqtaṭaf* 29, no. 7 (July 1, 1904): 610–18.

21. Ḥamdī Sakkūt, *The Egyptian Novel and Its Main Trends from 1913–1952* (Cairo: American University in Cairo Press, 1971), 11, quoted in Wen-Chin Ouyang, *Poetics of Love in the Arabic Novel: Nation-State, Modernity, and Tradition* (Edinburgh: Edinburgh University Press, 2012), 5. Ouyang has a very informative discussion of the history of this particular argument on pages 4–5 of her book.

22. Muḥammad Ḥusayn Haykal, *Zaynab*, 6th ed. (Cairo: Dār al-Ma'ārif, 1999), 27.

Index

Note: Pages in *italics* refer to illustrative matter.

CPSIA information can be obtained
at www.ICGtesting.com
Printed in the USA
LVHW090330141220
673734LV00033B/121/J

9 781501 753060